I0797033

THE NAVIGATOR'S LETTER

THE NAVIGATOR'S LETTER

The True Story of Two WWII Airmen, a Doomed Mission, and the Woman Who Bound Them Together

JAN CRESS DONDI

UNION SQUARE & CO.
NEW YORK

Jacket design by Pete Garceau
Jacket images by Getty Images: Mondadori Portfolio (photo), NoDerog (stamp), kyoshino (texture)

Union Square & Co.
Hachette Book Group
1290 Avenue of the Americas, New York, NY 10104
unionsquareandco.com
@unionsqandco

First Edition: February 2026

Union Square & Co. is an imprint of Grand Central Publishing, a division of Hachette Book Group, Inc. The Union Square & Co. name and logo are registered trademarks of Hachette Book Group, Inc.

Interior images courtesy of the author, Shutterstock.com, and © ICRC ARCHIVES (ARR), 1944, Guerre 1939–1945. Bucarest. Camp école Ste Catherine. Prisonniers de guerre aviateurs anglais et américains et soldats de garde roumains.

Library of Congress Cataloging-in-Publication Data has been applied for.

ISBNs: 978-1-4549-5635-8 (hardcover); 978-1-4549-5636-5 (ebook)

Printed in Canada

MRQ-T

10 9 8 7 6 5 4 3 2 1

AUTHOR'S NOTE

In three years, I delivered three eulogies—my mother, my only sister, and my sister's daughter, my niece—all at the cost of breast cancer.

As this difficult time was unfolding, I discovered a footlocker in the cellar of my mother's home. Inside were hundreds of letters, timeworn with age spots and musty from at least seven decades of humidity and stagnate air. Aside from sneezing, they got my attention. As I started to read, I realized the treasure chest before me.

While the early letters revealed a prewar innocence, as they moved into 1943, reading turned to a curiosity of how war impacted family. As for WWII itself, I found how little I understood about this major event. But now, the war years were unraveling before my eyes—a time so foreign yet so familiar. As I read, I made notes. Clues sent me on a journey to learn more about the parallels shared by two men with ties to the same woman.

Insightful and moving, the letters became the backbone of this book. I didn't realize it then, but the journey was a major distraction at the right time. What better way to see how folks from another time dealt with circumstances they couldn't control. And what better way to experience history than through those who'd lived it.

The events in the book were derived from primary sources

including hundreds of letters; interviews with the main characters and the people who knew them; a POW diary; videotaped recordings; memoirs from crewmembers; scrapbooks; newspaper clippings; and other verities. The narrative has been based solely on these materials, interspersed with italics (representing the writings and recordings of John B. and Bob) and quotation marks throughout the story, as referenced in the source notes. A large portion of the story, including dialogue and narrative, was actually written by the two navigators. Official records, including those from the National Archives, both American and German, corroborated these resources.

Having spent my childhood summers at *Cress Hill Farm* and the Whites' home in town, I have a unique perspective of where and what the main characters experienced while growing up in and around Hillsboro. And although I was not present during the war years, I have re-created the texture and atmosphere of the time founded upon a lifetime with Bob and Polley, including anecdotes told to me, and family stories of John B., which are also referenced in the source notes. While the history is accurate and each event happened as portrayed, I have shared this story in a way that evokes the feeling and meaning of what took place, which in all instances is authentic although sometimes not written to represent word-for-word transcripts. No characters have been invented, nor have any names been changed.

The B-24 Liberator, somewhat of a character in this story, is an American four-engine bomber but may also be referred to as a Lib, an airship, a ship, or in the plural as *heavies*.

At its heart, *The Navigator's Letter* is a personal narrative: a true story about three youths growing up at the advent of WWII. The main characters, John B. and Bob, drive the story through Polley's eyes—a journey that took two young men from the heartland of America to a cauldron of Hitler's crude oil at Ploesti, Romania.

This book could not have been written without
help synthesizing material and thought by
Nancy,

the love and support of
Beda,

the need to share with
Lauren and Caroline,

and the desire to honor
Bob, Polley, and John B.

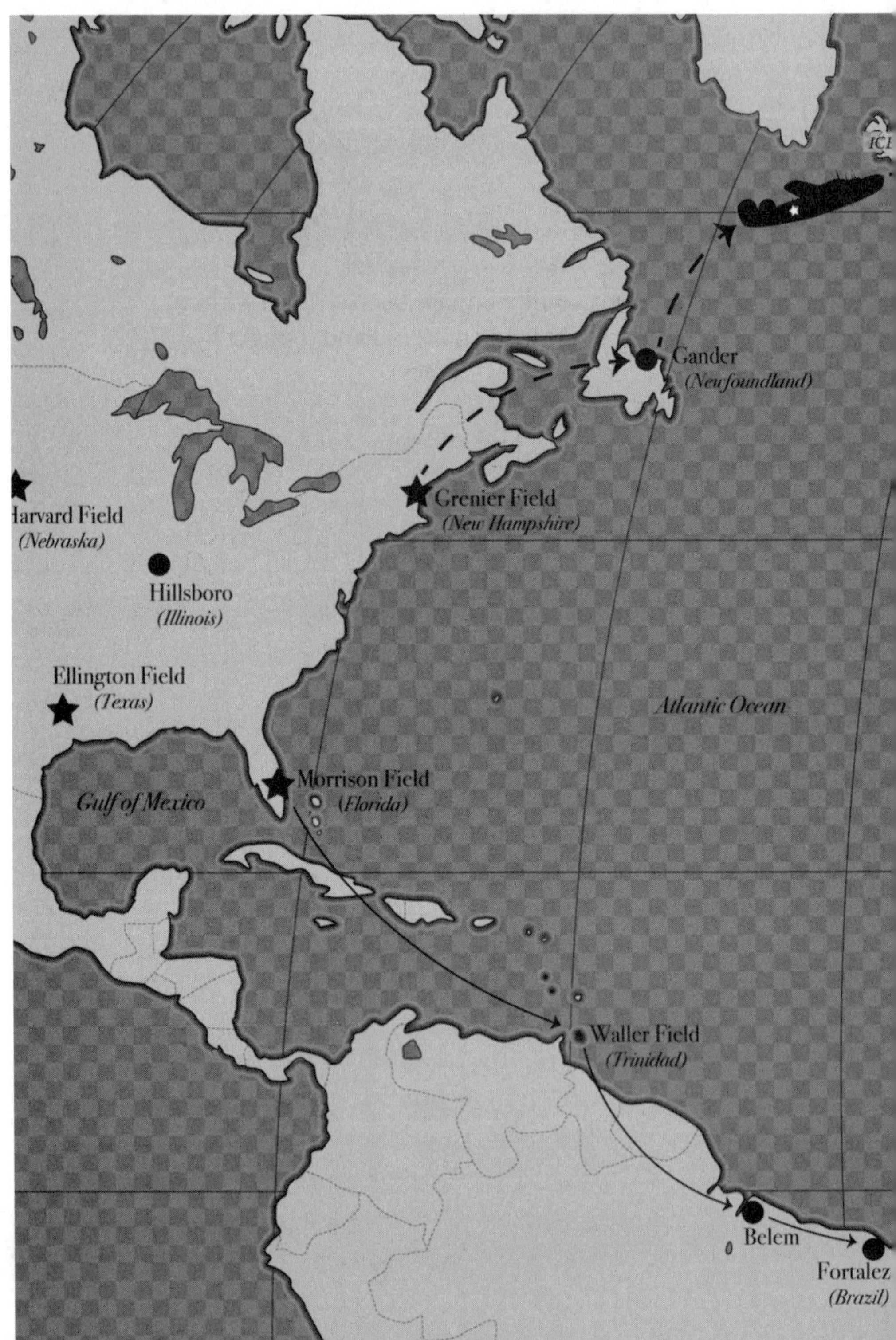

Gander
(Newfoundland)
Grenier Field
(New Hampshire)
Harvard Field
(Nebraska)
Hillsboro
(Illinois)
Ellington Field
(Texas)
Atlantic Ocean
Gulf of Mexico
Morrison Field
(Florida)
Waller Field
(Trinidad)
Belem
Fortalez
(Brazil)

UNITED KINGDOM
Hardwick
(England)
Bay of Biscay
Ploesti
Bucharest
(Romania)
Torretta
(Italy)
Algiers
(Algeria)
Djedeida
(Tunisia)
Casablanca
Marrakech
(French Morocco)
Benghazi
(Libya)
Dakar
(Senegal)
World War II
8th Air Force based in England
93rd Bombardment Group at Hardwick
Route taken by John B.
15th Air Force based in Italy
484th Bombardment Group at Torretta
Route taken by Bob
Equator
0 Kilometers 600 1200
0 Miles 600 1200
Map design by Jessica French

History thrives by being shared.

INTRODUCTION*

Each generation has its own heritage of popular music. The sound and lyrics portray the mood of the country, and the message of the lyrics expresses and influences the thoughts and imaginations of the young.

As the Great Depression was winding down, big bands, with their featured vocalists, came into prominence. Radios were coming into common usage, and the jukebox was appearing in most of the places where young people gathered. On the radio, nightly, you could listen to live broadcasts of the big bands as they played at America's famous hotels. We didn't have television, and this was our entertainment.

While I was in high school, I listened to the theme songs of the various bands and would memorize the lyrics of the popular songs. The lyrics helped in memorizing the tune and, if I could whistle the

* Years ago, Bob began writing his memoirs with anecdotes about growing up and his service during WWII. Excerpts are scattered throughout the book, and in particular, this *Introduction* (down to the asterisk break) was entirely written by Bob as was *Chicago*, which has been included as part of Chapter Fifteen.

tune, I could play it on my horn. I would try to imagine the grandeur of places like the Brown Derby in Hollywood or the Empire Room in Chicago, never dreaming that within a few years I would see these places.

On the jukebox for a nickel, you could select your favorite tune and let the lyrics express it for you as you danced with your partner. Because of radio and the jukebox, the big band sound swept the country and prevailed throughout the World War II years.

The war years were a time of uncertainties, coupled with long and indefinite separations of husbands and wives, families and sweethearts. Many of the lyrics were about romance and love. They told of parting and hopes and dreams of being together again.

Of all the great songs of this era, there were two that recall more memories than any others—the original Tommy Dorsey arrangement of "Stardust," and his theme song, "I'm Getting Sentimental Over You." My attachment to these two songs began when I was a sophomore in high school. I used to sit up in my room on a summer's evening, windows open, playing these two numbers on my horn. The cows in the pasture out front lined up, looking at the house. They were my audience.

Because music appeals to the emotions, our country used it for the purpose of morale, both for those who remained at home and for those of us who were away. The Armed Services Radio Station in Foggia, Italy, played music in the early-morning hours as our bombers circled to get into formation and to gain altitude before heading off to the target. The pilots were busy during the form-up, but the rest of the crew could flip their intercom to the music during this thirty- or forty-five-minute period. We would usually only allow five or ten minutes of listening but it served nonetheless to calm some tight nerves.

The enemy also recognized the power of music and played all the most popular love songs for propaganda purposes. *Axis Sally,* who was the German DJ in Italy, would talk to us between numbers and tell us what that sweet little thing back home was really doing while we were over there "getting our asses shot off . . ."

PLOESTI

Along the way, Bob and John B., the main characters and both B-24 navigators, became familiar with Ploesti, a town rich in oil reserves. Recognized as one of the top-producing countries of crude oil, Hitler took notice. Black gold was capital, a bounty for war-sustaining fuel. In 1939, Germany became Romania's primary trading partner.

In modern warfare, "no other item is more essential than oil." And Ploesti lay at the core of the German oil supply.

The Ploesti refineries kept Hitler's war machine in business, an economic relationship the Allies* became interested in. Early US Army Air Force studies estimated that the oil plants in Romania provided Nazi Germany with "60 percent of Axis† crude oil requirements." (Months later, the number was revised to 35 percent.)

Knocking out Germany's petroleum production at Ploesti meant shortening the war.

The occupation of North Africa opened an opportunity for the Allies to meet east of the Atlantic. In January 1943, US President Franklin D. Roosevelt met UK Prime Minister Winston Churchill in Casablanca. The conference formed a blueprint for the strategic bombing campaign in Europe. Eliminating the Axis energy stream

* In WWII, the term "Allies" refers to the coalition of nations, primarily the US, UK, Soviet Union, and China that fought against the Axis powers (Germany, Italy, and Japan).

† "Axis" refers to a military alliance composed of Nazi Germany, Fascist Italy, and Imperial Japan, who fought against Allied Powers.

moved to the top of the agenda. The oil fields of Ploesti became a priority target.

The plan for Ploesti's demise was not without complication. There were issues of reaching the target and returning; evading enemy radar; and striking a target with accuracy while battling Reich defenses.

Using its *state-of-the-art* weapon, the B-24 Liberator, the solution suggested flying some two hundred ships, redesigned for the long haul, low to the ground to avoid radar detection yet close enough to drop bombs spot-on, resulting in the complete destruction of Ploesti's oil production. Unable to fuel his trucks, tanks, and planes, Hitler would have little choice but to surrender.

On paper, the idea was brilliant.

While the Eighth Air Force out of England covered western European objectives, it loaned three groups of *heavies*, B-24 Liberators, to the Ninth Air Force in North Africa to take on the matter of Ploesti. As trailblazers, the B-24s flew at zero altitude, "a height of fifty to one hundred fifty feet" above the ground, in the first orchestrated raid over the oil city on August 1, 1943.

Months later, the Fifteenth Air Force out of southern Italy continued that initial drive on Ploesti at an altitude of nearly five miles high. Repeated poundings persisted through the summer of 1944.

PART ONE

PROLOGUE

Making It Through Hell

TEN MINUTES AND FORTY MILES OUT, John B. could still see the black clouds of destruction billowing above the target. Only the vibration of his B-24 Liberator climbing to altitude masked the adrenaline hammering through his veins. Like others, he didn't think they were going to make it.

Flying a hundred feet above Nazi Germany's anti-aircraft artillery had been a blur, but now, on the other side of the target, John B. couldn't shake what he'd left behind. Through panes of the ship's Plexiglas nose, a hailstorm of bullets drew lines of fire, as if stars blasting by at lightspeed, crisscrossing his path as his bomber flew in at treetop level, whizzing by, fearsomely close, knowing full well a direct hit would have ended it all. And a flash out the window meant another bomber was forced down. Friends lost. How did his ship make it? And why?

Over the target, the unknown was more frightening than the ride. Entering a blinding curtain of smoke swallowed any hope of making it through. In total darkness, John B. had no control. When you're on the edge of life itself, what do you do? The will to survive is a powerful weapon. But so is luck. And fate. Somehow, they kept flying and with it, burst out of the netherworld.

While he couldn't say he was happy, he was alive. And so was his family, the crew.

Holding on to the edges of his navigation desk, John B. struggled to steady his hands, surely thinking of what and whom he'd left behind. Hoping to forget but he knew it wasn't over. And it was time to call out the course back to Benghazi.

Not one to be a flag waver for combat, John B. recognized the need to join the fight. For a year, his crew had performed *a mixed bag of tricks* for the Air Force, all efforts aimed at knocking out the Nazis. And today, he'd just pushed through the toughest anti-aircraft artillery ever designed by the Germans and at point-blank range. Terrifying, Ploesti was pure hell.

The night before, ground crews had worked furiously to ready the ships. Installed were new Pratt & Whitney engines and "auxiliary fuel tanks retrofitted for the long haul." Despite the noise, John B. would have found it difficult to sleep. Not for the distant sounds of trucks making urgent deliveries to ships or the sputtering of engines being checked out. It wasn't the clanking of bombs being loaded or tools tightening bolts; but with his letter home, *I've had some of the most awful dreams in the world*, John B.'s tensions were no doubt fueled by the tough mission ahead.

ONE AUGUST 1943. On the Libyan desert, by the light of a lantern under a moonless Terria airfield, the orderly jumped from tent to tent. Pulling the tarp aside, he announced the morning's wake-up call. It was 0200 hours.

At the final briefing, the objective was understood—knock out the Ploesti oil refineries and Hitler's war machine would grind to a halt. John B.'s B-24 Liberator, together with some 175 others, would fly 1,200 miles one-way to the target, drop their bombs from zero altitude,* a height below 200 feet, while dodging enemy anti-aircraft artillery. Finally, they would fly the return trip of 1,200 miles back to the air base in Benghazi, all in the same day. If successful, the mission touted "shortening the war by six months." For certain, John B. sat proud knowing the contribution he would make, but he also knew *it was a huge risk*—such a strategy had never been tried before.

As navigator, John B. had already noted the headings and an alternate return course. Operations personnel outlined weather advisories and updated anti-aircraft estimations. "Expected losses of 50 percent" were no secret for a mission that professed an abbreviation of the war. Fifty percent? Muffled whispers were surely quelled as the final *good luck and Godspeed* message was delivered.

Five distinct US Army Air Force bombardment groups† were responsible for carrying out this bombing mission. Crews came together bearing names such as *Liberandos*, *Ted's Traveling Circus*, *Pyramidiers*, *Flying Eight-Balls*, and *Sky Scorpions*. To a certain extent, nicknames were coined to avoid enemy notice on eavesdropping radio transmissions. Each airman gleamed with pride, living the moniker that represented the soul of his bomb group.

John B. was part of the 93rd Bomb Group, dubbed *Ted's Traveling*

---

* "Zero altitude" refers to a USAAF term used on this mission of flying a heavy bomber at a height of "fifty to one hundred fifty feet" aboveground while maintaining flight below an altitude of 200 feet.

† "Bombardment group" refers to a USAAF aircraft unit made up of squadrons of planes designed to carry out bombing missions over enemy targets. Each bomb group consisted of some three dozen B-24 Liberators.

Circus,* hereinafter called the *Circus*. Having earned a considerable reputation for their daring combat missions, his "group was also referred to as *Hell-Pro* (Hell Dare Devils)." In a convoy of the five bomb groups, the *Circus* was the second group behind the lead, *Liberandos*.

Each airship was a B-24 Liberator, a *heavy bomber* with four engines that carried a crew of ten airmen. A huge warbird, it had a wingspan of 110 feet and its fuselage stretched 66 feet in length. On this mission, each Lib exceeded the maximum load allowance, carrying some 21,000 pounds of fuel, eight 500-pound bombs, and bandoliers of .50-caliber machine gun bullets. With each ship so heavily burdened, "the first, and possibly suicidal, problem of the flight to Romania was simply to get off the ground," according to James Dugan and Carroll Stewart in their book, *Ploesti*.

Approaching his ship, John B. could look up to see her name: *Exterminator*. He would have boarded *her* with confidence, knowing his crew had worked cohesively through many combat missions over Western Europe. But that day was different. Hitting the target while flying a hundred feet above the ground was a thought not easy to brush aside.

Tanker trucks awaited each ship to top off her wing tanks for the long haul. As crews loaded their Liberators, engines fired up and propellers swirled up grit. The ships made their way down the taxiway toward the end of the runway.

Routinely, John B. would stand behind his pilot at takeoff. With a view down the length of the airstrip, *Exterminator* dipped her nose

* *Ted's Traveling Circus* (a.k.a. *Ted's Flying Circus*) was nicknamed for its commander, Colonel "Ted" Timberlake. The nickname reflected the group's frequent movement across different theaters of operation during WWII, giving the impression of a traveling circus constantly on the move.

as she braked, seemingly to take a breath in anticipation of the long journey. Certainly, John B. felt the same.

At half-minute intervals, the ships roared down the pierced steel plank runway. In a fog from the ship before her, *Exterminator*'s revved engines created a cloud of sand obscuring the view of the Lib awaiting takeoff to her rear. As pilot Hugh Roper released the brake, John B. was yanked back as the bomber lurched forward. Bounding to gain enough speed, the wheels bucked until the craft left the ground with a heaved lift. As the airstrip fell distant behind them, they rose to meet formation.*

Pilot of B-24 *Let 'er Rip*, Victor Olliffe, flew right wing† to John B.'s leading ship, *Exterminator.* Born and raised in Napa, Olliffe was a rancher prior to flight school. He was a "very muscular man," a cowboy on the column who flew "his B-24 as if a Piper Cub. He was holding in so close to Roper, the wings of the two planes seemed welded together."

Russ Longnecker, in *Thunder Mug*, flew on *Exterminator*'s left side. Originally, he was assigned copilot of the B-24. But his pilot, suffering from a "recent outbreak of dysentery affecting a third of the men that day," was ordered to stand down minutes before takeoff. Longnecker would now take the controls of the bomber. It was his first time flying left seat or pilot on a B-24 Liberator.

The three B-24 Libs—*Thunder Mug*, *Exterminator*, and *Let 'er Rip*—now flew side by side as if one unit.

Nearly three hours out of Benghazi, formation was still northbound

---

* "Formation" in the US Army Air Force refers to the organized arrangement of aircraft while flying, typically in a V-shaped pattern, which allowed for mutual protection and coordinated attacks, with the most common formation for heavy bombers being the "combat box" designed to defend against enemy fighters while concentrating bomb drops on the target.

† "Right wing" refers to a brother airplane that flies off the right side of another aircraft's wing.

over open water approaching the Nazi-held Island of Corfu. Out the window, John B. would have observed the bluest water he had ever seen—a momentary respite along the route. But back to his maps, it was time to alert the pilot of the northeasterly turn at Corfu. Advancing the mainland, they climbed high above the Albanian Alps before descending low over Bulgaria. Passing the Danube River, they flew at treetop level just above the Romanian countryside and on into the target area.

As the American B-24s reached Pitesti, the first IP (the Initial Point*), the leading *Liberandos* group banked northeasterly. John B.'s *Circus* followed. (Due to radio silence and varying speeds together with hazy skies, the three remaining bomb groups had dropped back, out of sight and no longer flying together in the original formation of five groups.)

Gaining on the second IP at the town of Targoviste, the *Liberandos* made a ninety-degree turn. Again, the *Circus* followed. But it was a mistake. They turned "several minutes and tens of miles short of the planned turning point," as later noted by General Smart. The turn was supposed to be over a third landmark at the town of Floresti, not Targoviste. The *Liberandos* and *Circus* were now mistakenly headed away from the target at Ploesti.

With the directional change, John B. would have feverishly compared the topography and streams below to oblique views on the map. But the bombers were traveling at such speeds, they were on top of a landmark before a comparison could be confirmed. *It's wrong*, he surely thought. The mission's lead plane carrying the group commander had turned too soon. An error. Radio silence prevented clarification.

---

* "Initial Point" or "IP" refers to a crucial reference point or landmark. It is the designated geographical location in the airspace over the target area where bomber formations would begin their final approach toward the target.

Out the window to his left, John B. would have seen a dark haze rising over the Ploesti refinery complex. With that, he would know they were headed south to Bucharest—away from the target. As navigator, he undoubtedly reached for his throat mike to alert Roper of the wrong turn, but in doing so, navigator and pilot would be at odds. With communications between aircraft forbidden and in such tight formation, there was little his pilot could do other than to follow the lead plane.

Precious minutes were lost headed the wrong direction when the navigator broke radio silence. "Mistake! Mistake! Wrong turn!" and a dozen others joined in. "Discovering the mistake, [the *Circus* lead] maneuvered the group north toward Ploesti," no longer following the *Liberandos*. John B.'s group, as one-fifth of the original full-out force of 175 B-24 bombers, would now drive to the target as a single unit.

The original plan directed the airmen through the less-defended northwest sector of Ploesti. John B. and his brother Libs were about to confront Ploesti's fiercest installations on the south side. They were headed exactly where the Allied Command wanted to avoid.

Flying above cultivated fields, as low as fifty feet, the ground raced beneath them as the Libs drove in to target at top speed. "We were going in from the wrong direction at 245 mph, 65 miles more than our usual speed, pulling emergency power for so long that it was a question how much longer the engines could stand the abuse," said Longnecker.

The B-24 Liberators were entering the heaviest defenses found in Europe. And at point-blank range! Facing fast-firing cannons, *Exterminator* was driving through a gauntlet of enemy flak batteries*

* Flak batteries: clusters of anti-aircraft guns on the ground that fire explosive shells of metal shrapnel (flak) into aircraft, American B-24s in this case.

that straddled the bomber on both sides. It was "an eight-minute road to target," a seemingly endless barrage. At close range, the noise level was deafening.

"An *eighty-eight* cannon was hidden behind a row of trees at the crossroad." As the projectiles rocketed in the air, John B.'s left wingman in *Thunder Mug* pulled up, exposing *Exterminator.* Before pilot Roper had a chance to make an evasive maneuver, the shards battered *Exterminator*'s portside.*

As *Exterminator* pushed forward, she entered an angry web of white-hot strands of gunfire. The artillery intensified. Bullets rattled against the Liberator's thin aluminum skin. The starboard† side jerked upward and a basketball-size "hole ripped through the right wing." The intense concussion blasts forced confusion as John B. surely struggled to remain upright. Undoubtedly, a vision of terror and hollow disappointment overshadowed any feelings as hope willed his Liberator through the chaos.

Over the oil complex, the wing of a fellow Lib snared a detonating cable that hung from a low-floating barrage balloon, igniting the ship into a ruinous blaze. Ten airmen gone. *God help them.* Simultaneously, at three o'clock ground level, a B-24 slid out of control, stopping only as she smashed into a storage tank. Ten more? *God help them all!*

The pounding persisted as the three ships remained side by side in formation.

Suddenly, a flash of light must have caught John B.'s eye. "A huge oil tank exploded directly in front of my [far] right wingman, *Let 'er Rip*," said Longnecker. Out the starboard side, no doubt, John B. watched in terror as the bomber headed into the explosion. With

* "Portside" refers to the left side of the aircraft.

† "Starboard" refers to the right side of the aircraft.

no choice, pilot Olliffe of *Let 'er Rip* dropped his B-24 to deck level, heading to his left side below *Exterminator* on a path leading under *Thunder Mug*.

With *Exterminator* on top of *Let 'er Rip*, John B. would brace for a collision. Only inches separated the ships with even less clearance to the ground. As *Let 'er Rip* passed below *Exterminator*, John B. could follow her path portside to see the ship emerge out from under *Thunder Mug*. He made it! But as *Let 'er Rip* rose up, the pilot faced an oncoming smokestack. It was a breath-stopping moment, but the bomber hurdled the structure. A lucky maneuver over a perilous field—but there was more.

As the bombers closed in to target, the toll surged. With intent to obscure the refineries, German smudge pots burning oil created a blanket of blinding black smoke that rose above incoming ships. Charging into the mouth of uncertain death, John B.'s ship was consumed in total darkness. It was any wonder his pilot could even see out the window to fly. But they powered through.

Exterminator led the next wave as they flew over the refinery complex. Framed in the crosshairs, bombs were salvoed. A boost from below lifted the bomber as she released her heavy load. It was time to turn homeward.

Behind them bombs had dropped, shells had burst, and battle wounds had been inflicted. Plexiglas nose sections shattered. Wings battered. Tail assemblies chewed. The aircraft still flying had been peppered with flak strikes. Many airmen had suffered injuries from direct gunfire. But still there was more.

Beyond the refineries, the swarm of Luftwaffe* fighter planes awaited them. Out of nowhere dozens swooped in, strafing the

---

* The Luftwaffe was the German Air Force during WWII, essentially the air component of the Nazi German military. In 1940, it was the largest and most formidable air force in Europe.

B-24s with streams of bullets. But as soon as they flew in, they were gone. *Exterminator* was not the chosen prey—perhaps the only reprieve of the day.

As the Libs exited the outer ring of the target, the battle was over. The bombers that had survived Ploesti reversed a course that mirrored the morning's flight. With formations shattered, ships at varying abilities were left to their pilots and navigators to guide them home. Wearied crews sat back for the long journey to Benghazi.

John B. was on the return route, having outlasted the tougher half of the mission. He had made it through the flak, the fire, and enemy fighters but conceivably would wonder what else could get him from the rear. Or what was hiding ahead in the clouds. Well on his way back home, but still another twelve hundred miles to go.

Out the portside window, John B. could still see the black clouds of destruction over the target, no doubt revisiting the ride while trying to shake it off. With wind rushing through the nose, he would have struggled to anchor the map as he steadied his nerves.

As the ship rose to reach cruising altitude, power was reduced to conserve fuel, easing the engines for the long trip back to base. Other Libs were passing them in a race home but three stragglers merged in.

With *Exterminator* in the lead, John B. called out the course heading home.

ONE

Hillsboro, Illinois Years Before

OFTEN, THE BOY ROAMED the rolling hills as they dipped into meandering watercourses, a landscape primed for adventure. Traipsing through sandbars, he uncovered artifacts of Indian tribes marking their territory in times long before. As he held an arrowhead with pride, he would ponder the warrior who'd once used it for hunting. But distracted again, he spotted a rising bluff that invited his climb. Crawling to the top, he could see the army-green waves of cornfields and patchwork pastures dotted with dairy cattle. He was certainly proud. This wide expanse of land was his home.

In the distance he could see rooftops of businesses in Hillsboro, a small community located in south-central Illinois. Boasting natural resources, the town's economy grew with its coal fields, zinc smelters, and glass and brick factories while still relying on its rich farmland.

Built along the crest of a flattened ridge, Hillsboro's Main Street had transitioned from horse-drawn carriages to streetcars connecting its nearby industrial district. To the north was the courthouse, a stately redbrick Napoleon-III style that stood proudly with two towers. Framed in limestone, the distinctive arched windows were as imposing on the outside as the law it upheld inside. As the county seat, Hillsboro attracted attorneys and businessmen as well as statesmen who often rallied their causes on the courthouse square.

Just as other booming Midwestern towns, Hillsboro thrived in great prosperity until the Crash of 1929. But rising from the Great Depression, government relief projects initiated by the WPA* alleviated unemployment, helped local contractors, and improved infrastructure. The town rebounded. In 1940, with a population of 4,435, Hillsboro boasted two movie theaters, three banks, and two newspapers. With renewed prosperity, salaries were on the upswing, youth sought higher education, and there was reason for optimism.

It was in this Norman Rockwell community that both the White and the Cress families lived.

A respected businessman, John White, Sr., made his name buying up property during the Depression years. He had a hand in multiple enterprises, including the launch of White & White, a lucrative insurance agency on Main Street. Having chartered the country club, John Sr. often hosted golf tournaments and champagne dinners that went late into the night. As nephew to the owner and publisher of the *Montgomery County News*, he was closely connected with all that went on in the community and beyond. And given their social and political associations, the White family was once considered *Hillsboro's version of the Kennedy clan*.

* "WPA" refers to the Works Progress Administration, a New Deal program created by President Franklin D. Roosevelt in 1935 and designed to help the unemployed during the Great Depression. The WPA employed millions of people to build public works such as roads and schools across the nation.

Only blocks from the southern end of Main Street, John Sr. lived comfortably in a three-story clapboard house with his wife, Ada, and five children. Sugar maples lining the walkway, red geraniums in marble planters, and an American flag flowing from the porch column welcomed visitors into their home. While talk about political affairs often floated from room to room, the Whites loved entertaining friends with games of charades, vibrant sing-alongs in their Music Room, or croquet on the lawn. 1940 was a presidential election year and as party delegate, John Sr. rallied support in Chicago for the nation's neutrality while advocating a stronger defense for America. No doubt he believed in the country, a thought that began at home.

Located a mile west from Hillsboro's courthouse square was a large dairy farm homesteaded by the Cress family in 1818, *Cress Hill Farm*. Built on one of the highest points in the county, the home's redbrick Federal style commanded a grand view of the valley below. Massive corbels, adorned with cutout stars and white scrollwork, flanked the overhanging portico of the front porch. A vision of America, the home had been handed down generations to the oldest son. The character of this grand place embodied the bloodline that preserved it.

The old road between Vandalia and Springfield had split Cress Hill Farm as it wandered past the home's front door. Years before, the clomping of horses pulling wagons and the tinkling of metal rings on leathered leads interrupted the stillness of a late-summer day. Travelers waved as they passed by or tied their steeds to the hitching post where the trough watered the mounts. *During Abraham Lincoln's time, Vandalia was the state capital and Lincoln used this road as he traveled from his home in Springfield to the capital* and would have stopped long enough for conversation.

Involved in general farming and stock raising, Jim Cress, Sr., managed the homestead, a *showplace*, using cutting-edge techniques and novel systems. When bovine studies were needed to advance the dairy industry, Cress Hill Farm provided the necessary four-legged participants. In 1920, the University of Illinois named the *Hill* the "best farm-to-market dairy south of Chicago." On the farming side, the University used the *Hill* as an *early prototype for terrace farming*, the same method used in growing grapes on Tuscan hillsides. Jim Sr. served on the county's board of education and his father was president of the Illinois Farm Bureau, an organization touting 6,000 in membership across the state. No doubt the family was influential in the state's stock and agricultural development.

Both families were solid in the community. They knew anyone who mattered. The Cresses' prominence and the Whites' affluence made for tight-knit relations and their children—Bob Cress, John B. White, Jr., and John B.'s sister, Polley—benefited from their parents' prosperity.

As the Great Depression wound down, big bands like Glenn Miller came into prominence. Radios were coming into common usage, and the jukebox appeared in most of the places where young people gathered. This was also the golden era of ballrooms and dance casinos. On the radio, nightly, live broadcasts played from America's famous hotels simulcasting the likes of "*. . . live from the Empire Room of the Palmer House is Louis Armstrong . . .*" Inspired by the music of the day, youth's energy and innocence danced through the night. Life was good.

The oldest of five children, John Brown White, Jr. (John B.), was born into a family that instilled the belief of giving back to a life given much. Groomed for limitless potential and an interest in elite sports, he competed in fencing, played squash, and excelled at chess.

Handsome and charismatic, he was a natural at communicating and handily won debates broadcast live on national radio.

After years of schooling in Chicago, John B. graduated from Kent College of Law and returned home the summer of 1940 to open his law practice on Hillsboro's Main Street. With command of the language and a wit that could charm the most discerning skeptic, he was going places. "He imagined a broader future, running for public office and becoming a senator one day—perhaps even president of the United States," recalled Mary Hartline.*

John B. believed politics was the avenue toward positive change, a seed reflecting his upbringing. He had faith in the power of a single vote, underscoring the importance of an absentee ballot while away from home. One vote leading to a collective voice directed the country's course—a way to shape a future John B. envisioned.

While John B. was a lawyer filtering through the courthouse, Bob Cress's track was a few semesters away from attending law school. As best friend to John B.'s younger brother Bill, Bob was a regular in the White home. And he looked up to John B., not only as a big-brother figure but someone who seemed to have it all.

The youngest of Essie and Jim Cress's four children, Bob was christened Robert William after his maternal grandfather, a prominent attorney. Children of farmers were funneled into a one-room

---

* Mary Hartline was a Hillsboro-born actress and ABC radio and television personality (hosting shows such as *Teen Town*, *Super Circus*, and *Princess Mary's Magic Castle* in the 1940–50s). Married four times, her last husband was the heir to the Woolworth fortune. She entertained politicians (Spiro Agnew); Hollywood stars (George Hamilton); and royalty (former king of England Edward VIII and Wallis Simpson) in her home that was a couple doors from Mar-a-Lago in Palm Beach, Florida. After several years and four husbands, she returned to Hillsboro. She had saved a detailed scrapbook filled with newspaper clippings and personal references of John B. When asked why she kept the memories, she said, "I always preferred older men."

country schoolhouse accommodating eight grades, but Bob's parents, both university graduates, settled into paying tuition for in-town learning. Skipping first grade, Bob attended the better-equipped city school district.

To keep up with his older siblings, Bob was encouraged to handle matters as soon as maturity allowed. He and his brother, Jim, were brought up to understand what it took to run the farm as a thriving family business. External influences from economic, social, and political events were discussed during mealtime. These roundtable discussions in his formative years shaped his character and groomed him to confront life's moments.

Cress Hill Farm was ready-made for adventure. In the spring, Bob and his brother dammed up Bremer Creek to make a pool of water to swim in. When autumn yielded to winter's freeze, the pond transformed into an ice-covered surface where they skated in bladeless boots long after daylight surrendered to the stars above. As kids, there wasn't a corner of the fields and watersheds they hadn't explored.

There was time to have fun but there was also a mountain of chores. Cleaning out the chicken house or weeding the orchard, the family had duties around the farm. Bob and his brother worked with the hired hands in caring for the cows, sheep, and pigs. Everyone had to pitch in—mow the yard, mend fences, or bring in the crops—all for a smooth flow of operation.

Growing up on a farm in southern Illinois homesteaded by his third great-grandfather was a great empowerment but, at the same time, it was hard work. It was Bob's job to maintain the county cemetery that rested on Cress Hill, where tombstones dated back to the mid-1800s. When farm machinery was at rest, deer kept company with the departed as hawks flew guard overhead. It was a peaceful place.

Cress Hill Cemetery was a twenty-acre parcel. Working the tractor, power mower, and power rake, I cut the twelve undeveloped acres in a few hours. But the eight acres around the headstones took a good five full days. While I lived just up the hill, the real reason I got the job was because no one else would do it for the budgeted two dollars.

Bob's grandfather, DadDad, had retired from farming but still owned the homestead. He was the bank's vice president and had a reputation for being fiscally conservative. And he managed the cemetery likewise. His primary residence was in town. *I was sitting with him on his porch one day and finally got up the nerve to suggest that two dollars was a little low for cutting the cemetery grass.*

The courthouse was fifty yards from DadDad's home. Bob's great-uncle through his mother was Judge Thomas Jett. A four-term congressman, his political connections included William Jennings Bryan, who had twice run for US president and was a frequent visitor in the Jett home. Uncle Tom passed DadDad's house daily on his way to work.

After greetings were exchanged, DadDad got back to Bob. "Well, you saw Tom there. He makes a lot of money as a judge. But Tom spends more money than he makes, and he owes some people. I'll bet those shoes he was wearing cost at least twelve dollars. Hell, I never paid more than two bucks for a pair. And mine will last just as long as Tom's. You keep putting those cemetery checks in your savings account, and you'll never owe anybody." *That was the end of negotiations.*

Life's lessons were often learned on his milk runs. In the still of darkness, his father opened the back of the truck as Bob loaded crates of bottles. It was early but it didn't stop him from bringing up a variety of subjects. One Sunday morning he asked about his father's trip abroad while in college. The trip to Europe was structured around *blending of breeds to improve dairy production and taste,* but his father also discovered London's wealth and politics at a July Fourth reception hosted by the American ambassador, Whitelaw Reid. Invitation only, the event was held at Hyde Park's Dorchester House. The reception brought together American citizens as well as local politicians, business owners, and London's high society.

His father had said, "Amongst these elegant folks, my mother's voice whispered, *Stand tall with strangers.*" He had stressed that a broad stance always made an impression. There at the party, a top-hatted Brit had pulled Jim Sr. aside to talk about an incident in North Africa. Headlines had rumored German military intervention in Morocco. The year was 1911. In the days before July Fourth, Berlin had dispatched a gunboat and troops to the French-controlled port of Agadir. The French were outraged at the provocation. At the same time, the British Royal Navy feared Germany's increasing potential. English pundits deliberated involvement but were not inclined to support France given a position of isolationism.* At the time, Germany was gaining as a world power. His father's reflections paused as they turned onto Main Street. It was time to unload the crates.

In Seymour's Drug Store, greetings were exchanged before father and son were called to the front counter. With the stack of newly delivered newspapers, *Bob Seymour said, "Take a look at the headlines."* In three-inch boldfaced typescript, the *Chicago Sunday Tribune* proclaimed BRITAIN GOES TO WAR. *Hitler had invaded Poland.* Hitler had invaded Poland on September 1, 1939. Even in his youth, he recognized the impact of such a headline. But having just heard about the First World War, he tried to read his father's expression. Bob was sixteen.

As patrons entered the store, what promised to be a quiet Sunday morning turned into debates between townspeople. *The rest*

---

* Isolationism is a government policy to avoid involvement in foreign conflicts, not entering into alliances or providing military aid to other nations.

of the day we fielded questions, but all reduced to my father's reflection, "Sounds like the start of the last one." Bob considered what the headlines intimated: Germany's invasion had unleashed the European war. But with an ocean between them, there was some solace.

This was Bob's senior year in high school and much lay ahead of him. Before, being the youngest in class had cut down on his social life. The girls had been inches taller, but a growth spurt over the summer brought him added confidence. More captivating thoughts—basketball, graduation, and the university—were upon him. His reverie melted into a date with Polley. *Just maybe this would be the year.*

Talented and athletic, Bob was a star on his high school basketball team and played a mesmerizing trombone. An academic wiz, he excelled in Latin, science, and math. Bob could get along with anyone, and loyal, he would do anything for a friend. Growing into his tall frame, Bob's boyish good looks preceded him as he coasted through his senior year. He had long harbored feelings for John B.'s youngest sister, Polley. And while she hadn't always reciprocated in the same regard, Bob had always been there for her, even throughout her *boyfriends list*.

Wrapped in the latest fashion, Polley White had a warm smile framed by brunette waves. With a devilish humor, she had a bevy of friends and a sea of socials to attend. Playing the field, she avoided being tied down but fancied having a *beau-of-the-week*. As with all flirtations, boys threw compliments her way, lining up for a chance to take her out and perhaps eventually marry on to her well-to-do family.

While she relished the flattery, she knew John B. recognized her passing fancy as just that, seldom weighing in on the drama. But even still, he always had an opinion, and she would reluctantly listen. Polley adored her oldest brother and hung on to his every word, looking to him for guidance in making big decisions. He was her *North Star.*[*]

Polley had known Bob *forever*, mostly as a steady pal who had always been there for her. But through the years as Bob started to show an interest, she brushed him off. Being her brother's best friend first, it just seemed strange. While Polley fell for the attention, anything more than a friendship with Bob was premature. Was someone better out there? Although Bob had made romantic overtures, she was still hard-pressed to look at him as anything more than a friend. But there were times her intentions vacillated.

One day at school, Polley stopped Bob in the hall and said, "Mother thought you played well at the basketball game . . . Would you like to take me to the Hiltop dance this Friday?" And I said, "Sure, I mean, yeah!" *Up until that time I had only had one date, and I didn't know how to dance. My sisters hadn't taught me, so I went to the store and bought an Arthur Murray Dance Book. At home I did two steps up and one step back.* His moves came naturally, given each step was to a count of eight, not unlike playing music. Finishing a last rehearsal, he thought, *Mission accomplished.*

Through the school year, Polley would see something different about Bob. But it didn't alter her *list* much. Not being one to commit, *Polley had always kept a boyfriend list of at least five.* There were days her mood was hard to read. Voices in her head reminded her to keep all options open. But for a short time in their senior year, Bob had become *first chair*[†] in Polley's affections.

---

* The North Star, also known as Polaris, is a fixed position relative to other stars and makes a reliable guide for finding true north. Philosophically, the term refers to a person's moral compass, a guiding force or beacon of inspiration.

† "First chair" refers to the lead musician for a particular instrument in an orchestra or band.

As was his weekend routine, John White, Sr., got out of bed at sunrise. His plans promised an early morning of quiet, poring over the news with a steaming cup of hot coffee. Descending a second set of stairs, he reached the basement's garage. Turning the ignition of his Studebaker Champion, John Sr. let the car idle long enough to warm its thickened oil. The time gave him pause to think about who was left at home. The youngest of his five children, twins Bill and Polley, would soon finish high school and make their path to college. Surely he chuckled, imagining how a big house would behave with less drama.

With the car warmed up, he would head to town to pick up the *Chicago* paper. Glancing at the headlines, he'd see the editorial cartoon celebrating Lincoln's birthday while poking fun at his log cabin. Considering that a local boy, Lincoln, could become president was not far from the family's vision of John B.'s future. Headlines also captioned a warring pact between the Balkan countries. Being a businessman, certainly John Sr. would have wondered about the impact on commerce, particularly in oil distribution.

While John Sr. was still in the store, Bob was making an early-morning delivery. Balancing a metal crate filled with bottles of milk, he reached for the opening of the refrigerated casing, releasing the load before extending his hand and voicing a good-morning greeting.

In his commanding style, John Sr. greeted Bob before saying, "Mrs. White and I watched you play the other night—looks like you're headed for the conference championship."

As if buttressed by his son's talents, Jim Sr. was at Bob's side. After an exchange of cordialities, John Sr. exited the store but not before sharing details of the night's broadcast—John B. would be delivering another live debate on the radio.

Later that evening, John Sr. and Ada sat in their living room awaiting John B.'s debate. Dialing in to the popular Chicago radio station, the clock, in perfect synchronicity with the WLS broadcast, chimed ten *bings*. His parents must have swelled with pride knowing their son would soon be heard.

John B. was finishing postgraduate work at the Chicago Kent College of Law. The Presidents' Day presentation of February 18, 1940, was a final match delivered on behalf of his soon-to-be alma mater.

Prairie Farmer Radio Station hosted the presentation.

Headlines had publicized German dominance while hometown discussions questioned whether America should join Britain in her battle against the Nazis. At the time, cartoonists editorialized positions of isolationism. But the conflict was widening. Public sentiment was split. In response to the division, educational institutions put their finest debaters forward to present opposing political views. WLS offered multistate coverage of the issues.

As the radio host boomed with competitive shards toward each school, he handed the microphone to Kent's law school director, who opened the broadcast. "Tonight's program will focus on the proposal of whether the United States should form an alliance with Great Britain."

John Sr. would recognize his son's position of youth's optimism but knowing the consequences from the First World War, he remained on the fence for a second involvement. Surely ardent debates were ahead.

John B.'s opponent, Marquette's Anthony Palasz, a fervent defender of the isolationist, began. "International relations have been an important issue ever since George Washington sounded his warning against foreign entanglement, which he called the greatest enemy to a democratic government . . .

"Now, the affirmative tells us that we need this alliance; that Hitler, who is the modern version of the *bogeyman*, will soon be knocking at our doors to spread his domination over our fair land . . ."

Palasz continued, "Our military experts, the boys down at West Point, tell us that the 2,000 miles' distance between us is a pretty good defense against invasion."

Supporting the negative, Palasz concluded, "Since our shores are impregnable against invasion and since we don't need England's help, we must drop the idea of this British alliance."

Unconvinced, John B. would pencil in finishing touches to his rebuttal. The idea—leaving Britain to fight alone precluded war from approaching America—didn't add up. The Kriegsmarine had shown increasing superiority roaming the North Sea. Inventive German scientists were revamping ships to travel farther and carry bigger weapons. The range by sea was closing in.

Standing at the broadcast lectern, in true Lincolnian style, John B. began with a story of two hunters—one with a high-powered rifle and the other, the familiar shotgun . . .

The question now is, which gun, under the circumstances, was the best? We argue, a shotgun sort of an argument, in favor of an alliance with England . . .

. . . My opponent asks, "Do we want an alliance with England?" Before we can give an answer, he then asks, "Are you willing to fight and die for England?"

Of course, we don't want to die. He hopes the emphatic NO we answer to his second question will also serve as an answer to the first. None of us are fooled that easily . . .

. . . The arguments of the negative side are like the shot from the hunter's rifle. They argue against one kind of an alliance and unfortunately, like the hunter who didn't aim well, the rifle missed and the shotgun gets the rabbit . . .

. . . Mr. Palasz claims that England would be a ball and chain around our necks . . . that only tradition holds the Empire

> *together. What's weak about tradition? . . . In the last few weeks, tradition moved 100,000 armed and provisioned Canadians to the defense of England. Tradition is sending hundreds of Finnish Americans to aid Finland, to face privations and dangers they have never known before. And on tomorrow, tradition bids us pay tribute to a man whose deeds will ne'er be forgot . . .*
>
> *. . . The negative position says there can be no invasion by Germany or Russia because there is two thousand miles of open water between our nearest enemy and us.*
>
> *Finally, we are told, "Britain does not need our help." This is the last straw . . . An economic, political, or moral alliance, which we favor, is to be primarily for the benefit of our own United States of America. We want no other kind.*
>
> *After all, in 1914 we had no treaty . . . and yet we were drawn into that conflict. What have we to lose by an economic alliance? If we co-operate with England by selling materials and supplies, we might not have to sacrifice our lives. That is why we say that we, the United States, should form an alliance with England.*

With judicial scores in, John B.'s team had delivered a winning debate. Destined for more, his future was as limitless as the stars in the night sky.

SPRING 1940

Considered the most beautiful campus in the state, Hillsboro High School sat on top of a hill that dropped down to a winding creek bed. When the final dismissal bell rang, Bob often met Polley outside. In the shadow of the two-story schoolhouse, he helped her with math assignments, Latin, or history. He was a good student, but his help was part of an undercover scheme.

The serenity of a lazy afternoon was broken as Bob jumped to his feet, urging her to roll down the hill. Polley looked down at her dress as if to remind him, *No, I'm not playing any tomboy games.* Ignoring her pleas, Bob laid on the ground before tearing down the hill. At the bottom, he motioned his arms as if waving Polley toward him. Unwilling to resist a dare, she scanned the green carpet falling in his direction. The idea of tumbling uncontrollably into the creek terrified her. But at the same time, the thought was exciting. With her arms securing her skirt, Polley thrust her left shoulder to begin a slow roll. And again. It wasn't long before her body picked up momentum barreling down the grassy bumps. Rotations of heaven and earth were quickly bringing her closer to the creek. Polley was out of control. But before reaching the sandy rocks of the creek bed, Bob stopped her free-fall, whirling her up until her face was an inch from his. The feeling combined joy and letting go. Bob took her breath away. And that scared Polley.

With their high school graduation approaching, Polley was too comfortable with Bob's affections. Perhaps she was leading him on. Knowing they were heading to different colleges, Polley's imagination conjured random thoughts that excluded Bob. She suggested they see others. Bob reluctantly agreed.

Their high school graduation day arrived. As Bob had done at prior ceremonies, he played a trombone solo. It was made more poignant considering he had won the 1940 National Trombone Championship at Battle Creek, Michigan, just weeks before.

Keynote speaker Judge Fred G. Bale of Columbus, Ohio, stood primed to speak. He had presided over Juvenile Court and had spoken at graduation commencements across the Midwest. For the past nine months, a predominant conversation had been the war in

Europe. Headlines had made it clear the Third Reich was gaining ground. In closing, Judge Bale talked of the rise of Nazism. "Youth of today and all democracies face a conflict such as youth of no preceding generation ever has faced. The conflict is against youth in other lands that were brought up to think that their countries' anti-democracy should dominate the world. American youth must face this situation and struggle with it."

While the idea made an impression on Bob, war was still not a clear reality.

The summer before entering college, Bob's work on the farm was no different except it was harder. Likely because he was at an age where responsibilities accelerated. More tasking with the dairy business was expected of him. Before daybreak, he rolled out of bed and made his way to the barn for the first milking of the cows followed by bottling the milk. Milk runs made for the easiest part of the day. But returning from deliveries, he was back to the grind of unloading the truck, washing the bottles, and finishing up paperwork for the business end of his job. Mending fences or mowing the fields filled his day but by late afternoon, he saddled the horse to drive the milk cows from the pasture to the barn. There, he washed their udders, fed them, and did the final milking of the day. Hands-on and physical, maintaining the family business was hard work.

After a long day, Bob hoped for some social interaction in town. He didn't always have access to the family car and often bummed a ride. A couple hours fooling around with his friends was a welcome reprieve, but fatigue always coaxed him back home. Every minute of his day, seven days a week, was calculated. It was tough.

Bob's summer schedule was not conducive to dating. Girls usually wanted to stay out later. Polley was no exception. Not much had been going on between the two since before graduation. But Bob remembered a momentary change on July Fourth. Bill White had invited Bob to the Independence Day event. The celebration had long taken place at the country club where Polley's father was a founding member. The clubhouse soon swelled to a shoulder-to-shoulder swarm.

Seeing Polley, Bob navigated through a sea of elbows to reach her. The approach rekindled their friendship. At sunset, he took her by the hand and led her down the golf course away from others viewing the fireworks. On a bluff overlooking the lake, they cuddled as bright bombardments illuminated the sky and thunder boomed around them.

Following that night, Bob tried to carry on with Polley, but little time presented itself to meet up again. As the summer progressed, college days neared. Polley was headed to a girls' school, Gulf Park College, on the Mississippi coastline. Bob would be hundreds of miles away at the University of Illinois. Again, at her insistence, they agreed to date others.

TWO

A First Call to Serve

Across the Atlantic, the conflict widened. After Poland, Hitler charged into Denmark, Norway, Belgium, Luxembourg, and the Netherlands. But in mid-June, the "certain eventuality" in British minds became reality. France fell. England could only imagine Hitler's next move.

By the end of summer, Nazi Germany's bombing campaign screamed headlines with London in its crosshairs. While England had already been in the war, all battles had been fought across the channel. Until now. As prime minister for only a few months, Churchill stood tall against the siege. While an immediate counteroffensive was launched, Londoners were subjected to months of devastating air raids, famously nicknamed *the Blitz* from the German word *Blitzkrieg.**

President Roosevelt could see Nazi Germany consuming Europe. America needed a defense against the growing threat from the Axis

* "*Blitzkrieg*" is a German word for lightning warfare. It is a military tactic that involves a surprise attack, causing shock and disorganization in the enemy.

nations—Germany, Italy, and Japan. Time was ripe to train young men for military service. Just as Bob was unpacking at the University of Illinois, Congress enacted the first peacetime draft in the history of the country. With the Selective Service and Training Act signed on September 16, 1940, a call for young men to serve echoed across the nation.

Friends returning to Hillsboro for Christmas break dodged the reality of a foreign war. For those young men facing the draft, minds gnawed at the notion. But for now, stories sharing college escapades brought some semblance of peace.

With the exchange of letters, Bob believed he and Polley would see each other exclusively over Christmas break. When he first got home for the holidays, they shared a Coke at Mobley's, poring over crazy blind dates and pranks pulled off at school. When it was time to go, Bob walked her home, where they sat talking on her front porch. But Christmas vacation didn't end up quite the way he thought it would.

Polley had something on her mind, but she dared not change the mood. She would tell Bob soon enough about her date with another guy for New Year's Eve. Besides, she looked forward to going with Bob to the Christmas dance.

The holiday event was a few days later. At the dance, Polley could see Bob had learned some new moves. Putting aside silly thoughts of the girls he might have been with, she fell into his arms as he swung her to the tunes of jazz. And when they slow danced, he whispered the lyrics in her ear. But the evening would soon come to a close.

Bob memorialized the following exchange. After the dance, he took Polley home. He reminded her, "We'll do this again on New Year's Eve."

"Oh, I've wanted to tell you, I already have a date."

"I don't understand. I thought we . . . Who with?"

"Allan."

"That guy from Litchfield?"

"Yes, but, Bob—"

Bob was steamed but he chose not to press the matter. He opened the door to be sure she was inside before making a quick exit back to his car. Allan was two years older than Polley. Driving home he thought of the hours he'd spent writing her. *She seemed so appreciative. Now, on the biggest night of the year, she's going out with this other guy? He probably hasn't even written to Polley.* He thought about the character of the Litchfield boys. *I know from personal experience that Hillsboro boys took more liberties with Litchfield girls, and I assumed Litchfield guys thought the same of Hillsboro girls.*

He trusted Polley. But he didn't trust Allan.

A few days later, they saw one another in town, and she asked if he wanted to share a Coke. *I explained I didn't have much time because I was meeting my lawyer to get a divorce.* That was the last time Bob saw Polley before returning to school.

Back at school, he pulled out her letter. She had mentioned the Christmas dance but nothing about New Year's Eve. *I could have resolved everything with a straight letter . . . but I was still upset about Allan.* When he learned it wasn't a double date, Bob was good and mad. Admittedly immature at seventeen, he wrote Polley a letter casting doubt upon her character.

His direct language was like none she had ever received from him before.

A few days passed when a very thin reply arrived in his mailbox. The letter didn't have a *Dear Bob* greeting. Rather, it was, *What kind of a girl do you think I am? You don't own me. And you can just write your poems to someone else. Polley.*

Bob had often written original poetry to Polley. But the *Daily Illini*, a university publication, had a poem summing things up. Copying it verbatim, he put no greeting or signature on the card. Before mailing, he reread it. Since *dizzy dame* was underlined, it stood out. Although Bob believed the term "dizzy" in no way applied to Polley, he left it in and mailed it out. After dropping the card in the postal drop, he went over to check his incoming mail. An envelope from Polley dropped out. She had sent a birthday greeting. Her tone had lightened, or it seemed she had moved past his earlier accusations. Included was a cordial note. *For the next week, we will both be 18. But on Feb. 2, I'll pass you up again. Love, Polley.*

Bob felt like a dope given the *dizzy dame* card. He tried but couldn't retrieve his scorching note from the mail drop. Still at the post office, he immediately penned a message aimed at repairing the impending damage. He dropped the envelope in the same outgoing mailbag hoping she would get the postcard and letter on the same day, two very contradictory messages. Weeks passed.

Then, Polley's letter came. *You referred to me as a dizzy dame, so I'll answer you like a dizzy dame. You are jealous. You are conceited. You think you are cute. And you think you are so clever. You are just plain mean.*

Polley used the word conceited *a lot, usually a left-handed compliment, but she had nailed me very close to the way I probably was.* But not able to let it go, he buried his reply with sarcasm. *Brrr-rr-rr. I'll bet they use you to freeze the ice cubes at Gulf Park College.*

Concerned the *Brrr-rr-rr* card was a final break in their friendship, Polley wrote Bob to explain. *Last summer, Allan asked me to go to the New Year's Dance with him. I had hoped he had forgotten about it, but he called the day before Christmas to remind me. I tried to tell you on the porch, but you wouldn't listen. I'm sorry about the mix-up. Now I think you owe me an apology.*

Bob replied, *I am afraid I jumped to conclusions. As for anything I have written, I would like to apologize. There was very little of it that I meant.*

While they ended it on friendly terms, no more letters were exchanged.

Nazi Germany was sweeping across Europe. Recent casualties included Bulgaria, Yugoslavia, and Greece. Great Britain stood alone against the German Empire. While a formidable force, England could no longer be expected to do it alone. After weeks of intense debate between internationalists and isolationists, the Lend-Lease Act became law on March 11, 1941, authorizing military aid in the form of munitions, ships, and aircraft. For now, Britain had American invention at her side.

Germany's surge in the North Sea posed a threat to American trade and, more importantly, her shorelines. From the White House on May 27, 1941, President Roosevelt proclaimed, ". . . Unless the advance of Hitlerism is forcibly checked now, the Western Hemisphere will be within range of the Nazi weapons of destruction." While production of warring materials had boosted the Brits' efforts, the president urged additional engagement. "The nation will expect all individuals . . . to play their full parts, without stint, and without selfishness, and without doubt that our democracy will triumphantly survive." He reiterated the nation's call for young men to serve.

On Hillsboro's Main Street, a barrister's sign with his name written in bold script hung over the door of his second-floor office. John B. was approaching his one-year anniversary since taking a job with attorney Omer Poos, who was later appointed a federal court judge by President Eisenhower. As he climbed the narrow stairway, surely a glint of pride seeped through his smile as he reflected on the milestone. Although gaining experience in the field of law, John B. was not far removed from headlines coming from Europe. He couldn't help but wonder when America would join the fight.

Before the university let out for the summer, Bob came home for the weekend. He joined friends at the Ariston, a local tavern listening to swing on the jukebox. Toasting to old friendships, Bob looked to the door and saw a familiar face. He maneuvered through the crowd to give John B. a sincere handshake and shoulder pump. The two had not seen one another in over a year. Wasting no time, they exchanged recent exploits before crossing lines into hometown chatter.

With Bob in college and John B. a freshman lawyer, the two expressed aspirations as well as thoughts on the war in Europe. John B. had coursed his path while Bob was still steering toward his dreams. Looking ahead, they faced a future with youth's bravado, lighthearted and optimistic. Their goals were lockstep as they parleyed over drinks.

Colonel Albert Linxwiler's name came up in conversation. Bob had met the colonel at the Whites' home. Linxwiler was the family's link to FDR. Bob asked, "*You heard Roosevelt's last speech, right?*" John B. threw a questioning look before Bob shared a joke with a mid-Atlantic elitist accent. "*. . . I do not want wah, Eleanor does not want wah, Eliot does not want wah; but Franklin D. Jr. wants wah. He married a Du Pont . . .*" (The Du Pont family supplied nylon for parachutes, war materials, and nearly half of the explosives that US forces used during WWII. With a rise in the war effort and increased defense spending, Franklin D. Jr.'s marriage to a Du Pont meant not only power but big money.)

Dismissing the joke, John B. moved on, asking about Bob's sights on Harvard Law.

Admittedly, Bob was looking to attend the prestigious university—a goal he had been working toward. But the conversation flipped back to Linxwiler.

A frequent visitor in the White home, Colonel Linxwiler had wide connections that crossed political parties and state lines. In 1934, President Roosevelt appointed him postmaster general of Jefferson City. He had also served as vice president to then-senator Harry S. Truman, who served as president of the veteran's association Linxwiler had chartered. Pro-military, he had been encouraging young men to join up since the end of the *Big War.*

With Europe's troubles brewing, John B. had been thinking about his future, his law practice, and perhaps politics. A military post might catapult votes toward becoming a lawmaker. While he knew it was the honorable thing, he wasn't exactly thrilled with joining the ranks, but he told Bob that he had received *the* letter—his call to serve. John B. had not mentioned it to anyone else, not even his parents. Was telling Bob a mental exercise? Perhaps a flow of words made easier if he hadn't practiced his thoughts out loud. Besides, Bob was his little brother's closest friend, almost family. He would know Bob's character as one that would protect a confidence.

John B. had his eyes on the Air Corps. Certainly, he would have wondered how this detour in achieving his goals would affect his political trajectory, but at the same time, there was excitement at the thought of flight, a completely new concept. The exchange shifted to aircraft, engines, and wings as thoughts rallied to adventure high in the sky. Surely . . . *off we go into the wild blue yonder* . . . resonated in their minds.

As the evening turned to midnight, the two offered good wishes to one another. No doubt, Bob envisioned flying alongside John B. and soaring with eagles.

After a rocky beginning to the year with Polley, Bob knew any mention of John B. would make her smile. It was a brief note that said: . . . *I was out with John B. on Friday night. We had quite a time together.* She'd learn more soon enough.

John B. held *the* letter for over a week. He couldn't wait any longer. It was time to tell his parents.

In the short months since registering, it was never a question of if, but when John B. would be called to serve. With headlines that America's greatest ally was floundering in Germany's wake, he would know that *the* letter, together with thousands more, was the president's whispering lifeline to Britain.

Although an incessant planner, the *when* of life caught John B. at a time when he was settling into his law practice, gaining confidence with each hearing covered. While he believed his next chapter was destined to argue the issues of law, he didn't realize his service would come quite so soon.

To be sure, he had apprehensions. A shade of uncertainty, perhaps fear, harbored within. No longer would he be in control of his next move. At least not while under the government's thumb. Granted, military service had advantages in post-service leadership roles. And certainly, he wasn't afraid of the fight. But his present track was compromised. Or at least detoured.

He would consider his time at home. After years of schooling in Chicago, he had returned to Hillsboro. It was there he found comfort on a sidewalk where neighbors waved from a front porch. And kids on bicycles cruised along with pet dogs trailing behind. While only a temporary assignment, he knew full well this news was not something his parents would relish.

He would wonder how long this mad war would go on. But America had yet to join the fight. His confidence broadened, believing he would join the Air Corps and do his part to help Britain bomb the brutal regime with smashing precision. Soon he would return.

With his last turn he could see the family home, rising three stories above the ground. Many a day he'd spent climbing the maple trees that lined the entrance. Black-green shutters framed his bedroom window on the second floor. From that sill, dreams of distant travels were born.

In front, the home's foundation was covered with verdant plants in bloom. Mint and rosemary perfumed the side yard, as Old Glory waved freely from the porch column but for the stillness in the air. It was home, where lightheartedly he referred to his "tribe," a term of endearment for the family that flourished inside.

On hot afternoons, his mother indulged him with a glass of iced tea garnished with fresh mint or baked cookies still warm from the oven. He would spend hours on the wooden swing trying to catch a breeze or playing word games with his sisters. And in the corner sat his chariot, an oversized marble urn adorned with carvings of Roman goddesses that he commanded as a toddler, now filled with a fern draped in feathery fronds.

Once inside, John B. walked into the room that had long tendered a loving devotion to family. Memories. Christmases past brought to life with endless sing-alongs. Laughing. Watching the twins make a mess of the room only made worse when he scattered chair cushions to make a fort. Or a vision of suitors calling on his sisters. Gathering around the radio for Illinois football. And dinners of popcorn and apples meant Mother's Sunday night off. Gratifying thoughts of family.

He followed the sweet scent of tobacco. Over the years his father had sat beside a wooden humidor weaving tales of princes slaying dragons to his children, who circled around wanting for more. But now he was hidden behind the newspaper, no doubt absorbed in the business section. With John B. in the room, John Sr. lowered the paper before welcoming his son.

As long as the family could remember, John Sr. had engaged his children in the centuries-old game of chess. His father inspired a purpose with each move, a calculated action to follow a predetermined strategy. John B. wrote home of words learned from his father: *Always reason one or even two steps ahead of your opponent.* In a subtle way, it was his father's attempt at preparing his children for the complex choices in life. On the board and beyond, John B. would keep options open and make sacrifices count with a goal to win.

Looking for a distraction, of course, John B. suggested a game.

Usually, the games came out after dinner, accompanied by drinks and spirited conversation. Perhaps tonight an aperitif seemed apropos. His father would have poured each of them a shot of fine scotch whiskey.

As often done in the White home, a checkered board of walnut and ash would be placed on the father's footstool. The board became a link between the two men. With an eye on his seasoned opponent, John B. would wonder if his father had any idea of what he was about to reveal. Would he be proud? Or would he use his political associations to procure a deferment?

John B. would begin. It was not unusual to move the queen's pawn forward to center block. Waiting for his father's next play, FDR's speech of engagement likely flashed through his mind. As the game played, John Sr. would have studied his army of pawns, narrowing his choice to one chessman countering his son's move.

Conceivably preoccupied with his upcoming departure, John B.

would pause with his forefinger on the knight. A noble character, daring and bold, dangerous and powerful, it was complicated by emotion as protector. But before committing, he would switch to the queen's bishop, moving her diagonally until satisfied with the proper resting spot.

Not unlike poker, each man held his gaze—would the student gain the teacher's advantage? A father-son connection was a most telling bond. John Sr. made the next move.

John B. would again deliberate his move with his gaze likely locked on the queen's knight, a steed filled with energy awaiting the opening gate. It was time to make his move. Putting a north hold on the horse's head, he would lift it slightly before exhaling the news—his call to service. John B. was to report the end of June.

While not surprised given the escalating news from Europe, John Sr. would have been taken aback. His oldest child had been drafted. His emotions, no doubt, widened. He had eyed such promise in this son. Born with an infectious can-do spirit, John B. had been shaped for limitless potential and had an advanced education with interests in elite sports. A future in politics was not beyond reason.

The question of deferment came up. After some discussion, it was agreed that it was time to give back to the country. And right now, to England. Certainly, John Sr. was proud his son would serve the country, accepting America's responsibilities to England. But the isolationists still offered a strong rebuttal especially now the reality of war had reached out to his son. Not yet prepared to accept the inevitable, he hoped his son's military exercises would stay on home turf.

It seemed a hastened calling. There were many good-byes at the courthouse and down by the lake pavilion. John B. would focus his remaining time at home with like-minded politicos, school friends, and neighbors sharing gallant stories and promises to keep. He would be missed.

The sun cast long shadows as a bus carrying military recruits rolled into town. John B.'s friends gathered around to witness the departure of Hillsboro's native son. As Hartline recalled, "everyone offered him good luck and hugs. With suitcase in hand, John B. climbed up to greet the driver before turning around to wave good-bye."

On June 24, 1941, John B. left home to begin basic training at Camp Grant in Rockford, Illinois.

Cushy classes had softened Bob's hands, but no time was lost getting back into chores. College life and parties had made him realize just how hard work on the farm was. Gearing his studies toward law, his desire of becoming a farmer was fading.

One Friday afternoon, he had finished early and headed into town where Polley was interning at the bank. In an exaggerated fashion, he mimed a wide-mouthed *Mobley's* and held up four fingers. Later she met him at the soda fountain counter, the place where they had often gone over the years. After sharing a Coke, she asked Bob to walk her home. The sunporch on the backside of the house offered space where teasing and jabs were exchanged. They mulled over the latest town gossip. Time escaped them.

Probing one another about dating, Bob noticed a car pulling up to the curb. He memorialized the following exchange.

"Who's that?"

"Oh good Lord, that's Jim!" Polley had forgotten she had a date to the show. She continued, "He mustn't see you."

"Jim Dagon? Polley, I don't go out the back door for anybody." Bob knew Jim well; he was a pretty good guy even though Bob had lost to him for senior class president.

"He is so jealous of you. Please don't cause any trouble."

Bob paused at the *jealous* part, wondering what she meant. "Okay, I won't but—"

"Quick, go somewhere . . . anywhere!" In a panic, she pulled him by the arm through the kitchen before pushing him into the powder room. Then she regained composure before opening the front door.

Bob perched an ear. Jim's drivel would be great fodder for future teasing of Polley. It wasn't long before he heard the front door shut and he was *free* to go.

Given the rise in the military build-up, fewer eligible bachelors were in town. Bob chuckled as Polley had one hidden in the bathroom and another taking her out. As he made his way to the lake pavilion, he laughed knowing his own list of girls awaited.

In September, Polley transferred to the university. When their paths crossed on campus, indifferent exchanges were met with proposals to meet. But they never did.

Not until one night after Thanksgiving.

Back from an early dinner, Bob began a four-hour accounting assignment. In the common area of the men's dorm, the phone rang. The resident advisor sent a freshman upstairs to advise Bob of the call. Thinking it was his parents, he bounded down the flight of stairs. Picking up the handset, he heard *loud music in the background* and recalled the exchange.

Over the phone she whispered, "Will you come get me?"

"Polley? Where are you?"

The background noise became all too clear. He could hear girls chanting "*Herman the German*"* but the melody drifted into laugh-

---

* "*Herman the German*" was a beer-drinking chant at the time of WWII. The author is not aware of the roots of the song; however, the name Hermann etymologically means "man of war." Additional references may be to Hermann Göring, the commander-in-chief of the Luftwaffe during WWII. He was a fighter pilot in WWI, a prominent Nazi leader, and an associate of Adolf Hitler. Ultimately, he was tried

ter with words he couldn't understand. Bob sighed disapproval. But at the same time, at the first sign of trouble, Polley had called him.

Again, she pleaded. "Please come get me." Polley was at Bidys on a pledge walkout.*

Bob responded, "Call your brother!"

"I can't. Please?"

Grabbing his jacket, he made the fifteen-minute walk to Bidwells in ten. Inside, tables had been pushed together. Heckled as he maneuvered through the room, Bob spotted *twenty of the prettiest girls [he] had ever seen*. Mixed in the group, he could see Polley's head was listing as she leaned heavily on the table.

"Hey, kiddo—you all right?" She offered little response. Grabbing Polley's arm, Bob found her body wilting. As they left the bar, he learned she couldn't return to the house until later—*walkout rules.*† *[Bob] thought, Oh gee, what have I gotten into? What the hell am I gonna do with her until 11:30? And when am I gonna study for accounting!*

Out the door and with little patience, he began his interrogation. As he learned, she had become sick the first time she started drinking. Her condition played on his sympathy. She hadn't been the first victim of the chant "*Herman the German*" and certainly would not be the last. Bob opened up about an incident that had happened in his freshman year.

The Hillsboro brood had gone to the Victory Tavern in downtown Champaign where a pitcher of beer was fifteen cents cheaper

at the Nuremberg trials and found guilty of war crimes and sentenced to death by hanging.

* A "walkout," in a sorority, was a required get-acquainted gathering for pledges (new members).

† "Walkout rules" refer to guidelines/consequences in a walkout. Early departure could mean being grounded.

than bars closer to campus. As Bob explained, *"Banging our fists on the table, we chanted, '*Herman the German *has lost his Messerschmitt and no one knows where to find it' . . . then all fingers point to one, saying, 'YOU know where to find it' and he has to chug a beer. Well, no surprise—at the end of the first chant all fingers pointed to me. After more chants and beer, it was final call. And again, no surprise—all fingers pointed in my direction. I started to chugalug and about halfway down I got choked, letting it out all over the table [and] showering Polley's brother with the suds."*

Later, Bob and his friends walked back to campus. *Between Champaign and school was a little creek they called the Boneyard.* It inspired student folklore and provided ample setting to act out impulsive behaviors, often called *boneyard baptisms.* Boneyard Creek was a place where fraternities fought over tugs-of-war, upperclassmen pushed unsuspecting freshmen into the chilly waters, and too much libation was expelled. Many a girl had been courted there, naïve to her suitor's true intent. It was said the remains of students who couldn't hack the tough curriculum jumped to their demise and lay hidden under the muddy waters of the creek bed.

With the three of us feeling no pain, we went looking for bones. The two double-teamed and pushed me over the bank but not before I grabbed their ankles and we all face-planted in the creek. I told Polley the story to make her feel better and said, "If you had stayed with that crew, you might have ended up in the Boneyard too!"

The clock tower chimed ten. Still too early to return, they hid behind a hedge at her sorority house.

When two cabs arrived at the curb unloading a gaggle of girls, Polley joined her pledge sisters on the front walkway. Going through the door, she turned back to wave, wearing a look Bob hadn't seen before.

The next afternoon, Polley called me to deny any foolishness she may have pulled. She asked me, "So did I say anything I'm going to regret?" and I reminded her of the very sweet time we shared. Of course, she denied admitting to anything.

Surely, he believed, his collegian act of chivalry would begin to unlock her heart.

THREE

America Joins the Fight

John B. pushed through basic training, but he wanted to fly. He did all he could to steer his course toward the stars. By November 1941, he'd enlisted in the Air Corps, where changes came swiftly.

Having matriculated through a series of medical evaluations, John B. was told to wait. After what seemed an hour, a young lieutenant, another doctor, passed through the curtain. After brief introductions, he turned a somber face to John B. "I have to disqualify you." Seldom did anything catch John B. off guard. Racking his brain, he would wonder *what in hell* the doctor could be talking about. Then he heard it. *Hay fever. Anyone with the condition was precluded from becoming a flying cadet.* John B. couldn't imagine that an obstacle so minuscule could cut him from the program. Never one to give up, John B. conjured his debating days and spoke with another lieutenant. How would he minimize a lifelong condition? Perhaps it was simply an acute condition, a short-lived virus. Certainly not a chronic case.

Keeping the conversation alive, John B. went up the chain of command to a senior officer. In a letter home, he wrote, *I talked some more and finally went to see a captain who was over both lieutenants. After a few words, he was convinced to overlook whatever I might have thought was hay fever. Any such history was scratched out of my examination and my record was sent to Washington, DC, as being physically qualified to become an aviation cadet.*

After days of passing rigorous testing, he was transferred to flight school. Having *met the government train*, he scored a *tourist sleeper.* Two days later, he arrived in San Antonio for his next adventure: Pilot Replacement Center.

There was such excitement in being on an air base. The perceptible change was in the sound effects. *Planes flew overhead with the regularity of streetcars day and night.* As for ground transportation, jeeps purred loudly but were drowned out by thunderous roars of aircraft ruling the skies.

On December 3, 1941, Randolph Field hosted a grand military parade. Joining the rally, *nine squadrons from Kelly Field arrived in 200 trucks.* The field was saturated with flights of cadets. Any observer could feel the rumble beneath one's feet. It wasn't the marching, but as John B. would look to the skies, he was spellbound. *I saw upward of three hundred planes in the air at one time while the parade was going on.* When much younger, he had seen airshows in St. Louis of biplanes from the last war. But on this day, it was the biggest show of military pageantry and might that he had ever witnessed.

On the following Sunday, alongside the paved taxiway, John B. joined a game of touch football. Trainer planes lined the gridiron. Deep in the game, the tower squawked its prequel transmission. With the message delivered, players reduced speed to slow motion. Pearl Harbor had been attacked. It was December 7, 1941.

A call to active duty was imminent. Missions. Combat. The reality of his service would sink in that Sunday afternoon. An all-out defense would soon be dispatched and undoubtedly John B.

recognized his name would top the list of deployment. Not exactly what he had in mind.

At the same time John B. heard the news, Bob was huddled with college friends around the radio. They were listening to WGN's broadcast of the final game of the regular NFL season. Kickoff at Comiskey Park thrust a Chicago rivalry between the Bears and the Cardinals. *Most of the Illinois boys backed the Bears, who, if they won, would be tied for the Western Division championship with Green Bay.* The Bears were in the lead carrying the ball when rookie reporter Ward Quaal interrupted the broadcast with a special news bulletin. "The Japanese have attacked Pearl Harbor by air!" *We knew at that moment that we would have to get into the war.*

Later that night, thousands of us marched out to President Willard's home to try to get classes suspended the next day so we could listen to President Roosevelt's address. Being football season and with the Illinois cheerleaders in front of us, we chanted, "B-E-A-T, beat JAPAN" over and over again. In spite of our enthusiasm, he wouldn't allow us to cut classes to hear FDR speak. But the next day in English Lit, my professor brought a radio into class, so we did get to hear it after all.

Following class, Bob deliberated his next step, knowing his call to service would be escalated.

With war declared on Japan, three days later Germany declared war on the United States.

Washington was a frenzy of activity with this new declaration. Telephone operators were in constant movement aligning the wires of spaghetti connecting lines on switchboards. Messengers on bicycles delivered classified memos between the White House and the War Department. Strategies were proposed and timelines were directed.

Before Pearl Harbor, an independent Air Force had not existed except to augment ground troops—the Army Air Corps. Recognizing the air supremacy of two hostile opponents, America would now react. President Roosevelt ordered a mass production of planes to counter the enemy. The directive also included men to crew the aircraft.

Initial plans had aimed at arming England with American air power, men, and munitions. But now America needed a defense along its shores. The military's mission became to fuel the Pacific and Atlantic wars, both at the same time.

On January 28, 1942, the Eighth Air Force was born. And in months, the blueprint became reality. The landing of heavy bombers, fighter aircraft, and energized Yanks would soon awaken the tranquil East Anglian countryside.

That week, all plans at John B.'s air base were in disarray. Classes were hit-or-miss as the officer instructors were pulled to confidential meetings, shifting cadets on lists to fill requisition forms into the next layer of training. John B. was catapulted into the mix.

Just eight days after Pearl Harbor, John B. was pushed through aviation training detachment into classification. Aptitude and psychological exams followed. Classes continued but in a more demanding style.

On track to becoming a pilot, John B. wrote home, *I'm in very low spirits. I've just gotten back from a check flight with our flight commander, and I don't believe I did very well on it. If I didn't, it will mean I get transferred again and into some other branch of the service.*

But with the country in attack mode, the War Department made decisions forthwith. Just a month into the program, John B. was eliminated as a pilot. News came of his transfer to navigation.

Ellington Air Force Base outside of Houston was his next stop. *Navigators are the ones who tell the pilot where to go and how long to steer in a certain direction in order to get there when you're supposed to . . . The studies we take up all pertain to subjects that will teach us how not to get lost in the air.*

February 1942. John B. had *been moved again, back to Kelly Field to advanced navigation school.* Coursework was designed to build upon work completed in the previous phase. Layers of new knowledge stacked so tightly that techniques became second nature, hastening the rush to advance cadets to the next level.

In the classroom, they studied the intricacies of navigation by radio beams. A *right handy system*, wrote John B. But the radio compass was subject to errors. Atmospheric conditions. Signals confused by magnetic poles; a lesson few aircrews would experience firsthand.

Increasingly more complicated, navigation required considerably more mental work than any post in the army. *By week six, the exams were geared to be the Waterloo for a lot of us.* A *washout* was the military's plan to weed out substandard abilities.

On one flight, a photographer was escorted into the small fuselage of a trainer plane. She started snapping away. John B. would learn the photographs were part of an upcoming issue in *Life* magazine's feature on *Aerial Navigation*. As photographed with his headset properly adjusted, John B. sat in the third seat of the trainer. With pencil in hand and chart on his desk, he started dialing the E-6B,* his speed and wind-drift computer, likely before explaining what the equipment was for. As they took off, John B. no doubt smiled at the thought of his picture appearing in the magazine.

* The E-6B flight computer is a slide-rule-based tool used by the navigator to perform calculations for wind correction, ground speed, and fuel consumption.

In the air, John B.'s focus would return to the flight. *We were given a course to fly, such as 270°, which means straight west. We start flying by dead reckoning and hold that course by allowing for wind figured by a maneuver called a double-drift.* In a simulated mission, *the instructor passed a note indicating an enemy ship was sighted at 20°00 N 98° 00 W sailing a course of 300° at 30 knots.* The exercise was to *course a heading and time interception if a turn was made in twenty-five minutes.*

John B. started the problem. Many factors figured in: *ground speed, direction, force of wind, pressure altitude, true air speed, etc.* By hand, *we compute how far along the course before initiating the turn.* At the same time, *we figure where the enemy ship was, given its heading and speed. The idea is to intercept the ship by flying a straight line to a point where both enemy and interceptor are at a certain time, given all conditions remain constant.*

The second problem was almost as much work except it was a radius of action problem factoring in fuel supplies. The exercise required patrolling an area until the last possible moment, returning to base with only the reserve gasoline left in the tank. In actual tactical duty, the reserve was usually minimal so that additional bombs could be carried. Guess it pays off to work the problem correctly.

That stuff he could do. But as John B. felt confident with dead reckoning, coursework moved to the stars.

In a new classroom, his group began celestial navigation. The concept surely prompted childhood memories of western travel with his grandmother; of dirt clumps hurled behind as he urged his stallion along a game trail; of navigating the corridor, a gauntlet flanked by burly limbs; and when the valley opened, John B. would have taken in the enormity surrounding him. Magnificent, oversized trees. The rugged mountains of Mt. Rainier. The vast skies above. His grandmother, *Nellie* to her friends, had inspired a love of nature nurtured by a spiritual binding. Nightly walks fostered conversation, creating a bond between the two. Her keen interest in the stars led to a curiosity of infinite galaxies that lay beyond. Nellie often encouraged tracking skyward, pointing out Polaris or Cassiopeia, and describing the maps the stars created.

In class, John B. would listen as academia resonated from his instructor. Celestial navigation would be the navigator's guide in the night sky. Although his body had been grounded in the classroom setting, his mind shifted from the heavens his grandmother had described to the lecture before him. He wrote home, *I wish I had gotten Grandmother to teach me more about the stars, it would sure make it a lot easier to grasp now.*

Clearly, John B. looked forward to a time when techniques would become instinctive. *Celestial navigation is no cinch.* It was not long before night flights put to practice what he was learning by day. *If I put my mind to it, I will do well enough.* But upcoming evaluations could cost him considerably. In previous exams, John B. had made some foolish mistakes. If he kept from making blunders, he *ought* to get by. His father's words whispered in his ears, *It's all right to make mistakes, but don't make the same one twice. Words of wisdom if there ever was any.*

Flights were at higher altitudes and to greater distances. Reaching an altitude of *13,500 feet was the highest I have ever been. We used oxygen most of the way. It was quite an experience shooting stars with an oxygen mask on.* Tethered to an oxygen canister while wearing a mask covering much of his face was cumbersome. John B. would soon discover the difficulty as his mask would bump against the bubbled glass of the astrodome. And he recognized the added challenges given adverse weather, or worse, combat.

On a training flight on May 30, 1942, his plane stopped in Albuquerque. Waiting for the fuel truck, John B. would go inside to get the weather updates.

At the same time, *a transport plane had flown in from Chicago to refuel.* As John B. stood at the desk in base operations, the door opened. Addressing the senior airman, John B. would extend a quick salute. Immediately recognizing whom he was speaking with, he surely congratulated the officer on his recent promotion. A conversation would begin. Brigadier General Doolittle discussed details of his recent raid over Tokyo. "Fifteen minutes and fifty miles out, the crew could still see the black smoke billowing from the target," as quoted in the *Austin American*. Still classified, the mission had originated from an air base the president quipped as *Shangri-la*. From several directions, sixteen bombers flew in at low level, a height of 1,500 feet, "to cause as much confusion" as possible while navigators quickly made calculations confirming sights below. It had been a risky raid over the Japanese capital.

With John B. headed for his wings, he had no idea that one day soon he would be involved in an infamous low-level mission not unlike the Doolittle raid.

On June 13, 1942, John B. earned his wings as a commissioned officer, a navigator in the US Army Air Force. At his graduation, his parents would revel in John B.'s achievements. "Later that evening a dinner dance was held on the Gunther Hotel roof," wrote his mother, Ada. For years, champagne hailed celebrations, christened ships, and launched marriages. Signaling the bubbly to be poured, John Sr., not unlike tributes he had made before, toasted to his son and the other young men embarking upon daring endeavors in the name of peace. His mother would join in, raising a glass with love and admiration, although concealing her reluctance to the job her son would soon face.

After being cleared with final orders, John B. had a weeklong furlough and drove back to Hillsboro with his parents. He spent time at the courthouse, down at the lake pavilion, and at the

Lutheran Church. But time was dwindling. The night before he left, a family dinner was planned. Polley came down from Springfield and Bill from Urbana. It was a joyous evening, ending a wonderful week with their oldest son.

Before going to bed that night, Ada opened her journal and wrote, "Nearly a year since he entered service and no furlough till now? How long before we see him again? War news is decidedly bad."

But John B.'s furlough was ending. It was the longest day of the year, June 21, 1942. Ada and John Sr. drove their son to St. Louis. On the tarmac at Lambert Field, the stairs to the plane awaited John B. After an embrace of arms between parents and son, he boarded the passenger plane bound for San Antonio. As the plane gained speed down the runway, his parents would follow it as the wheels left the ground. They tracked the airliner until it was only a dot in the sky. And then it disappeared from view.

The trip back to Hillsboro was surely a quiet one. Ada would reflect on her son's departure. An overseas deployment? When would she see him again? Arriving at home, she likely headed straight upstairs. Before slipping into bed, she composed a message in her journal. ". . . how we hated to see John B. leave. Watching the plane rise, he pulled back the shade and waved—left me with an empty feeling."

The Balkans topped ongoing diplomacy between Russian and Allied dignitaries. The Romanian military, fighting on behalf of the Nazis, provided resistance on the Eastern Front. There was a Soviet push for the American military to flex more muscle in the region, perhaps a declaration of war on the Balkans. And while the Allies counted on Soviet strength to further split Axis capacity, Russia wanted assurances their assistance would reap benefits after the war. While no commitments could be made, the Allies needed to keep Stalin interested.

On June 5, 1942, the US Congress declared war on Hungary, Romania, and Bulgaria.

Simultaneously, an attempt to avenge Pearl Harbor was initiated. Thirteen heavy bombers, B-24 Liberators, were on a transatlantic journey via North Africa with a final heading to Tokyo. But during travel, a last-minute decision to abort the mission was made and the B-24 engines were reduced to idle in Cairo.

Fate triggered swift changes in military planning. The recent declaration of war required a show of force in the Balkans. On June 12, 1942, those same Tokyo-bound B-24s were redirected to deliver an immediate airstrike on Europe's top-producing oil facilities at Ploesti. But with too few planes to inflict damage, the raid only served to alert the Axis of Allied intent.

General Gerstenberg, commander of the Luftwaffe in Romania, knew Ploesti would one day be the prime objective of the Allies. Plans were initiated to build a fortified loop around the oil complex. These rings of defense housed "forty separate batteries." In the surrounding fields leading up to the oil refineries, a gauntlet of fast-firing cannons was positioned. *Acht-acht*, as referred to by the Germans, or *eighty-eights* by the Allies, were anti-aircraft cannons recognized as one of the most fearsome weapons in the German arsenal. Each cannon had four barrels aimed in square formation. The advanced weapons system was designed with variable fusing and timed to explode at the formation's altitude. When an *eighty-eight* made a direct hit, it often destroyed the bomber.

To strengthen Ploesti's defenses, "barrage balloons trailing detonating cables" designed to snare the wings of bombers floated above the refinery complex, and "smudge pots" fanning oily smoke obscured the facilities. Positioned on the outer ring were lighter batteries with hundreds of machine-gun pits and towers. Additional gun emplacements were mounted on factories, bridge approaches, water towers, and church steeples; some "topped oil derricks" while others were concealed in "whirling haystacks"; others were hidden under the cover of forests and groves. The trip to and from Ploesti was further endangered by Axis fighters at multiple aerodromes ready to pursue the American aggressors. The Third Reich tenaciously defended its oil refineries.

Gerstenberg built the first air fortress in the world: *Festung Ploesti.* The name implied unconquerable redoubt. The refinery complex was a colossal land battleship, armored and gunned to withstand the heaviest aerial attack.

During the summer of 1942, Bob attended school in Champaign-Urbana. With no way to avoid the draft, he hedged his options for an officer-training program available to college students.

Often, Bob mulled life over a beer with Polley's twin brother, Bill. The military was a primary topic, not only because of John B.'s service but recruitment offices were popping up in every major town across the country. Recruitment trailers accompanied motion pictures at movie houses. He had just seen the film *Winning Your Wings*, narrated by Jimmy Stewart. The Air Force aroused his senses like no other.

With final exams over, Bob pursued the US Army Air Corps.* Not far from campus, Chanute Field had been designated the Air Corps Technical Training Command since the war in Europe began. At the enlistment office, a recruiting officer took Bob by the arm.

* The terms "US Army Air Corps" and "US Army Air Force" were used interchangeably during this time. The USAAC became a training and logistics component of the USAAF while the USAAF was responsible for frontline combat operations.

Crowning his sales pitch, he surely pointed to a poster-sized caricature of a single-engine fighter. *"Just picture yourself, commander of the cockpit!"* And from a background speaker, the melodic mantra proclaimed, *We live in fame or go down in flame—nothing'll stop the Army Air Corps!*

It was an exciting proposition. Bob phoned home. *"I'm joining the Air Corps."* With Bob's brother having joined the Naval Officer program, his mother replied, *"Airplanes? You know nothing about them."* To which he replied, *"And what do I know about boats? Besides, they sink ships too!"*

The following day, Bob returned to Chanute to commit to the program. As for matriculation, he was told there was time to finish college. What was not mentioned was the mounting speed in which the military needed cadets to fill vastly deficient requisition quotas.

FOUR

First in Combat

For years, Germany had crippled British supply lines in the North Sea. Fast, well-armed, and long-ranged, the *Unterseeboot** widened its prowl to shipping lanes along the Atlantic coast. Twenty kilometers off Florida's northern coast, a German submarine, a U-boat, skulked just beneath the surface of the water.

When the lookout spotted an object headed northbound, the German captain rushed to the bridge. With one eye on the periscope, he would make a 360-degree turn before scanning the water along the coastline. Adjusting the viewfinder, he focused on the vessel. His pulse likely quickened. It was an American tanker. Heavy at the high-water line, it cruised along Jacksonville Beach without escort. The captain didn't know it then, but the *Gulfamerica* had come from the Texas coast carrying 90,000 barrels of fuel. For some time, the U-boat stalked the ship before gaining position. The crew of the tanker was none the wiser.

---

* *Unterseeboot,* or U-boat, was a German submarine used in WWI and WWII. These subs were armed with torpedoes and deck guns to sink Allied ships, block shipping routes, and starve out the enemy.

The submarine positioned its bow to the starboard side of the tanker. Waiting for the right moment, the German captain would need a perfect strike. Releasing the torpedo, an explosion erupted. It was a direct hit.

Before, Americans had worried little of war on domestic shores. But with the harsh spectacle of a direct hit, America had reason for concern. It was April 10, 1942. World War II had come to Florida.

The US military took note. Headlines were censored. Radio silence along the coastline was mandated. Cargo ships and fishing vessels were banned from relaying any transmissions to coastal authorities, including seemingly inconsequential weather advisories.

In the coming months, German submarines loitered like barracudas in the Gulf Stream before coursing the Gulf of Mexico.

America would respond.

There is a rumor that we are going to England within a month. If I can find out that we're not, I'm seriously considering matrimony. It was the first time the family had ever heard any mention of marriage from John B.

Lucille Saliba, a classical dance teacher from Colorado, had been visiting her brother, a gunnery instructor for bomber crews, when she met John B. After a weeks-long courtship they married in the post chapel at Barksdale AFB in Shreveport, Louisiana, on July 12, 1942. A hasty affair, the nuptials were only witnessed by a few of John B.'s classmates from Kelly Field together with Lucille's mother and John B.'s sister, Anne White, and cousin, Bruce White. The day before had been John B.'s twenty-seventh birthday. In her journal, Ada wrote, "I am happy for John B., but it does something to me to not be able to see him married. I hope he can celebrate many more happy birthdays at home with no war clouds hanging heavily above."

Two weeks before their vows, John B. had been put to work on the Gulf. His first assignment was Fort Myers, in what he termed *a jumping-off place*. He called the camp *practical, no barracks of any kind, just tents. No hangar for planes, just sheds for tools and supplies.* The rudimentary accommodations were likely preparation for what he was headed for overseas.

A jeep pulled up as he stood in a group of new navigators. In a letter, John B. wrote that the driver shouted out, *"Hey, fellas, we need a navigator to hunt submarines." So I went.*

It was the first time I'd ever been in a B-24, which is a large bomber. Except during landing and takeoff, I'm up in the glass nose right behind the bombardier. . . . There is also a place for a gun to be fired by the bombardier or navigator thru the nose of the ship. If I should want to get out in a hurry, we open the front bomb bay doors & drop through the bottom.

The pilot gave me hand-printed orders from headquarters, and said, "Go ahead." John B. set the course. *We had to patrol the shipping lanes, 500 miles west of Tampa. I figured a search pattern, and we started looking for the submarine that had been reported.* It was not unlike the German U-boat off Jacksonville Beach.

We couldn't verify what we thought we saw as being a submarine. Murky waters and shadows from clouds obscured any definite sightings, but following a few leads, their brother crew bagged a confirmed *kill*. John B.'s message home relayed, *I've talked to navigators and pilots who have been in ships that [have] sunk subs . . . From the time the sub is sighted to the time an oil slick from the destroyed sub appears is scarcely three minutes.*

After that assignment, pilot Hugh Roper requested John B. serve as his permanent navigator on his crew. Anti-sub patrols "widened to the Yucatán Peninsula and the Caribbean" as John B. bolstered his position in the group.

Earlier in spring, the 93rd Bombardment Group had been established. The summer's anti-sub patrol was preparing the group for combat. At the same time their commanding officer, Colonel Timberlake, was in Washington advocating a move to the British Isles to engage the enemy. As word spread of sunken U-boats, three victories decidedly put the 93rd into being the first B-24 group to travel to England. When Timberlake returned to Fort Myers, he called select officers to share the group's trajectory. John B. wrote, *I was in on a secret confab discussing our flight plans for leaving the country.*

With mobilization nearing, John B. called home. He still didn't know his exact deployment date or ultimate location, but it was imminent.

His mother, Ada, wrote in her journal, "John B. called to tell me good-bye . . . I think a piece of my heart is gone. God grant he will come safely home again." A few days later, she wrote, "I wish I knew where John B. was going to be . . . I've got a dreadful uneasiness caused by this frightful war."

The 93rd Bomb Group, including John B., moved to Grenier airfield, just outside of Manchester, New Hampshire. But course heading soon turned to Great Britain. After topping off fuel tanks in Newfoundland, the crew's new B-24, which they named *Exterminator,* crossed the North Atlantic. It was an overnight journey. "Winds were stronger than anticipated."

Having relieved the pilot, the copilot asked for an updated heading. John B. would have looked left out the small portal before stooping to look forward through the nose. Likely, he glanced out the blister window above. Polaris! *I can't believe it.* The ship was headed incorrectly toward the North Pole.

In an instant John B. pressed his throat mike, issuing an immediate course correction. "Turn One-Eight-Zero. Now! John B. went through his briefing notes and found that sometimes when flying the North Atlantic, the magnetic pole will make the compass inaccurate, so celestial navigation must be used. John B. then took star sights, and we navigated by that method until we were out of the troubled area," wrote Roper.

"All during the trip we could see the Northern Lights, which at times caused the radio to go dead." With *Exterminator* back on track, they headed toward the British Isles.

SIX SEPTEMBER 1942. As the wheels of his B-24 touched down at Alconbury, England, John B.'s heart surely twinged with relief hitting the mark, especially knowing the crew had relied upon him to safely reach their destination. No doubt, he was proud that their ship was "the sixth B-24 Liberator to land on British soil." But as part of the initial wave of bombers to land, he also knew his crew would be the first to face active combat against an enemy known for its first-class fighters.

At the time, the entire Eighth Air Force Bomber Command in England was comprised of only three Fortress groups and the 93rd Bomb Group Liberators, which John B. was a part of.

Combat training and ground sessions continued. When coursework discussed planes being forced down, "training sessions were held to teach the airmen how to cope if captured by the enemy, how to escape from prison, and how to return to home bases." It was a very busy time.

The Officers' Club routinely kept a cache of reading material. Likely, John B. would have seen the issue of *Life* magazine dated September 28, 1942, headlining an article on aerial navigation. With his photograph on a double-page spread, he had become the face of dead reckoning. As captioned, "Science, the sun and stars paired with a sextant identified their ship's position as a dot on the map. But for the achievements of the navigator, precise flying would not happen." All of John B.'s hard work had come down to this while back home, his parents would be trumpeting the publication.

Before combat missions began, John B. wrote home that he ventured into Cambridge. The Eagle pub was one of the oldest taverns in town. A regular haunt of the RAF (Britain's Royal Air Force), brown ale was consumed to the tune of endless dogfights in the air. The setting and brew released the tensions of flights to warring targets. The antics of the English officers played out as one pilot climbed up onto a chair atop a table. Balancing a beer in one hand and a candlestick in the other, the pilot would scribe his name on the ceiling above in the black soot rising from a burning candle. Then another would step up to mimic the same precarious action. Initials and names memorialized lives of the day on the ceiling. Undoubtedly on his next visit, John B.'s name would be burned into Cambridge history.

It was late when they headed to the transportation truck. Getting around in a strange town under blackout conditions was no easy feat. Cobbled stones underfoot, John B. would navigate narrow alleys lined by ancient facades. Reaching out to feel stonewalls lining the sidewalk took the mind traveler back to the Renaissance and Shakespeare. *Time has brought the Middle Ages to modernity.*

But the war called. What training they had was complete. True combat missions were set to begin—no doubt a taste of war John B. hadn't asked for.

NINE OCTOBER 1942. John B. entered action for the first time. The day also marked the first-ever combat mission flown by B-24 Liberators from an English base. It was a historic day.

To his group of a hundred or so officers, Colonel Timberlake concluded the briefing with encouraging words. "I know you Joes can do it!" Timberlake's own argot was that if he called a man a *Joe*, then he was in. With the rumbling of benches, an armada of young men headed to their ships.

The target was Lille in Occupied France. Engineering facilities. Fifty German fighters responded by attacking formation inbound to target. As the Libs began the bomb run, the skies were filled with flak, black clouds of exploding shrapnel. One ship fell victim. Ten airmen gone. The narrative of the group's first mission stated, "Most of the fellows were frankly scared, some showed their feelings, and some had enough self-control not to. Captain Al Simpson, a favorite, was lost. The loss of his crew hit most of the boys pretty hard."

After debriefing, John B. sent a telegram back home to Hillsboro.

The next morning was game day in Champaign, Illinois. Ada and John Sr. drove up to see Polley and Bill, and to cheer for their team from the bleachers in Memorial Stadium. Illinois played Minnesota, winning the duel 20–13. It had been a long day by the time they arrived back to Hillsboro. But at the front door laid a real win. A telegram. Bold letters typed on tape affixed to the message spelled out *MY THOUGHTS ARE WITH YOU. KEEP SMILING. JBW.* The dispatch implied John B. had faced combat and that he was okay.

From that day forward, John B. flew as often as weather permitted. Attention turned to submarine harbors along the French coast. By the end of October, he was relocated to Bournemouth along the southern coast of England. Not unlike his work on the Gulf of Mexico, John B. was headed for anti-submarine patrol over the Bay of Biscay.

In November 1942, Churchill addressed Parliament in London. With headlines of a push into North Africa, he declared, "Allied forces will soon have far greater facilities for bombing Italy." A staffer placed a memo in the prime minister's hand, interrupting him. Looking down through his spectacles, the leader tried to maintain composure before smiling at the group. "Casablanca has just fallen to the Allies." Cheers and applause thundered through the chamber. Churchill would have wondered if Hitler saw the tsunami headed his way.

Plans could not have been achieved without superiority in the skies. In the weeks leading up to Churchill's address, aircraft had reduced Axis supply lines at sea, preventing enemy troops from getting food, munitions, and fuel. The American Air Force, John B. and others from his group, joined hands with the RAF Command out of Bournemouth, undertaking coastal patrol.

Missions seeking German U-boats were not unlike those John B. had performed as a newly commissioned officer. Only this was not the Gulf of Mexico but rather a mission that extended over the open waters of the Bay of Biscay and was complicated by intruding fighters manned by enemy pilots. According to the 93rd Bomb Group archives, "In late October, one bomber in the group was jumped by five German Junkers, Ju 88s,* during one mission." John B. wrote home, *We're on a special job which resembles the work we were doing in Florida and we're on an incomplete field again as usual.* John B.'s message implied the B-24s bombers had no friendly escort† to protect them from German fighter aircraft.

From late October through November, John B. and his crew continued to fly missions over the Bay of Biscay. At the time, they were "making an impact on the North African campaign by providing

* Ju 88, also called Junker, was a twin-engine German multi-role aircraft (a fighter airplane) used by the Luftwaffe in various combat roles.

† "Escort" refers to friendly fighter aircraft designed to protect bomber formations on combat missions.

protection for the American Naval Task Force sailing to the Mediterranean for Operation Torch," wrote Roper.

ELEVEN NOVEMBER 1942. As Churchill spoke to Parliament, *Exterminator* was flying over the Bay of Biscay. Earlier at briefing, the target was announced: Saint-Nazaire. Located at the mouth of the Loire in Brittany, it was home to one of Germany's most notorious U-boat pens and became known as *Flak City*. It was their second trip in as many days to the French port. John B. would wonder whether this day would be a repeat of quiet waters.

As engines fired up, word was radioed that a German merchant vessel had been spotted cruising north along the Spanish coastline. Roper wrote in his diary, "What a prize it would be to sink that ship." Certainly John B. agreed. It would mean earning another painted moniker, an image of a ship, on the forward left side of their Liberator, adjacent to the bombs representing missions completed.

An hour into the trip, daybreak rose from the east. The light forced its way through chinks in the steely skies. Flying along the coast of France, spotters scoured the seas below. As the sun climbed, waves crested and sunk as reflections bounced from white to gray. It was difficult to confirm whether a spot was a ship or simply nature playing tricks on their eyes.

With the Pyrenees ahead, the top turret gunner would stretch his neck as he sharpened his gaze. He alerted the pilot of a ship at eleven o'clock. Roper would scan forward and portside. Confirming the sight, he pulled back on the column, bringing *Exterminator* to an elevation sufficient to drop the bombs. At the same time, he banked easterly. As they closed in over the target, control was handed to the bombardier.

As was habit, looking through the crosshairs of his bombsight, the bombardier waited to hover over the hull. At the precise moment, the switch was toggled to drop the bombs. But in looking out the Plexiglas nose, no bombs had fallen. He toggled again but the bombs remained in their cradle.

The bombardier returned the controls to Roper, who quickly climbed and circled around for another try. And again, the doors failed to fully open, preventing the bombs from releasing. Curse words undoubtedly filtered through the fuselage at a failed second attempt. They weren't directed at the bombardier or the pilot. The hit would have been dead on but for the malfunction.

Now aware of the bomber overhead, the German ship retaliated by returning shellfire high into the sky. POMP-POMP-POMP came screaming toward *Exterminator.* Bursts of flak surrounded her. She was hit. Initiating a third attempt, a direct hit jerked the right wing-tip. Fire was too close. It was time to turn away, but not before communicating "the [enemy] ship's position to another B-24, *Hot Stuff,* commanded by Captain *Shine* Shannon."

Two hundred miles south of their English base, the tail gunner spotted a group of planes. He identified them as six British Beaus* at three o'clock low. But in that split second, the black cross on one of the wings came into view. "WRONG! WRONG! Six German Junkers! Junkers closing in fast." Out the window, the enemy fighters would "climb and crest in attack formation" before diving toward the lone bomber. Roper pushed the column forward, urging the B-24 toward the sea before leveling out "just above the waves." The fighters aimed shellfire as they chased the bomber downward. But flying at twice the speed, the enemy was forced to pull up to avoid diving into the ocean. The fighters circled around and regrouped. And soon, two Junkers were headed back with the other four not far behind.

* "British Beaus" refer to Bristol Beaufighters, fighter aircraft used by Britain's Royal Air Force.

In greeting the aggressors, the Lib's gunners began thumping away with their *fifties.**

As the lead Junker crossed over the bomber, the Liberator's turret gunner struck the enemy pilot. The fighter crashed to sea. And with another right behind him, the B-24 gunners hit a second enemy Ju 88. Too much fight for the other four attackers, they turned tail heading east to a French air base.

That was the most action the crew had ever seen.

On the ground, the crew chief began his rant to the pilot and said, "You can't land my ship with a full bomb load!" As the crew chief looked closely, his gaze locked on the track of the bomb bay doors. With a screwdriver, he lifted "an empty cartridge casing," spent from a gunner's machine gun, that had lodged in the narrow rail of the opening and prevented the door from fully retracting.

With a confirmed *kill* and a *probable*, two small swastikas were painted on the left forward section of *Exterminator*, illustrations used to show successes against enemy aircraft. Having faced incoming enemy fighters firsthand, one can only imagine the danger behind the symbol of a painted swastika. The German pilot was working just as hard to earn a like victory rendered on his plane. Combat in the air was pure chaos. And so was landing with a full bomb load.

John B.'s little brother had recently signed on for the officer candidate program. Were headlines of bravado lionizing the Air Force? He couldn't imagine bullets aimed at his kid brother. Later that night, hidden between lines to avoid any censorship, John B. penned a letter home: *Tell Bill to take any and all deferments he can get.*

Breaking from anti-sub patrol, John B.'s crew returned to Alconbury, where strategy was again redirected. The Air Force was drawn

* "Fifties" refers to .50-caliber machine guns used here for defenses on a bomber.

to a sophisticated electronic navigational system developed by the RAF, the same brains that spawned radar. The equipment allowed navigators to fix a precise course for bombardiers to release bombs through heavy undercast. They referred to it as *blind bombing*, or *moling missions*. Military minds banked on the method, touting it as the answer to carrying out missions in poor weather.

The Bomber Command narrowed the list to the most experienced crews to take on the experimental mission. As one of a handful of navigators, John B. carried out the trial approach, newly coined *intruder* missions. *At a station near Oxford, we are learning some more tricks about navigation . . . and some high-powered secret stuff.*

Four B-24s, including *Exterminator*, were outfitted with the classified device, the Gee box.* John B.'s crew and three others were the first-ever American airmen to implement this new phase of bombardment.

Christmas was approaching and this was John B.'s second away from home. Following the English custom, the officers of the 93rd Bomb Group waited tables and served the enlisted men. After John B. delivered the blessing, Lieutenant Linck and Major Sullivan (the commanding officers at the time since Timberlake was in Africa) rendered a couple songs in what John B. referred to as *whiskey tenors—mellow and smooth*.

A week later, four crews were ready for what John B. called a *historical trip*. According to the Air Force Historical Research Agency, it was "the first US raid on Germany." In addition to high-ranking officers of the Eighth Air Force Bomber Command, which included a general, John B. wrote home that *there were about thirty-two news reporters that came to interview us about it*.

---

* A Gee box, a British radio system, is a device the navigator uses to track radio pulses in identifying the target.

It was a big deal.

On January 2, 1943, packed with full bombs and boxes of bullet-fed cartridge belts, *Exterminator* was prepared to make the US Army Air Force's first lethal appearance over Germany. Bremen was home to *Flugzeugbau*, assembly works of the Focke-Wulf aircraft factory. Intelligence found they produced scores of fighter aircraft each month. It was payback to the swarms of Fw 190s* for wreaking havoc on Allied bombers.

Airmen paraded in front of parked Liberators before stopping to pose. The day was overcast "with heavy cloud cover" and undoubtedly the dewy chill of the English countryside. As crews boarded the B-24s, the clicking of cameras surely followed the Libs as they lifted off. Beyond the runway, the ships would disappear into the heavy fog.

German airspace touted the strongest defenses. Nerves were secondary as John B. no doubt beamed at the implications of the trip. It was the first time American bombers would fly into the industrial heartland of Germany—everything that made for strong headlines back home.

After crossing the channel, the Dutch coastline soon fell behind them. The weather remained a mess. But as they reached Germany's Ruhr Valley, the cloudy muck dissolved into broken skies. Visibility increased. On any other day, John B. would have welcomed the sun, but clear skies called for disappointment. An assured victory was ripped from the crew's grip.

The navigation system was designed to identify the target through thick cloud cover. The intent of the mission was to fly blindly into enemy territory, salvo the payload, and turn back before

---

* The Fw 190, or Focke-Wulf, also known as a Focker, was a German fighter aircraft with heavy armament and speed used during WWII. Along with its well-known counterpart, the Messerschmitt Bf 109 (Me 109), the Fw 190 became the backbone of the Luftwaffe.

German tracking got a fix on the flight. Clearing weather conditions put a snag in the plans.

Earlier at briefing, explicit orders were not to risk the loss of aircraft or classified equipment falling into enemy hands. But also, with the presence of a large press, the Air Force feared headlines would drop morale if ships went down or if they failed at the first attempt at bombing Germany. Success was primary, and if not, abandon the mission.

After a back-and-forth, a decision was made. Words bled through the radio. "Abort mission." The ships turned around short of mission complete. Like others, it was not what John B. expected, a feeling that filtered through *Exterminator*. The crew would return deflated.

A handful of intruder missions were attempted into January, but with negligible results, the plan was scrapped. Air Force strategy returned to the more conventional methods of altitude bombardment.

While January 2, 1943, marked the very first American bombing mission over Germany, albeit the last-minute reversal, some three weeks later John B. was headed for an encore—a second chance at notoriety.

On January 27, 1943, *Exterminator* flew lead position, joining another group as they headed for Wilhelmshaven to bomb Germany's greatest naval base housing U-boat pens. But for the earlier date, it was the first American bombing mission into Germany.

At 25,000 feet, the thermometer dropped to minus sixty. With frigid winds breezing through the open fuselage, temperatures were too much for *Exterminator*'s two waist gunners. The freezing conditions precluded any function in their hands and fingers. And without guns, the ship was unprotected.

Responding to an alert called over the interphone, John B.

would have raced to the open waist window. In writing home, he said, *Two boys in my crew got frozen hands and one a frozen face*. Neither had any movement in their hands. Timing was critical. *I took my tin helmet and filled it with water and soaked their hands until motion returned, likely saving their fingers. One of them passed out for lack of oxygen.* At high altitudes, moisture from an airman's breath could condense and freeze inside the mask, blocking the flow of oxygen. Similar to an episode over the Bay of Biscay, John B. was familiar with this danger. He pulled the mask from the boy's face, beating it against a strut until ice particles dropped out. Grabbing a portable oxygen bottle, John B. hooked into the line and shoved the mask over the gunner's nose, shaking the boy until he regained consciousness. According to the *Hillsboro Journal*, "Local relatives are of the opinion that Sergeant Dagon (gunner from Hillsboro) may have been one of the two men whose lives were saved by Lieutenant White." (Coincidentally, this Dagon was the older brother of Jim Dagon who dated Polley.)

It was unavoidable. With crew injuries, *Exterminator* was forced to turn back.

The Allied invasion of North Africa opened an opportunity for the Allies to convene east of the Atlantic. In January 1943, Prime Minister Churchill met President Roosevelt in Casablanca. The conference became a blueprint for the strategic bombing campaign in Europe. The next phase of World War II was devised.

Churchill declared the Romanian multiplex of oil fields and refineries as the "taproot of German might." Initial estimates projected that Ploesti provided Nazi Germany with up to 60 percent of its crude oil requirements (the number was later reduced to

35 percent). Shut off the fuel valve—the Allies reasoned—and Hitler's war machine would grind to a halt.

Knocking out Ploesti meant shortening the war.

The leadership's plan required gutsy crews to fly a 2,400-mile round-trip mission deep into enemy territory, low to the ground to evade radar detection, and drop their bombs onto a heavily defended eastern European target before returning to their North African base—all in a day's time.

The mission would be the first-ever "zero-altitude" air raid ever attempted.

FIVE

A Second Call to Serve

JANUARY BROUGHT A BOOM of war activity. The first American bombing mission into Germany proper had just been flown. Unbeknownst to those back home, John B. was part of the historic flight.

After returning from Christmas break, word spread like wildfire that cadets were getting called. It was hard to stay focused. With little motivation, Bob skipped many of his classes as he tracked the status of those around him.

Back in Hillsboro, Bob's mother would thumb through the mail and spot an official-looking letter. Handing the envelope to her husband, an exchange of concern likely mirrored one another. They called Bob. It was *the* letter—his call to serve. With his twentieth birthday a couple days away, Bob returned home.

As was his habit, long walks fostered thoughts that were best blanketed by the tranquility he found on the *Hill*. Quiet sounds prompted his reflections. Of his trombone solo and seldom seen pride across DadDad's face when Bob won the National Title. And Judge Bale's address at graduation, "Youth of today . . . face a conflict against youth in other lands brought up to think their anti-democracy should dominate the world . . . American youth must face this situation . . ." His closing words were never more poignant.

Familiar ground had always been a welcome partner, a comfort given the times. Bob had much pride in his home, *Cress Hill Farm*. The *Hill* had forged confidence. Resourcefulness. Everyday challenges had demanded solutions on the fly. *Anything is possible if I put my mind to it.* He had an emotional bond to the ground upon which he stood, inherited from those before him who'd toiled to improve it. His roots went deep into the black soil. No longer a piece of property, the Hill ran through his veins. It was a source of strength and security, a constant when so many things in life come and go.

Along his walk, he would have passed the barn with its towering brick-lined silo that stored the annual harvest; and the milking parlor, where hours were spent preparing for milk runs followed by friendly faces greeting him at daybreak; marching through pastures, serenading attentive cows with his trombone; and down the hill, a frozen Bremer Creek that brought memories of skating on bladeless boots long after dusk. As he made his way up through the cemetery, old souls gathered around him. Scenes inspired by a family farm. Adventures. Rootedness. Empowerment.

While he met his next step with apprehension, he wasn't alone.

The next day, he returned to school. A couple weeks later, his father called with the news he was expecting. Report to Fresno. February 25. Bob would think of a myriad of details to attend to. Check out of the university. Pack up his things. Arrange travel. Plan a farewell gathering. When he got off the phone, he called Polley. Although she was dating another guy at the time, he knew that his relationship with her was more solid than anything she had ever had. *We were still good friends and depended upon one another*, said Bob.

Fraternity brothers and friends packed Midway Saloon to deliver a grand send-off. Polley brought a large group of girls, adding panache to the party. The kegs quickly drained. A roasting came Bob's way, mostly mimicking a charismatic crooner, swinging the slide of a trombone or his quick-witted academia. The tavern resonated with *Off we go into the wild blue yonder . . .*, a mantra that bellowed against the timbers, it would seem, a hundred times. There would be countless hugs, backslapping, and talk of returning when the war was won.

A month after his twentieth birthday, Bob responded to the call. Following the morning service, his mother prepared a lunch rivaling the breakfast she'd served earlier. But it was time for Bob's biggest adventure yet. After his father's embrace, Bob left the familiar and hopped the train bound for Chicago.

At Union Station, the pace of hustled travelers, mostly boys studying signboards signaling a departure to a military destination, energized him. But as his eyes tracked upward, Bob would be spellbound. Suspended from the ceiling-wide skylight were thousands of miniature warplanes, all in paper white. Fighters. Bombers. Trainers and transports, all flew above. The tribute, a gigantic patriotic display intended to stimulate the sale of bonds, was commissioned after President Roosevelt ordered thousands of aircraft for the war effort. At the sight, he was *jazzed by the Air Corps* challenge.

Arrangements were made to overnight at the YMCA. Never before had he slept in a hotel room alone. In between consciousness and sleep, anticipation of future exploits surely danced in his head. By morning, he secured his *orange and blue necktie before sporting a blazer.* Bob's reflection in the mirror offered the final okay. *Good enough for a Rotary Club convention.* He was ready.

Exiting the hotel lobby, cold governed a brisk pace. With the station in sight, he would step off the curb onto cobbled streets where taxicabs crisscrossed his path dropping young men at the entrance. Dearborn Station was a hub of transient action. This passage was unlike any other. Inside the double doors, archways bordered the cavernous room accommodating ticket counters, oversized wooden benches, and passenger lounges while the clacking of signboards shuffled through distant departures. And over in the corner was a military post, where he would have been directed.

Hundreds his age tracked cordoned trails. *College boys clad in tweed blazers and ties bearing school colors* congregated in one area. Bob, in his of Illinois, mingled with others from Notre Dame, Wisconsin, and Northwestern. The station was also packed with servicemen wearing fatigues of olive drab who were relocating their lives to bases in all corners of the country and beyond.

Standing in the queue, friendships merged as they advanced to check-in. One by one, each young man signed the log and was ushered to a location to await further instruction. Called to attention by the sergeant-in-charge, each boy raised a right hand and accepted the oath. No doubt, big smiles befell them, as they became privates in the US Army Air Corps.

The rookies would be steered to one of many Pullman cars towed behind a diesel-powered red and yellow locomotive, the *Super Chief.* Twice weekly, the train traveled between Chicago and Los Angeles. It was made fashionable by Hollywood celebrities, movie stars, and famed singers. But for now, it was transporting young men to a military purpose.

In unison, the wheels of the locomotive muscled into momentum as the youths' energy dwarfed the sound of clacking wheels. "Nothing cemented friendships like a long train ride."

Nearing sunset, the dining car transformed into a social hall where recruits deliberated on service expectations, travel, and adventure. The valiant warriors would raise swords to battle and drinks to friendship. Returning to the Pullman, it was another night on the train.

Bronzed prairies were soon replaced by an evergreen panorama of hills. To the west, dual snow-topped masses of the Spanish Peaks emerged from the foothills.

Rolling into California, the steward knocked on the door, advising curtains were to remain closed through the night. *Blackout conditions. Lights after dark, a simple mark—no need to be an easy target.* Concern had been raised about attacks from the Pacific. Japanese patrols had been spotted over shipping lanes from LA to Seattle. The Ellwood Oil Company had been the subject of a surprise attack. As a result, coastal defenses were fortified while nerves were heightened.

After four days on a train, Bob arrived in Fresno. There was excitement in being on an air base. *Airplanes are going overhead all the time with the regularity of trains at Dearborn . . . Must close now and enter into my army life. Chin up because I am having a wonderful time so far.*

County fairgrounds housing shelters that once paraded prize-winning livestock had been transformed into a pre-aviation training facility where the basics began. In the rawest sense, a foul-mouthed sergeant molded boys from callow youth into the discipline of the army. The terse delivery of orders took Bob back to the milking parlor where, hidden from view of the hired hands, crude language was splayed across the stockroom.

While the army expected mastery of technical instruction and rote memorization, drilling was the mechanism that turned inexperienced civilians into compliant soldiers. Repetitive drilling was designed to galvanize discipline and build a cohesive bond among the recruits.

As Bob marched with his flight, they hammered out a melody: *If this is the Air Corps, what the hell are we marching for?*

A couple weeks in, Bob would have a lift in his step. So did the others. It was moving-on day and they were headed for preflight training. They only awaited the final okay. But fifteen minutes before the scheduled departure, the sergeant entered the barracks and said, *"Tough luck, boys of barracks 179. One of you has the measles and you're all quarantined."*

It was discouraging news, but the Army would not risk an outbreak. Spirits sank knowing drilling was on the rise. Quarantine translated into a delay in advancement. Base leaders were left with little plan to keep the recruits occupied. With no equipment required, physical conditioning was the answer. *Honestly, the life of an army private is so damn simple. All you do is take orders, exert physical energy, and get herded around like sheep. And brains aren't even required, why, I'd be better off without any. And dinner is not the evening meal but it is chow. You don't eat out of plates, but out of a mess kit that acts as a terrific laxative if you don't wash [it] thoroughly.*

With the war advancing at a faster pace, the military struggled to make camps available for the next phase of training. Soldiers could hardly be supplied at the rate requisitions were being written. At the same time there was a tremendous *washout* rate for those in the officer training program. In navigation, the military found deficiencies in math, physics, and science, courses necessary to complete the program. To remedy this, the Air Force sent cadets to College Training Detachments for intense coursework in hopes to reduce *washout* rates. But until colleges were under contract to take on vast numbers of recruits, Bob, like others, was locked in at Fresno.

March 20, 1943

Dear Polley,

I was so glad to hear that you got a letter from John B. When he comes back, he certainly will have some experiences to talk about . . .

With quarantine over, the recruits were moving on. As transfer orders were completed, they boarded another train. The full moon was rising as they rolled into Las Vegas. Taverns and gambling places branded by huge signs lured an entry. *It looks like a big carnival, only the Ferris wheel and merry-go-round [were] missing.* Bob had *never seen such bright lights on one street*, seemingly irradiating across the northern hemisphere. *No blackouts here* and no ordinary adventures would be met. But by midnight, they headed out on the last leg of their trip. After a thousand miles of traversing desert flats and mountain highs, they arrived at their destination—Cedar City, Utah.

During the summer of 1933, Polley had ventured to the same place Bob received his next military assignment. Cedar City was linked to other cities by the Union Pacific Railroad, luring tourists to the gateway of three national parks—Zion, Bryce, and the north rim of the Grand Canyon. The train line promoted the region as a "Celestial Circuit of Painted Parks." The illusiveness of the mountains, majestic and magical, created a scene conceivably from an artist's canvas.

A decade before, Polley had stepped onto the same railway platform and viewed the same mountains Bob had never before experienced. If they had joined dimensions, they would have shared the same moment. But for that day, Bob and his comrades began a new adventure, poring over books as aviation students at a mountain retreat.

Bob would have glanced down at his watch. It was only eight in the morning. Then he looked up. Before, he could only imagine the splendor of the Rocky Mountains from inside the cover of *Life* magazine. *Cress Hill* was his baseline for heights, certainly huge in his heart, but now he witnessed massive peaks reaching through the clouds.

On arrival, he was directed to a hotel named El Escalante. In days gone by, the hotel offered a peaceful respite to tourists escaping a frenzied city lifestyle. Facing vacancies imposed by war, the lodge was transformed into a dormitory for aviation students shouldering coursework at the nearby college. Feeling as if it was *like an oversized fraternity*, this would be Bob's home for the next phase of training.

From the hotel, it was a brisk walk to the Branch Agricultural College. Studies began, ranking was scrutinized, and each private's military course was determined. Initial exams unraveled ability and motivation in determining rank. With high academic scores, a *seventh-place ranking overall*, Bob was regrouped into A flight, placing him on an accelerated path.

Fantasizing about flight, Bob would follow John B.'s exploits and make headlines in the hometown newspaper.

April 4, 1943

Dear Polley,

. . . I am glad to hear that John B. is doing so well and is still ok. You really have to be a crack navigator to get recognition like he has received, so if you write him, send him my congratulations and best of luck . . . You certainly have a right to be proud of that brother of yours.

The days led up to flying. While this phase focused on advancing book studies for further classification, it was also a vivid reminder that aviation students became airmen driving the war from the skies. As part of the program, ten hours of flight training was required. Civilian instructors were under contract to introduce recruits to flight capabilities. The process further ranked aptitudes. If a trainee failed to reach Air Force expectations, he was eliminated, or *washed out*, from the program.

After completing theory of flight procedures and instrumentation, it was time to fly. Bob had never been in the cockpit of an airplane and certainly was never a passenger or student pilot. Flying was a totally new venture. His academics, especially his math abilities, would likely earn him the navigator position. But to be a pilot, dexterity was key. Experience with basketball and training on the slide of his horn had refined his coordination on the right side, but his left hand needed sharpening for any aspirations of being a pilot.

A small plane, the Piper Cub assumed an L-4 military designation. Powered by a Continental 65-horsepower engine, it reached cruising speeds of 80 mph and handled well at low speeds for a controlled landing. Split by a Plexiglas skylight, high wings hung over its riveted steel-framed fuselage. The bright-yellow craft functioned ideally for training purposes.

After Bob met his instructor for the first time, the elder's coarse grip matched his knuckled disposition. The two walked around the fuselage, nose to tail, in an abridged version of the preflight inspection. The instructor first relayed warnings of loose riveting, holes in the skin, and instability of flying wires. At the tail, the old man reached for the control surfaces while delivering standard instructions: *"Make sure the stabilizer is firm, the elevator moves freely, and the rudder shouldn't go beyond the stop."* He gave no opportunity for feedback before moving to the other side. Lifting the fuel cap, he looked at the gauge stick, noting fuel was okay before he said, *"Always check the dipstick. If you don't have oil—you're screwed!"* Given Bob's work on tractors and farm machinery, he recalled thinking, *Does this guy think I'm a complete idiot?*

The procedure for start-up was simple enough. He would have pulled the primer knob, giving the engine two steady shots. As a safety precaution, standard procedure required yelling *Clear!* out the left side before engaging the starter. Waiting at the nose, the mechanic forcibly swung downward on the blade until the propeller rotated on its own. The aircraft sputtered and smoked, increasing momentum. Looking forward, the blade appeared to turn as if the frame-by-frame of a silent movie, but in fact, it was powering up for the flight ahead.

Bob taxied to the end of the runway. In front of him lay 5,000 feet of flat field with a backdrop of mountains. He glanced at the oil temperature and fuel gauge. *All okay.* Sensing pressure on the stick, Bob would know the instructor had control for takeoff—maneuvers monitored from the back seat, insurance on the novice at the start. Releasing the brake, the Cub sprinted down the runway, grabbing enough air until the tail lost its grip. Balanced by a furrowed brow, Bob's excitement widened as the plane inched upward. Cedar City was already at an elevation of 6,000 feet. Winds challenged the climb as the plane pushed through dips as if waves at sea before reaching cruising altitude. Once level, the real flying began.

A standard exchange would follow. "Soldier, the stick is yours."

"Roger that. Stick is mine."

Avoiding risky updrafts from the mountain air, Bob turned a southerly direction. As the plane tilted, golden fields lay below. And in the distance, the rising mountain ranges were topped with winter's remaining snowfall.

Bob banked over town. He spotted the football field and followed the road to the train depot. Not far beyond was the Escalante. The landscape drifted from town to farmland to rolling hills as he flew the plane wide open. The terrain became more rugged. Startled from his air-powered stroll, expletives roared through the speaking tube. *The instructor gave me hell through the earphones.* In a blink, there was nothing but a panorama of solid rock and snow blocking the horizon. In short order, a memorized passage from his textbook told him to *yank-and-bank*. Surely he puckered in his Army-issued khakis as he banked wildly to the left while counting off the distance to the peak. With the mountains alongside, Bob would hear fragments echoing through the speaking tube: *"Take this goddamn bird back to base!"* Which was exactly where Bob led the Cub.

At the end of his initial flight, he wrote, *I am proud of myself since I didn't get sick. So many fellows did . . . Usually the instructor gets part of it in his face if the student doesn't hold his head far enough out of the window. At least my instructor didn't get any on him from me . . .* But Bob worried about his performance on his first flight—distractions that could have ended his training or cost him a commission. Or worse. *It will just kill me if I wash out. I hope I get classified as a navigator since it is a job that requires more brains than a pilot and I think I would have a better chance to get through.*

Days later, *it was cloudy and plenty windy.* Visibility was on the fringe. But encouraged by the Corps, takeoff was promptly at eleven. *At 2,000 feet it was snowing and the wind was bouncing this light plane around considerably but I was flying very well.* Bob had completed the maneuvers, satisfying his surly instructor. It was time to return to base. With the field not yet in sight, he used the mountains, the same range he nearly flew into days before, as a directional guide paired with his gut of the runway's path. At three miles out, faint images began to appear; and at one mile, the airport environment came into view.

It was time to initiate the landing. Normally a gratifying task but with only four hours under his belt, Bob would feel a knot building in his stomach as the runway neared. In his mind he repeated, *throttle for altitude, pitch for attitude,* while gingerly banking the plane to set up for landing. A slight crosswind prevented the nose from a straight-on heading. Bob described *flying at a 30-degree angle to the airstrip . . . a crabbing* of sorts. But with no disparaging comments from behind, his brief training kept him on track.

Landing with a crosswind required more finesse than pure theory as he well knew that many a pilot dinged a prop or bounced embarrassingly down the runway. Descending over the runway threshold, Bob pulled the throttle to a stop, gliding soundlessly as the wheels touched the ground. A textbook landing. Relief washed through his body.

As they entered the building, his instructor uncharacteristically acknowledged a good landing and for the first time didn't give Bob hell for anything he'd done. Now bordering on good humor, he turned further training to another instructor.

After brief pleasantries, it didn't take long to recognize the new instructor, *a prince of a fellow,* was the antithesis of the old man. Before, instruction had meant being *jumped on for any move,* putting both pilot and student on edge. But now, Bob was allowed to think through the mechanics behind a maneuver in flight, albeit swiftly. Unexpected maneuvers were called at a moment's notice. *Without warning, the instructor closed the throttle and said, "Forced landing!"* The propeller came to a choppy stop. Immediately Bob looked around for a field large enough for a simulated landing. He wrote, *I glided down to about twenty-five feet to make a fake landing. The farmer, scarcely forward of the nose, was fixing a broken fence. With the throttle off, I glided right over his head. I could see the expression on his face and he looked plenty scared.* But with a quick look over his shoulder to confirm the maneuver was accurately performed, Bob engaged the throttle and gently pulled on the stick to regain altitude. With a hefty whirring, the plane climbed before heading back to the airfield.

Instructor and student became fast friends. At the airport restaurant they hashed out maneuvers, how best to react and other ways to improve his flying.

At altitude, Bob's instructor asked if he had ever done loops or rollovers. *While the maneuvers were taboo for training, the instructor said he was tired of straight flying and asked me if I would like to have him do some aerobatics.* As the instructor pulled back on the stick, the nose was forced upward. Heavy, Bob's weight pressed back into the seat. As the tail slid below, the instructor jammed his right foot against the rudder pedal, throwing the nose into an immediate downward rotation. It happened so fast Bob hit his head against the window before being pulled forward from his seat. Instead of the horizon ahead, he accelerated downward as the earth rose to meet him. That was when the instructor reduced the throttle and applied steady pressure on the stick. The plane flipped over backward before pulling out of the shallow dive. The force of gravity was like nothing Bob had ever experienced, *definitely not a ride on the family tractor.*

Bob had reached a point in flight training where responses were expected to come as second nature. If he nailed the maneuvers, he would move forward in the program. His next sequence was approach-to-landing stalls. At altitude, the instructor reduced power. Not long after, like a falling dart, the nose started its awkward turn downward before the instructor returned the controls to Bob. In his head, words would reverberate: *stick, throttle, rudder . . . keep it level.* It was time. *Recover! NOW!* He pushed the stick forward, careful not to push too much lest the plane roll into a spin. Gaining air speed, the plane took its long swoop forward and back on course. *There is quite a sensation in a dive . . . and in a pullout you can't lift your feet off the floor and your chin drops.* It was time to turn the plane toward home.

May 21, 1943

Dear Mother and Dad,

. . . This week has just been hell, flying and carrying a full schedule. Tomorrow, I have my final 10-hour check flight, which will either pass or flunk me. I think I will pass if I have a good day but this flying is just like playing basketball. Sometimes you do well and other times you just do everything wrong . . . I want to pass tomorrow because I have never flunked anything in my life and this is no time to start.

His final flight evaluated procedures from performance to judgment. It was an opportunity to show the instructor his skill level. But without notice, the instructor could append the plan to see how Bob handled himself under pressure. If pilotage was his path, this flight was short of flying solo.

Facing the length of the runway, Bob would throttle up, creating a rumble laced with adrenaline. With brakes released, the Cub lurched forward. As the tail lifted, the wheels picked up speed until the air provided enough lift to leave the runway behind. He was airborne with the power in his hand, flying above the highway coursing alongside the Cedar Mountains. Bob's final flight was a cross-country simulation of maneuvers under pressure.

After doing the 500- and 1,500-feet maneuvers, the pilot who was checking me out told me to fly over the mountains so that he could hunt for falcon nests . . . Falcons? I thought it was some kind of a trick and that he was going to pull a forced landing over the mountains. Bob assessed the valley floor, continuously looking for potential landing sites when his instructor delivered another order to lower his altitude to get a closer look for nests. Again, Bob didn't want to be on the short end of a joke, especially flying through mountains known for updrafts and granite peaks. He kept a sharp eye fixed on the terrain below as he floated closer to the mountainside. That was when his instructor pointed to the *white spots on rocks and I realized he really was looking for falcons. He wanted to find a nest, then return and climb up the mountain to get a couple of young falcons to train as pets for hunting. We went flying above the mountains looking for white splotches on the rocks. Once found, I noted the coordinates so that my instructor could find them on his return.*

Finished with the *falconing* task, Bob turned the Cub south. Before leaving forested valleys and rock-ridged mountains behind, *I counted mule deer on sloping meadows. Then I went on and finished my test flight with stalls and spins. I think I passed.*

In the closing days of his College Training Detachment, it was time to render preferences. His future course was now in the hands of the Air Force. With scores considered, the field of capable aviation students was made, and they were pushed to the next rotation.

Bob would have packed his belongings into the army-issued canvas sack before pulling the cotton drawcord to secure the contents within. Storing big-country experiences, he would head for the depot but not before considering his track. Home endured as a constant, inspiring him to focus on the present, a mission of service to country. Cedar City had been a reminder of the man the Air Force was shaping.

Classification, the process of evaluating and assigning recruits to specific roles within the US Army Air Force, would be his next step.

SIX

Diversions Over Europe

JOHN B. MOVED ON FROM INTRUDER MISSIONS. Air Force strategy was on a learning curve, and the airmen of *Circus*, a nickname coined for John B.'s 93rd Bomb Group, were called on to audition changes in tactics. Churchill himself had advocated American *heavies* join his RAF bombers on nighttime missions.

Only minutes into February 15, 1943, mission details were complete. Crews headed to awaiting ships. Takeoff was 0215. Rendezvous went as planned. Leading the second flight, John B. would set the course to the shipping docks at Dunkirk. The target was a German raider, a warship named *Tojo*,* berthed in the harbor.

Over the target, bombs were dropped and the docks were blown to smithereens. But through a gap in the smoke, fanned by flames lighting the quay, John B. would track the destruction. *We bombed all around the warship and tore up the docks but somehow the warship survived.*

After giving an initial heading back to base, the plane ahead of

* *Tojo* may also refer to the MS *Togo*, formerly a civilian freighter that transitioned into a German naval auxiliary cruiser and radar ship during WWII.

them suddenly nosed straight down. With no flak seen, why was he losing altitude? Looking for parachutes, John B. would see none as he tracked the ship plunging to sea. With no time to mourn the loss, a swarm of German fighters fast approached.

As they rallied from target, *Exterminator* held up the rear of the formation. A group of enemy Fw 190s jumped the ship, taking a bite out of her tail. *The tail gunner, a substitute from the frostbite incident, was blasted forward as 20-mm shells eliminated part of his turret.* But as British Spitfires swooped in, the enemy fighters dispersed. *Three of our ships were ruined, one was shot down over the target, one over the channel, and one cracked on the English beach.*

With the hits that *Exterminator* took in the tail, Roper would have struggled with the controls. One of the engines wouldn't slow when he pulled back on the throttle. *We had to shut that one engine off while landing, which was a pretty tricky job but my pilot did it very nicely,* wrote John B. With holes all over *Exterminator,* she was down for a couple weeks.

The RAF flew nighttime missions to avoid notice and disrupt by surprise, at least to reduce the accuracy of anti-aircraft weaponry and fighter opposition. But nightly bombings were proving inaccurate. And the Air Force took note.

Again, strategy shifted. The *Circus heavies* would resume daylight bombing. Commanders added a new tactic: diversion missions. The Air Force coordinated two bomber units, the B-24 Liberator and its older but smaller brother, the B-17 Flying Fortress.

John B.'s *Circus* Liberators were called to implement the new plan. Diversions. The B-24s would sweep foreign territory, luring Luftwaffe fighters away from larger formations of B-17s and allowing the Fortresses to bomb their objective. As a result, enemy aircraft focused on chasing the Liberators. Fortress crews were always happy to see the Libs arrive, knowing the enemy would leave the B-17s alone.

EIGHT MARCH 1943. The target was the railroad yards at

Rouen, France. Takeoff was at noon. *Exterminator* was leading the second flight when "five minutes in from the coast, we were attacked by about sixty fighters," wrote Roper. The group had been jumped by the Abbeville Kids,* the Luftwaffe's best known Fighter Wing. But British Spitfires soon came out of nowhere, swooping in to strafe the enemy Fw 190s. "The squadron leader of the Spitfires said it was the toughest aerial fighting he had ever seen."

And while *Exterminator* had held course through the dogfights, John B. would later write home, *The movies had nothing on us.*

Visits to coastal targets went as planned. Brest. Amiens. And on to Rotterdam. Diversion tunnels continued. They flew over submarine repair facilities and transportation hubs. Flying at 25,000 feet, it was solid undercast. Unable to see the target, no bombs were dropped. But random flak from ground defenses made a direct hit on one B-24. *I watched a friend of mine go down—my chief chess opponent*, wrote John B. One can only imagine the emotions felt at that moment—perhaps a flashback to their last chess game, a friendly but measured competition. But now his friend, Lieutenant Wilhelms, was on a failing ship, cornered in checkmate.

Between missions, John B.'s crew settled in at Hardwick, a base in the East Anglian countryside. With the airfield established, on occasion dignitaries would stop by. While King George VI visited the 93rd Bomb Group at a previous base, Lord Trenchard would be the first distinguished visitor on the newly acquired US airfield. John B. would have a chance meeting with the marshal, also known as the father of the British Royal Air Force. John B. wrote, *He appears to be a very fine man. Looks to be close to seventy and still has more energy than nine out of ten men half his age.*

---

* The Abbeville Kids, also referred to as the Abbeville Boys, were a group of Luftwaffe pilots, Jagdgeschwader 26 (JG 26), whose skill had earned them a fearsome reputation among Allied aircrews.

EIGHTEEN MARCH 1943. The shipyards of Vegesack, Germany, were next on the mission list. With *Exterminator* down for repairs, John B. would fly as substitute navigator on another ship. On what had become routine, black mushrooms of exploding shrapnel dotted the target area. The official record reported bombing results were excellent. The *heavies* suffered battle damage but not before returning the favor. By the end of the day, the count was in. Nine enemy aircraft were destroyed and as many probables.

The Luftwaffe took notice.

By the time the Liberators landed at Hardwick, crews would be drained physically and emotionally. Except for an occasional celebratory shout at having survived another flight, most airmen waited silently for ground transportation back to quarters.

John B. was in the middle of writing a letter home. Suddenly the silence was broken as the air-raid alarm revved its whining sound. A rumbling was heard overhead. Running for cover, surely he spewed expletives. *Damn those Germans!* When the all clear was sounded, he returned to writing. *This evening the neighborhood close by our post was bombed. I was as close as I want to be to the explosions I saw. The raid caused most of us to lose sleep. . . . It's probably a reprisal for something this afternoon in Germany.*

The Luftwaffe had delivered payback to an American base on British soil.

TWENTY-TWO MARCH 1943. The shipping docks and sub pens at Wilhelmshaven stood as the target objective. Takeoff was at noon. As the B-24s approached the German coast, three-dozen enemy fighters jumped John B.'s group. Repeatedly, the tinny sound of machine gun shells knocked at the ship's skin. A few penetrated through. But the B-24 powered on, dropping her bombs before rallying home.

Air Force strategy widened the course and the *Circus* Libs were brought to the head of the line. Targets exceeding the limits of reasonable distance had to be covered. Shipbuilding facilities at Bordeaux kept the Kriegsmarine in business. John B. was about to embark on "the Eighth [Air Force's] longest mission to date."

SEVENTEEN MAY 1943. Over the Bay of Biscay, they "flew at an altitude of 2,000 feet for over two hours before climbing" easterly at the coastline. Due to the heavy bomb load, they were only able to reach an altitude of 23,000 feet. Out the window, John B. would have seen that "southern France was beautiful" with its cultivated vineyards, just as Roper had. But "as we neared the target, we could see Jerries* shooting at the group ahead. As we made the run to target, flak started to burst all around us." Motoring through the quaking current, bombs were salvoed. On the rally, pilot Roper turned homeward but not before a couple *Fockers*† made passes around the ship. Through the Plexiglas nose, no doubt, John B.'s eyes would have locked on one fighter racing head-on toward the ship. With a standoff imminent, John B. likely braced for collision. The Focker "came within fifty feet of the nose of the plane," seemingly at arm's reach before fast banking away. But in that fleeting instant, the German pilot had made his mark.

After the long journey, their ship landed at Portreath, short of her home base. "The mission was considered a success and for once we really outfoxed Jerry," said Roper. But the bomber's thin skin revealed another score. John B. wrote, *We picked up at least seventeen flak holes over Bordeaux and had to get some new gas tanks because of it. Our ship has been in the hangar for about three weeks for repairs so what flying we've done has been in other planes.*

---

* "Jerry" (pl. Jerries) was a nickname used by the Allies to refer to the Germans during WWII.

† "Focker" is a nickname for a German fighter plane, the Focke-Wulf 190, or Fw 190.

Allied press trumpeted headlines of the Eighth's success over Bordeaux.

That night, Axis Sally* delivered her regular radio broadcast. In it, German radio claimed the Americans lost "seventeen bombers on this raid and also hit a hospital." She regularly ended her broadcast with "Next time we're coming for you . . ." as she played an American hit the airmen would likely recognize. While Axis Sally exaggerated claims, John B. had seen the score. The Luftwaffe was taking out his friends on each mission. It was tough to shake the notion—her broadcasts, at times, were eerily spot-on.

TWENTY-NINE MAY 1943. Bordeaux was followed by another long haul: the submarine pens at La Pallice housing a deep-water port along the French coast. Bombs were dropped and their Liberator returned to base. The same dance was becoming routine. With two long missions behind them, yet another change in Air Force strategy was in store for the Roper crew.

Along the North African coast, the Allies had marched eastward from Morocco claiming new territory. They advanced on Algiers and while the enemy held at Tunisia, Allied determination prevailed. With a last desert battle fought in Libya, control of the African sand was now in Allied hands.

By early summer 1943, the Axis's retreat from North Africa opened logistical opportunities to advance into Italy and Eastern Europe. Hundreds of ground and aircrews, many from the Eighth

* The voice of Axis Sally from Berlin was Mildred Gillars, an American-born showgirl hired by the Nazi government to broadcast propaganda. Playing nostalgic songs, she speculated about the fidelity of wives and sweethearts left back home and warned of horrors the airmen would soon face against the Luftwaffe.

Air Force, were beginning relocation efforts to a new Ninth Air Force on the southern continent.

With another strategy on the horizon, John B. was destined to leave the emerald landscape at Hardwick.

In early June, crew lists were refined. John B. and his brother airmen were pulled from the mission board and redirected to an untested strategy of flying. Challenging the limits of reasonable flight, *Exterminator,* together with two-dozen ships flying wingtip-to-wingtip at speeds of more than 200 mph, screamed a hundred feet above the fertile landscape of the British countryside.

According to the Historical Narrative of the 93rd Bomb Group, "Following the La Pallice mission, a specialized training set in; almost daily low-level formation flying was rehearsed. As the big B-24s go roaring over East Anglia at treetop level, it is apparent the 93rd is being groomed for another special job." The 329th Squadron Diary noted, "No one can imagine what the B-24s could be doing at treetop height."

While an American-run operation, the RAF played a supportive role in the planning. According to the Historical Narrative, "the RAF brought out several of its mobile ack-ack* guns to take beads on the ships and to estimate what effect fire would have" on bombers flying at low level. Artillery experts would then analyze the potential of ground resistance. The simulation was scrutinized. Military minds deliberated. Findings were deferred.

Crews were finishing up specialized training for an unknown task they nicknamed the *Super-Duper.* Rumors were flying and now

* An ack-ack gun was an anti-aircraft gun used during WWII. It was an artillery piece designed to shoot upward at airplanes.

they were told to don their finest. Hopping a jeep to the airfield, John B. would watch as a convoy of sedans stopped all traffic. *Something big was going on.*

With all the low flying and now the bigwigs stopping by, he would wonder, *Africa? Eastern Europe? Another change?* Recognizing their track—anti-sub patrol, night raids, blind bombing, intruder missions, diversion tactics, high altitude, and now treetop level—it would seem his group had become the *guinea pigs* of Air Force change.

Colonel Timberlake had been intimating John B. and Hugh's experience was ripe for getting their own squadron. *My ship is probably as well equipped for navigational purposes as any in the group. It's just as well as we lead the squadron now. I've been made the squadron navigator lately. That job entails considerable work but I could stand more than I was doing. Most of the work is in directing training and training new navigators who have had no operational experience here . . . Roper and I are working on a deal whereby he gets a squadron and we need an adjutant*, wrote John B. Being a lawyer, he would gladly take the adjutant position.

On June 23, 1943, *General Devers, General Eaker, General Hodges, and a couple others I didn't recognize came to inspect the group. It was one of those before-the-big-game pep talks*, wrote John B. Clicking of cameras went off, memorializing generals mingling with aircrews.

Timberlake would pull Hugh and John B. aside and make introductions. The two had been with him since work on the Gulf. They had shouldered everything thrown at them and had come back under the worst of circumstances. John B. wrote, *We were picked out as the most experienced crew operating in our group.*

While Hugh was paired with one of the generals for a one-on-one discussion, John B. escorted General Devers, commander of the European Theater of Operations, to a parked Lib. *I explained to him some of the high-powered equipment we have for navigation systems that were the finest anywhere on earth.* With Timberlake's introduction, the general would know that John B. was leading the squadron and directing the other navigators on where to go when. Certainly, John B.'s calculations made for a fine course, but what the senior officer really wanted to hear about was being in the middle of a half dozen fighters trying to shut them down. *I told him about some of our recent flights.* While the encounters were occurring more often than not, John B. would characterize enemy fighters swarming in from nowhere at a speed of 350 mph—less than the blink of an eye.

John B. would have become animated describing the encounter at Bordeaux. After bombs away, "two fighters made a few passes at us; one came within fifty feet of the nose of the bomber." But just before an assured collision, as if barreling right through the bomber, kamikaze style, the enemy plane fast banked away. But in that instant through the fighter's clear canopy, John B. would be close enough to see his eyes.

Before General Devers left the field, he asked John B. to circle back after his next tour. The mention confirmed John B.'s guess that they were leaving the Isles. Focus had turned to North Africa—a closer reach into Eastern Europe.

John B. awaited his next assignment.

SEVEN

Classification

IT WAS AN OVERNIGHT JOURNEY as a hundred aviation students pushed into LA's Union Station. With a brief layover in a town known for glitter and glamour, Bob would have wasted no time in hailing the first cab he saw. *Reaching Hollywood and Vine, we saw movie starlet and calendar girl Ann Miller, posing on a German Messerschmitt.**

Located near the movie studios and known for attracting celebrities, the Brown Derby was the place *to see and be seen*. Bob and his buddies would soon learn that service in the dining room was reserved for the rich, the famous, or the beautiful, none of which the boys qualified as. Even their uniforms couldn't sway the host in procuring a table as the eyes of elegant patrons tracked the young cadets.

The maître d' suggested the café next door. "On the house, boys!" It was a gesture of the establishment's contribution to the war effort.

---

* While Bob mentions a Messerschmitt in his letters, his video interview refers to a Japanese Zero. Both are enemy aircraft fighters.

Later, Bob wrote home, *There certainly are a lot of beautiful women in Hollywood—perhaps the Brown Derby wasn't exactly the place I should have been. . . . Maybe the reason they all looked at us was because we walked in with gaping mouths wide open looking for celebrities.*

His Hollywood stint was short-lived as he stepped from the bus. Santa Ana was designated the West Coast Command Training Center. Being a coastal base, the paint scheme was intended to camouflage—gray buildings on a monotone landscape. Considering the Utah mountainside, the steely change partnered well with the rigid classification he soon faced.

May 29, 1943

> *. . . We were slightly spoiled in Utah. From all indications we are going to be so busy the next two weeks we won't notice the change in living . . . I am not worried about mental exams and I shouldn't be worried about the physicals but you never know—my dreams will be shattered if I wash out.*

THIRTY-ONE MAY 1943. The day marked the beginning of Bob's progression toward becoming a commissioned officer. While the process was meant to advance the aviation cadet, if the grade was not met, a student was released with a humiliating *washout*. For those making the mark, results collated a predictive score in branding the three distinct aircrew positions—pilot, navigator, or bombardier.

Bob took a battery of examinations. With papers distributed, the timed exam would commence on the command "Begin!" Bob would reckon each computation, completing each query with utmost focus. With a click of a stopwatch, the proctor proclaimed, "Pencils down." No time was allowed to double-check answers before moving on to the next query.

Hands-on testing followed. Since perceptual motor skills were important when flying, the military designed performance-based evaluations to identify mechanical aptitude, mental alertness, and ability to respond under pressure.

A first task was a hand-eye coordination test. The device resembled a turntable topped by a nickel-sized target. Placing a hand on each of two handles guiding perpendicular tentacles, the objective was to connect the angle made by the two arms as the dot circled around. The process continued until a number of one-minute trials were completed. Bob's mark would be one part of the grading system, important if he wanted to be a pilot.

Every few minutes Bob moved to another sequence. There was a test using controls to synchronize light patterns; a test for manual dexterity through peg placement; an exercise measuring speed by pushing a toggle in response to a signal lamp; and more. Scores were tabulated; marks were placed in a recruit's folder, only to await a ranking.

Psychologists conducted interviews to pair civilian experiences with filling Air Force positions. Bob was quizzed about his hobbies and upbringing. The interviewer honed in on his national trombone title, paired with his sense of the dairy business. Being fluent in German didn't hurt.

The demanding pace was beginning to wear on Bob. *Truly this is the busiest rat race I have been in all my life and everyone is really dead tired at taps.* For the first time, he was feeling homesick. *Maybe it is because it's the time of year for school to get out or else this pace is getting me down. Wallie Davis is feeling about the same way so maybe it is contagious or else it is the grind. So much for feeling sorry for myself . . . If I can just get through this physical tomorrow and get my Cadet rating everything will be peaches and cream.* Part of it was the waiting—the tests, the doubt all weighed on him, compounded by boys in his flight who had washed out—*it could happen to me.*

Following tests and interviews, the classification board convened. While some were marked to move on, others *washed out* or were reduced to noncommissioned calls.

June 7, 1943

. . . Yesterday I had M.M. (Mess Management, which is the name applied to K.P.) Ironically, I was the milkman of the mess hall, and if we sold as much milk at home as I passed out yesterday, we would really do all right.

I am definitely sold on the Air Corps and can't wait to get through my training and into the air . . . 32 out of 200 have washed out. I hope I am fortunate enough to get through . . .

The War Department understood the power of cinema. Even Hitler knew its value when he commissioned *Triumph of the Will*, an example of Nazi propaganda. After Pearl Harbor, Washington enlisted Hollywood to create informative films. Perhaps a response to Germany's cinema, but more likely, it was to forge public opinion as to why America was entering the war. From a darkened room, the cadets spent a day viewing movies. *As part of a series, we saw* Why We Fight, *primarily to show us how the war in Europe and Japan started and to instill a fighting desire in us. They are very effective.*

The camp had its share of celebrities. *Movie actors William Holden and Alan Ladd are here as organizers of entertainment. There are four coast-to-coast radio programs broadcast from Santa Ana weekly. Joe DiMaggio is one of the physical instructors here.* With *Joltin' Joe* coaching baseball, Bob's team hadn't been beaten.

But one day while *on the athletic field playing ball, a runner came out to the field.* Everyone stopped to hear who was called. "Cress. Robert Cress?" Bob was to *report to Room 14 of the classification building.* The room number was where all the fellows to be washed out had to report. With *the wits scared right out of me, I hurried to my barracks for a shower.* Worries dickered a conversation in his head. *I must have failed something. But what?*

As he got to the building, others were lined up. *In the hall were about a hundred fellows who had washed out, waiting for interviews to see where they would be sent. They all welcomed me to their little group of washouts, which I didn't appreciate too much.* Bob checked in with the orderly before he found a spot to stand. He waited. Checking his watch, it seemed he had been waiting for hours. Then his name was called.

In the major's office, Bob would have extended a stiff salute. After what seemed an eternity, the major grabbed a folder with Bob's full name written boldly on the outside. The officer paused, thumbing through papers, before he pulled out a single document. *It was really quite trivial since I had made a mistake on my classification folder when I filled it out. All I had to do was change it. Boy, was I relieved. I think it would be my life's biggest disappointment if I washed out. I have my heart set on that commission.*

The next morning, word circulated that classification was posted. With his visit the day before, Bob would know right where to go to view the notice board. Over another boy's shoulder, he saw it. Cress. He tracked over, seeing "Preflight Navigation" next to his name. *The way I feel right now I don't think anything can stop me. I just got my classification and I am a navigator. Isn't that wonderful? There were only 10 of our 200 that were classified navigators.* Bob could hardly see straight as the words reverberated in his head. *Navigator! My choice!*

The stars had aligned to make his reality. Although the hard work did not end with classification, his dream of becoming a navigator was materializing. Real training would soon begin with the onus on him to course his path. And he was good with that.

Departing the Pacific Coast Command, it was another two days, long and hot, by train. Arriving in Houston, Bob boarded a bus bound for Ellington Air Force Base. With over 5,000 miles behind him, he could only imagine the thousands more he would log in before entering active duty.

At Ellington, he became a full-fledged aviation cadet. Outfitted with a new uniform, Bob would sink his energies into the bona fides of becoming a navigator on a heavy bomber.

During World War I, Ellington Field had been an advanced training base. Biplanes were the first to fly from its grassy airstrip. But with economic hardships brought by the Depression, postwar mindset considered the land as surplus. It was abandoned to the more prominent Houston field.

As American support of Europe grew in 1940, there was a push to reopen the airfield. Politicians touted consistent flying conditions while businessmen promoted the need to defend nearby oil reserves. Following Pearl Harbor, aviation intensified. Ellington became the Gulf Coast Command Center, producing officers to staff bomber crews requisitioned for America's war machine.

John B. was one of the first to funnel through Ellington. Hundreds more followed. And now Bob was passing through.

Wake-up came early with the bugler's call at 0500. As with mornings on the farm, Bob was soon indoctrinated to rising before dawn. Morning mess obliged an eye-opener. The guy running the food was a former restaurateur and had a crew of cooks preparing bacon and eggs to order. The meal was his best, by far, since leaving home. Signaling the close of breakfast, the staff sergeant called, "Atten-hut!" before gesturing cadets to pile out.

Falling in, the group formed a parade. Three abreast, trailing lines of twelve cadets, marched along the main thoroughfare. Stepping in unison with shifting arms, the group made snaking turns through the barracks to classroom buildings. As they marched, duty-honor-country radiated as they commanded a baritone: *Off we go into the wild blue yonder.*

At hourly intervals, Bob moved through classes beginning with *math, ground & air force organization followed by code class. In this code class we sit with earphones & take dot dash. We have to be able to take 12 five-letter words a minute before we finish the course & be able to send 8 words.* Coding caused him concern with its new language. But he would lean in to maps and chart interpretation knowing it was a critical course in navigation. The day was rounded out with lecture class and physical training. *Then at night we have to study, shine shoes & sometimes do extra work or have meetings. All in all, it is a pretty busy day.*

With insignias on shirt collars, superiors treated cadets more like officers than privates. And they were expected to act accordingly. A cadet faced being washed out for small infractions to bigger offenses like cheating, stealing, or lying.

The flag was raised at reveille and also honored at the close of day. At 1700, all flights* met for retreat.† As *Old Glory* slid down the pole, salutes were hailed. There was pride in becoming an officer in the US Army Air Force.

To add balance to a strict schedule, cadets earned passes for good behavior. Like most towns during wartimes, Houston was well stocked with females. Bob would soon figure out the score. *The Aragon was a pickup place filled with stag women, divorcées or girls working the shipyards.* While spot-on for impulsive servicemen wanting a one-night stand, it was not a place Bob was inclined to return to.

---

* A "flight" of cadets refers to a training group of aviation cadets designated as trainee pilots, navigators, or bombardiers undergoing the military flight-training program to become a commissioned officer in the USAAF.

† Retreat is a military ceremony that marks the end of the duty day in the USAAF.

Bob soon befriended a like-minded navigation student, Park Chetwood. An ATO* from the University of Washington, he had studied aeronautics before being called. And as a part-time ski instructor at Sun Valley, often Park could be found racing downhill. Competing for the Silver Ski Trophy at Mt. Rainier, he had been photographed carving a turn in the snow that had made front-page news of the *Seattle Post*. Park was only ten when his father died. A family friend, a surrogate who was a photographer by profession, taught him how to ski. Dabbling in filmmaking, the friend had filmed a life-sized Coca-Cola cutout girl hanging out of the back seat of Park's convertible.

After the first week of preflight, Park's car arrived. A 1941 Chevrolet Super Deluxe Cabriole, her yellow exterior shined a cameo cream with an interior of red leather seats. Maple-grained wood paneled the dashboard and moldings. She was sweet. With a three-speed manual gearshift commanding ninety horses rocking six cylinders, she was fast. And she was cool. Three ski racks mounted on her trunk accented the fender skirt and fog lights. With liberty passes, Bob and Park cruised the Rice campus. Girls would have waved, wishing for a ride. Few were left behind.

From Polley's letters, Bob would know that she was also writing other guys and sending homemade cookies to them. Not knowing whether she would be available when the war was over, Bob dated a variety of girls throughout his service.

Houston's Junior League organized parties for the cadets. The first was held in the Crystal Ballroom of the Rice Hotel. Surrounded by girlish chatter, *I danced with girls who attended Smith, Vassar, and Wellesley* while closing down the band. And with more parties, his

---

* ATO (Alpha Tau Omega) is a social fraternity on college campuses that focuses on brotherhood, leadership, and community service.

modest grin told the story. *I went from Barracks 868 to an exclusive members-only River Oaks Country Club in one day.* Given the parties, his service stateside wasn't all that bad.

News from home arrived by way of Hillsboro's local paper, the *Montgomery County News*. Scanning the latest issue, he fixated on the front-page story with headlines in boldfaced type: LT. WHITE IN AIR RAID. Bob focused on words written about a fellow airman. On track for navigation, he was particularly interested. The paper echoed the *Chicago Tribune*'s correspondent William J. Humphries, who described John B. as "one of the group's crack navigators. He must, and does, know his way around Europe." Bob would have become energized knowing John B. was at the top of his game—a standing he hoped to one day share.

July 9, 1943

Dear Polley,

. . . I got a paper with John B.'s letter in it. Being squadron navigator is a very responsible position. Someday, I hope to make as good a navigator as he has turned out to be . . .

As Bob faced coursework, US generals were launching resources northward from Africa. Sights were set on Italy, Hitler's fascist partner. The offensive not only reduced distances to Axis targets, Allied leaders were banking on another strategy. With the conflict building on the peninsula, German assets would be drawn away from northern France, where another plan was in its infancy.

Sicily became the objective. A jump step, it hung from the toe of the Italian boot. Code-named Operation Husky, the invasion began on July 10, 1943, and in intervening days, the American flag was raised. Facing significant pressure from the advancing Allied forces, the Italian king had Benito Mussolini arrested on July 25, 1944. (Mussolini was eventually executed at war's end.)

At Ellington, *Texas heat was breaking records. It was 109 degrees yesterday with 92 percent humidity.* Escaping the swelter, he would join his friends at a tavern in town. It *was quite reminiscent of college with practically a Greek council** *huddled around innumerable quarts of beer.* Songs of *Patty Murphy* were shared over the brew. As flights warbled the Irish rhyme, the influence of alcohol murdered the tune. *It reminded me of good times at Bidys.* But at the same time, he thought of the changing world.

July 26, 1943

Dear Polley,

. . . Two cadets in advanced pilot training were killed yesterday when their plane crashed. With so many planes flying here all the time, I'm not surprised . . . Ellington field has had a remarkably fine record but there are bound to be some accidents, and I guess yesterday was that day.

The resignation of Mussolini seems to be the talk of the day. Boy, I hope Italy drops out of the war. That would be another nail in Hitler's coffin. Gosh, I wish this war would end.

I got the Journal with John B.'s picture in it. You have a darn good-looking brother . . .

---

* A Greek council is a governing body that oversees Greek organizations, such as fraternities and sororities, on college campuses.

EIGHT

The Plan to Destroy Ploesti Begins

NINE JULY 1943. While brother ships had already left for North Africa, John B.'s crew had an unexpected delay.

At Boringden, an airfield outside of London, *Exterminator* stayed back awaiting the schedules of two very important passengers, an Englishman and an American. John B. would waste no time getting acquainted with the extra travelers. Their backgrounds hinted at the upcoming *Super-Duper.*

Lord Arthur Patrick Hastings Viscount Forbes was an RAF Wing Commander and former Air Attaché at the British Embassy in Bucharest. He held valuable intelligence regarding the Ploesti oil refineries and was instrumental in creating a blueprint of the complex. When Romania broke relations with Britain, Lord Forbes advocated attacks on Ploesti to deny Nazi Germany its oil supply.

Exterminator also carried Gerald Geerlings, formerly a WWI infantryman and Connecticut architect. He had designed a three-dimensional table model, a miniature representation of the still-classified Ploesti refinery complex, to be studied by officers flying the mission. Major Geerlings also created "oblique drawings to show how places look as you approach them," to be used by navigators in identifying the lead-up to target.

While Lord Forbes would feign control, Geerlings would sit quietly clutching his briefcase packed with top secret briefing materials. Next to the two was a box containing film canisters. Forbes, together with "a Texas-drawling New York newspaperman, had produced a professional 45-minute sound film to brief Ploesti fliers." It was the first time a motion picture would be used to prepare airmen for a single battle.

While the mission remained under a shroud of secrecy, only a handful of brass and a few dedicated designers were aware of the plan's objective. Should the materials fall into enemy hands, the entire mission would be scrubbed. "Consequently, Intelligence had bet on one [crew]," *Exterminator*, to safely transport the secret yet to be disclosed.

From Portreath, *we left England at 3:00 a.m. in a rain that continued for 5 hours, all of which time we were on instruments*, wrote John B. While brother airmen were leading the invasion of Sicily, *Exterminator* journeyed from England to their provisional base on the North African coast. With Roper at command and John B. coursing the route, the rest of the crew would be at relative ease believing it was a standard transport trip with two stodgy passengers.

But this was no ordinary voyage.

The resources on board, a mound of anonymous parcels, were the essence of intelligence for the upcoming operation—the plan to cripple Nazi Germany in a manner few had considered before. If executed properly, it would "shorten the war by six months."

Extraordinary measures had been taken to ensure the secret materials remained classified. Thermite sticks, incendiaries prepared to set an instant inferno, were strategically placed on board *Exterminator* should the plane come under enemy hands. "If we were hit, the entire contents of the ship would go up in a single splendid flash, leaving no trace of the secrets," said Geerlings.

At times, Hugh would glance beyond his rudder pedals through the forest of instrument wires and hydraulic lines to his navigator below, before requesting the ship's location.

Beneath the flight deck, John B. stood at his navigation desk. Remembering the half-dozen *Junkers* that had jumped the ship on their last visit, it was a place he knew well. "Navigator to pilot: approaching Saint-Nazaire to the east."

Sightings of enemy planes had been reported. *Since we were a single ship, we had to take a circuitous route to avoid patrols of Ju 88s,* wrote John B. In a time before GPS, it was a constant reworking of calculations. His head undoubtedly pounded knowing this trip was far more critical than all others. Privy to the secret, John B. had to make sure the heading was followed with as much precision as ever.

Familiar with the Bay of Biscay, John B.'s course skirted its western borders across an open ocean. With only water below and sky above, they flew with no land in sight for a long while. From a briefing in the days prior together with newspaper accounts, John B. would have known of a recent incident over the same route he was flying. British actor Leslie Howard, who portrayed Ashley Wilkes in *Gone with the Wind*, had been linked to anti-German propaganda. The month before over the Bay of Biscay, the actor was flying in a civilian ship, a DC-3, when it was attacked by eight fighters, sending it crashing to the sea. With the flight plan Lisbon-to-Bristol, John B. would be put on the defensive. The enemy was nearby. And recently.

Not far off from Saint-Nazaire, John B.'s bombardier, Ted Brannon, called out, "Junker 88s below!" But moments later, he added,

"Looks like they're chasing a big fat Sunderland* in and out of the clouds."

Exterminator continued south.

We were a long way from land for quite a while. Eventually I figured it was time we had gotten beyond the German patrol area and headed east for Portugal, which we saw about nine in the morning. John B. would change course eastward, passing the Rock of Gibraltar before heading into Oran, Algiers. At Tunis, their Liberator was grounded for repairs.

Due to the critical nature of *Exterminator*'s cargo, Colonel Timberlake flew in to pick up Hugh, John B., and their distinguished passengers as well as the mission materials. The remainder of the crew stayed with *Exterminator.*

Exiting Timberlake's ship at an air base near Benghazi, John B. would look around to see a 360-degree view of the desert. Could there be any more contrast from the Hardwick landscape? Arid clouds of choking sand replaced the English fog that reeled in the romance of an English novel. With *Casablanca* in the movie theaters, John B. surely mused, *No Ingrid Bergmans here.*

New airfields named Berka, Benina, and others dotted the North African coastline. A couple hundred American aircraft, thousands of supporting ground crew, and airmen converged on the desolate Libyan sands.

John B. was assigned to Terria Airfield, designated Benghazi #7, a barren stretch of sand topped by a few dry and lonely scrub bushes. On the east side of the base was the Tobruk-to-Tripoli highway where Rommel's Afrika Corps had retreated. Trashed military vehicles dotted the landscape.

* A Sunderland was a British flying boat, a seaplane, used by the RAF in anti-submarine warfare.

On July 11, John B. spent a third birthday away from home. The day was marked with pitching a tent in the pink African sand. It was one of many staggered far enough from the next, so as to make a more difficult target should there be a strafing attack by enemy aircraft.

Living conditions were rugged. "Crawling with scorpions, in dust blowing shoulder-high, the Americans [slept] . . . in threadbare tents patched with scraps of aluminum from neighboring junk yards of Axis air wrecks." An oil drum doubled as the company privy, offering neither privacy nor comfort. Poor water conditions and constant wind made cleanliness and order more difficult. While letters were censored to prevent sensitive information, like troop movement and location, from reaching the enemy should mail be intercepted, there were times when references slipped through. *It's hot and dusty but swimming in the Mediterranean is convenient and almost necessary daily from a hygienic standpoint*, wrote John B.

Colonel Timberlake had been assigned to oversee and administer the countless details of the upcoming top secret mission. The colonel would rely upon a handful of officers, John B. included, in defining the mission parameters. The airmen had been with Timberlake since forming the group in Louisiana, a relationship sealed by a shared history.

In handling the final details of the still secret *Super-Duper*, John B. guided Timberlake's ship between bases. Plans and logistics. Flying over the pyramids, no doubt John B. conjured Cleopatra and an ancient civilization, a ground trip saved for another day. After a week of travel, they stopped in Cairo. Egypt's capital had all the modern conveniences of any American city, mixed with antiquities of impressive mosques and shady bazaars.

At a nightclub in Cairo, a Yogi was the featured entertainment. The performer *had remarkable control of his muscles and was very interesting to watch. The floorshow was the best I've seen anywhere since Chicago,* John B. wrote. As the entertainer finished his act, a clatter of voices entered the room.

Captain Edward "Eddie" Rickenbacker took a seat next to John B.

Best remembered for the high example he set, at the request of General Henry "Hap" Arnold, Rickenbacker had stopped at bases along the North African coast on a morale-boosting mission. During the first World War, the captain had been part of the first American unit to go over enemy lines and had "claimed twenty-six victories over France." No doubt, he described fearsome dogfights against German pilots with arms flaring. And likely, he impressed upon the flying airmen seated around him, as Rickenbacker had been quoted, that "courage is doing what you're afraid to do."

With the dogfights John B. had seen firsthand, surely he thought of his own fear in battle, an image not easily released.

Rickenbacker knew the aviators had a big job to do. Likely he would have emphasized they were flying planes with performance second to none; the finest navigation systems anywhere; and, looking at those sitting around the table, the best aviators in the world. John B. surely smiled as he considered the empty bottles surrounding them. More drinks were poured as Rickenbacker continued his rounds of what John B. would later write home as *spirituous talk on fighting spirits, and the spirits had the best of the match.*

In the days that followed, John B. continued to navigate Timberlake's ship to bases along Libya's coastline. *As I look below—10,000 feet—all I can see are remnants of tanks, planes, and trucks lost to the sand. The tracks were made by various military vehicles, which lastly fought and maneuvered here in the desert. The sand is reddish brown and reminds me of the Badlands of the Dakotas. It's certainly a contrast to the green of the Nile valley. The Nile separates the desert and the garden, the most abrupt change of scenery I have ever experienced. And the desert is as empty and desolate as the ocean—more so I guess because the ocean has fish and I don't believe the desert supports a solitary creature.*

Out the window to the undulating sand below, no doubt John B. was reminded of his former copilot, Lieutenant McKelvey, whose B-24 had crashed in the desert. In the dark of night, the crew was returning from a mission to Italy when they missed the base. *We have dropped supplies to them; however, they will have to stay for a while as it is impossible to reach them except on foot over a hundred miles of broken lava beds. The RAF rescue service is sending trucks, donkeys, camels, and Arab tribesmen in after them. They are in a bad predicament anyway . . . It's about time to start our let-down & for me to see just where we are. About a week ago I was in London. Yesterday in Cairo. Tomorrow? What a war!*

NINETEEN JULY 1943. Pilots and navigators entered the briefing room. Colonel Timberlake opened with mission details. The day marked the initial assault on Rome. Roper wrote, "This was one of the biggest days in my life—the first time in history [Rome] would be bombed." John B. surely felt the same.

With Roper and White leading the Wing* in B-24 *Utah Man* (*Exterminator* was still in Tunis down for repairs), the target was identified—the Littorio marshaling yards. Situated a narrow three miles from the Vatican, John B. would have considered its proximity to the global headquarters of the Catholic Church. "We were briefed on precisely what parts of the city were not to be bombed." John B.

* A Wing is a large USAAF operational organization that controls many combat groups made up of several squadrons of bombers. On the July 19, 1943 mission, Roper/John B. led "5 groups of B-24s," some 112 Liberators who bombed Rome for the first time. Official records reported that "this was a big raid in which nearly all available American aircraft in Africa participated"; some 300 total aircraft of the USAAF were part of the mission.

would have understood that each mission was becoming even more critical, given the civilian population nearby. At an altitude of 24,000 feet, accuracy in navigation was crucial.

From the North African airstrip, takeoff was precisely at 0735. In the lead plane, John B. would have called out the course with an armada of more than one hundred ships in tow. On approach to the city, a barrage of flak and aerial fighters met the *heavies*. But at 1319, the rail yard was centered in the crosshairs and bombs were dropped spot-on. John B. would have then marked the return course to base.

It was a long day, clocking in over ten hours in flight, but "all crews returned." "Photoreconnaissance indicated a high degree of precision bombing." Given the accuracy of navigation, the commander tendered personal commendations to John B. on the course flown. Official reports concluded the raid on Rome as "one of the most successful raids in the annals of the USAAF, which proved probably more than any other mission that high altitude bombing was precision personified."

July 20, 1943

. . . We led our group on the trip to Rome. It turned out ok. Didn't lose a ship. One ship turned back over Sicily & was jumped by 11 fighters. Got the tail gunner. They landed on a field near Syracuse that was still under fire from Snipers. Got engine repaired & got to base the next day. We saw about 3 fighters but they stayed out of range. Flak was moderate & accurate.

What scared me most was flying thru clouds of pamphlets dropped by the group ahead of us. We didn't know what they were but it looked serious. The trip was 1,800 miles & took about 10½ hours . . .

Don't know when the next job will be pulled but we're training for it now. Anything local girls teach the English lads, who have been taught by English girls, which they don't already know is preposterous to the point of unbelievability.

. . . Love & kisses, John B.

Following the raid to Rome, crews were quarantined in anticipation of the next mission. A day shy of two weeks, John B. would take to the skies in his most historic, and heroic, mission ever.

With days to go, group leaders expressed apprehension of the upcoming mission. Considering distance and the low-level danger, the best-case scenario was destruction of half the oil multiplex at a cost of half the American fleet and airmen. Alternatively, repeated pounding attacks from high level were recommended until the target was rendered inactive.

Concerns were forwarded to General Lewis Hyde Brereton, but final approval came from Eisenhower. After some debate, the mission at low level would go forward as planned.

NINE

A Storm on the Horizon

IN NORTH AFRICA, John B. awaited his next mission. The *Super-Duper*, as nicknamed by the airmen, was now revealed. A historic operation, it took on the name of *Tidal Wave*. Given the high losses expected from the upcoming low-level raid, commanders urged the airmen to write letters back home. While John B. wrote home regularly, tonight would give him pause.

July 22, 1943

> *. . . We've been sitting around the last couple of days not doing much of anything but a little practicing for our next job. It should make headlines about the first of August or within two or three days one side or the other.*
>
> *Yesterday there was a sandstorm, wind & dust all day. I look pretty brown now but it will wash off pretty quickly . . . It sure is barren here. Think I'll take my laundry with me when I go swimming. The waves & sand should get a lot of the dust & dirt out. Our plane is still in Tunis but we have hopes that it will be fixed soon, we'll be riding in it in a few days.*

Our next one is longer & tougher & a real "Purple Heart" specialty. However, the colonels, generals, & S-2 people are all trying to go along so it's either so big they'll stick their neck out or else so easy they'll do the same.*

What our plans are after that, I have no idea. Rumors have us everywhere from the US to China by way of India. That wouldn't be so bad, would it? Give everyone my regards.

Love, John B.

John B. would soon write Polley.

ELLINGTON AIR FORCE BASE

Prowling off the Texas coastline where Bob was stationed, German submarines were still rumored to be in the vicinity. Home to shipyards, oil refineries, and aircraft suppliers, the Bolivar Peninsula provided a wealthy cache of exiting cargo ships.

This was where John B. started his combat experience—tracking U-boats in the Gulf of Mexico. And although reports of sightings were rare, the Air Force remained vigilant.

Before the war, weather advisories had been called ahead by shrimpers, freighters, or aircraft. But as required for wartime secrecy, radio communications were silenced in Gulf waters. No one would be the wiser until all hell struck.

Military lecture was dismissed early from news of an incoming storm. Rain bands had reached Ellington. *We got the order to go to our barracks and to put on our fatigue uniforms.* Stand-by orders were issued until military supervisors could get a handle on preparations.

* The Purple Heart is a military decoration awarded to service members who are wounded or killed in action.

We are having something right now that may develop into excitement. There is a hurricane on the Gulf Coast and we are getting pretty much of it here in camp. The wind is blowing strong enough to knock you down and it is blowing shingles off all the barracks around here.

Before that morning, there had been no advance warning of the storm. (Satellite imagery was still twenty years in the future and aircraft reconnaissance was soon to be born, but not yet.) With no time to transport aircraft out of the area, military planes were left unsecured on the tarmac. Windows had not been boarded up and construction materials had not been secured. No plan had been put in place for such an event. After writing his parents, Bob took a moment to write Polley.

> *July 27, 1943*
>
> *. . . There is supposed to be a big tidal wave coming into Galveston so we might be put on rescue work. Then again, we may do something less exciting such as holding down airplanes. . . . This is the worst storm I have ever witnessed . . .*
>
> *These barracks are built very strongly, but right now they are shaking quite a bit. A fellow just came in the door, and the wind threw him through the doorway and the door slammed, all the glass panes were broken. The rain is pouring through that hole.*

In a surprise attack, a war of winds and tidal waters hit the Texas coast. In a tempest, the storm surge traveled up the ship channel, dealing its share of damage before making a hit on Ellington. As the hurricane was fueled with higher winds and lower pressures, shifts of cadets were called out to the flight line. With no means to tie down the aircraft, plebes acted as human stakes holding down the planes. *The peak of the storm will hit around 4:00 p.m. and we just got our orders. I guess we will be out holding down the airplanes three or four hours.*

The wind was blowing so hard that the only way you could walk was to lock arms with five or six other fellows and even then, it would throw you to the ground sometimes. The rain was coming down so hard that you couldn't see 10 feet, and it was impossible to try to look into the wind or this hard driven rain would knock your eyes out, and that is no exaggeration.

It was Bob's turn on the flight line. As one of eight, he was assigned a twin-engine trainer weighing over two-and-a-half tons. *I got hold of a rope with three other fellows on one wing with another four on the other side. There were also two Flying Fortresses with about 150 men on each trying to hold them down.* With ropes thrown over its wings spanning some forty feet, Bob was tethered to the craft. Tightening his grip, he pulled with his full weight but the plane still bucked doggedly in the wind.

As the storm's intensity peaked, gusts of wind whipped in with the roar of a freight train. Objects were hurled in slapdash directions. Loosened shingles and shards of glass launched through the air. *Swirling sand pricked like thorns.* A roof from a nearby hangar peeled away. But not before the anemometer, secured to its ridge, was catapulted to the ground, shattering into pieces. Its dial "clocked a speed of 132."

And then all hell broke loose. As the tempest crested, the wing jerked upward, popping away frayed lines. *The rope I was holding snapped, throwing me to the ground.* In an instant, the winds heaved the right wing upward and over. *The big plane collapsed and flipped over, pinning under it two fellows on the opposite side. I got clear of the wreck and the ambulance took these fellows away.*

I then went over to another plane and was helping hold down its wing. All of a sudden, a lot of debris started flying and I glanced around and the plane right behind me had broken loose. I moved in a hurry as the plane scooted across the big field toward us before stopping.

When the peak passed, we were relieved at 8:30 p.m. I got a cup of coffee and came back to the barracks . . . I heard a few cadets had been killed and a great number were injured. I was not looking forward to going back out again one bit, but everyone had to pitch in so that all the planes would not be lost. I was scared to death about going back out on the line.

The eye of the hurricane tendered a brief respite but before long the swirling increased and rotations fueled the fury's second act.

At 9:00 p.m. we went back to the flying line. Ordered to another plane, Bob met his next human-staking assignment. *The second phase of the storm was not near as bad as the first*, he wrote. *Dodging a piece of lumber, a shingle made a direct hit.* Avoidance was not possible. *At 2:30 a.m., we were relieved by some soldiers that were brought in from Camp Wallace.*

While the breeze continued to blow, it paled in comparison to the agonizing ten hours that had just played out. Strained tensions and physical energy took a beating. Bob would return to his barracks to see windows blown out, standing water on the floor, and personal effects sodden and scattered about the room.

At the light of day, the score would be revealed. The barracks had taken a beating. Windows were broken. Rooflines were peeled from walls. Overturned benches and untied construction materials were haphazardly laid among the clutter. Trees were uprooted. Airplanes toppled. Rubble and fallen branches blocked roadways as tangles of distorted debris littered the tarmac.

Ellington resembled a war zone.

Power and water remained out. Schedules were upturned. Cadets were awakened to large-scale cleanup duties. *All day today we have been picking up boards and shingles and cleaning up the camp somewhat. It has been raining most of the day so it's pretty hard to get the mud off of the streets.*

A hurricane is much different from a tornado. Instead of lasting ten or fifteen minutes, this terrific wind lasts for hours without a letup. That wind driving the rain right through your raincoat and clothing knocks all the vitality right out of you. I feel none the worse for my experience today, but I definitely would not like to go through it again. There are a lot of rumors going around as to how many cadets were killed or injured . . . I know of at least six cadets that were killed and the hospital is overflowing with injured . . . None of my close friends were hurt and for that I am especially thankful . . . I consider myself damn lucky to get out without getting more than some scratches . . .

The *Galveston Daily* reported "it was the worst storm since 1915." Any military reference of the hurricane was downplayed by design. For the same reasons no advance weather warnings had been issued, the same held true afterward. Evidence of the storm's impact was censored.

Oil derricks, refineries, and plants along the ship channel were impaired. The making of high-octane gasoline for aviation fuel was interrupted. Shipyards and the tankers' abilities to move supply had been hampered. Military production, and lack thereof, was considered a matter of national security. Extraordinary efforts were taken to prevent Axis powers from gathering information of any such deficiencies.

July 29, 1943

. . . It really was funny at 5:10 this morning . . . Our lights, of course, wouldn't work and the loudspeaker over which they play the bugle wouldn't work and besides it was raining outside. Our cadet officer tried to get us up to fall out into the rain for reveille. No one would move and he was quite frustrated, threatening us with gigs, etc. We just laughed at him. Gigs sound so foolish after what we went through the other night . . .

That was really a terrific storm . . .

TEN

Tidal Wave August 1, 1943

WHILE BOB WAS WRESTLING NATURE'S TEMPEST in Texas, John B. was on the northern coast of Africa in final preparation of his most challenging mission.

In Hillsboro, on his usual run into town, John White, Sr., would have stopped by the local drugstore. A display of current periodicals included *Life* magazine, a weekly publication that regularly circulated stories of WWII. Its issue dated July 26, 1943, featured Eighth Air Force bomber crews in England. As if huddled for the next big game, a sea of some fifty airmen graced the cover.

A father's pulse would have quickened as he scanned each face looking for his son. Having tracked nearly the entire group, his gaze undoubtedly stopped just above the emboldened *LIFE* spelled out in white against a red background. John B. was in front of all the others with his pilot right next to him.

Other customers would quickly move in to get a look at John B.

His oldest son would be all he could think of. Admiration. A recent letter marked him as squadron navigator. No doubt his heart burst with pride as he pictured his boy.

Following the raid to Rome, the Libyan base bustled with intensity fueled by the mission ahead. With its complexity, the operation went through a series of name changes. Being a low-level raid, the intent was to quake the earth below as waves of airships roared overhead. Not unlike Churchill's reference to a tsunami, the objective was to leave a path of destruction. The mission took on the name of *Tidal Wave*.

In a dark hut, John B. and other officers viewed a colorless movie, the first-ever film used at briefing to describe details of a single mission. It was the same film brought to North Africa on John B.'s B-24 bomber, *Exterminator.* Due to the operation's significance, cost, and risk, "the principal purpose of the movie was to insure uniformity of briefing and no omission of any important information."

Like the revving of an air-raid siren, the protracted drone of the movie's narrator decreed their next mission: "Romania, a country rich in petroleum reserves." The film affirmed Hitler's need for oil to sustain his war machine. When Ploesti was revealed, compounded by the scheme of zero-altitude bombing, muffled calculations of distance surely filtered through the room. The round-trip with a full bomb load was beyond the reasonable range of the Liberator.

Although there was pride in taking on a mission that touted shortening the war, this was a tough one for the flyboys.

Words from John B.'s chance encounter with General Doolittle the year before might have crossed his mind. Doolittle's low-level mission was at 1,500 feet; John B.'s group was flying in at deck level—zero altitude—a height under two hundred feet.

Crucial to the low-level operation was the element of surprise. Without tactical surprise, the American B-24 bombers would be highly vulnerable to anti-aircraft cannon fire from a range as close as fifty feet away. The film continued.

The mission was divided into three objectives code-named the *Red*, the *White*, and the *Blue*. Each target was well outlined on the film but John B. would have been particularly interested in the direction he would lead his element. "*White Force* Section Two" targeted the Vega Concordia Oil Refinery. No doubt, *White Force* crossed his mind as good a name as any coursing the way.

As the film went on, Ploesti's strongest defenses were described to be on the south side of the complex. According to plan, the mission brought the American *heavies* in from the north, away from southern fortifications.

The film's narrator drew his conclusions, and said, "This is a tough job, but one worth doing. If you knock out the Romanian oil, you will screw up Hitler's future plan."

By the last week of July, all flying officers, in particular the navigators, had studied the relief model, a three-dimensional representation of run-up to Ploesti, imprinting the peaks and valleys of the Balkan route as well as streams and steeples along the Danubian plain. Not a detail was missed on the ingress to target.

In the days before the mission, intelligence rolled off the telegraph that "heavy guns [from the ground] would be unable to direct accurate fire at the low-flying formations because of the inability to follow a fast-moving target." But at the same time, "a captured Romanian pilot" contradicted the information, saying Ploesti "was the most heavily defended target in Europe."

The last rehearsal was conducted on July 29, 1943. Ships flew the tightest formation, some roaring a thunderous "fifty feet" above the sandy complex. "Executed without a hitch," bombs dropped perfectly on mock targets. "In two minutes, five groups had completely destroyed the dummy targets." "It was something beyond belief, when from nowhere there was a sound of power and fury, coming and going before one's reflexes could do anything but duck," said Major Geerlings, one of two VIPs that had traveled on John B.'s bomber to North Africa.

Upon landing, ground crews hailed the exiting airmen, overjoyed at their success.

Later, the three senior officers were grounded. Their classified knowledge was considered too high a risk, given the expected losses. Would such a move deflate morale on a mission that needed unquestioned optimism for success? But the order was final. With only hours before takeoff, reshuffling of crews had to be made. Yet another challenge imposed on a difficult mission.

General Brereton had flown in from Cairo to Benghazi to view the final practice. With him was Frank Gervasi, a war correspondent at *Collier's* magazine. "As far as I could tell from Brereton's poker face," said Gervasi, "it was somewhere between worry and outright anxiety." To Gervasi, Brereton said, "This is it. This is where the Ninth Air Force makes history or wishes it had never been born. Hap Arnold* has handed us a tough one."

While success of the mission depended upon the courage and conviction of each airman, the mission would hit the heart of the Axis—its oil refineries—leaving the powerful calling card of a great nation.

Superiors had created the impression that this mission was in a class by itself. Historic and game-changing. Low-level and dangerous. Courage by a few making a major impact on the war. And if for no other reason—a movie, models, and an enormous amount of money had been spent in the planning. Likely due to the close relationship he had with Colonel Timberlake, John B. would have recognized that the preparation for this mission had been unprecedented.

---

* General Henry "Hap" Arnold, commander of the USAAF, played a crucial role in the planning and execution of Operation Tidal Wave.

With training complete, the men left the final session with mixed emotions of dutiful bravado. John B. must have realized that he was "participating in one of the greatest experiences of our generation." Surely, he felt he would play a vital part, albeit small, in a mission that would impact the world. There was satisfaction for the privilege given him. But while proud to play a part in shortening the war, John B. would be keenly aware of what lay on each man's shoulders. And his.

July 30, 1943

. . . Time has been going by quickly here on the desert. We're almost ready to go on the trip we came here to make. There certainly has been a lot of preparation.

The cost must be immense but the objective is worth it, I guess . . . I was trying to figure out the amount of money tied up in the venture—the first figure I used was about $50,000,000, then next $20,000,000, and that was just the beginning, so I didn't pursue the subject any further. It's the most completely prepared job I've been involved in yet & if it works the effect will be worth any cost. If it doesn't work, well, it was still a good idea.

Tomorrow or the next day we'll take off on what will be either our easiest or our hardest job. Rumors have it that some of us may get a chance to come back to the States when this campaign is through. Guess I could stand it. Best we not count on it too seriously for the present.

. . . Love from John B.

That evening, a ceremony was held announcing commendations. As part of the formality, Colonel Timberlake presented John B. with the *Distinguished Flying Cross* for heroism, and he was promoted to captain. The following day the men were quarantined, awaiting the next big assignment.

ONE AUGUST 1943. Wake-up was early that Sunday morning. Rolling out of bed as if routine, this day was worlds apart from prior missions.

At final briefing, chatter among the crews raised "unofficial estimates of the chances of returning ranged between 50 percent and suicide," as noted in the US Army Air Force archives. (The mission was so important that General Ent* confided that "if nobody comes back, the results were worth the cost.") Commanders had made clear that the target was "worth the price." "The raid on Ploesti was the biggest thing" the US Army Air Force had ever taken on. To win the war, this target had to be destroyed. The thought undeniably lay on John B.—a heavy yet proud place to be.

"The armada [of B-24 ships and airmen] was the most intensively prepared and the most experienced large force that had been dispatched in the history of aerial warfare," wrote Dugan and Stewart. Many of the men had reached mission quota,† John B. included, and had long since used up their odds of missions against the enemy on staying alive or out of captivity. "They flew to shorten the war."

An awaiting truck dropped John B. off at the flight line. As the engines were tested, he would have stood at his navigation desk preparing his charts and tools.

As habit, John B. moved to the flight deck for takeoff.

From down the tarmac, a jeep spitting a cloud of sand raced toward *Exterminator.* Another pilot, and friend of the crew, was waving his arms wildly. With the bomb bay still open, Captain Jack Jones vaulted through the retractable doors. "Since his plane had

* In Operation Tidal Wave, General Uzal Ent served as mission commander leading the raid on the Ploesti refineries.

† "Mission quota" in the USAAF refers to the number of bombing missions that airmen are required to complete before earning leave, which usually meant a trip stateside or home.

been grounded, and not wanting to miss this one, he hopped on as an unofficial stowaway," said Karl Casanova, Jones's great-nephew. As part of the historic flight, official records listed him as pilot observer.

The ship now carried eleven on board.

At the end of the runway, the engines revved to a screaming pitch as a red flare signaled takeoff. With brakes released, the ship shot forward, hurdling down the runway. At half-minute intervals, a montage of ships followed. One hundred seventy-seven heavy bombers successfully took off from a handful of desert airstrips "carrying a cargo of demolition bombs well in excess of a half million pounds," according to Air Force archives.

As soon as *Exterminator* met formation, steel nerves relaxed a bit. But not much. Banter, albeit reserved, eased the tensions of the mission ahead. With rations of canned meat and dried crackers, one-liners might have spread through the interphone. Somehow, talking about dinner that night and the idea of returning to base ensured a return trip home.

Five separate bomb groups joined in flight as they headed north over the Mediterranean Sea. John B.'s *Circus* Liberators were second in the convoy behind the lead *Liberandos*. The three remaining groups of B-24 Liberators had dropped back, out of sight. A mandated radio silence and "varying styles of leaders" combined with hazy skies contributed to a "wider spread between the five bomb groups." A vast sixty miles lay between the first two groups and the trailing three.

As the *heavies* moved north, John B. would need to alert the pilot of the upcoming turn at Corfu. The coastline passed below them. Securing the map on his desk, likely he would have traced the penciled line from Corfu across Albania, noting the 9,000-foot summit. The ship climbed to 16,000 feet. At that altitude, John B.

undoubtedly secured his oxygen mask, tightening the strap. As the Libs climbed the Albanian Alps, rough air jostled the ships. And the sun shined in their eyes.

Clearing the mountain range, Roper would have leaned on the controls to lower the ship's nose as she descended. The B-24 hugged the mountainside before leveling out to minimum altitude. The power descent brought the ship under German tracking.

Unbeknownst to the B-24 aviators, German military had been tracking them since takeoff from Libya. "The Luftwaffe had recently placed a crack Signal Interception Battalion near Athens. It had broken the Allied code and was reading Ninth Air Force transmissions." Although the destination was unknown, the Germans were aware of a large formation of American bombers driving north. An alert was sounded.

When the Libs passed over the Balkan range, the Germans narrowed the target to Bucharest or Ploesti. Axis defenses engaged. But just as the American Liberators were detected high above the mountains, they descended low over the Danube River valley to an altitude below German radar tracking.

It was market day across the Wallachian countryside. A harvest of colorful produce was seen in stands across town squares tended by women in embroidered wraparound skirts. Although the Libs had vanished from radar, the plunge was close enough to be seen by villagers "waving from the ground." And from German spotters who conveyed the groups' trajectory.

German ground trackers reported sightings to the Luftwaffe Fighter Command at Otopeni, an aerodrome* between Bucharest

---

* "Aerodrome" refers to a military airfield.

and Ploesti. The center had a sophisticated tracking system manned by women dressed in military uniforms "wearing headphones facing [a wall-sized] map." According to Dugan and Stewart, "When they received the location of a plane . . . they directed a narrow flashlight beam to its map position and airmen on ladders crayoned its location on the glass." As the ships advanced, a proposed track was formed. "Full alarm" was called to the outer-lying aerodromes.

Nearly seven hours into the Liberators' flight time, air-raid sirens on the ground sounded.

The German High Command still questioned the intended target. Bucharest or Ploesti? The two leading groups were headed to Bucharest. The three trailing groups were still northbound as if to Ploesti. Confused by the two directions but also astonished the Americans would attempt a simultaneous attack on both cities. "Damned cleverly done," said German Air Controller Zahn. "They send planes to tie up fighters at Bucharest while the main force hits Ploesti."

The Liberators picked up speed. Crops nearing harvest passed by in rapid frames as the bombers roared over the Danubian plain. Out the window, streams and orchards mirrored the landscape back home. Surely Hillsboro crossed John B.'s mind. But gaining on Pitesti, it was time to advise the pilot of the two-minute warning for the easterly turn at the Initial Point.

As the armada turned at the first IP, as standard practice, Roper would have advised his crew to ready their positions.

Stationed at his nav desk, the navigator faced the back of the ship with his eyes just below both pilots' feet. John B. would have been able to see through the spaghetti of tubes and wires leading up to the flight deck. No doubt, mindful eyes were exchanged as

John B. reached for his throat mike. "Navigator to pilot: Forty miles to target!"

Turret gunners perched in greenhouse positions at the nose, tail, and crown while the waist gunners roosted for battle aft the wings. Each airman would scramble to confirm bullet cartridges were within arm's reach and the view down the gun barrel was clear. And finally, they stroked a Bible or good luck charm before taking a quiet moment.

As the ships roared over the second IP at Targoviste, the lead *Liberandos* mistakenly made a right bank south toward Bucharest, away from Ploesti.

The *Circus* followed.

John B. would have surely questioned the turn. They had just passed the monastery in Targoviste but the course, as planned, was to continue northeasterly to the TP, or Turning Point, at a third town, Floresti. John B. likely shook his head, knowing they had just "turned at Targoviste instead of Floresti." He reached for his throat mike to relay the message: "Navigator to pilot: This is NOT the turn."

In such tight formation, pilot Roper "had no choice but to follow the lead plane."

No doubt, John B. reiterated the wrong turn, requesting his pilot to open the command channel. While communication between ships was forbidden, John B. would know precious minutes were being wasted heading away from the target.

Pleading the mistake, radio silence was broken. "Mistake! Mistake! Wrong turn!"

Air Force archives noted as they "got to within ten minutes of Bucharest," John B.'s *Circus* leader made the decision to cut away, pivoting from the lead *Liberandos*. As a single unit, wingtip-to-wingtip, some three-dozen ships of the 93rd Bomb Group made a sweeping ninety-degree turn to the north.

No longer following the *Liberandos*, John B. and his brother Libs would now enter Ploesti's fiercest defenses on the south side as a single group.

John B. would have tried to make sense of his maps. Frustration surely compounded his angst, knowing full well they were headed in from the south where defenses were heaviest—exactly where the Bomber Command wanted to avoid. Out the window, the ground was racing below him. So low, treetops reportedly stroked the bombers' bellies.

Nearing the target, enemy guns were imposing. The Germans defended the *inner ring* with their mighty eighty-eight cannons. At point-blank range, explosive shards of fire pelted *Exterminator* as she raced through a web of silver tracer bullets aimed at the nose.

The Liberators were charging into the mouth of hell itself.

Flying as low as "fifty feet" above enemy anti-aircraft fire aimed at "point-blank range" was, no doubt, surreal. *Circus* B-24 guns were in a "direct fire fight with the larger German [cannons]. The noise was beyond decibel measure as the choir of 136 fourteen-cylinder engines, with a total of more than a half-million horsepower, roared among muzzle blasts, shrapnel crumps, and the ship-shaking clatter of 230 machine guns in Liberators," wrote Dugan and Stewart.

As to ground fire, "I could see the muzzle flash and the projectile as it came toward us," said the pilot of *Thunder Mug*. "The shell removed the left aileron, left rudder, and half of the elevator of [*Exterminator*]."

Then, "suddenly, a huge oil storage tank exploded directly in front of *Let 'er Rip*. He couldn't possibly avoid it. The next instant I glanced out and saw [*Let 'er Rip*] crossing under [*Exterminator*] and [*Thunder Mug*], barely clearing us, and then going over a pair of stacks like a hurdler before putting his bombs in a cracking tower. How he missed the explosion, our ships, and the stacks is a mystery."

Ground artillery grew stronger as the B-24 gunners were pounding away steadily. "*Circus* planes trailing smoke from smashed engines and men were bleeding and dying on the air decks among hot bullet casings, and taking new wounds through the thin-skinned planes, their cries drowned by the deafening air-ground battle," wrote Dugan and Stewart.

Walt Stewart, John B.'s former copilot whose B-24 was flying near to John B.'s Lib, said, "Going over [Ploesti] all I could see was fire, flame, smoke, broken and crashing airplanes, gun flashes, and horror. It was the first time we ever heard the guns that were firing at us. We not only heard them but we could smell the burnt powder."

All the airmen "wanted was to get beyond that inferno of tracers, exploding storage tanks, and burning aircraft," said Longnecker. With the target beneath, bombs were dropped. *Exterminator* heaved relief before initiating a wide turn. But danger wasn't over. Beyond the refineries, a swarm of fighters awaited them. But somehow, *Exterminator* was spared.

As the B-24 Libs exited the *outer ring*, the battle was over.

Following the cacophony of shrapnel exploding, machine gun fire, and people yelling, certainly the drone of four engines was ironically calming as they climbed to altitude.

Decidedly pausing to control the rush of adrenaline, John B. would have returned focus to his desk, straightening maps thrown in the frenzy. He and his crew "had made it through hell." No doubt shaken, he would have steadied his nerves as he began to mark his biggest course yet.

Their lives now depended upon four engines and a depleting fuel supply. Brother ships *Thunder Mug* and *Let 'er Rip* rejoined tight formation. Another three ships moved into Roper's lead element. Their armada now stood at six "with *Exterminator* in the lead."

John B. would set Roper on a course heading home.

With the fight left behind, John B. would have recognized the challenge was far from over. Not only was their Liberator severely damaged, but they still had another 1,200 miles before landing in Benghazi.

As was habit, John B. would head upstairs to the flight deck but likely not before eyeing the damage to the ship. "Hanging from *Exterminator*'s vertical stabilizer was a guy-wire," presumably snagged passing the refinery stacks or perhaps a dead cable from a blocking balloon. Shells had removed "part of her left aileron, left rudder, and half of the elevator." And there was a gaping "hole in her right wing." Although *Exterminator* looked like a "flying junkyard," she was still in the air as their B-24 "passed over the Danube."

Through the catwalk, John B. would have seen the tail and nose gunners had joined the other gunners; all were jockeying position "at one waist window, waving to a passing Lib. Both crews of enlisted men shared quarters and were overjoyed seeing their buddies had made it through the target," said Joe Avedano Duran, nephew of *Tidal Wave* pilot Joseph Avedano.

The flight deck would have been a different story. With wavering gauges and severe damage to the bomber, both pilots would have struggled to keep *Exterminator* level and in the air. While the mood on deck was tense, John B. surely scanned his maps for the most direct route to base.

Looking forward beyond the instrument panel through the heavens, distant but not beyond reach, John B.'s vision would have undoubtedly drifted to home. After all, having reached mission quota (twenty-five combat missions), only a few hours and a thousand miles stood before an earned leave and a trip stateside was his.

John B.'s B-24 Liberator motored on.

Exterminator was gaining on Greece, where she would skirt the border back to Corfu and a final hurdle over sea. An hour had passed since leaving Ploesti but they had been in the air well over eight and had another five or six to go.

As they flew over southern Bulgaria, weather conditions changed.

"Clouds soon forced the planes to space out. But *Exterminator* and *Let 'er Rip* remained close together. They had flown the whole mission tight as a team of aerobats," said Longnecker, John B.'s left wingman.

Buffeting winds defied the best of pilots. Visibility decreased. Haze challenged judgment. One ship drifted. A collision occurred. With her left wing severed, *Let 'er Rip* instantly "broke away into a steep dive" before crashing in flames east of Brod, in Yugoslavia.

Exterminator's tail assembly snapped. John B. would have been thrown off balance. Caught by surprise, there was no missing the impact. With the force of the dive, he would have reached for an exit as gravity pulled on him. The ship's right aileron and rudder were useless. With her nose heavy, she was forced down.

Multiple parachutes were seen descending over enemy territory. John B. went missing.

Back at Cairo, smoke and nerves pervaded the War Room. On the conference room table, an ashtray was filled with half-smoked butts. Over strong coffee, the commanding officer and his staff would have spent the afternoon awaiting word of the mission. According to Air Force archives, "by 1700, with no returning Liberators in sight, the atmosphere grew tense." Up from his chair, no doubt, the general would begin pacing.

The phone rang. Presumably Brereton's aide picked it up. The *heavies* were spotted on radar over the Adriatic. Relieved his crews were returning, the general surely flexed a clenched fist in a triumphant pump.

At 1810, planes were landing at their home bases. The ships had been in the air nearly fourteen hours. As fuel gauges registered empty, more Libs trickled in.

By midnight, of the "165 that had reached the target," "seventy ships were accounted for." Those that returned carried battle scars of shredded fuselages, fractured wings, and shattered turrets. Some landed with fragmented elevator sections or gaping holes in tails and many with failing engines. It was a wonder the planes managed to fly the returning thousand-plus miles in such broken condition.

The airmen were debriefed. They provided the last known coordinates of still missing ships as well as a count of parachutes seen. Surviving airmen told stories of *hellfire*, barely escaping with their lives, leaving commanding officers to wonder why such a risky mission was executed in the first place.

But especially, they shared "the nightmare that was Ploesti."

Each base commander scrambled to determine where his remaining planes were. While not reaching the African coast, some ships made it to Allied-held territory. Damaged beyond repair, most ran out of gas, some landed on Cyprus, while others coursed to Syracuse and Malta. Within days of the mission, another third of the crews were accounted for and eventually returned to Benghazi.

But so many others were lost—missing, killed, or captured. Or unknown; and for those, a question mark appeared next to their names on official reports. Air Force archives reported "of the 1,726 officers and enlisted men that took off that morning, 532 airmen failed to return," including John B.

The reality of 50 percent losses anticipated at briefing hit hard on the *Circus*. The 329th Bomb Squadron history reported "of the group's thirty-seven B-24s that took off that morning, seventeen failed to return." Nearly half of John B.'s group went missing.

Reports were prepared. And thoughts of sending next-of-kin letters were put off.

The Air Force suffered a major loss that day—the highest cost of men and machines ever. Due to the dreadful loss, *Black Sunday* was conceived. *Tidal Wave* was the Air Force's darkest day, by far.

While losses were censored, the War Department touted success, as did news accounts. But in reality, the ferocity of the Axis was confirmed in the raid over Ploesti. Due to the high casualties, the Air Force ceased low-level missions. Strategy was deliberated. Future trips to Ploesti were deferred.

What was learned? Ploesti was fortified second only to the German capital. Had they ignored the memo? Days before the mission, Air Force Headquarters sent a memo to the adjutant general of the War Department that "greater losses are to be anticipated in *Tidal Wave* than in any other operation."

The failure to conduct aerial reconnaissance, a conscious decision made early on by Allied leaders, overlooked the Axis capacity. The complex was armored beyond imagination.

Earlier in May, German barrage balloons had been discussed. The Brits had developed a cable-cutting device known as the Martin-B that had been installed on RAF aircraft. But American leadership deemed the device "impracticable" through a low-level attack, especially when taking avoidance actions from flak.

As early as June 16, they knew the score. In England, on a practice raid to determine feasibility, the RAF brought in mobile ack-ack guns that took beads on formation of twenty-four low-flying Liberators. Hardwick Airfield was the designated target and Hugh Roper, together with John B. in *Exterminator*, led the flight in the mock mission. The British major conducting the simulation concluded "that his men could have shot down an appalling total of the planes." Was it too late for Allied leaders to make an about-face?

In June, two months before the raid, the RAF offered three of their expert crews flying Lancasters (Britain's heavy bomber not unlike the Liberator) to assist in leading formation on the Ploesti mission. But again, the offer was deemed "impracticable."

In Algiers, England's Prime Minister Churchill met with General Jacob Smart (the principal architect and planner for *Tidal Wave*) and again offered his best RAF navigators to join crews in the lead B-24s. In his words, the RAF had "damn good navigators." But at the time, the offer was declined.

The attack altitude had been fiercely debated. Did egos ignore intelligence?

And while extraordinary measures were taken to ensure *Tidal Wave*'s secrecy, a dummy target laid out in the Soluch desert was no secret. Practice raids were performed. Two hundred bombers roaring at zero altitude broadcast a message of things to come. No secret there.

General Ralph Royce reviewed official reports noting "security around [Brereton's Cairo] headquarters was practically nonexistent." Cairo was a city "full of people gathering and selling intelligence." A typist, a local girl, had been hired because she was multilingual. Was she exchanging secrets for a price? Were others? Around the mock target in the desert, wandering Arabs had been stopped for questioning. Did they pass on information to German spies who only awaited the day the *heavies* would drive north? Everyone was suspect. Or what about known enemy reconnaissance that frequently scouted the staging area from Cretan bases? And Axis Sally with her broadcasts—how did she know? Whatever the source, the German Wehrmacht* was prepared.

---

* Wehrmacht was the German Army in the Third Reich; also sometimes referred to as the unified armed forces (the army, navy, and air force) of Nazi Germany during WWII.

Tidal Wave was the costliest Allied air raid of WWII. Long after the smoke settled, military superiors suppressed the idea that the raid on Ploesti gambled with recklessness. And that human stakes had danced with suicide.

While damage to the oil complex was severe, it wasn't long before the Germans restored the refineries and Hitler's crude oil was again flowing to his war machine. But Allied focus didn't leave Romania. Crushing Ploesti remained the objective in the Air Force's assault offensive.

In spite of the setback at Ploesti, the war in Europe was moving. The Allies were gaining ground. *Circus* survivors returning to Benghazi were given a two-week rest before resuming efforts against the Axis. By August 16, 1943, they were moving up the Italian peninsula with a first bombing mission on Foggia. In coming months, the Air Force would secure bases around Bari. Strategy was reset with sights adjusted to a nearer Ploesti.

ELEVEN

The Pressure Chamber

DETAILS OF THE MISSION TO PLOESTI remained unknown to those back home. News would be forthcoming.

In Hillsboro, the cabbie was waiting at the curb. Rushing out, Polley stopped long enough to give her parents a farewell hug before grabbing John B.'s letter that had just arrived. It was late summer before returning to her senior year at the University of Illinois. She was traveling to her sister's apartment in Alabama. Anne had recently married George French and his service took them to Maxwell Air Force Base where he was a flight instructor.

This was to be a reunion, of sorts, for the White siblings. If his military furlough was granted, Polley's brother, Bill, would join them in meeting John B.'s bride, Lucille. Polley's sister Jane, whose husband was serving in the South Pacific, also had plans to be there. And while their family was scattered all over the world, a rousing time was in store to welcome Lucille into their clan.

As the cabbie turned onto the hard road, Polley would have wished her parents had given her a proper send-off at the station. In pre-war days, they would have driven her in the family Studebaker. But with the economy shifting to war production, they all did their part to put the military's needs first. What an imposition this *mad war* was becoming! The OPA* put a ceiling on everything from sugar to gasoline. And silk stockings! Tokens were issued to families to purchase consumer goods. For personal use, weekly gas rations were set to a few gallons but businesses requiring gas to survive were provided with more, thus the taxi. Perhaps this leg of her journey was not meant to be a family road trip.

Arriving at the station and once seated in the Pullman, Polley pulled out John B.'s letter.

Reading his words in present day, Polley could still hear his imposing, yet lyrical voice resonating. A beacon of light, John B. had often kept her on the straight and narrow, especially when making big decisions. Seventy years after his letter had been written, Polley held on to the envelope, running her fingers across his script as if to draw John B. closer from a place far away.

Looking at the postmark, *July 25, 1943*, more than a week had passed since John B. dropped it in a military mailbag. But it had made its way to Polley as she slipped it open and began to read. *Somewhere in Africa . . . Got your letter before leaving England but had no time until now to catch up on my correspondence . . .* Polley could only imagine what John B. must be experiencing as she read more from his letter. *The pyramids are just a few miles and a few centuries away from modern apartment buildings . . . Small children speaking two or three languages had to help me, an educated man by US standards. The US knows a lot but it has a lot to learn . . .*

---

* "OPA" stood for the Office of Price Administration, a government agency responsible for controlling prices of goods and managing rationing systems to prevent inflation and ensure fair distribution of scarce resources like food, gasoline, and clothing during the war effort.

Cairo is a most interesting place. Probably one of the most cosmopolitan cities in the world and truly a place where old meets new and east meets west. Merchandise that comes into the city on a camel train goes out by plane. As John B.'s letter went on, Polley imagined the women he described, *still holding veil over their faces while wearing high-heeled shoes on stockingless feet . . . Respectable girls do not go out at night unless accompanied by their mother or an aunt or some suitable chaperone.* Hanging on the *chaperone* part, Polley had wondered if the mention had been made for her benefit. . . . *But during the day until sundown, they're just like you or Anne or Jane.*

Never one to hold back big-brother guidance, his voice rang clear as Polley continued to read. *When you get back to school, don't just coast along and figure you're done studying for life when the diploma is yours. You've only just begun, no matter how much you think you know—you've still got lots to learn . . .* In spite of his casual authority, John B.'s approval meant the world to Polley.

While his letter went on about family, friends, and hometown gossip, she would gloss over more words before racing down to the last lines. *If there's anything I can do for you here, let me know. I hope to go over to Cairo again before leaving this theater of operations and if I can, I'll try to find something to amuse you . . .* At his closing, she paused. *Love from John B.*

John B.'s letter arrived after he had roosted on foreign soil, a third continent since leaving the States. His military service had taken him through the rigors of navigation as chronicled in *Life* magazine—his picture had appeared in two issues. A recent write-up in the newspaper cast him as squadron navigator. Of course, Polley didn't know the significance of what that meant but as she recalled, *"Daddy was certainly pleased."* And although she didn't know exactly what John B. was doing, she was certain that whatever it was, he was surely commanding adventures.

In Texas, Ellington was rebuilding and Bob was doing his part with post-hurricane cleanup. For days, drinking facilities and electricity remained off. While the camp showed signs of recovery with debris and vegetation piled alongside the road, broken windows and torn roofs burned a permanent memory in Bob's mind as he wrote home. *You can be thankful that you don't have hurricanes in Illinois. You just can't imagine the intensity of one of those storms. Out there the other night, I realized how small man is, when put up against one of nature's worst concoctions. There has not been one bit of braggadocio from any of the fellows who were out on that line hanging onto those planes. Every one of them will admit that they were damn scared and damn thankful when it was over.*

Although buildings remained storm-ravaged, classes resumed. The military had no use for downtime. Next on the agenda was the *pressure chamber . . . used to determine how we react under high-altitude flying.* In several letters, Bob shared his experiences with pressures that began with coursework.

We had a lecture and one thing struck me as funny although crude. As you go up in altitude the pressure gets less & at 18,000 feet the gases in your body expand. The lecturer told us to remember that we were not in Mrs. Astor's drawing room and . . . that the more vociferous we were, the less our pains through expanded intestines would be . . .

Ever hanging over his head was the possibility of washing out, the disappointment of being transferred to a lower branch of service. *I hope that I am okay at high altitudes. That will wash you out if you don't have the right reactions.*

Following classroom studies on the effects of pressure at altitude, there came time to put into practice what was learned. *The pressure chamber is a large tank that looks like a boiler. The sealed compartment is designed to chart reactions at the different altitudes as simulated by lowering or raising the pressure.* With air sucked from the chamber, *it gives you the experience of going to altitude. At 38,000 feet the gases in your body are expanded to four times normal, but most of us had gotten rid of our body gases by that time by various & sundry means.*

Having reached the intended pressure, the instructor would point to an oxygen mask and describe its lifesaving attributes. If the students failed to follow orders, a reprimand was given. If perception was lost, it was noted.

We stayed there for an hour. Of course, we had oxygen masks on. After about 30 minutes, quite a few fellows got the "bends," which is caused when the pressure is not great enough & nitrogen bubbles get into your blood. It is similar to the effect deep-sea divers get when they go too deep & the pressure is too great. I had no ill effects at this altitude.

Then we dropped to 18,000 & took off our oxygen masks to get the effect of anoxia (lack of oxygen in the blood). The reactions are much different for different fellows. After about 10 minutes your fingernails get blue & you either get very happy, pugnacious, or sleepy. It is much like drunkenness, in that you react in about the same way. I got happy & then I got sleepy. Just as soon as you slap the oxygen mask to your face you come out of it.

Then we climbed to 30,000 feet & made a 2-minute drop to 20,000 to simulate a parachute jump. For those fellows who could not keep their ears cleared or had sinus trouble, it was a terribly painful process. Some people are just not built for high-altitude flying and the low pressure affects them. However, I was okay throughout the process.

Any inability to handle the chamber's pressure meant *washing out*. But Bob held on. Another step closer to advanced navigation.

TWELVE
The Telegram

In hillsboro, three knocks would be heard at the front door before an announcement of words followed. Western Union was making a delivery.

Previous telegrams had been confirmations to keep smiling. It was John B.'s code indicating all was okay. John Sr. would expect the same as he approached the foyer to sign the delivery.

With cable in hand, he opened the envelope. A man of solid structure, no doubt his posture weakened with each word he read. Blood would have pulsed between his ears as the words rang in disbelief. *Missing in action.* Incensed at the military's term, he denied the possibility.

For certain, a jumble of chaos dashed through his mind: bombs bursting, clouds cradling lifeless engines, weightlessness. And shouts fought to be heard above the roar of battle, blind images of his son urging others toward an open bomb bay. Forces out of control. A father's mind raced, searching for a way out.

How powerless he would have felt—an inability to pull his son from danger. Reflecting on a last chess move, his son's fleeting strategy. A chute, surely John B. had one.

Controlling a surge of emotion, he would have called his wife to the music room where over the years many memories had been born: at the grand piano, the game table, or atop the oriental rug he'd given his wife as a wedding gift. It was in this room that grand announcements—pregnancies and achievements, academic or other—were made. No doubt he was numb with shock as he looked around the room filled with a garden of picture frames: a family cultivated with love.

Ada would have passed through the double doors marked by grids of paned glass. With the telegram still in her husband's hand, Ada listened as he shared the news that their son was missing in action.

A mother's thoughts can only be imagined. Surely, she had not heard him correctly. Perhaps he was joking, although he was never so cruel and certainly not about such a serious manner. No, perhaps he'd missed a cue or read something into it that wasn't there. She had to see the words for herself.

> I REGRET TO INFORM YOU THAT THE COMMANDING GENERAL MIDDLE EASTERN AREA REPORTS YOUR SON CAPTAIN JOHN B WHITE JR MISSING IN ACTION SINCE ONE AUGUST PERIOD IF FURTHER DETAILS OR OTHER INFORMATION OF HIS STATUS ARE RECEIVED YOU WILL BE PROMPTLY NOTIFIED

No doubt her heart was broken.

A fear, perhaps a premonition, long repressed was now on paper before her. So direct the dispatch, it lacked emotion of a missing life. But that was it. Other than the capital letters imprinted boldly across tape affixed to the telegram, it left a void of details. And with only the time and closing by an impersonal adjutant general, the text relayed that her son was missing. A mother would believe they must be wrong.

"What this telegram says is that he is missing, nothing more," a sentiment John Sr. shared with members of the family. The Whites were optimists. They maintained a positive spin on any situation and, of course, this was no different. Especially knowing hope was the only way to deal with such tragic news. John Sr. shared his beliefs in a way others would remember. "John B. is resourceful; has a *top-notch pilot and crew*; and [is] likely hiding out for resistance fighters to help him return to the Allies. We must stay focused; he will return."

He would need to call John B.'s wife, Lucille. She was still in Alabama at his daughter Anne's home. Polley was also there.

The news was difficult in any situation. But now, sisters would surround their brother's bride as a father spoke to his son's wife. Certainly, he tried to be as gentle as he could, but there was no soft way to impart the news. John Sr. would have reiterated, as he'd done with family members, the strong possibility that John B. could reach Allied territory. But most of all, he would have stressed that John B. would return.

Polley's brother was missing. How could this happen? What went wrong? Was he hurt? Surely, he'd find a way home. He had to be found. Polley wouldn't believe anything different.

Hearts were fractured but they held on to hope. Family mantra demanded a positive face. As Polley left her sister in Alabama, Lucille would return to her mother in Colorado.

As the wheels rolled from the train station, Polley would have looked to the vacant seat beside her with relief, knowing she wouldn't have to pretend to exchange idle chatter.

Out the window to the fast-passing landscape, a woolgathering of scenes may well have emerged of Polley's home. From the sleeping porch three stories up, the late-night sounds of summer critters would conjure dreamscapes. Behind Polley's house, one street over was Oak Grove Cemetery, where owls and nighthawks sent cautionary messages to eavesdropping ears beyond the burial grounds. The locals called it Hope Cemetery. The graveyard predated the Civil War, where epitaphs revealed earthly ancestors entering a world beyond. Marbled monuments of angels stood guard as lambs offered peace to visitors. Headstones inscribed a life laid beneath and cenotaphs marked others somewhere far away. Pioneers and politicians, beloved mothers and devoted sons rested under weeping willows.

While it was hallowed ground, the rows of gravestones ignited childhood imaginations of haunted souls. The entrance closed at sundown, but it didn't stop wayward kids from entering, who would then weave tales of restless spirits under the moonless night.

One summer night, as Polley recalled, neighborhood kids had ventured into the cemetery. Beyond the gates, an endless sea of clouded markers rose from the earth. And shadows would scurry as if they had their own agenda. The sound of the whip-poor-will followed them deeper into the graveyard as an owl clapped its wings, warning of intruders. Polley hastened her pace, but she was falling farther behind the group. Running to keep up with the others' longer-than-her legs, she tripped on a tombstone, falling hard on her knee. John B. must have had eyes in the back of his head as he turned around and jogged back to help her. Shielding her skinned knee, Polley was more embarrassed than hurt, being the youngest in the group by at least two years. She could hear *John B.'s booming yet kind voice* as he leaned over her. He had a way of smoothing things out despite her clumsy little-girl moves. In one fell swoop, he scooped her up and sat her on his broad shoulders. On top of the world, she was safe and ready to take on the scary stories told by the older kids. *"Oh, John B.!"*

Once Polley arrived at home in Hillsboro, focus remained on John B. She would have gone straight to the living room, where her father often sat reading the paper. Sitting on the arm of his chair, she would find comfort snuggling next to him. With her eyes shut tight, she could sense John B. in the room. The feeling was so palpable, Polley recalled, she didn't want to open her eyes, fearing a crumbling apparition.

With John B.'s plight, Polley thought of others, guys she'd been writing overseas. She had just learned about Lloyd Handshy, whom she cared about deeply, receiving news that he'd been killed serving in the Pacific with the Marines. And then Bob. That's when it struck her. His letter. What was it that John B. said?

Rummaging through her handbag, she pulled out John B.'s letter. Scanning down to the fourth page, she found it. *Bob has a fine reputation . . . If he's okay by you, he's okay by me.* Bob? Okay by me? Had John B. known all along? While Bob had always been there for her, Polley hadn't given him a second thought. But now, John B.'s words gave her pause.

As weeks passed, John B.'s whereabouts remained unknown. Because his plane had gone down behind enemy lines, the military was unable to enter German-occupied territory to get answers. Then came a letter from his former copilot, Walt Stewart. He was on the same mission, in another plane. He didn't have much information but wrote: "Two pilots reported two large planes crashed on the ground and they also saw several parachutes around the region too." A few weeks later, in another letter published in the *Decatur Herald*,

Stewart wrote, "Fliers returning from the raid indicated that all or most of the crews of both planes were able to parachute to safety following the collision." Stewart went on to say, "If any pilot could get his crew and himself out safely, Hugh Roper certainly could—he was the best pilot I have ever known."

Hope was on their side.

Not long after that letter, Pat Dagon, a local boy who had served on John B.'s crew and had been on the same mission in another plane, wrote to his family. A portion of his letter was published in the local Hillsboro newspaper. "When you are forced down in enemy territory it may be months before you can get communications out to let your Bomb Group know where you are. I know how Captain White was—he was one of the best navigators in the Group. He always looked things over for the worst-case scenario . . . I have a strong feeling that Captain White is okay." As Dagon continued, he wrote, "I lost a lot of good buddies on that raid but in this 'racket' we live today and are gone tomorrow."

While John B. remained in Polley's thoughts, she would have to gear up for her last year in college. Although grades were not her forte, she was inspired to do well so that when John B. did return, she could proudly show him her diploma.

So, as they waited for word from Europe, life for Polley went on at the university.

In disbelief, Bob read her letter. Moments before, hearing his name at mail call would have brought on a brightened smile as he reached for the postal delivery. As his eyes targeted the personalized stationery, a lifted mood would deflate. Although hope was relayed, her sadness eclipsed his heart.

Before now, war had been a distant notion—Bob would go in,

do his job, and return. With John B. missing, reality hit hard. At the time, Bob ran through a million scenarios of what might have happened. How was he forced down? What ground resistance did he encounter? How would he escape? He would escape. And return. He *must return*, for the Whites.

Bob mulled ideas in his head: an accurate flak strike, mechanical failure, bailing out, or a crash landing in enemy territory. He plotted his own stratagem, given the same circumstances. If anyone could, he believed in his heart John B. could get out of it.

August 21, 1943

Dearest Polley,

. . . I just now received your letter and was quite taken aback about John B. I realize what a great shock it was to you and your family. "Missing in action" can mean many different things, so chin up, and let us hope for the best.

It is very likely John B. and his crew could have been forced down somewhere, and with a plane as big as a Liberator, it is very possible without injury to the crew. By the term "missing in action" the Air Corps means the plane did not return to its base and its whereabouts are not known.

If John B.'s plane had been forced down, to me, John B. has a very good chance to be well and safe. Your father did the right thing by contacting the Red Cross, since they will do everything possible to gain information. I know what a trying circumstance it is for you and your family, but about all we can do is [to] hope and to pray . . .

Knowing his parents would soon learn the news, Bob wrote home. *I hear John B. is missing in action. Of course that doesn't mean that he has been killed because a plane as large as a Liberator can be forced down—the crew has a pretty good chance. And navigators are in about the least vulnerable place.*

At the same time, he wondered, *Where is John B.? How is he?* Then his thoughts turned to *Hell, I could be in the same position . . .* Making a vow to himself, Bob would set a course to find out what happened to John B. It wasn't easy in the middle of the war, but Bob started asking questions to his instructors and commanders about the raid, hoping to hear anything that might indicate where John B. was.

In the meantime, word spread that the list of those advancing had been posted. Bob was one of many that hurried over to the admin building. A crowd formed, blocking his path to the list. The front recruit scanned the roll for his name before retreating. More young men would shuffle in and out to get a view of their future. With Bob's turn at the signboard listing names alphabetically, he would have first seen that Chetwood made the cut. And just below was Cress. Bob was on his way to a commission. No doubt he would have motioned a fist pump and a laudable YES! He was moving on.

Orders came down. They were shipping out the next day. Bob would have returned to the barracks, packed his things, and said his good-byes. Early the following morning, reveille sounded. Those who remained in preflight faced replicating routine. But for those destined to wear wings, changes were only a horizon away.

Advanced navigation would be the next phase.

PART TWO

THIRTEEN

Ut Viri Volent

Facing the next phase of training, Bob pushed forward into Advanced Navigation, specialized instruction using complex techniques to accurately plot long-distance flight paths. Given the structured program, *We will be going to class from 8:00 a.m. to 10:00 p.m. every day . . . Please write as often as you can. This is going to be a grind and I'll need all the encouragement I can get.*

San Marcos Air Field was fifty miles northeast of San Antonio. The newly constructed base had been the Air Force's response to war when it opened a year after Pearl Harbor. Designated the region's Technical Training Command, its grids of roadways laid out in organized blocks surrounded one-story barracks and classrooms. On the far side, large hangars housing twin-engine trainer planes lined the airstrip.

Funneled into a single line, *we were issued navigation watches, a great number of books, mostly containing astronomical charts and graphs . . . all kinds of drawing instruments, and three very complicated-looking computers*, tools that would soon plot their future course.

Orientation was an eye-opener. After delivering an initial list of expectations, the commander would shift to a darker tone. An anticipated 50 *percent* of the navigation candidates would not finish. *About half of those who come here wash out. I hope that I can get through*. Eyes would have tracked from side to side making predictions of the lucky ones or those destined for failure.

I think I am going to like this navigation, and it will just about kill me if something goes wrong and I wash out. I'm going to give it everything I've got and trust my native intelligence. I always tell myself that dumber guys than me have gotten through . . . Forty out of the last class were made instructors. What chance I have for that, I don't know but I may look into it as I am not much of a flag waver or impatient for combat duty.

With a rush-to-the-skies strategy, planes were flown around-the-clock. Mechanical burnout resulted. With planes exceeding manufacturer recommendations, mechanics worked tirelessly to keep up with the hours of training. *Last night the siren sounded . . . I found out today that four were killed when their ship caught on fire. Not exactly a morale builder for the first night in camp but I guess I will take the fatalist idea on things and hope.* Priority dictated trainers in the sky.

Training had been a robust competition with everyone in his flight. From Cedar City to classification through Ellington, rivalry among the cadets was keen. Before, names had been placed on a bulletin board for all to see how one was doing in comparison to others. It was no different when Bob reached Advanced Navigation. From dead reckoning to celestial to flying training missions, he kept on course knowing his track depended upon his successes.

More mental work was required than any post Bob had before. While the education focused on how not to get lost in the air, he knew it was his responsibility to guide the pilot where to go, and how long to maintain heading while adjusting destination with enough reserve fuel for the return.

Pilotage, the least complicated, was the first of many new concepts. As Bob explained in his letter, *Pilotage is looking at your air chart & the ground, paying attention to the roads, streams, and towns to determine how you are advancing on your course and how long it will take you to get from one town to the next along your route. Mind you, though, you don't just sit up there & have a scenic ride. All the time you are making 5-minute entries in your log of all instrument readings, besides trying to keep your ground position accurate. It is a busy job.* The method was easier in fair weather but additional systems were needed during inclement weather, unmapped land, flying over the ocean, or flying at night.

Classes were all business, a place to make or break. It was his first introduction to dead reckoning. With the term *dead* relating to a fixed object, *reckoning* incorporated allowances made for wind. The instructor waggled a circular slide rule, the E-6B. The front factored numbers on the ground while the back determined how wind affected speed and course, solving problems of fuel consumption, distance conversion, time, speed, correction of altitude, and airspeed with temperature differences.

With all calculations made by hand, *one small mistake in the beginning would ruin the rest of the problem. This course is harder than anything I ever took at college because we go so fast . . .*

I can't explain the complicated procedures that we have to go through in correcting the different instruments in a letter. But every time we read any of our instruments, we have to correct for various factors. Before we can get the ground speed from the air speed meter, which registers in mph, we have to change that to knots. Then we have to correct for altitude and temperature since the indicator registers from barometric pressure outside the plane. Then you have to factor in wind to tell how fast you are going along the ground. That is one of the simpler calibrations. Of course, you can set that up on your computer [a slide rule] *&*

if you read all the lines out on the various scales you come out with the answer. It sure is easy to screw up the works. Even an instrument like a compass has to be corrected for the metal in your plane and the difference between the north pole & the magnetic pole.

September 3, 1943

Dear Polley,

. . . I think John B.'s friend was right in saying it took a smart person to be a navigator. We certainly do get a lot of material shoved at us in an awfully short time. I am concentrating about 10 times as much as I ever did at college . . .

Course loads required more than the preceding classes. *Daily, reports come back from combat zones of additional systems that we should be taught. It makes [for] much more material to learn and the course just that much harder. We're reminded daily that the washout rate is high with only half of the cadets who start, finish the program.*

We are living navigation every minute of the day and computers keep revolving in your head when you sleep at night. In the weeks that followed, navigation consumed him.

Occasionally Bob wrote home about amusing things that happened in class. *The instructor asked how many of us were interested in the Ferry Command. I immediately stuck up my hand, real eager like. The instructor said, "All right, Mr. Cress, you can pick up this big suitcase of instruments and ferry it over to the building next door." I guess I bit on that one . . .*

NINE SEPTEMBER 1943. *I made my first flight mission.* Surely Bob's stride picked up as he crossed the tarmac toward a Beechcraft AT-7 trainer plane. The flying classroom carried an instructor and three students who each would take turns practicing their navigation skills. On the right side were three desks, trainee workstations similar to those used in bombers and transport planes. John B. had been photographed earlier in the same third seat that Bob had taken. The talk of Hillsboro, John B. had been featured in *Life* magazine the year prior. Pictured on the double-page spread, he became the face of dead reckoning in an article on *Aerial Navigation*. Bob's assignment was to use the same E-6B computer that John B. had used in the issue's photograph.

With fickle weather patterns, there were plenty of jolts and bumps in the air. *It was quite rough and the majority of the fellows got sick. Even many of the instructors got sick, but Sir Robert William didn't even get butterflies.* At one point, the plane hit an air pocket, dropping so fast that Bob had to reach above to catch instruments in midair, before they caught up with the table. It was a turbulent orientation, but Bob held on.

Tonight, I have to plan out tomorrow morning's flight. It is a flight in which we calibrate our air speed meter and the deviation of our compass. It is a low-altitude mission and involves an awful lot of turns. We look through a telescopic instrument called a drift meter that lets the ground go whizzing by. It is used to improve dead reckoning by measuring the wind effect while flying.

With a first open post in some time, Bob and Park Chetwood jumped in Park's convertible. *We drove to the University of Texas to get a line up on operations but campus was very quiet for a Saturday. Then we stopped at the Phi Gam* house.* Bob was prepared to give *the* handshake to an unassuming brother when a uniformed fellow opened the front door. To Bob's surprise, *the Fiji house had been taken over by the Navy.* While a passing camaraderie was kindled, uniforms and

* Phi Gamma Delta, aka Phi Gam or Fiji, was Bob's social fraternity at the University of Illinois. On college campuses across the country, its core values are friendship, knowledge, service, morality, and excellence.

war shadowed the times. Headed back to base, the realization that a fraternity house had transformed to military operations sank in—a new normal.

Open post was extended through the following afternoon. With the top down in Park's convertible, *we drove to New Braunfels. His car is so good-looking that we didn't have much trouble finding female company. Of course, we had to leave right in the middle of the afternoon so couldn't extend any real offers . . . It is so swell out there that you just about forget that you are in the army & that there is a war going on. At this point I can stand a little of that sensation.*

But the pace hastened. *All this week, we had three flight missions, three ground missions, and one heck of a lot of new problems. On top of that, our schedule has been pushed ahead with class all day on Saturday and only a few hours of open post on Sunday.*

October 2, 1943

Dear Folksies,

. . . We had a terrifically hard exam this morning. To elaborate, our plane is at a certain base and a battleship is reported at a certain position going a certain direction at a given speed. We have to figure out what direction we should fly, what speed, and the point we can get to the battleship in the quickest time.

By the time the ship alters course a few times, the problem gets rather complicated. On top of that we have to figure out whether we'll have enough gas to get back to base. It is an interesting problem to work but also very easy to screw up . . .

His letters were sounding much like John B.'s. So similar were his words and experiences that it was as if Bob had stepped into John B.'s shoes.

As work intensified, long days offered little free time. Bob faced a four-hour final exam on the first phase of training. He made it through pilotage and dead reckoning. His next jump would be celestial navigation. There was no letup as he coursed forward.

As the military advanced young men through technical training, the Air Force prepared for the next phase: practical training. Stateside, new bases were needed to prepare combat crews for overseas deployment.

Around the country, airfields carved from rural farmland supplied the staging areas.

In Nebraska, crews flying heavy bombers found a home at Harvard Army Air Field. The 484th Bomb Group, part of the 49th Bomb Wing of the Fifteenth Air Force, was born. As one of four squadrons within the new group, the 825th Bomb Squadron was destined to include Bob's name.

Just when Bob thought he was getting to be a pretty hot navigator, new concepts were introduced. *With a final exam on dead reckoning, we then start celestial navigation.*

Absorbing strange new names of *some seventy stars and identifying each one's location relative to the night sky was only part of what was required in class. Wish I remembered more from our walks, Dad . . .* With each new constellation introduced, reflection wasn't far away.

The stars would evoke memories of walks on the farm with his father, who had often pointed out star formations. With an outstretched arm, Jim Cress would connect a locus in the heavens as he directed his son to the stars before building upon a vision using more stars. When Bob would point to the brightest star in the northern sky, he remembered his father's words: "*Polaris. The North Star—from there you'll find your direction.*" His father revealed more to life on darkened trails guided by the heavenly blackboard above.

Coursework became more complicated with the use of sophisticated devices. Celestial navigation relied upon the use of a sextant, which measured vertical angles and used the height above the horizon of named stars to locate the substellar point relative to a dead reckoning position. Results required a double-check as the flight course depended upon precise accuracy.

Bob would have taken this phase of navigation even more seriously. As missions to and from enemy territory approached reality, he recognized the significance of his position—and the responsibility it carried. His crew would depend upon his expertise in guiding them home from treacherous skies. He knew the course he formed upstairs would rely heavily on lessons learned on the ground.

On clear nights, Bob spent hours roaming the skies through the ocular lens of the sextant. Repetition of stargazing would make identification at altitude less complicated given the stress of the plane's pitch and motion compounded by combat.

Saturday night, Chetwood and I drove over to New Braunfels to look at officer uniforms and then we drove out to the Oasis. We hashed out the latest fighter aircraft in the US arsenal before having a great big steak and a little airplane beer. Wisecracking with the drink in his hand, Bob said, "*You know, Park, you drink one bottle of this and pee-38.*" (Bob's reference to pee was the P-38 Lightning, an American single-seat fighter aircraft used during WWII.) Talk of fighter planes deteriorated from there.

We didn't have dates, so we drove back to San Marcos where there was a costume ball . . . I had a few dances with a girl who was wearing a gruesome mask . . . turns out she had not been wearing one. Following the party, Park had asked Bob if he'd had any luck at the masquerade.

"*Nicht sehr gut*"* said Bob.

Bob had learned German from his mother, who had been raised in Nokomis, Illinois, a town made up of immigrants mostly from Switzerland and Germany. At play, she had absorbed the sounds from foreign-speaking friends and, having played the piano at the German Methodist Church, she fine-tuned her language skills speaking with adults. It was only with the advent of WWI that German was discontinued in worship services. But during childhood lessons with her young son, Essie would impart the German language. As Bob entered high school, German classes came easy, and he continued them through college.

An exchange of jabs, one-liners, and the German language followed, before Park wrapped it up. "They're gonna love you in Intel."

A continent away, the Fifteenth Air Force was establishing bases on foreign soil. Major General Doolittle took command at Bari, Italy. Heavy bombardment groups were activated in the Mediterranean Theatre. From the Italian Peninsula, Allied operations prepared for a strategic bombing campaign over targets in northern Italy, France, Austria, and the Balkans.

By early December, Doolittle turned command over to Major General Nathan F. Twining. The number of combat-ready airmen was increasing. Soon, full strength would be achieved.

Classes were graduating. Some were given furloughs. Others not. As anticipation for a commission intensified, only rumors floated

* In German, "*nicht sehr gut*" translates to "not very good."

dates. Much depended upon weather, scratching flights, test schedules, and trajectory to the next phase.

With no timelines posted, deadlines were uncertain, and plans had to be put on hold. Best guess put graduation on Christmas Day.

Bob had never been away from home for the holidays. *One night looking at the stars, I considered the trip.* At best, if he could find someone with a car it was a twenty-hour drive to St. Louis with a final two home. *I looked into train schedules, south to north and west to east, but the train just wouldn't work out. I could only get home after Christmas. After riding in planes, it sure gripes me to think that it takes 24 hours to get to St. Louis by train. That would be about a 6-hour trip in one of our planes.* But still, much depended upon the timing of graduation.

As soon as Bob learned when the ceremony would be held, he wrote home. *Looks like I will be commissioned on Friday morning, I think I will get in to St. Loo at 8 a.m. Saturday morning. I will send a telegram just before I leave here and I'll have you meet me at Union Station (the big railroad station) in St. Louis.*

On Christmas Eve, flags framed the stage as a hundred cadets took their place at the Post Theatre. Class 43-18 was graduating.

Next to him sat Park. Random thoughts of adventures would certainly have flashed through Bob's mind: of picking up girls in Park's convertible; or getting jazzed on beer; playing basketball. How proud he was to be among this exceptional group. *Great guys! No washouts here!*

Raising their right hands, "I," followed by a chorus of names, took the oath through to a resounding "so help me God!"

Being a student of Latin, as his wings were presented Bob considered the meaning behind the Air Force insignia, *Ut Viri Volent.* But internalizing the mantra, *That Men May Fly,* he was now among them. Commissioned an officer, a Second Lieutenant in the US Army Air Corps, he was pretty proud of himself.

John B. had stood in the same place not long before. But now he was missing. *Missing in action.* Surely, *he parachuted, maybe [was] captured or [is] hiding out until he can get free passage through underground efforts.* Upon his commission, Bob thought, *I knew I was more closely related to John B. than I had ever been.*

Bob learned the top twenty were headed directly into bomber crews. The remaining eighty officers were dispatched to gunnery school. He ranked third in his class and for that he would bypass gunnery. Orders required he report to Harvard, Nebraska, on January 3, 1944. *A ten-day furlough!* Undoubtedly beaming, he scrambled back to the barracks for a last inspection before his final orders were signed. Gathering his gear, Bob headed to the parking area where he met his ride, *a navigator from Carthage, Illinois.*

Two newly commissioned officers would depend upon weather conditions and open gas stations for the trip north. With a full tank and the car in gear, four tires spit a cloud of dust and gravel trailing behind them. Out the side view, San Marcos would become a fading image. Turning on Post Road, their course was initiated. The two had their sights on the objective. They had just completed 500 hours of ground instruction plus another 100 in the air. Of course, this was a journey on four wheels guided by a map, a compass, and some genuine intuition.

Pilotage was the method of navigation they relied upon. In the days prior, Bob had marked each point along the course, cognizant of *the most direct route with the best roads.* Timing was tight. Estimating each leg of the route, a course reckoned no holds barred. With hours of road ahead of them, the trip required steady, and speedy, driving. The intended *target was an eastbound train coming into*

Jefferson City for a 5:30 departure. Only minutes lay between making or missing the connection. Most roads posted a speed limit of thirty-five, but his driver *accelerated to seventy* on straight stretches of rural farmland.

While the dark of night obscured road signs, Bob still would have guided directional turns with accuracy. He was anxious to get to the *Hill. How fitting that as a new navigator, I was directing my course home.* Texas prairies and good weather boosted spirits—they were ahead of schedule. *My driver was doing everything possible to get me to the train, but until I stepped on that platform, I kept thinking, I've just gotta make that connection.*

As they hastily carved the way to Arkansas, the weather changed. Driving into a haze of ice particles, the ceiling closed in—an *unexpected sleet storm shut down the flow.* Any gains they'd made in Texas quickly evaporated. In Missouri, visibility cleared as they powered on. With renewed momentum, the pace picked up again. But still, they had another hour on the road. The calculation predicted a window of minutes either way to the station. A final push to target was initiated.

Approaching the train station, there was no time to spare. But still, there was nothing either one of them could do to get there sooner—finer calculation put their ETA at five minutes late. As Bob got to the ticket counter, *the incoming train had been delayed. Ten minutes late!* Luck was his windfall.

His folks were waiting on the platform when his train rolled into Union Station. After a drive to *Cress Hill*, Bob was home at last.

While he had not slept, certainly adrenaline kept him energized. The idea of being a second lieutenant, a commissioned officer with a brand-new uniform topped by sterling silver navigator wings, gave him added confidence to take on anything.

His bedroom was just as he left it, trombone in the corner and fraternity paddles above his desk. In the ten months he had been away, his bed had never felt so good. He hardly remembered laying his head on the pillow before drifting off into a deep sleep.

His time home became a lasting memory of events with family and friends. He spent every night with Polley. Promises were made. Upon his return, Bob would finish his degree before entering law school. A future presumed.

By year's end, the *Big Three*—Roosevelt, Churchill, and Stalin—met for the first time at what became known as the Tehran Conference.

While a summer invasion on the French coast topped the agenda, the more pressing strategy moved US and British forces northward through Italy as the Soviet Union launched an offensive from the east. But for his efforts, Stalin demanded Allied bombing campaigns over Eastern Europe as well as vehicles and equipment for ground support.

The fate of the eastern territories was begun, and soon Russian dominion would hover over the Balkans.

FOURTEEN

Combat Training Stateside

Bob was wrapping up a ten-day leave at home when his small-town life would soon give way to a new world. It was time to report to Harvard Army Air Field in Nebraska.

His parents redeemed some gasoline vouchers for the nearly two-hour drive to the St. Louis train station. With so many unknowns of war, there was no telling when they would next see their son. Surely, Essie tightened her embrace as Jim Sr.'s hand gripped Bob's shoulder. But the whistle signaled final boarding, beckoning a forlorn call to farewells.

On the train, Polley didn't escape his thoughts. Nor did music. As a melody played in his head, he whistled the tune softly. He could almost hear Vera Lynn singing the lyrics to "We'll Meet Again."

It was pretty hard to say good-bye to the folks, but I am rapidly beginning to realize again that I am in the army and my playing is over for a while. My parents, you, and everyone have been so swell to me over my furlough. With the gratifying times behind him, he had to share one more with Polley.

January 3, 1944

. . . Something pretty funny happened last night after I took you in. I came back to my car and that dear old automobile of fashion & passion suddenly decided to turn against me. To my embarrassment I found the battery was dead. Needless to say, I didn't want to stay parked in front of the White manse any longer since we had already been strongly hinted at by either thy mater or pater that hospitality was definitely at a low ebb.

Anyway, I couldn't get the darn thing started. I was about to walk uptown to find someone to help me. For some reason, I thought your father would not be exactly hilarious to get out of a warm bed to give me a push. Luckily a man happened to be walking along the street and helped me push the car and we got it started. I was afraid I was going to have to stay in front of your house all night, and that wouldn't have been much fun since you had already gone in.

I guess you'll be busy next month with exams and all. You are a pretty smart girl, and I know you'll come through ok . . . I love you and "we'll meet again some sunny day."

It was late when he arrived in Hastings, one stop short of his new military home. A last night as a civilian, he checked into the Hotel Clarke.

The next morning, he took the *7:10 bound for Harvard.* After a short hop, he stepped onto a concrete platform that became the demarcation from his personal life to becoming the property of the Army Air Corps. *A light freezing rain was falling.* To his right, flat plains disappeared into a mist of fog. And to his left, it was just the same. *That old north wind gets up a lot of momentum across the Nebraska flats and feels icy cold.*

The town's name was carved into a wooden signpost. HARVARD. *The prestigious university and a law degree crossed my mind, as did thoughts of initiating my wartime experience.* Bob would have pondered his reality—ambitions postponed.

He caught a military bus bound for the airfield. As it rolled along the newly paved road, vast prairies extended in all directions. Emerging in the distance was the three-story crossbeam control tower, framed by the rising sun. Around the base was a scant wire fence secured by eight-foot posts that enclosed an enclave of wooden buildings. They entered the compound through a gate where winged airships, fierce and powerful warbirds, awaited the next course.

Originally Harvard was a satellite base to nearby Kearney Field but with the war escalating, more men were needed and more places to house them. Harvard Army Air Field was the last stop of an around-the-clock program of training bomber crews bound for the European and Pacific theaters.

Bob was ushered in and out of doors handling initial paperwork before having a one-on-one with his pilot, Jack Crumbliss. *I immediately liked Jack and felt the feeling was mutual.* The two would become roommates and in time good friends given their close relationship on a heavy bomber.

At the Officers' Club, the formal conference turned to informalities over beer.

At twenty-five, Jack was the *old man on the crew.* Considering the side conversations Bob witnessed, Jack usually got what he wanted. He had a proclivity for *bending the rules and could weave a story to get out of any trouble* he faced. The pilot was *well liked* and most certainly a character. *I felt lucky to be a part of his crew.*

With beers in hand, the other two officers on the Crumbliss crew stopped by to check out their new navigator.

Just twenty-two, copilot William Martin had grown up in

Sulphur Springs, Oklahoma, where his wife was living at the time. As Bill went through the classification phase, he wanted to be a fighter pilot, but the military elected him to the right seat of a heavy bomber. *First impressions laid him out as a pretty good guy.*

The copilot roomed with bombardier Richard Parsons. A *likable guy,* Dick hailed from Jamestown, New York. He was a good-looking twenty-three-year-old and as for marriage, *in his words he was undecided.* No question, *he was a smart guy* and likely a military lifer.

Jack would hint at the rest of the crew, experienced but a discerning group. Bob had said, *I came in as a brand-new lieutenant, a title I barely owned two weeks prior . . .* The crew had formed in Utah two months before coming to Harvard. While finalizing their training to go overseas, they only lacked filling one position. Navigator. *I was the final component to this ten-man crew.*

Bob was the outsider based on the crew's presumptions of *the A-grade fraternity boy from Chicago. By the look on their faces, I knew I had to gain their respect.* Six sets of enlisted men's eyes exposed quick judging concerns about the *skinny new kid. Suspicions of the college-boy-turned-airman were compounded in that I had more college than the enlisted crew combined. I didn't tell them I graduated third in my navigation class. But as far as first impressions, I liked them . . . And in time I was sure I'd win them over, or at least, I was going to give it my damnedest.*

With meeting the crew behind him, he would have stopped by the hardstand* to view his new office, the B-24 Liberator. Just like soldiers lined up for battle, ships painted an Army green would be flown during this final training phase.

Seeing the bubbled dome in front of the cockpit, Bob wrote,

* "Hardstand" refers to the designated paved area on an airfield where the aircraft is parked and serviced.

From there I'll take star sights. As he faced the warbird, humbled by her size, he noted how panes of Plexiglas formed her nose. *Through there I'll navigate the world.* No doubt he marveled at the thought of this king-sized aircraft soaring through the skies. Four imposing engines with one-story propeller blades hung from wings spanning the width of a large barn. Behind each wing was a large star, a moniker of the country he was proud to represent.

Connecting with the crew was crucial, but the primary objective at Harvard was combat training. Flights began with short hops that progressed to full practice raids dropping dummy bombs in a designated area. They flew in formation with other ships in the squadron. And they flew at night.

One day, Bob's crew went out to the pistol range for a qualifying target shoot to carry a sidearm. *I got the 3rd highest score, high enough to be qualified as a sharpshooter. Surprised the hell out of me but helped in gaining the respect of the crew. Boy, having the respect of your crew means a whole lot. In fact, it means everything.*

The pace hastened. *I have been busier than heck since I last wrote you. I have put in over twenty hours of flying topped by classwork, celestial groundwork, and extra duties. I have been flight control officer for a five-hour duty, each two out of three days.* Working seven days a week, the Air Force designed a new schedule—*we will work eight days straight and then have the ninth day off. Not exactly a banker's vacation but it will afford some relief from the monotony of a routine with no letup as we have now.*

One night, *we flew to St. Louis for a simulated bombing attack on Eads Bridge. Using celestial navigation, I guided the ship to St. Louis within a half minute of our ETA.* After the bombardier sighted the bridge through the crosshairs for the mock bombing, *I adjusted course to the bombing range at Broken Bow before returning to Harvard.* Overall, *it was an eight-hour flight and required quite a lot of navigation*. As Bob looked at his log of time and distance between points, the Harvard to St. Louis leg stuck out. *Only two hours and fifteen minutes*, a stretch not far from home.

On that flight Bob realized his luck of being placed on this crew. Each man handled his position as if seasoned and were ready to assist in any way possible. Bob reeled in the coordinated efforts as he wrote home. *People unacquainted with bomber crew training can't understand what an intertwining, closely knit teamwork is required of every man in order to operate the plane successfully. You really learn to appreciate the other fellow and his job. Every fellow has too much to learn to become cocky so that eliminates that possibility.*

January 26 marked Bob's twenty-first birthday.

Many days *John B. was in the back of my mind. What happened that day? Where is he? What is the Air Force doing to find him?* Often and with regularity, Bob sought answers that might offer some solace to Polley and her family. Along the way he met a bombardier that had flown *Tidal Wave*.

February 1, 1944

. . . I just finished talking to this bombardier who was on the Ploesti raid and said he remembered John B. . . .

As you probably know, the raid was practiced for many weeks in advance on an exact replica of the refinery that had been set up on the African desert. It seems there was an English colonel who had been an engineer at Ploesti before the war and was able to reproduce the setup of the refinery very accurately.

He said the Germans knew something was up since Liberators almost always bomb at high altitude and here they were practicing on the desert at an altitude of about 100 feet and lower. In fact, they were flying so low during this practice session that many of the planes scraped their bomb bays on the sand.

A few days before the mission they were all called together and told to write all their friends and relatives as they were going on a very dangerous mission, and in an undertaking of that type, many casualties were a certainty.

They were also explained the complete underground system of Romania so that any of those who were forced down would know how to make the right contacts to get back.

He then told me that he had heard some of the fellows had recently gotten back by way of the underground. How long ago "recently" meant, I couldn't pin him down, but I imagine it was a month or so ago.

I didn't realize just how important that raid really was, but he said if Ploesti had not been knocked out, the invasion of Italy could not have been accomplished. It seems Ploesti supplied the big part of oil and gasoline to the Axis forces in N. Africa and Italy. I didn't know that, but I guess it was a big factor.

Well, that is what he told me, and even though it doesn't tell us too much about John B., I thought you might find it a little enlightening to know just what kind of mission John B. was on.

I realize it has been a long time since John B. was reported missing, but if he was wounded and in friendly hands it might take a long time before he could travel the underground back to our bases. So, don't you dare give up hope for a minute.

Probably you knew most of what I have just told you, but this was firsthand from a fellow who was on the raid, and didn't contain the "Print what the readers want to read" newspaper element. So much for that, and I'll keep my ears open and try to talk to some of these other fellows who were on that raid. There are quite a few of them around here and I may be able to find out something or find somebody that knew John B. . . .

. . . Tomorrow night will be a long one before my B-24 comes into roost. B-24s are very fine planes and right now I wouldn't want to go into combat with any other . . .

When they weren't flying, evenings were spent at the Officers' Club. But with a pass, some nights Bob and Jack would go into town. One night, *the lights burned quite late at the Hunt Club. My pilot slipped on ice and fell on his right hand. He was carrying a quart of liquid joy and broke the bottle and cut his hand pretty badly.*

Due to his injuries, Jack couldn't fly for a couple of days. A training exercise followed with two pilots, both squadron captains. As lead officer, *I pulled the crew aside to let them know the pilots were checking procedures and gave them a pep talk to outdo ourselves.*

One of the pilots, Captain Gordon, was a fine fellow to have when navigating. Although the other pilot had rank, he was not holding his heading very well. Bob figured he was testing him to see how well Bob handled under pressure. *I called him up over the interphone and told him that he would have to hold my heading or I wouldn't be able to do good navigating for him. My voice didn't have any of the "Please, Sir" inflection in it either, but after all, when I am navigating, the pilot does what I say and that is the way it has got to be . . . Later, Captain Gordon caught up with Jack and told him I was a darn good navigator—that I wasn't taking any of the other pilots' nonsense.*

Bob knew his time stateside was almost up. Crews attended ground school in final preparation for deployment. Flight training was double-booked with two formations a day, leaving little free time on the ground. They ate, they slept, and they waited. The days were long.

The idea of war was closing in as he wrote Polley . . .

February 3, 1944

. . . I don't know whether it's a feeling of excitement, anxiety, or what; but when I stop to think where I will be in 30 days it makes me feel rather funny inside. Europe or the Orient? Either place is no picnic but personally I prefer Europe.

Others have done it & although any fellow in the Air Corps knows his card is in the deck somewhere, we all feel we will be fortunate enough to evade that card. I guess you would call it a fatalistic view on life, and it is about our only outlook. I don't know why I developed this into such a grim letter. Maybe I'm getting something off my chest . . .

As combat training continued, Bob set up shop in the forward hold, or nose, of the bomber. For safety reasons, *on takeoff and landing I would move to the flight deck. But once the plane was airborne, I would return to my station* by crawling through a narrow tunnel alongside the nose wheel. At the front of the bomber, panes of Plexiglas formed a transparent enclosure that offered visibility for navigation while safeguarding the crew from potential attack. A step back was his desk, a flat piece of plywood where instruments and mapping tools were arranged.

Viewing access through windows was just as important as the instruments he used. Above his head was *the astrodome, a bulged window used for making celestial observations.* With a view through the bubble, *I take out my octant and shoot the stars,* tracking the ship's location in space. To his right was a small, flat window. And to his left was the same. Through the windows, he would have identified landmarks using pilotage.

I am more pleased every day [at] my fortune of getting a B-24. Although the navigator is quite crowded, rides backward, and does have to stand up the entire mission, I still like it. Training missions were

White siblings c. 1926
From left: John B., Anne, Jane, Bill, and Polley

Cress siblings c. 1927
From left: Louise, Marian, Jim, and Bob

Of the nine White/Cress children, four sons and the husbands of four daughters all served in WWII.

John B. White, Jr.

Left: Portrait of John B. while attending Chicago Kent School of Law. During his time there, he delivered *radio debates* to a multi-state audience over WLS Radio. (1939-40)

Below: Portrait of 2nd Lieutenant John B. White, Jr., a newly commissioned navigator. He was destined to join the 93rd Bomb Group commanded by Col. Ted Timberlake at Barksdale AFB, Shreveport, LA. (1942)

Below, left: Last visit home before John B. deploys. At the time the White family had four sons serving in the military. From left: George French, Bert McWilliams, John B., Ada, John Sr., and Bill White. (June 1942)

Above: John B. uses the E-6B flight computer, a circular slide rule that calculates ground speed, wind correction, and fuel burn. [Double exposure shows airfield in background.] (1942)

Above: John B. shoots the sun and stars with a sextant through the astrodome of an AT-7 trainer. Given space constraints, one can only imagine the difficulty taking star sights wearing full gear and an oxygen mask. (1942)

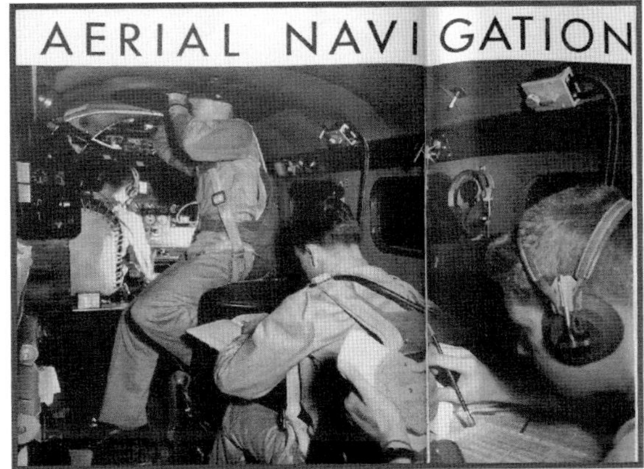

Above, left: John B. (highlighted) and the airmen of the 93rd Bomb Group pose in a *before the big game huddle* on the cover of *Life* magazine, July 26, 1943.; Above, right: John B. (on right) becomes the face of Dead Reckoning in *Life* magazine's September 28, 1942 issue. (*Both photos courtesy* Life *magazine*)

Above, top: On top of a B-24 Liberator, 93rd/329th crews pose at Hardwick AFB—May 28, 1943. John B. is below engine #2. (*Courtesy AFHRA*)

Above, bottom: As part of the 93rd Bomb Group, John B.'s Liberator nicknamed *Exterminator* is the sixth B-24 Liberator to land on British soil on September 6, 1942. The tail designation "H" and serial number 123717 make identification easier in the air.

Right: Just east of Terria #7, John B. stands next to the Tobruk-to-Tripoli Road where months before Rommel's Afrika Korps had retreated. (July 1943)

Left: *Exterminator* and her crew at Hardwick AFB, England. (April 1943)

(L to R) Pilot Hugh Roper, Copilot Walt Stewart, Navigator John B. White, Jr., Bombardier Ted Brannon, Walt Zablocki, Henry Loyd, William DeFreese, Earle Lemoine, Frank Young. Bombs painted below the pilot's window note missions complete, swastikas note enemy fighters claimed. (*Courtesy NARA*)

B-24 Liberators pass plumes of fire and smoke, a result of the *Tidal Wave* mission of August 1, 1943. (Photographs *Courtesy National Archives*)

In the nose of his ship, the navigator's desk is just below and forward the two pilots' feet and shared with the bombardier and nose gunner. Equipment, ammunition, and guns limit movement for missions lasting eight to twelve hours.

Pictured with his back against the Plexiglas nose of the ship: Captain John B. White, Jr., Navigator of a heavy bomber—Consolidated's B-24 Liberator, U.S. Eighth Air Force, 93rd Bombardment Group, 329/330th Bomb Squadrons. (1943)

Polley White

Polley and her cat, Tom. (1927)

High school portrait. (1940)

Portrait of Polley taken in her sophomore year at the University of Illinois. (1942)

Bob carried this photograph of Polley with him while overseas.

On leave from the Air Force, Bill (Polley's twin brother and Bob's best friend) stands for a photo with Polley. (1943)

Robert "Bob" William Cress

Above, left: After winning the 1940 National Trombone Soloist title held in Battle Creek, Michigan, Bob is featured in the national ad campaign of the Conn Instrument Company. The headline touts *"Champions prefer Conns."* (1940)

Above, right: With aspirations of becoming a trombonist in a big band orchestra, Bob sits before famed photographer, Paul Stone of Chicago, who was known for taking *Glamour Shots* of celebrities, athletes, and politicians. Here, Stone captures Bob as a sophomore at the University of Illinois. (1942)

Left: Bob's portrait is taken as a cadet in College Detachment Training, an education and training program for pilots, navigators, and bombardiers, combining military training with civilian academics. (Cedar City, Utah, 1943)

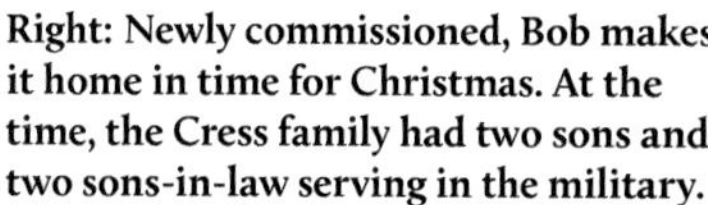

Right: Newly commissioned, Bob makes it home in time for Christmas. At the time, the Cress family had two sons and two sons-in-law serving in the military.

(L to R) Bob, Bill Durrett, Harry Beckemeyer, and a framed photograph on the radio of Bob's brother, Jim Cress. (1943)

Screamin' Demon and her crew at Harvard AFB, Nebraska.

Front row (L to R): Jack Crumbliss (P), Bill Martin (CoP), Bob Cress (N), Dick Parsons (B). Back row: Bardwell, Lou Tatum, Lynn Chinn, Harry Harris, Warren Townsend, Buzz Shuttleworth, and Moe Bayer. (February 1944)

In Tunisia, Bob (on right) explores remnants of former battles. (March 1944)

Above, left: A group of officers in front of the 825th Bomb Squadron Headquarters, Torretta AFB, Italy; Bob is second from left in front row. (April 1944)

Above, right: A resident of Munich before the war, Jagdgeschwader 53's Erich Gehring, pilot of a German Me109, claims victory of *Screamin' Demon* on May 31, 1944. (*Courtesy Jochen Prien*)

Left: With Romania's capitulation rumored, guards appear jovial, likely to curry favor with the Americans. On the steps of Lagarul #13 (formerly a boarding school for girls), POWs ponder a bridled freedom ahead of them. Bob is in 4th row, 3rd from right. (*Courtesy Swiss Red Cross / ICRC taken on or before August 23, 1944*)

Far left: Repatriated back to Italy and in a press release to families back home, Bob shows the German Luger he acquired during the chaos of escape. (September 7, 1944)

Left: Lt. Robert "Bob" W. Cress, U.S. Fifteenth Air Force, 484th Bombardment Group, 825th Bomb Squadron, Navigator of a heavy bomber Consolidated's B-24 Liberator. (1944)

Above: B-24 Liberator, *Screamin' Demon*, flies another combat mission. "42" identifies her revetment; the 484th's insignia, an hourglass turned sideways on her tail fin, symbolizes time running out for the Axis powers. These images together with the serial number make identification of a downed ship easier. (*Courtesy Joan Crumbliss*)

often eight hours long. *Metal boxes of ammunition lodged at each foot limited any legroom*. It was cramped. But he was so busy making calculations and calling out corrections to course that any worry of space or comfort was secondary.

The navigator made calculations by hand and head, a human computer of sorts, directing the course. There was no GPS.

Nearing the target, I would move to the flight deck to allow room for my bombardier to do his job. Stretched out on his belly and with his eye hovering the Norden bombsight, Bob's bombardier, Dick Parsons, would have looked down through the greenhouse window. The earth was in full view as it passed rapidly below him. Over the target, Jack would *hand the controls to the bombardier to fine-tune the ship's position.* With the objective framed in the crosshairs, he would have toggled the switch for bombs to drop and mission was complete upon return to base.

Training stateside was the best opportunity to see how things could go wrong quickly without the pressure of combat.

Today while flying I had an experience that was both amusing and yet of the most serious nature. Dick (my bombardier) and I share the same tight space in the nose. We had been flying at 25,000 feet for several hours with our oxygen masks on. All of a sudden Dick called me over the interphone to say he was getting sick. I laughed and told him sarcastically that I hoped he had fun throwing up in his oxygen mask. About 10 minutes later I felt a tugging at my leg. I looked under my desk and there, with his oxygen mask in his hand, was Dick. He had thrown up in his mask and all over the front of his flying suit . . . and all of that had frozen . . . At that altitude it didn't take long without oxygen to feel silly and get anoxic. Without oxygen for a few more minutes, Dick would have been in bad shape. *I grabbed his mask and knocked out what frozen chunks I could and slammed it back on his face and turned on the emergency oxygen.* Dick recovered pretty quickly. *All was okay until we came down from altitude and the stuff started thawing out.*

With each training exercise, Bob was increasingly impressed with his pilot. Lieutenant Crumbliss fit the role of an aircraft commander perfectly. *I'd rather have him than anyone else in our squadron.* Before the service, *Jack had been a merchant marine and lived a rough, but colorful life.* He had plenty of strength to handle the controls of the B-24 and more moxie than most could carry. With a genuine concern for his crew, there wasn't anything Jack wouldn't do to defend them. With a *clever sense of humor, Jack was good-looking and a darn husky boy. If I was ever to get in a brawl, I'd want Jack on my side.*

February 10, 1944

Dear Mother and Dad,

. . . I was showing pictures of home to my copilot . . . he got the impression that I came from a family [that was] pretty well-to-do. I took the defensive because I thought I had given him the impression I was conceited but he added you could pretty well tell by a fellow's bearing and the way he handled himself what kind of family he came from.

I guess I always had everything I wanted, and I appreciate everything that you have done for me. You have given me twice as many advantages as most families who have much more money. I hope that when my time comes, I can look back with as much satisfaction as I know you must have.

I am still looking at this period to earn some money to finish school and get a Harvard Law degree—I just hope this doesn't last too long that I lose sight of that. . . . I don't think I have ever set out to do anything yet [that] I haven't been able to do and I don't think that will be any exception.

As deployment neared, *my pilot and I are trying to pull some strings to schedule flights to each of the crews' hometowns so they can see their folks . . . and their families could meet the entire crew.* Bob felt showing the families who was handling the bomber might offer some comfort as their sons headed overseas. *We pitched the flights as training and navigational exercises.* It would take them from New York to Texas, South Dakota to Oklahoma, and places in between. While efforts continued to press for a green light for the operation, including a bribe of spirits, the trips remained doubtful.

February 12, 1944

Polley,

> *. . . I took my physical fitness exam today—about killed me. My stomach muscles feel like a tangled mass of barbed wire from doing sit-ups. Oh, how I grunted and strained to [eke] out those last few. Then we had to make a 300-yard run at top speed. My left lung collapsed in that event, but just like a B-24, I limped in on one motor.*

It was the first clear day in a week. Still blustery cold, the crew was called out to one of the B-24s. All had showed up but one. They were awaiting their navigator for the crew photograph. *I was tied up in another advisory when I got the message to join the crew. I didn't have my class A uniform on but was told to put on my trench coat and report to the flight line, pronto. I made it to the ship just in time for the picture to be taken.* When his copy of the photograph arrived, Bob identified the crew on the back. On the front, he personalized it to his grandfather, hoping *DadDad* would have been proud.

Briefings began hinting of overseas travel.

Bob spent the night of Valentine's Day on a photo-bombing mission of Navy Pier. *The flight to Chicago to camera-bomb a steel mill in*

Milwaukee and back was six-and-a-half hours. The conception of distance and time changes when flying. A trip home by plane is a short hop when I think that it takes a full day by train.

Flying over the target, Bob would have known he was not far from where Polley attended school. He studied the map on his desk, wondering, *How could we land in Chicago? Just for one night.*

During this period, each crewmember was graded on details performed on training missions. Bob's crew ranked as one of the top two in the group. As a result, his crew was presented with a brand-new B-24 Liberator. Getting one of the first two ships flown to the base was recognition of excellence in training.

Bob met his new B-24 Liberator on the flight line. A real beauty, she sat silent against a backdrop of cleared snow darkened from road dirt. Menacing, she hovered on wheels like a mad cat with wings and, painted an olive drab, avoided notice. She was a workhorse, a force to be reckoned with. Her tail, with its twin oval fins, was her signature. As part of the 484th, she would soon wear the bomb group's insignia, an hourglass signifying time running out for the Axis. With space constraints on the fin, the image was turned on its side topped by her serial number. Logging in long hours, the crew worked out snags inherent in a new ship and cared for her as if she was their first hot rod.

With plans set in motion, Bob's crew was on schedule. Within weeks, they would travel overseas. And a few weeks beyond that, they would be flying combat missions over enemy territory. *The real deal.*

FIFTEEN
Chicago*

Urbana, IL: Thursday, February 24, 4:00 p.m.—The telephone rings at her sorority house. She acknowledges the call and immediately calls Chicago. She leaves a note for her roommate, takes a cab to the Illinois Central Railroad station, and at 8:15 p.m. checks into Room 748 at the Stevens Hotel in downtown Chicago.

Harvard, NE: 8:47 p.m.—A lone B-24 Liberator with full crew takes off from Harvard Army Air Field on a combat training mission. The bomber is to fly to Chicago, carry out a practice bomb run on Navy Pier, and return to base. Navigation is celestial to and from the target.

* Years ago, Bob began writing his memoirs with anecdotes about growing up and his WWII service. Excerpts are scattered throughout the book, and in particular, *Chicago* (down to the asterisk break at *Diversions*) was entirely written by Bob.

Chicago: Friday, February 25, 12:19 a.m.—Midway Airport tower gets a request for an emergency landing. A B-24 bomber over the city has lost oil pressure in #1 and #2 engines. Clearance immediately granted. The bomber lands, is parked and secured at 12:43 a.m.

Chicago: 1:37 a.m.—The telephone rings in Room 748 of the Stevens Hotel. She answers on the third ring and hears a familiar voice. “Hi, I’m in 746, right on the other side of this wall.”

For this navigator, this was the only perfect mission of the war. It took a lot of quick planning, and we could have ended up in a lot of trouble.

We were about three weeks from the time we would get our orders to fly overseas to enter the real air war. We didn’t know whether we were going to Europe or Japan, but we were in the final phase of an intense combat training program to condition us for whatever and wherever. What we did know was that we would be flying combat missions within forty-five days.

Jack, my pilot, and I were in the Officers’ Club at the air base. We had been down for two days because of a blizzard that had stopped all flying. I had just talked to Polley, by phone, and Jack was on the phone talking to his wife, Louise, who was pregnant. He hung up the phone and came back to the table.

“How’s Polley?”

“She’s fine. Jack, how’s Louise doing?”

“Well, she figures she’s going to have this kid sometime the next few days, so she doesn’t feel too hot with me here and her in Chicago.”

“I know how you feel. It’s not the same situation, but I know I’d sure like to see Polley before we head out.”

During the past four weeks, I had been calling Polley regularly and writing her about four or five times a week. We had talked about meeting at some midway point like Kansas City. But in this type of training, I knew three-day passes were out. We talked about her coming out to Harvard or Hastings. But because of limited accommodations, I mentioned it would probably be better if her mother didn't come with her.

I had noticed a pattern on Friday nights. She was always out when I called. I didn't really like it, but I had encouraged her to date. I knew the Alpha Chi house was not exactly like living in a nunnery, so as noble as this may sound, it was the only way to handle these long separations. She had encouraged me with the same freedoms, particularly in places with a low female population like Harvard, Nebraska.

After another drink or two, Jack turned to me. "Call Polley and see if she can meet you in Chicago." We talked for a couple of minutes, and I saw Jack was dead serious. I got another stack of quarters for the pay phone and put in another call. Some pledge answered.

"Can I speak to Polley, please."

"Polley has already gone to bed, and I can't wake her. Rules, you know."

"I've never heard of that rule. This is Lieutenant Bob Cress calling from Harvard. If you don't get her, you're gonna be in a heap of trouble."

"Oh yes, Bob, I didn't know you were at Harvard. Do you like it there?"

"Look, I'd like to talk to you about Harvard but it's important that I speak with Polley, now."

Polley came on the phone, not very awake. It was 11:30 p.m. on Monday night, February 21, 1944.

"Can you meet me in Chicago?"

"When?"

"This Thursday night."

"How are you going to do that?"

"Jack and I will have it worked out tomorrow."

"Have you and Jack been drinking?"

"No, well, just a couple, this is for real."

"Where will I stay?"

"Jack's wife has an apartment on the north side. It's all set."

"I have to get a letter from Daddy to be away overnight."

"You'll have to work that out. Call him tomorrow and I'll call you back tomorrow night."

"Well, all right."

"Good luck with your daddy."

I wasn't confident that Polley could get her father's permission. He was not the type of person to give her a letter to stay with someone he didn't know (Jack's wife). I also had no idea how Jack was going to pull this off without the whole crew ending up in the brig. All I had to do was to get with the squadron navigator and get a celestial navigation mission approved to Chicago and return to base.

I was proud of Polley and the way she handled her end of it. The next morning, she made arrangements with her cousin to stay at her Chicago apartment. Polley then called her father, who not only sent his letter of permission but also included some extra money to take me out for a nice dinner. Her cousin then suggested that Polley and I could have more time together if we stayed at the Stevens Hotel. She knew the general manager and could get us two rooms on short notice. Polley had her part set up.

We had one thing going for us. During this period of training, every member of each crew was graded on every detail we performed on each combat training mission. We knew we had graded out as one of the top two of the 36 crews in our group. In a ceremony two days before, we were presented with the "keys" to our new B-24.

All crews would get new planes, but these first two were the reward for excellence in training. It was a big deal.

Jack was an extremely popular pilot and knew how to get things done. He didn't tell me about this until later, but this is the way he pulled the trip off. Jack went into Captain Gordon's office, our Squadron Commander, and explained the situation with Louise. He asked for permission to fly to Chicago and for an overnight pass. He was immediately turned down.

"Captain Gordon, I'm going to be with Louise on Thursday night. Either I'm going over the hill or I'll divert from a flight plan and end up in Chicago. I'm going one way or the other. My navigator has just cleared a celestial mission to Chicago. What if I had engine failure over Midway?"

"I can't approve that and you know it." Then the captain picked up the phone and called Colonel Keese's office. That's just what Jack wanted him to do.

Colonel Keese was our group commander. Jack had flown with him a number of times and Jack was probably his favorite pilot in the group. Col. Keese's favorite story involved us . . .

Jack and I were partying in the Hastings Hotel. About midnight, we decided we better head back to the base. Walking down the street, Jack had a whiskey bottle in his left hand and a drink in his right. He slipped on a patch of ice and the bottle went flying in the air. He fell on the glass, cutting the inside of his wrist pretty bad. I took him to the Hastings Hospital and while they were stitching him up, one of the staff called the base. In about fifteen minutes, Col. Keese called and wanted to talk to Jack.

"How bad is it, Jack?"

"Not too bad, Colonel. My navigator caught it in midair and saved almost a full bottle of whiskey."

That's the way the colonel liked to tell the story.

Back on the phone, Colonel Keese told Captain Gordon he would handle Jack. By that time, Jack was in the colonel's office.

Colonel Keese had told Jack previously about a time he dummied up a "loss of oil pressure" on a flight just for a chance to see his wife. Jack told me he approached the colonel in this way. "Sir, we both know that loss of oil pressure can just happen, and I know my engineer can fix it in about eight hours."

Colonel Keese responded, "You're full of it, Crumbliss. You have no intention of going AWOL. This is your ass if anything goes wrong. Now get out of here."

All was set except for the possibility of weather. I called Polley on Thursday. "I'll see you at the Stevens about 1:30 a.m. Don't miss your train."

An hour before we were to meet on the flight line, Jack called the crew together. He told them what was going on, emphasized security, and suggested they wear their class A uniforms under their flight suits. We had blended together as a good crew, and there was a shared excitement.

At 9:45 p.m., we were 10,000 feet over western Iowa.

"Pilot to navigator."

"Navigator to pilot: go ahead, Jack."

"Are you seeing your stars all right?"

"Roger, have just plotted my first fix. We are a little north of course and have a little tail wind. Will correct on my next fix."

"Roger. What's the name of that bright star dead ahead?"

"That bright one just above the horizon?"

"Roger, that one."

"That's Venus, named for the goddess of love, and she's hanging right over the Stevens Hotel, Michigan Avenue, USA."

"Engineer to pilot."

"Go ahead, Harry."

"Should I go down and check Lieutenant Cress's oil pressure?"

"That's a negative, Harry. We'll leave that up to Polley."

"Tail gunner to pilot."

"Go ahead, Chinn."

"Can I ask Lieutenant Cress a question?"

"Got time, navigator?"

"Will always make time to answer Sergeant Chinn's questions."

"Do we get to meet Polley?"

"Sure hope so, she's anxious to meet all you guys."

"Another question. Do we get to stay with you at the Stevens Hotel?"

"That's a negative. Better watch out for bogeys back there."

"Okay, let's knock it off. Navigator, what's our ETA over IP?"

"I have ETA over IP at 2352."

"Roger, 2352."

After making our bomb run on Navy Pier, we radioed Midway about our loss in oil pressure. An emergency landing was granted. But Midway's longest runway was short for a heavy bomber. We had to come over an eight-story building, drop down, and hit the end of the runway. We were the first B-24 to land there. We parked the craft and assigned guard schedule to the crew. I was to call Jack at 8:00 a.m. to confirm takeoff no later than 2:00 p.m. Weather was coming in and, at best, we only had a few hours. I took off for the terminal and grabbed a cab to the Stevens Hotel.

I checked in at the Stevens about 1:30 a.m. Friday morning, went to my room, and called Polley's room next door. The rooms were connecting.

It is hard for me to describe emotions. We both knew this was our last time to be together for a long time. Until I called Jack in the morning, we didn't know whether we had twelve hours or a shorter time. Polley and I were each well aware that I would be on my way overseas and would be flying combat missions shortly thereafter. Those uncertainties hung over us.

During this entire 36-hour period, neither of us spoke of these things. It was expressed in the way we held each other—the kisses, the hand-holding, the repeated declarations of our love for each other. At about 3:30 a.m. we went downstairs and walked up Michigan Avenue. I was hungry but also anxious to see what the weather was doing. It was beginning to get very foggy, and I hoped it wasn't just because of the nearness to Lake Michigan. I felt certain a front was coming in, and if it did, it would allow more time together. By the time we finished our walk, I knew we were okay on the weather. It was turning bad and getting worse. I was getting all charged up to do the town at 4:30 in the morning.

Scanning the morning *Chicago Tribune*, we saw that Jimmy Dorsey's band was at the College Inn in the Hotel Sherman; Del Courtney's band at the Blackhawk; and Hildegarde was the feature at the Empire Room. These names and places were the famous nightclubs and ballrooms of Chicago that broadcast on the radio nightly. It was an era of the big dance bands. All through high school and college, we had listened to the radio broadcast: ". . . live from the beautiful Empire Room in the Palmer House in downtown Chicago, we present . . ." It was a part of our lives. Now, if the weather front added hours to our visit, we could step into places that before we had only heard of.

We went back to our rooms to try to get a couple hours' sleep but being so wound up, we couldn't sleep. At 8:00 a.m., I called Jack. He had been busy.

"Are you a daddy yet?"

"No, we're still just sitting here drinking coffee."

"The ceiling here is low. How does it look your way?"

Jack replied, "I called the airport. We probably won't get out today."

"That's great! Have you talked to anyone back at Harvard?"

"Only Gordon. He's a little nervous about this whole thing. I told him I'd bring him a bottle of whiskey. You and Polley getting along?"

"Polley wants to know if we'll be here long enough to get married."

"Louise says there's a quickie place over at Crown Point, Indiana, but it may not be quick enough."

Polley leaned into the phone. "I didn't say that, Jack!"

I got back on the phone. "Okay, I'm in room 746. Later, I'll check the desk for any messages and get back with you at noon."

"Bob, I don't plan to take off till tomorrow afternoon. Gordon is raising hell, but I'll handle him. You and Polley relax and have a good time."

"Thanks, Jack. You take care of Louise."

"Roger that."

The most memorable evening of our lives was spent in the Empire Room that night. About 8:30, we took a cab to the Palmer House. Chicago was a Navy town, and this was a Friday night. There was a long line of sailors and their dates waiting to get in. Polley and I went up to the doorman to see how long the wait would be.

He asked, "Just you and the lady, lieutenant?" I nodded and he said, "Come this way."

He led us to the maître d' who then took us all the way to a table, front and center, right in line with the entertainers' view. It was the best seat in the house. How or why this happened, I will never know.

Waiting for the show to begin, I moved my chair toward Polley's so we were sitting shoulder to shoulder and holding hands on the table. When the champagne was served, we toasted each other but barely touched it beyond that. We had been doing pretty good in keeping our emotions under control.

Hildegarde was a top talent, a torch singer and comedienne with an act playing the piano. Between numbers, she would tell jokes keyed at the Navy guys and their dates. We were the only non-Navy in the audience, so she'd tell a joke, and then look at us and ask, "How'd you like that one, Air Corps?"

Like any good entertainer, Hildegarde could read her audience. She had captured us, and she knew it. She sang lyrics seducing every word and phrase for expression and meaning. And the way she used her head movements and eyes to make everyone feel she was singing directly to them was unbelievable.

Her next to last number was a slow blues ballad, one I had never heard before, "Temptation." I still remember the last four lines . . .

My throat had a big lump in it. As Hildegarde caressed each word, her eyes never left us. All the loveliness, charm, expression, and sensuality that this superb entertainer used to possess every person in this large ballroom was focused on the two of us. But she wasn't finished yet . . .

At the piano, she played a soft interlude as she introduced her last number. "And now I dedicate this beautiful new love song to each of you who are thinking of your lover . . . and especially for the Air Corps lieutenant and his lovely lady." And she began . . .

I'll be seeing you in all the old familiar places
That this heart of mine embraces all day through . . .

Singling out people in the audience was all a part of her act but this did not diminish the effect. We both whispered a "thank you" and she kept her eyes on us for another few moments, nodding her head with an expression on her face of "I understand." Standing up from her piano, she tossed kisses to the applauding audience; then she looked down at us and threw a tender kiss our way before walking off the stage.

We were both numb. I looked into Polley's eyes and whispered, "Wow!"

We had planned to see Jimmy Dorsey at the College Inn, but the mood had changed. We walked back toward the Stevens Hotel, hand in hand, saying nothing and thinking our own thoughts. About a block in, I took Polley in my arms and said, "Sweetheart, this isn't like us. We have a lot of time left." So we went to the Oak Room in the Stevens, where we cuddled, smooched, laughed, and listened to the rhythm and blues combo. I finally said, "Polley, we've got to try to get some sleep," so we went up to our rooms.

Jack called me at eight on Saturday morning and told me takeoff would be at 2:00 p.m.

In the cab to Midway, Polley asked, "You'll write every day?"

"You know I will."

"So I'll know you're all right?"

"Don't worry, I'll be okay. I love you, Polley."

The crew was already preflighting the plane. With the activity, a crowd had gathered behind a fence outside the terminal to watch us take off.

Jack knew how to play the crowd as he spoke to his crew. "I want y'all to line up on the other side of the plane facing the terminal. Come to attention and then parade rest. Bob and I are going to walk over and get Polley and Louise. If we do this right, all those folks over there will go back home and buy war bonds."

As we approached the crowd, we could hear the murmurs. *He's the pilot, and he's the copilot, no, those are navigator wings . . .* Then the crowd became almost reverent as a very pregnant Louise took Jack's arm, Polley took mine, and the four of us walked from the terminal fence across the runway to the crew. Polley spoke with the members of the crew, giving each one a send-off hug. As the crew boarded the plane, Jack and I walked the girls over to a position in front of the nearby hangar. From there, they could see the full takeoff.

With all the crew on board, Jack fired up each engine before he taxied to the head of the airstrip. At the end of the runway, he applied full brakes and full throttle like he was taking off from a carrier. We were at about 75 feet as we passed where Polley was waving. And within seconds, we topped the building at the end of the runway before climbing into the low overcast.

The ground disappeared and *Chicago* was but a memory playing in my head . . .

I'll be seeing you
In every lovely summer's day
In everything that's light and gay,
I'll always think of you that way.
I'll find you in the morning sun,
And when the night is new,
I'll be looking at the moon
But I'll be seeing you . . .

DIVERSIONS

Back at Harvard, Bob and his pilot would have spent hours creating flight plans that would maximize experience. Eight-hour missions tracking multiple destinations became the norm. Not only would travel fine-tune tasks as second nature, but also the ship continued to work through glitches inherent to a new plane. These wide-ranging auditions would bolster a successful curtain call.

As the days grew closer to his wife's delivery date, Jack's anxiety level increased. *I got such a kick out of him last night when he was sweating out the phone call when he heard Louise went to the hospital. Truthfully, I was sweating it out too and every time someone would congratulate him, I'd say "Hell, congratulate me too. I was sweating it out with him."*

The next day, Jack got the call. Louise had given birth to a leap-year baby girl. She was at a hospital in Evanston, just north of Chicago. That night, Bob would plot another flight to the Windy City.

The next morning, their ship headed east. Hours into the flight they approached Midway. As they made a pass over the runway, *I saw the exact spot where we kissed each other good-bye. I got real sentimental, Polley.* Surely pulling himself out of a daydream, he would have reached for his throat mike to give Jack his next heading. By the time Bob crawled through the nose tunnel, the ship was nearing its turn north at Lake Michigan.

Up on deck, Bob pointed out landmarks to his crew: first, a domed structure, Adler Planetarium, the place his father first showed him the stars through a telescope; Grant Park, where Bob had seen a German Zeppelin flying over the Chicago World's Fair in 1933; and Northwestern University, where his brother had been commissioned in the Navy just months before.

But memories of his family adventures would soon be redirected. *I located the hospital in Evanston, and we circled it several times, surely giving the staff and patients quite a show. Then I gave Jack a heading south.*

One of the most treasured experiences for an airman was to buzz his hometown. Bob had been dreaming about it since he first entered basic training. *Everyone wanted to do it, but the Air Force frowned on such use of its aircraft.* And it was not easily done. Any crew that tried such a stunt would return to a guaranteed stiff reprimand. Or worse.

But pilot and navigator would push limits. Given an unexpected hospital run, Bob's home was just a hop away. Besides, to avoid getting the crew in trouble, he would spin the trip as a *diversion or circuitous route [to evade] enemy territory.* Well within a triangulated heading of Chicago, St. Louis, and back to base, *it was only a small detour.*

Approaching Montgomery County, Lake Hillsboro came into sight. Only the vibration of four engines could have muffled the adrenaline likely pulsing through Bob's body. Home would soon be within view. According to a *Montgomery County News* article, ". . . it became a common joke for the crew to ask when passing over hills, 'Lieutenant Cress, would this be Cress Hill?' However, it was no joke to him. Bob knew that the hill upon which stood his home would look pretty small to his crew, but it stood out in his mind as the biggest thing in his life."

Approaching the farm, Jack let down to treetop level. As they sailed through, the Liberator barely missed the silo as they banked around. Increasing the throttle, the ship gained speed and sound. Spooking the herd, cows scattered like buckshot. The crew lost composure. The Hillsboro newspaper noted, "The huge Liberator bomber flew over Lieutenant [Cress's] home west of Hillsboro four times and his mother felt sure he was saluting her as a birthday gift . . ."

Bob shared his conversation of what his parents saw from below. The family had gathered around the oak dining table to celebrate Essie's fifty-second birthday. The occasion was tempered by the palpable absence of her two sons, one serving in the Navy and the other in the Air Force. Across the table sat her nephew, who was on a brief leave before deployment with the US Marine Corps. He was Bob's age. Pushing back on her chair, it brushed across the hardwood planks, making a light, droning sound. When she got up, the sound continued. She surely mused, *Who the heck is running the hay baler?* But somehow it was different. For a moment, all conversation ceased at the table as ears stretched toward the window to identify the low rumble. As the sound intensified, everyone jumped from the table and ran outside. Hearing a thunderous roar overhead, Essie would look up. There it was. A huge warbird was making a wide circle. It had just passed the house when she reached the yard. Barely clearing the silo, it banked right to the milking barn. No doubt she hoped it would come back.

Mesmerized at the huge machine in flight, Bob's family, on the ground, followed the airship as it circled. Visible through tree branches still barren from winter's cold, they would track the ship as it became larger. Thunder amplified as the B-24 flew overhead. *All the people on the farm were out in our front yard waving dishrags, caps, and their arms.* As the Liberator was lost to the horizon, Bob's father was surely bursting with pride while Essie's son had delivered her best birthday gift of all.

Joy at the sight of his parents waving would imprint a lasting snapshot in Bob's mind. What a thrill he must be giving them—but no thrill bigger than the one Bob got sharing the *Hill* with his crew. *That was the most wonderful thing that could have ever happened to me and of course my crew got to see where I lived.*

Bob would have looked at his watch as it was time to head to St. Louis before a final trek back to base. But Jack would have one last gift to deliver as he turned the ship toward town. Flat-hatting, an unauthorized low-level maneuver, was frowned upon and would result in a stiff penalty. If caught. Challenging maximum speed, Jack pushed forward. The B-24 roared down Hillsboro's Main Street on its thunder ride as full-pitched prop wash swept a whirlwind below.

Townspeople scattered. Others looked on in awe. *Undoubtedly it was the fastest anyone had ever driven down Main Street, going over 200 mph, and it wouldn't surprise me if we broke some windows . . . Seeing the people look up and scatter, you would have thought it was an air raid.* Running out of roadway, Jack would quickly bank left, barely clearing the mansard tower of the county courthouse. No doubt Bob was overcome with laughter at his hometown's expense.

With the farm just west of town, they made a final pass over his home. Wings were dipped as if to say farewell, and Bob's laughter surely softened then.

But as fast as they had come, they would fly away.

At his nav desk facing the back of the bomber, Bob would have followed the web of tubing, wires, and equipment that rose to the flight deck. There, Jack would handle the ship with care, even if he pushed her limits. She had given Bob a lifetime's adventure in a few days—*we are certainly proud of our ship—a real honey of a plane.* Was he doting on a flying machine? His affection was surely growing.

Looking forward through the Plexiglas nose of the Liberator, Bob would have followed her path westward as she chased the sunset back to base.

After returning to Harvard, they would begin final preparations for the overseas trip. Only essentials would be allowed. *Fifty-five pounds was the limit in overseas packing. It takes quite a lot of thought to try to figure out what things you will need. If we had any idea where we were going, the task would be much easier.*

Before leaving the base, there was a party at the Officers' Club. *I got such a yearning to play the trombone that I went right up and took over the trombone position for about a half hour. The second number that we played was* "Temptation" *with a trombone solo all the way through. I surprised the hell right out of me and played it beautifully. I really "wowed" the other boys in the band and got a good hand from the floor. It was one of the few pieces that the dancers applauded. Oh, it made me feel so good and it was so much fun to play a horn again.*

A few nights later, Bob would have pulled out his Parker 51 pen to write his parents. Black and silver, she scribed with India ink. And as the advertisement touted—*Like a Pen from another Planet!*—it was designed by a company owner's passion for aerodynamics. Only fitting, Bob would circle the globe with it parked in his shirt pocket.

The pen and pencil had been a birthday gift. *I am still wondering how Mother was able to get hold of such a treasure in rationed times.* As he often said, somehow his parents always seemed to come through.

March 7, 1944

Dear Mother and Dad,

. . . It will not be long until I am many miles away from you than I have ever been. I want you to know that even though the distance will be much greater, you will be just as close to my heart as you have always been. I will be doing a job that may be unpleasant at times, but I know if I do my job to the best of my ability it will make it possible to be together again maybe sooner.

So many people have the idea that home is made up of tangible things. But to me, home is made up of intangible inspirations bestowed in family by the parents. You have done everything for me that could ever be expected of a mother and dad.

It takes a lot of guts to accomplish what you have done with our family especially when something like this mess disrupts what you have worked so hard to do. I appreciate all the things that you have done for me and have tried to do the best with the opportunities you have given me. Maybe I have in your minds, or maybe I haven't. But I will keep trying to do my best and do what I believe is right.

I have confidence that I can do anything I set out to do. I don't know where I ever got that confidence unless it was from you. I have always believed if a person sets a goal and wants to accomplish it enough, no matter what the odds, if he is willing to work hard, he can do it. My next goal is to get back home and I have just as much confidence in that as anything I have ever done.

I really do want you to know that I think I have the swellest parents in the world, and I will always try to do the things that will make them proud I am their son. I guess that is the least and most I can do . . .

In the days that followed, reality struck. *I was given a short haircut, and we became restricted to post. Physical exams* followed. The base buzzed, a bustle of activity. But still, there was no hint of where their final destination would be.

Crews traveled to a staging area before leaving for a port of embarkation. *From there, the compass needle spins and whatever direction we head will be an answer to a lot of questions in our minds.* The day was fast approaching.

With the word out, Lincoln would be the first stop before going beyond.

Early the next morning, it was moving-on day. *I heard a bird singing this morning and although I don't know exactly where it found a tree around here to sit in and sing, nevertheless I heard it.* Following the sound to the skies, he would have internalized ceiling and visibility unlimited or CAVU, an aviation phrase used on a clear day. *It really is a beautiful day . . . Perhaps springtime has finally come to Nebraska, at last.*

Although reservations of leaving home might have crossed his mind, he was excited as he coursed the next step.

SIXTEEN
Transatlantic Passage

WITH TRAINING COMPLETE, the crew left Harvard on their biggest adventure yet. First stop was Nebraska's capital city. From Lincoln, they flew to Morrison Field, a 1,400-mile flight and another overnight stay. Although the destination remained a secret, a West Palm Beach departure hinted Europe.

With new equipment and modifications made to the Liberators, they were restricted to base and sworn to secrecy at the final briefing. Each airman was issued a bail-out kit, a sealed packet of emergency rations in the event of an ocean ditch.

TWENTY-TWO MARCH 1944. For the last time on American soil, Bob's overloaded B-24 Liberator lifted off to begin her global journey. Given a route to Trinidad and a sealed envelope, *we were under strict orders not to open it until we were two hours out and over open water.* After setting the course to Waller Field, Bob would return to the flight deck to inquire about their destination. *Since I was the one guiding us there, Jack handed the orders to me.*

As Bob lifted the sealed flap, he pulled out a packet of documents. Across the top in bold script was written TOP SECRET—ITALY.

He lost no time reading through the list of layovers. The order took them to North Africa by way of friendly air bases along the South American coast before crossing the Atlantic. *Dakar, French Morocco, Djedeida—most of the crew had never heard of the places.* Bob would study the African coordinates before calling out the next heading.

The trip from West Palm Beach to Trinidad was just under 1,800 miles. Along the route, tiny islets and sea stacks protruded out of the ocean, offering a first such sight for a farm boy from Illinois. *We went past the edge of Puerto Rico, where San Juan came [into] sight, then I set the course straight south across the Caribbean. Eleven hours later, we circled the Port of Spain before landing in Trinidad where we spent the night.* It would be Bob's first overnight stay on foreign soil.

With an early wake-up, they were back in the air. *From Trinidad, I set the course from a latitude of eleven-degrees north to one-degree south*. Reaching the continent, he got his first look at South America. Flying at 9,000 feet, the altitude was low enough to appreciate the lush green canopy hovering over the landscape below. The vastness of the tropical rainforest extended inland as far as the eye could see. *I confirmed I had my escape kit while trying not to imagine a crash landing or a forced bailout. With the dense tropical forest below, it might be days before a downed ship was found even if a rescue was attempted.*

I was a good student of geography and being the navigator, I would point out to the crew the significance of places. I had quite a bit to say about the Amazon. As we crossed the equator and about a hundred miles later, we landed at our next destination. Belém greeted bomber crews every ten minutes . . . In town, there was no lack of budding entrepreneurs. Brazilians marketed trinkets, reptiles, and more. The locals quickly became aware of the seeming affluence of young America.

Showered in mosquito netting, Bob slept on a cot. The upcoming journey didn't escape his thoughts. The next leg, a few degrees south, was no problem. But beyond that, he would have to course the route over the long and dark Atlantic Ocean.

At Fortaleza, Brazil, their last South American stop, the final briefing to Dakar, French West Africa, was given. With a map spread out, Bob would have drawn his finger across the equatorial Atlantic to the bulge of the African continent and the *dot* upon which he had to land. After two thousand miles and twelve hours without the aid of ground navigation, hitting the mark would be no easy task.

It was a time before satellite-driven positioning or GPS. The journey was solely coursed from calculations charted by Bob.

His training would be tested to the limit. For the first time, as navigator, Bob would be over a wide expanse of black ocean *using a sextant to locate the stars, triangulate a point, and continuously plot adjusting our position as we advanced toward the destination.* To complicate matters, *the stars south of the equator were completely different from those in the northern hemisphere.* Along the route, he would become the star finder, trying to figure out which stars were which. Setting headings, adjusting for winds and speed, confirming fuel reserves, conveying a position at random times to the pilot, and calculating an ETA all compounded his task.

Bob made the final calibrations to his navigational equipment. *Because we were heavily loaded, we had just enough fuel to get across—a little reserve but not much on this particular trip. We had to travel at the most efficient speed. Ground speed had to be maintained at 160 to 165. And because we weren't carrying the extra oxygen tanks due to the added weight, altitude had to be kept under 10,000 or 7 to 9,000 feet.*

Mail sacks had been a last-minute add-on, letters from home to troops fighting on the front lines. I know what they meant for morale. Bob would make his calculations work even with the excess weight.

With the ship ready, Dakar was by far their longest flight ever.

TWENTY-SIX MARCH 1944. Facing the fading glow of sunset,

their B-24 postured for an overnight journey. *It was a 2,100-mile trip, by far the longest trip we had ever taken.* Jack revved the engines to max takeoff rpm before releasing the brakes. Barreling down the runway, the Lib struggled with her heavy load. As the ship gained momentum, Bob called out the airspeed. Jack tightened his grip on the shuddering column as he wished for "another quarter mile" of runway. Struggling with the weight of the overloaded bomber, Jack urged, "C'mon, baby, lift. Lift."

Nearly out of pavement, the Lib's wheels pushed from the ground. Straining to gain altitude, it became airborne. As the bomber rotated upward along the "mountainside," climbing on a *turn-and-bank*, she left just enough elevation to clear the peaks' crest. *It was not unlike our takeoff at Midway, ascending abruptly above an eight-story building.*

Flight engineer Harry Harris also stood behind the flight deck on takeoff, continuously checking the directional gyro, artificial horizon, altimeter, and other gauges on the instrument panel. Harry was responsible for the aircraft's mechanical, hydraulic, electrical, and fuel systems. Drafted at nineteen, Harry was a lanky fellow, tallest on the crew. On his first military physical, they cut an inch from his height to qualify for flight duty. From Wichita Falls, he left behind a girlfriend, Ruth, whom he wrote daily. With a distinct Texas twang, he put a spin on many a story, often revealing an underlying inspiration. He never met a stranger and aspired to become a preacher someday, likely after marrying Ruth. While each crewmember championed his part, Harry was the crew's wiz engineer. His battle station was the top turret and with a full view of the world, he was first to see incoming fighters. With his face inches from the firing chambers, he shot his twin *fifties* with precision.

To get the B-24 off the ground at takeoff, "the superchargers had to be turned up above the red line. The extra surge from the exhaust blew a manifold stack, a four-inch split near the top of an outboard engine." In his memoirs, Harry recalled that after a few minutes of intense scrutiny, they decided not to turn back for repairs. "When the cylinder head temperature rose to the high side of the safety limit, we used extra air to cool it down by cracking the cowl flaps." Any extra drag was minimal, and the issue was not considered their biggest concern. Pilot and engineer were aware of the concerns that a blown stack could cause a fire. But as Harris would later say, it "seemed so minor considering the storm systems and malfunctions in the generator and fuel transfer pump encountered" on the long haul.

As they entered the darkness over the Atlantic, they left behind city lights used for orientation. Cumulus clouds were building. *We had to go through a stationary equatorial front with clouds reaching up to 50,000 feet. They weren't particularly turbulent, but they would knock you around a bit.* Heading east, weather closed in. The rain and wind strengthened.

Sitting at my nav desk I could see flashes of light outside my window pulsing all around the four-engine bomber as she bucked in the gusting wind. "Winds clocked hurricane-force speeds," noted Harris. Updrafts lifted the ship before downdrafts dropped her a thousand feet. Bobbling through the front, tensions of the rough ride were rising. In a hollow of blackness below and at the whim of wind shear, there was no recourse. Any land was hundreds of miles away. They would push forward.

As Bob waited for a break in the clouds to calculate the next heading, his eyes widened. Out the window was a halo of fire, a blue and white billowing blaze consuming the leading edge of the wings, wickedly licking her propellers. At the same time, an urgent call came through the interphone. *"Gunner to pilot: fire along the leading edge of the wing!"* Others would look at the sight. Flames were swallowing the ship. Hearts surely paused as worry consumed those on board.

Bob recognized the fiery spectacle but had never witnessed it firsthand. *Is this what it looks like?* He wasn't sure. *Or is the fire some other explanation, a serious problem?* But confident in what he saw, Bob pressed his throat mike: *"Navigator to Crew: Hold tight, guys. It's called St. Elmo's Fire. We'll be okay once we clear this front."* Electrical currents charged by an unsteady atmosphere created the appearance of flames against the metal of the aircraft. A rare weather phenomenon but still, it was an intimidating sight.

In celestial navigation, we shoot three different stars and plot on your chart to show where you are. With overcast skies, Bob couldn't get a lock on enough stars to calculate their position. It was only through the few breaks in the clouds that he could determine their location. His celestial charting exceeded the entire surface of his navigation desk. *Finally, we got through the equatorial front, and I got one really good fix where our plane was in relation to our preflight training—we were a little north of course and our ground speed was pretty close. I knew we were going to have to make a correction sooner or later to the right of three degrees.* As the ship advanced, the storm settled. Calm returned. Stars began twinkling in the clearing sky.

Working my tail off standing at my desk, I was dealing with strange stars while continually tracking the ship's heading and calling out corrections to Jack. Navigating over a black ocean brimming with death-dealing consequences *was the greatest responsibility I had ever been handed. I knew full well the lives of my crew depended upon the accuracy of my course-plotting skills.* While the storm was behind them, they still had a vast ocean to fly over before sighting land.

All the crew had been sleeping except Bob and Jack. Bored with straight flying, Jack flipped through channels, playing with the radio dials. *After long hours with little else to do, that's just what pilots did.* As he turned the dial, *Jack picked up what he thought was Dakar's signal. [He] got on the interphone and said, "We're south of course and need to go seven degrees north." And I said, "No, Jack. We're north of course. We'll make a correction pretty soon to four degrees south." Jack then asked, "Are you sure about that?" And I said, "Remember? We were briefed that there is a German sub that sits out there putting out the same signal as Dakar—they're trying to get you off course so you go past Africa and run out of gas."*

The route taken by the American *heavies* was well known to German trackers. With a bogus signal, the Axis hoped to lure bomber crews north past the African bulge. The aircraft would follow the signal out to sea, run out of gas, and plummet into the ocean.

Jack agreed to follow Bob's course.

Four hundred miles out, *I told Jack to adjust to four degrees south and I said, "We will reach Dakar at oh-seven-ten."*

TWENTY-SEVEN MARCH 1944. At dawn and still over open water, *I made some adjustments and with celestial navigation I did what's called shooting sun lines*, which determined their ground speed. He then headed upstairs to the flight deck. Bob wasn't going to miss this landing.

After nearly thirteen hours of flight over a dark Atlantic Ocean, the ship descended through broken clouds into the landing pattern of the airstrip. Bob had hit a *dot* on the map. *We got there one minute early, and we were a half mile south of the field, which put us right in the traffic pattern of the airstrip.*

Relief washed through Bob's body as the wheels touched down in a flurry of pink dust that plumed from under the bomber. Hailing a fist pump, he reveled in mission complete, overwhelmed at having hit his mark. Dakar, French West Africa. Bob's biggest concern had always been the lives of his crew, which were dependent upon his navigational skills for safe passage. *From that time on, the crew knew "they had a real navigator."* Sharing the story, Bob choked with emotion—he had gained the respect of his crew, which meant the world to him.

Arrival in Dakar marked their landing on Africa's most westerly point, the Cape Verde Peninsula. The southern route was one of two corridors bringing American aircraft to the European conflict. In a week, Bob's crew had journeyed through three continents with one more to go.

The culture of French West Africa was unlike anything Bob had ever experienced. A garrison of Senegalese guards provided security for the ship. Pilot and navigator stood at the nose of the ship as a duo clad in sullied khakis ambled over. They each carried a long rifle, a relic from the last war, topped by a foot-long bayonet. It looked sharp. Bob said, *At six-foot-six, these guys had at least four inches on me. And with a height that towered, their appearance was intimidating. You didn't fool around with these guys.* They spoke little English. And Bob spoke no Senegalese. His attempt at sign language was returned with somber stares. Regardless of the language barrier, they worked out a password to access the area. These trusted sentries would not allow any unauthorized entry.

Following the next day's sunrise, the ship headed north 1,300 miles across the desert. The direct path would have taken them over a neutral country controlled by the Vichy French. *The only way to circumvent the area was to fly northeasterly inland to a point in the desert that was not marked. Changing sands offered no landmarks, therefore no pilotage. Dead reckoning was difficult as was reading a drift. Coursing was tricky navigation.*

All signs of civilization soon disappeared but for an occasional caravan trail. Only sinuous contours of sand lay below them. Ships losing course were known to crash in the desert, not unlike John B.'s former copilot. It would take days or weeks to locate the downed plane to drop water and supplies. Stories of rescue were meager.

Bob coursed a fine line between finding the mark or being forever mislaid. *We had to use celestial sun lines all the time to enable us to know the point in the sand.* A couple hours into the flight he spotted the first checkpoint. Atar, Mauritania. A remote outpost, it was a dot on the map in the middle of nowhere. Hours later they passed a second checkpoint. Tindouf, Algeria. A century before, it had been a Foreign Legion camp but was now lost to the desert sand. Both settlements were emergency landing locations. But more topography lay before their next destination.

From a distance, the Atlas Mountains rose from the desert floor. The elevation precluded the bomber, carrying excess cargo, from flying over. *It started to rain.* Bob was headed for a treacherous mountain pass known for fickle winds swirling through its corridor. *Because our plane was sluggish in gaining altitude, I did a good job of finding a pass, which we cleared, but not by much. After a left bank, we were on final approach into Marrakech.*

Given better base facilities and weather conditions, the Air Force moved operations from Casablanca to Marrakech. It was the crew's second African landing in as many days. The officers were quartered in a modern cottage, formerly occupied by the French military elite. *The buildings looked like they were right out of the movie* Casablanca. *Architecture of the homes was so different to us.* The enlisted men, on rotation, would sleep on the plane to keep strangers from tampering with the equipment.

Bob had crossed the equator twice in one week before the four engines roared again for takeoff on the last leg of their African journey. *After over 1,300 miles,* he rested his sextant before calling out the final heading into Djedeida.

John B. had arrived in July 1943. And now Bob was landing. It was April 1, 1944.

Remnants of a wicked battle dotted the ground. Like much of North Africa, Tunisia was a desolate tract of undulating dunes. The desert below revealed the ending to a supreme match between opposing generals, America's Patton versus Germany's Rommel. The Reich's *Desert Fox* (a.k.a. Rommel) succeeded in slowing the Allies in the beginning. But charred remains of German panzers declared the score. And American bombers were landing.

Still awaiting construction of the base in Italy to be readied with a runway, renovations to the outbuildings, and the arrival of ground crews by troop ship, Bob's crew settled in Djedeida, a town about ten miles west of Tunis.

Tunisia was Bob's first real introduction to war. *Right around this section was one of the most famous battlegrounds of the African campaign. There are still quite a few shell holes around.* He, with Jack's help, *confiscated a jeep.* Despite official "warnings of booby traps left by the Germans," the two drove through the *scrubby countryside exploring abandoned equipment and military vehicles, mostly German tanks and trucks.*

While the campaign ended the year before, the clash had begun years earlier. Hitler dispatched General Rommel. Field Marshal Montgomery led British forces. Both sides realized gains. But when American troops landed in November 1942, General Patton joined the Allied offensive. Fierce fighting continued until May 1943 when the Axis "was pushed into the sea at Cape Bon."

The post was an open compound. Neither fences nor sentries kept nonmilitary personnel from accessing the base. The men lived in a canvas bivouac staked along the airfield. With no guards, the quarters were easy game as locals came down from the hills to pillage in darkness.

We didn't have any guards, and the Arabs would come down from the hills at night. You might be sitting there, and a knife rips the back of your tent and a hand reaches in just trying to grab anything it can. We didn't take kindly to this type of behavior. During the daytime, the same nocturnal thieves tended sheep up on the hill about a half mile away. We'd sit with our .38 revolvers and lob a shot up there to see how close we could come. We'd see the sand come up but never hit anyone.

Mission training tightened. By day, crews flew formation over antiquities and hilly terrain. Upon return, officers attended briefings. Aircraft strategies, enemy sightings, and bail-out procedures were some of the topics covered. Work picked up. The inevitable was nearing.

Parked on a desert airfield, the B-24's onboard radio reached stations all over the world, including broadcasts from home on shortwave. There were nights where Bob sat right seat in their Lib as Jack skipped through transmissions muffled with static and rolling through shrills echoing hollow space. Turning the knob, he heard a woman. *With a sultry voice, Axis Sally welcomed the boys of the US Army Air Force. She would say, "Heard you boys of the 484th just landed from South America. We'll be watching to see where you land on your next journey." Adding more details, she would load another song. At that point, we all wondered how the hell she knew so much. But more unsettling was the fact that we knew they were tracking us.*

Often mistaken for Berlin's Axis Sally (Mildred Gillars), whom John B. would have heard in England, Rome's Axis Sally was Rita Zucca, an American-born radio announcer. She was hired to play American music and broadcast Axis propaganda to Allied troops in Italy and North Africa. While stoking fears of cheating sweethearts back home, she used intelligence from the German embassy in Rome to spread messages that the Axis powers knew their locations.

We got into the city of Tunis a couple of times; it was a teeming mass of humanity. While the Kasbah was off limits to military after dark, Dick and I found a bar where aircrews hung out. After last call, we left. It was dark but we felt secure with our revolvers on us . . . Walking, we noticed three locals behind us. When we stopped, they'd stop. Then again, we stopped, and they'd stop. This was scary as the devil. Finally, when they got too close, we took out our sidearms and turned around and shot at them . . . they scattered. No one was hit and we got back to our tent without incident.

Time in Africa was coming to a close. The base in Italy was ready.

FOURTEEN APRIL 1944. Slated for takeoff, the Crumbliss crew coursed a heading north 500 miles. The destination was the Foggia complex of American air bases in Italy.

The Germans were counting how many planes we had. To keep them from knowing where we were going, we flew a circuitous route, around the southside of Sicily [and] looping below the boot and on up the backside of the Italian ankle. Bypassing Air Force headquarters at Bari, we reached our final destination. Torretta Airfield.

And just as Axis Sally broadcast, with not a detail missed. German tracking was watching.

SEVENTEEN
Tempus Fugit

HUNG ON THE SIGNBOARD WITH TACKS was a four-page Operations Order that detailed who was flying the following day. Prepared by the commander, this order signified the 484th Bomb Group's very first combat mission. On the second page, Bob would have stopped. "Crumbliss crew. Position: Charlie 13."

It was dark by the time Bob and Jack headed to their tent. Training had prepared them for as much as was possible. Stretched out on his cot, no doubt Bob's mind moved beyond tomorrow's mission and focused on the countdown to quota—the reward of a trip home.

Two weeks before, their Liberator had landed at Torretta Airfield in southern Italy. As Bob exited the ship, he would have taken in the surrounding fields as jeeps packed with men crisscrossed his path. Bustling yet serene, acres of wide-open space created a cordial welcome. The weather even seemed to cooperate as Bob described in a letter home of temperatures *feeling much like late May back home*.

When the 484th arrived, base operations were rough. Outbuildings were run-down, some with chickens scampering about. The commanding officers resided in a two-story farmhouse used also as the group's headquarters. Next to it was a barn designated as the briefing hut. It was large enough to accommodate 150 officers sitting on benches made from tail fin bomb crates.

Home to the 484th and 461st Bombardment Groups, Torretta's twin 6,000-foot runways accommodated traffic imposed by their heavy bombers. Army engineers had designed the airfield from farmland, soil topped with a crushed gravel mix. Once level, Marston* metal mats were laid, extending the length of the airstrip.

At takeoff, ships grumbled down the pierced steel plank runway. And upon landing, the roar of rumbling wheels announced their return. When both groups were assigned missions on the same day, the noise level was deafening. And it made for a tight rendezvous, a term used for establishing formation in the air.

The four officers lived together. Bob's home was made of heavy canvas draped from a center pole. When it rained, beads of water seeped through the walls. And beneath their muddied feet, the ground swelled a spongy touch. On those days, the earth's scent of swamp musk filled the air. *When sleeping, we are bothered by small lizards that crawl over me at night.* Not much better than a hunting hovel, the shelter became an oasis after a day *upstairs*.

At night, the men would listen to the BBC or other broadcasts from a *small radio in our tent.* Bob was tuned into a station playing a Benny Goodman number. As the song ended, a female voice speaking perfect English came on. *I called the others over and said, "Hey, guys, listen up—this is what we were talking about in Djedeida."* The airmen leaned in to hear more. *She introduced herself as Sally—Axis*

* Marston Mats, or pierced steel planking (PSP), was used to rapidly construct runways on airfields during WWII.

Sally. "Welcome to Italy, you boys of the 484th. We've been awaiting your arrival from Africa." Everyone's eyes widened.

Axis Sally played good American dance music but in between numbers, she'd try to get under your skin with her propaganda. She would say, "Our fighters are knocking down B-24s every day." Or she had a different angle aimed at making you homesick. She'd say, "While you're over here, your girlfriends are back home with other men who have jobs in the defense industry. They have a lot more money than you—they're 4Fs and don't have to worry about getting shot down and killed. You'd be surprised what your girlfriends are doing." Her sultry tone relayed the score. "You know why you're here. You are replacements to crews lost at the hand of our Luftwaffe pilots. You'll be dead in 30 days, too." While Bob recognized it was propaganda, the Germans were tracking flights and Axis Sally's comments flaunted details daily with chilling precision.

Trained as his unit's morale officer, Bob was instructed to keep letters on the light side—no need to worry those back home.

> *April 18, 1944*
>
> *. . . A few English soldiers are a hundred yards away. We are noisy and high-spirited. I walked past their tents the other day and heard one say, "I say, don't those chaps ever quiet down?" It's easy to see they can't understand us. Here we just moved in and already have movies, good food, and a neatly arranged camp. We dress nicely and raise a little hell. They, in their conservative way, can't quite picture American life.*
>
> *I guess no foreigner can realize what America is unless they have been there. Our country is really something to be proud of.*

With camp set up, days were spent training for combat missions. Morning started with briefing. To the officers, details of the route were outlined. Watches were set to the second. Anticipated weather to target was described. And if the objective couldn't be reached, an alternate target was posed. With briefing complete, the airmen hopped jeeps to ships readied by ground crews.

They boarded the B-24 through the belly of the ship and prepared their stations. Harry's perch, inside a bubbled top turret, had twin *fifties* as did the others with Warren Townsend at the nose, Louis Tatum in the belly, Charles "Moe" Bayer at the waist, gunner Bardwell, who was later grounded due to ear problems, and Lynn Chinn at the tail. Radio operator "Buzz" Shuttleworth had a machine gun. Depending on the path to target, the officers carried handguns.

Mission success would depend upon the efficiency of each crew member. At takeoff, the pilot focused on rendezvous;* the navigator laid out the course; gunners tested their *fifties*; the bombardier took control of the bomb drop; and if all went well, they returned without incident. Training was becoming routine.

Some days, practice flights were made over the sea. *Intel suggested German spy boats were disguised as local fishing vessels. We were also told U-boats, [or] submarines, were lurking just below the surface of the water. Between the two, they were counting the planes and relaying our positions. Likely giving Axis Sally material for broadcasting.*

One day flying over the Adriatic, I said to Jack, "See those boats lined up? Why don't we go down and give' em a little show." Under the guise of an avoidance simulation against incoming fighters, *Jack pushed the column forward and our Lib headed straight down before Jack leveled out and thundered just above the masts. As we crossed over, their sails went flop, flop, flop, one sail after the other. The people down on the boat*

---

* "Rendezvous" refers to a predetermined location in the air where multiple formations of bombers would meet up and assemble before proceeding together to target.

were shaking their fists at us. Truthfully, I think they were Italians just down there fishing.

Rigorous field training had been exhausted—at least what was necessary to ready crews for what lay ahead. Mock missions gave crews bolstered confidence. And last-minute navigation classes covered mapping of northern Italy and eastern European countries.

Emergency kits were passed out. Included in each package was a compass and signaling mirror, a silk scarf designed with a map of the targeted countries, K rations, cigarettes, chocolate, chewing gum, an assortment of pills (including morphine, tranquilizers, and pep tablets), a razor knife, bandages, and foreign cash. The bundle was small enough to fit in an airman's pocket.

Time came to move forward with the crew's first mission—what they'd been preparing for. If strategy allowed, commanders proposed *first flights as milk runs, where little fighter opposition was anticipated and flak batteries were considered light*. It was the Air Force's attempt at gliding the airmen into combat. The real deal. But tasking was still the luck of the draw. Tough targets needed to be covered as well.

With the order posted, the Crumbliss crew was headed for their biggest day yet. The date marked three months and twenty days from the time Bob met his crew at Harvard—not much of an orientation period for a group of ten twentysomethings embarking on a first combat mission against live anti-aircraft fire and skilled enemy fighters.

Training was now behind them.

Flying their first combat mission, Bob and Jack made a final check of their B-24 before heading to their tent for the night. Their Liberator was easy to identify by the giant "42" painted on her nose and rear waist section. An hourglass turned on its side topped by an ID of 52773 was painted on her twin tail fins. The aircraft insignia and numbers were necessary for flight control and group assembly in the air, but also, they made it easier to identify a disabled or downed plane. With the identification in place, she awaited only the christening of her flying name.

Back in his tent, Bob wrote Polley . . .

April 28, 1944

. . . Your large picture is right above my bed, so it is the last thing I see at night before I go to sleep and the first thing I see in the morning. And just before I go on a flight, I always look at your picture and say, "Well, Polley, I'll be seeing you, in a few hours." It may be silly to talk to a picture but I know it will bring me good luck . . .

Well, as the immortal Caesar said once, "Tempus fugit, Polleyciae." I have to get up early tomorrow so I had better go to bed as I probably will need to be alert . . . I am always thinking of you . . .

At lights-out, all was quiet. Nerves danced circles in Bob's head as he thought, *Will I plot the right course? What about the return? These guys are depending on me—I can't disappoint them.* His mind turned to the target. And from the target, they floated to the mission. *Will our ship be hit? Will I shoot at something? Or someone?* His mind would have drifted.

Facing combat for the first time, certainly Bob had thoughts of John B. After all, John B. had flown the initial mission for the 93rd Bomb Group just as Bob was preparing to do for the 484th. Bob would wonder: Was John B. empowered at the notion of flying his group's very first combat mission? Was he anxious? Or both?

Italy remained a hot spot of battle. Rome was a German bastion and, as the crow flies, the Gustav line was only sixty miles away. As the Allies moved north to Cassino, the sound of war echoed in the distance. And with each bombardment, aerial combat drew closer.

TWENTY-NINE APRIL 1944. As the orderly pulled the tarp, the

aviators' sleep was abruptly interrupted. As if the first day of school, the men would jump to attention before stumbling around looking for pants or misplaced boots.

Before leaving the tent, Bob threw his wallet and Polley's letters in his footlocker. Reaching for her photograph, he recalled the directive: *Personal items are discouraged on missions.* Lest a downed airman venture into enemy territory, his captor would have great folly with such an item. *No need to give them a free ticket.* Only army-issued items would accompany him on this trip.

Chatter hummed through the briefing hut as the meeting was called to order. In front of a room filled with pilots, navigators, and bombardiers, the curtain was pulled. A red yarn stretched from a point marking the base to target. Tracking the route, Bob's pride overshadowed any nerves. *It was an honor flying the very first combat mission for the 484th.*

Extending a long pointer, the briefing officer would identify the objective. Drniš, Yugoslavia. The target represented a transportation hub, tracks moving combat vehicles headed for the German front lines. As a logistics center, it met the demand for the enemy's military deployment. The mission was to eliminate all ability for movement coming and going. Moderate flak was predicted.

Bob was a student of language but, admittedly, sometimes read too much into a word. As to the meaning of *moderate*, he was aware of the dictionary's definition and also understood the Army's term. But *moderate* was still a relative term when it came to flak assaults. *Moderate* meaning *reasonable*, perhaps nothing to worry about. Or *slight*, meaning flak was armed to fire at such a soft range as to miss the bomber. Or if *moderate* meant *average* as in *adequate*, it was potentially as deadly as heavy flak given a direct strike. Releasing a picture of moderate, he would have returned to mission prep as details were concluded.

Gathered at the plane, coffee was gulped, cigarettes were lit, and sticks of gum were chewed. Nerves were calmed by any solace within reach.

With the last bomb lifted into the belly of the bomber, Bob said to his pilot, *"Jack, you're buying me a beer after I whip your ass at cards tonight."* Somehow, talking about future plans ensured a return to base.

Anticipation would creep into each crewman's head as they boarded the ship and secured their respective posts. Today was different from all others. Today, they would charge the enemy's gate.

As was his habit, Bob assembled his instruments close at hand, securing them for a bumpy ride. He confirmed all lifesaving plug-ins were operational and within reach. *Oxygen canister, good. Heater plug, good. Interphone jack, good. Headset, good. Desk cleared, yes.* He would pause as he looked to the machine gun available for his use.

At takeoff, Bob stood between the pilots. One by one, each engine started with a cough, followed by a high-pitched whining sound before the steady rhythm engaged. Four engines roared a deafening vibration as Jack wheeled the ship to the head of the airstrip.

With another three-dozen ships following the same process, it became the sound of war.

Bob could see as Jack throttled up, revving the engines. When they reached max rpm for takeoff, he released the brakes and ripped down the runway. As the bomber gained speed, everything seemed to rattle and quake. Jack gripped the column, fighting to prevent the Lib from pulling herself over her nose. Fully loaded, it seemed a long breath before she was airborne.

The flight over was inconsequential. When they reached the target, there was broken cloud cover; but once in sight, bombardier

Parsons plugged in the altitude, speed, wind, and target coordinates into his bombsight. When the moment came, he toggled the switch while announcing over the interphone, "Bombs away!" The ship released her first-ever lethal blow, striking the entrance of a tunnel and smashing train tracks.

Forgetting to request permission from the ship's commander, as Harry Harris recalled in his memoirs, tail gunner Lynn Chinn piped in, "Let's get the hell out of here!" Jack pitched the nose downward, gaining speed before following Bob's course back to base.

A few hours later, they reached Torretta. Their first mission was now behind them. The group's graphic artist was a mechanic who awaited each plane's return to paint the first bomb on the nose of the fuselage. The image represented each mission's success.

That day, a single flak battery had responded. *Moderate?* Maybe. *The mission fit the description of a milk run and we commented to one another, "Hey, these missions aren't bad at all." We had our first mission under our belt.* Bob started the countdown. *They had just increased mission quota from thirty-five to fifty. I had forty-nine missions to go.*

THIRTY APRIL 1944. At preflight briefing, their second mission was announced. Alessandria, Italy. *The objective was another marshaling yard where Germans accumulated supplies from a munitions factory. Over the target, flak guns responded but no fighters.* Bombs were dropped and the return to base was uneventful. Another painted moniker was awarded the side of their ship.

As Bob left the flight line, home didn't escape him. Without breaking censorship rules, he wrote, *We weren't delivering milk, Dad, but I guess you could say we were in the delivery business.* Surely smirking at the thought, he would know there was benefit in being his group's mail censor.

The following day the crew was scheduled to be off, but Bob had to report to headquarters in Bari, a sixty-mile trek. The first part of the day, he was called to a meeting of navigators. Later, he met up with another officer. *I often went to see the Intelligence officer who I met when I first arrived in Italy. He was a history professor at Cornell before enlisting and we talked of places of interest that we flew over.* Bob was eager to match territory on maps and bring European history alive. *We covered local places, leaders (past and present), and politics. And we mulled over the boot of Italy with its outer lying islands, tracking battles and noting how control had changed over time.*

Bob would leave Bari a little smarter.

Every air crew depended on their airplane to get them safely through each mission. As a result, they became very attached to their warbird. Naming the bomber with a caricature painted on the nose was a rite of passage. The Crumbliss crew had yet to name their Liberator.

Before leaving Bari, Bob had stopped by the Officers' Club, where he picked up the March 4, 1944, *Saturday Evening Post*. When he got to page seventeen, he stopped. Pictured was a sleek fighter, a dive-bomber. The white star, shining against her dark body, stood out in the colorless photograph. *I focused on her lines. She looked fast.* The headline reinforced a vision. "Bomber, fighter, strafe and equipped with a terrifying wail, the new Invader plane has sunk ships, blasted bridges, scared the dickens out of the enemy." Seeing this article, Bob found inspiration for naming their B-24.

It was dark when Bob got back to base. Having the day off, his brother airmen were hunkered down boasting adventures over cards and lifted spirits. For days, the crew had thrown around names for their ship, but none seemed to fit. When Bob joined the fray, he showed them the article in the *Post*. *The Invader—the original screaming demon. But the name's got to sing . . . Then I suggested taking off the* g. *Screamin' Demon.* Jack was the first to step up with approval, then the whole crew was on board. Short of a paint job, their ship was named: *Screamin' Demon.*

Lots had happened in three days. As he reflected on home, Bob thought of his family. *I guess Bill and Harry John are both serving in the South Pacific*—a reference to his sisters' husbands. And Bob's brother was in the Navy. Word was, Jim had settled on the east coast of England. An ordnance officer on an LST,* he was charged with defending vehicles and troops being dropped directly onto shore. *I imagine he will be coming up for Lt. JG pretty soon.*

Rumors were spreading of a major amphibious operation along the Atlantic Wall: France. Not unlike the North African Campaign in November 1942, it involved all branches of the military. He would wonder how it might involve Jim.

* "LST" stands for "Landing Ship Tank," a naval vessel designed to transport troops, tanks, and other vehicles directly onto a beach during amphibious invasions, allowing them to land heavy equipment on hostile shores without the need for docks or piers.

EIGHTEEN
Corsica

TWO MAY 1944. Before leaving for the flight line, Bob would have grabbed some maps, stuffing them into his briefcase together with the items he always relied upon upstairs. This was his third mission, La Spezia, the west coast of northern Italy. The flight promised some of the most beautiful vistas of azure sea matched with rugged hillsides along the way. Of course, this was no sightseeing trip.

The yet-to-be-christened *Screamin' Demon* waited to advance the taxi lane. At the time, Bob was feeling cocky from two *milk runs* in as many days. On the flight deck, he stood behind his pilot and began another joke. *So, Jack, there were these two undercover German spies getting some local intel at an English pub. The older spy, in his finest British accent, approaches the bar, demanding, "Two martinis." To which the bartender replied, "Will that be dry martinis?" Incensed, the angry German grumbled back, "Nein, ZWEI!"* Waiting for his pilot's response, Bob said, *"Get it? Eins, zwei . . . How many do you want tonight, Jack?"*

Just prior to releasing his foot from the brake, Jack quipped back, *"You know, your German is taking us to hell!"*

The route took them over water, north along the western spine of the Italian boot. Before the coastline made its westerly turn, Bob could see the Mediterranean meet jagged rocks rising upward. Yellow, orange, and white specks were sprinkled across the steep incline, homes to fishermen who lived by the sea. Further west was Monte Carlo. But this trip would not offer a glimpse of fine dining, elegant women, or a jewel box of extreme gambling.

To the contrary, it was time to make their turn to the target, a munitions factory located east of the coastline. Up ahead angry black puffs dotted the sky. The Axis was ready with precision anti-aircraft flak timed to altitude. Shrapnel, soaring from the ground, met the ships as they entered enemy territory.

Flak shot up our plane and we were still ten minutes to target. Concussions knocked *Screamin' Demon* as they struggled to maintain tight formation. Anti-aircraft was heavy and direct. It riddled the underside of the left wing, jolting it upward. *Engine two received the brunt. We knew it knocked out our engine, so Jack feathered*[*] *it. Then we had to put the juice to the other three engines to keep up with formation.*

They stayed in formation long enough to dump the ship's payload. Then they rallied homeward. But with only three engines, the Lib dropped back. Two sister Libs reduced speed for her to catch up. Flanking either side, they escorted the wounded warbird out of enemy territory.

Working overdrive, number three engine started running rough. It sputtered black smoke and died. Jack feathered that engine. It was difficult to maintain speed and altitude, so we dropped out of formation. They lagged behind. And it wasn't long before they lost sight of their

---

* "Feathering" is a process that pilots use to adjust the pitch of the propellers' blades to be parallel to the airflow, which minimizes drag and improves flight performance and handling.

group. *I remained in the cockpit.* The ride had been a long fifteen minutes from bombs away when *Jack ordered the crew to immediately dump all nonessential items or anything not tied down.* Gunners tossed boxes of used cartridge belts, oxygen canisters, and gas masks. Anything easily dismantled was thrown out the hatch. If in doubt, it was pitched. The ship seemingly obliged as she maintained course. But still, Jack struggled to keep the plane in the air.

Bob didn't need to read the expression on Jack's face to know they weren't going to make it back on half power. Possibilities raced through his mind before conjuring a heading. Above the roar of exhausted engines and a wicked vibration, Bob said, *"Corsica!" And Jack said, "Are you sure about Corsica? I don't want to go into a bunch of Germans." And I said, "YES, the Americans have it, the Americans have it!"*

Jack didn't have time to argue. *Down to two engines, one and four, there was no way they could make a safe landing on the mainland.* Especially given enemy territory. The choice to ditch in the water, certainly not without risk, was an involuntary suicide. Or maneuver to Corsica, an option avowed only by this lone navigator. *I shoved the map in front of Jack, showing him where we were and where we were headed while calling out the course.* Although the island was not in sight, they were close.

As luck would have it, *I was the only guy in our entire group that knew about the airfields in Corsica. We had not been briefed on it as being an alternate landing site. Because I loved history, in my last semester I had taken a course on Napoleonic history and found out [Napoleon] was born on the island. The chance visit with the Cornell professor the day before had opened my curiosity. He showed me the American fighter fields on the map. I took the map and happened to stick it in my case that morning.*

But the ship's trouble was not over. Jack's focus sharpened as the island came into view. Crossing the coastline, the ship became increasingly unsteady. Heat rising from the ground rocked the wings left and right. Balance would be no problem flying on four engines. But with only two, passing through thermals compounded the difficulty. If Jack overcompensated, the plane would go into an uncontrolled roll. If he didn't give it enough, the ship's forward speed couldn't be sustained.

It was complex flying, at best.

Jack moved the yoke just enough, making the critical attitude* adjustments to maintain course, all the while dancing with the rudder pedals. The ship was struggling for lift when Bob sighted the field to the west. But just as Jack initiated a right bank, Bob grabbed his shoulder and pointed portside. *Coming in from the mainland was a fighter. We could see the P-47 was dirty,*† *with flaps and landing gear down on final approach. He was going twice our speed. With no way to reach the other pilot, Jack had to make a split-second move. Picking up speed, Jack forced her into a shallow five-degree dive under the pattern of the P-47.* It was his only option to avoid certain collision.

As Jack initiated a turn portside back around to the field, *the ship was shaking violently with the maneuver.* Jack coaxed the two remaining engines. *"C'mon, you mothers, you sweet mother of God, just a little bit more!"* With constant pressure on the rudders, Jack's legs were surely cramping when he shouted, *"Step on the right rudder!"* The copilot obliged. They banked left. As the teardrop turn was completed, they got her lined up on final approach about a mile out. As the bomber aligned with the airstrip, engine four sputtered, trailing a stream of black smoke. *As the ship lumbered down, we finally got*

* "Attitude," an aviation term, is the position of the nose relative to the horizon, crucial for controlling the bomber's path.

† "Dirty," an aviation term, refers to an aircraft with landing gear down and flaps extended in preparation for landing.

lined up on the runway and the third engine quit. If we had not been that close, we may not have made it on the one engine. We wouldn't be here.

We didn't know what their radio frequency was, so I grabbed the Very pistol, a flare gun, to let them know we were in distress. I'd shoot a flare, then say, "Hand me another one, Harry"; then, "Hand me another one!" I was shooting flares of red, yellow, and green in an attempt to alert the tower for a priority landing. While the colors meant that we had wounded and dead on board, which we didn't have, I was more concerned about landing.

The crew positioned for a crash landing. With the heavy bomber coming in, a crowd appeared. No doubt weak-kneed, Jack gave it his last effort as the plane tottered from side to side. The landing wasn't pretty, but it was all the ship could muster given her wounded state. She bucked and bounced as she rolled down the runway. At the end of the field, the Lib came to a heaved stop in a swirl of dust and smoking of spent rubber.

The bomb bay doors opened with a slow-grinding screech. Waist gunner Moe Bayer was first out of the belly. As soon as his feet hit, he *knelt down and kissed the ground*. One by one, each of the ten-man crew jumped down, jubilant the landing was a success. Pilot and navigator were last to exit the ship. On terra firma, Bob would have gripped Jack's shoulder. No words were needed as harried expressions knew there was no second attempt at landing.

Fearing the worst, the base responded with emergency personnel. From the other side of the field, a cloud of dust followed as two ambulances raced down the tarmac. Fire trucks and others carrying ground crews made their way to the wounded Lib. And *standing out of an open jeep, a guy with a movie camera was grinding away.* While the crew motioned all were okay, wearied smiles were keenly aware of what could have been. There were slaps on the back and stories shared of the mission: the flak strikes, the dubious navigation course, and especially the crack landing made by their pilot extraordinaire.

While the island base housed scores of P-47 Thunderbolt fighters, it was considered a distant retreat before the war. A seaside location, it easily passed as a summer resort. Not far from the base was a mountain lodge where guests once hunted for wild boar.

That evening the four B-24 officers were welcomed into the Officers' Club. *We were introduced to a number of P-47 pilots and were treated like royalty. The night resembled a fraternity rush week with joking, boasting, and backslapping stories. The flight surgeon said to me, "The way you were shooting those flares I thought it was either the Fourth of July or else everyone on board was dead!"*

Turns out we were on the field of the most famous fighter squadron of the war in North Africa and Europe. The fighter pilots countered with harrowing stories of escaping enemy ace pilots and how they maneuvered in for their own kill. Stories of strafing German installations and aerial dogfights were embellished. The airmen motioned with arms slanted, as if soaring with wings tilted through a narrow mountain pass, banking to the left or the right to confront another aggressor. *One pilot crowed, "I was on that mother's tail shooting dead center up Jerry's ass!" Another boasted, "I hit a train full of ammo—it blew up right under me. Ka-BOOM!" Those P-47 pilots were hell-for-leather, balls-out type of guys. Legendary. A terrific bunch of young men.*

And they shared the finest contraband found in the Mediterranean Theatre. *The P-47 pilots had been in North Africa and somehow confiscated a C-47 (cargo plane). They flew it to Cairo, loaded it with whiskey, and flew it back to Corsica.* Given the remoteness of the island, the pilots pilfered the libation and stocked up their inventory.

When Bob asked about the cameraman grinding away in the jeep, he was told *he was a famous Hollywood director doing a movie on the P-47 pilots*. It was William Wyler. Before the war, Wyler's credits included movies with such notables as Betty Davis, Henry Fonda, and Gary Cooper. He had already filmed a story about a B-17 Flying Fortress crew, but it hadn't yet been released. It was rumored he was preparing a motion picture on the P-47 Thunderbolts. And these Corsican-based pilots would soon be featured on the big screen. Who could blame them for being so cocky?

At daybreak, the crew was committed to getting back in the air. Their fortune was augmented by having two engineers on board, Lou Tatum and Harry Harris.

Lou was the crew's lower ball gunner. Barely five foot three, he was perfectly sized for the confined space. From Honduras, his vision was to start his own shrimping business after the war. He was a devout Catholic, and a decent guy ready to step up to any task. And being a mechanic adept in field repairs, he was a resourceful and strong link to a fine crew.

It wasn't long before they scavenged the parts they needed. Because the P-47 had a Pratt & Whitney engine, as did the B-24, replacement parts were remarkably available. First job was to repair the severed oil lines. *We worked all day and got three engines in good working order. The fourth was good enough for a takeoff and we would fly all the way back on three engines. By day's end, she was airworthy.*

Immediately on takeoff, we had to feather the number two engine and as a result, we didn't have enough power to get enough altitude to cross over the mountains. I laid out the map on my nav desk and found a crooked pass. After giving an initial course direction, I grabbed the map and crawled through to the cockpit. I remained on the flight deck [to tell] Jack where to go when. With some pretty delicate navigation, we made the turn through the pass and headed back to base. Before landing, we buzzed the tents in the officers' section. It was a bit of mischief for a stressful couple of days.

After landing, debriefing took place. Word quickly spread of their emergency landing. *Colonel Keese asked, "Jack, how'd you know about Corsica?" and Jack responded, "Well, my navigator knew about it." Colonel Keese went straight to me and gave me some pretty nice recognition for it. Between my transatlantic flight and Corsica, I got quite a reputation for my navigation.*

The ship was down for repairs the next few days.

May 4, 1944

Dear Polley,

. . . We had almost decided to name our plane "Two Naturals and a Crap." Our plane number is 773—we had two uneventful missions and then on our third mission we "crapped" and were forced down. If you know anything about shooting dice, you will understand . . .

We came back from that mission and were told we could stand down the next day. Nothing cemented a brotherhood of airmen like combat on a bomber. Or surviving a crash. *Our enlisted crew had a bunch of wine, and we were drinking it out of a canteen cup. Emotions of lost engines and near-water ditching made the spirits easily flow. About midnight, I crawled back to my tent and passed out.*

NINETEEN

I've Been to a Place...

BOB HADN'T BEEN SLEEPING LONG when the orderly entered his tent. *The sergeant said, "Get up, Cress. You're flying today." It was 4:00 a.m. and I was in terrible shape.* His eyes were glued shut, dehydrated results from the alcohol intake the night before. *I said there must be some mistake since our ship was down for service, but he said it was no mistake.* Bob had been called to substitute on a ship readied for combat.

In the briefing room, the objective was revealed. The group was headed to Romania.* *I knew the Ploesti facilities furnished a third of the oil, petroleum, and benzene for the German war machine; it was very*

* With censorship rules, Bob did not identify the target by name in his letters. It is unclear whether his mission was to Pitesti or Bucharest with the 484th, or to Ploesti with the group that shared the same airfield, all of which were Romanian cities in proximity. Years later, Bob made a handwritten notation on the envelope containing a letter to Polley dated May 9, 1944, wherein he indicated *1st time to Ploesti.*

heavily defended; and I was well aware that John B. had gone missing nine months prior. I was afraid, very uneasy, about that target.

An officer would have stepped up to the podium to describe the enemy's defenses. German radar was extremely accurate and anti-aircraft cannons were timed to the bombers' altitude. To distract German tracking, countermeasures in the form of aluminum slivers codenamed *chaff* or *window* would be tossed from the lead ships. *It was not unlike Christmas tinsel. You would break it up and throw it out the waist windows. It was supposed to generate a cloud of false signaling in an effort to confuse altitude settings.* Despite these measures, the airmen would face anti-aircraft guns producing intense and accurate flak from the ground. When the commander stepped up, he rallied the young men to the skies before the final *Good luck and Godspeed* message was delivered. No doubt a rumble filled the briefing room as the airmen got up and headed for trucks taking them to awaiting planes.

Ground crews had already readied the ships before airmen boarded for takeoff. It was nearly an hour before all bombers were airborne and rendezvous was made. As formation faced the sunrise, they headed east across the Adriatic before making a northerly turn. As was his habit on final approach, Bob headed upstairs. Bracing against a strut, he held on as the ship bucked through blasts, concussions made by each burst of heavy shrapnel from flak guns below. Looking out the cockpit windscreen to the Romanian farmland below, his mind floated to John B.'s whereabouts. But before he had much time to think about it, "Bombs away" roared through the interphone and some ten 500-pound bombs were salvoed.

As the ship made her rallying turn, the bombers reversed course. In between jolts of the plane, Bob headed back to his navigation station. *Out the dome, I watched as a half dozen enemy fighters closed in, swarming overhead. They were shooting at formation, and they were shooting to kill. It was fearsome. Our gunners started thumping away* until the friendly escort drove the enemy fighters out of the bombers' range. Beyond the battle and upon returning to base, he undoubtedly felt a sense of relief at having survived active combat against the Luftwaffe, who was known for its first-class fighters. The landing was uneventful, but the day's mission was certainly imprinted in Bob's mind.

Upon exiting the ship, he was met with a shot of whiskey to bring him down from the reality of the mission. It was the military's attempt to calm frayed nerves. He would have asked for a second shot, knowing tomorrow's task would come all too soon. As he caught a ride back to quarters, he would not be his jovial self. Flying with a hangover hadn't helped his mood. It had been a long day, and he was exhausted. He had a hard time releasing the thought that he had flown in the same airspace in which John B. went missing. Still nothing definitive had been issued about John B.'s whereabouts. Bob tried to focus on the underground. *He's got to be hiding out—but nine months? Or maybe captured. In prison camp. But where? Why hasn't word gotten back?* Bob would be more introspective than his usual upbeat letters. In a letter to Polley, he wrote, *The moon is making me very lonely tonight . . . things are tough all over.*

With his ship still down for repairs, the following days Bob was sent for training in Bari and Foggia. He would still process Romania. His first two missions might have been considered *milk runs*, the third a daring yet doable emergency, but the last one, facing blitzkrieg, would quickly induct him into the real deal.

Before heading to his tent for the evening, Bob sometimes took the long way back. Breathing in fresh air, it was not unlike his walks on the farm but for the distant bombardments. At the hardstands, the Liberators seemingly stood guard. As he reached his ship, he stopped. She stood peaceful yet readied for the call to action. Against the ship's *olive-green drab* color, the giant white star on a dark circle stood out. In bold script two feet high, *Screamin' Demon* was illustrated on her nose. Just below the pilot's-side window, three bombs were painted, representing missions complete. With each flight upstairs, another image of a bomb would be added. Nose art told a story of the crew, a name that personalized the ship. While lusty women and sweethearts were often the subject of art, so were cartoon and Disney characters. *Screamin' Demon* was no exception. Her name was spelled out, but her caricature had not yet been painted.

Bob hadn't expected to fly that morning, his fourth mission. *Facing fighters was fearsome . . . and violent.* But fortune was on his side. Was it luck? Or divine design? Bob would shake the thought, knowing fate governed his story. It was communications back home that helped recharge his soul. A nightly letter became a daily lifeline, a way to decompress from the day's stress. A letter was therapeutic—a way to focus on home and away from the perils of the day. Little was written, but he had to get something off his chest.

May 9, 1944

Dear Polley,

. . . There doesn't seem to be much to write about except I am well and everything is going okay. I will be missing you until we are again together, which I hope is not too far from now . . .

. . . I have been to the place that John B. mentioned in his last letters, and it is just as bad now as it was then. It is by far the worst place I have been, and I don't care to go there again . . .

Combat missions continued.

Wiener Neustadt, an Austrian city producing major components for the Me 109[*] fighter planes, remained one of ten priority targets. A successful attack on Aerodrome Nord would paralyze the Messerschmitt 109, the backbone of the Luftwaffe's fighter force. Nicknamed *Messer* not only for its designer but the German word translated to *knife*, razor-blade sharpness that cut through the skies at lightning speed.

With the briefing completed, wooden crates used for chairs rumbled as the airmen got up.

At the flight line, the aviators loaded awaiting ships. One by one, the ships roared down the runway, gaining speed and altitude before completing rendezvous over the Adriatic. In calculated choreography, three-dozen Liberators, wingtip-to-wingtip, banked left in a single motion, northward to the target.

Advancing into a "strong headwind," Bob's group was hindmost, flying 1,000 feet above and behind the leading group. The position offered a wide vantage of the skies as they motored toward the aerodrome where bombs were dropped.

On exit, the area was covered with Me 109 fighters. German reinforcements raced in from Vienna to add power in battering the bombers. Crossing over the group, the fighters split and circled around, firing into the wings of the lead ship. Flames rose from her right wing before it snapped in half. Some airmen bailed from the falling B-24.

I counted as chutes blossomed. "One . . . two . . . three, four. C'mon, guys, jump!" Bob followed the ship in its plunge to earth, hoping for more chutes. In noting the location coordinates, a flash from the left caught his eye. Another B-24 was on fire and losing altitude.

---

* The Me 109, a.k.a. Messerschmitt Bf 109, was likely Germany's most important fighter plane armed with a 30 mm or 20 mm cannon and 13 mm machine guns. The Me 109, together with the Fw 190, formed the backbone of the Luftwaffe's fighter force until the end of WWII.

As navigator, he was responsible for recordation of downed planes, coordinates, and number of chutes deployed. Things were happening so fast that processing his perceptions barely allowed enough time to transfer on paper. While important for rescue and recovery, it wasn't a task he swallowed with ease. In real time, Bob was seeing the enemy take out American bombers. And with it, good men.

By the end of the day, a count was entered. While the Fifteenth Air Force lost a couple dozen ships, Bob's group lost two planes. Twenty-one men went missing. Gone were comrades who didn't make it back to base.

After debriefing, Bob would pass by one of the missing crew's vacant tents. An eerie quiet came from within. For those airmen who failed to return, a transition of quarters was made. Operations personnel entered the tents of the missing men. They gathered mementos, photographs, and unread letters, packing the personal items into footlockers. Possessions were sent home to family but not before pulling materials considered classified. Once sanitized, any remnant of the prior crew vanished as a quick turnover of quarters was needed. With the tent emptied, Bob would know it was now available for a new crew. Replacements, men still green from the long trip over, took up residence in tents from airmen whose stories were never finished in the way a mother would hope.

Replacements, the idea of one life swapped out for another, would strike a nerve with Bob. Those gone had honored America. Each had obeyed orders. Each cared about his fellow man. Good men reduced to an untimely designation. *MIA* (*missing in action*) kept hope alive as *KIA* (*killed in action*) beckoned finality. Postponed were the official letters to families back home.

Each airman lived knowing the next mission could be his last. Bob knew he coursed a narrow path between the joys of success and a really bad day. A notion of returning to base. Or not. And there was guilt for those left behind. A downed ship meant lost friends.

Bob counted the days until he satisfied Army requirements. In the month he started flying, mission quota for the reward of a trip back to the States jumped from twenty-five to thirty-five to fifty. But with recent assignments, tough as they were, he wondered if that last milestone was even possible. Increasing numbers of ships were lost. *Planes were dropping from the sky before our eyes. We all wondered who was next?* As a result of the losses, *I began to compile my own list of downed planes and airmen.* That night he tucked the list under some papers in his footlocker before joining an ongoing card game.

The radio was playing in the background when they all perked up at an alarming broadcast. *Sally said, "Hey, boys of the 484th . . . heard you lost two planes today—twenty of your closest friends. Our Luftwaffe won't stop until all of your tents are vacant."*

How did she know?

Weather precluded flying the following day. The mission had been planned for Ploesti. With the cancellation, the crew's navigator especially felt relief.

TWELVE MAY. Bologna. The city housed German Army headquarters, its communications and transportation hub. With complete cloud cover over the target, Bologna was aborted. Formation turned to Viareggio, a shipbuilding town. With marshaling yards in sight, the bombs were salvoed. Opposition was slight. And Bob would be appreciative for the milk run as he wrote home, *I am okay and going strong.*

THIRTEEN MAY. Rail installations at Cesena. The morning briefing outlined ground opposition and weather, followed by a concluding *Godspeed* message, sending an alliance of young men to carry out the War Department's campaign.

After jockeying for position during rendezvous, the armada

traveled westerly across Italy. Although the city hadn't been taken yet, the Allies were closing in on Rome. As the ships flew over, Bob, being a fan of history, would hone in on the Colosseum and later write home, *I saw The Eternal City for the first time today.* While far away, its antiquities were clearly seen from altitude. After tracking north over blue waters, they banked east, leaving the Mediterranean behind before crossing the hilly terrain of north central Italy. More ancient cities came into view.

Earlier at briefing, the commander's message was clear. "Do not attack Florence!" Bob understood the obvious reasons why Florence was spared, but why weren't so many other villages of ageless architecture? The ships powered past the pardoned city toward the target. Unbeknownst to the crew, warning sirens would be heard on the ground as the *heavies* roared above Cesena. Townspeople surely took cover. It was early afternoon when the bombs were released over the ancient town, a first the residents had ever experienced. But not the last.

FOURTEEN MAY. Padua was a center for transportation, with double-lined railroad tracks stretching between Slovenia and Vienna and Milan to Bologna. On approach, the lead bombardier believed he was over the target. Bombs were unloaded. The Libs collectively "dropped ninety-five tons" of explosives south of the intended target. Once *bombs away* was heard, the group rallied eastward toward the Adriatic. *Milk run?* Definitely. But they missed the mark—they hit *Bungdoo. An expression we use to denote when the bombardier misses the target is that he dropped the bombs out in Bungdoo.*

Weather grounded all bombing operations the following days. Jack and Bob headed to Bari but missed the truck back on the return. The two came across a military vehicle secured with a chain. *We saw this jeep, broke the chain, and drove it back to our base. So many jeeps were stolen in this way. Although the ground crews complained, we weren't punished as long as we told them where to find the jeep. Our attitude at the time was "we're the combat guys going out on missions, getting shot at. We didn't give a damn about the vehicles because we knew we were going to get killed anyway."* About that time, Bob was beginning to realize that they were only a number and that each of them was expendable.

Bob's perspective was not far off from what was happening in the skies. Combat crew strength of the Fifteenth Air Force was about 20,000 airmen on any one day. While numbers were still being tabulated, year-end losses of the reported 20,570 airmen were astounding. In newspapers throughout the States, hidden between rooming vacancies and ads for women's hosiery, back-page headlines revealed the score. General Ira Eaker, air chief in the Mediterranean Theatre, reported "the Fifteenth Air Force was losing 100 percent of its combat crews in 1944." With jaw-dropping rates, airmen—Bob's friends—were alarmingly becoming military statistics.

SEVENTEEN MAY. Portoferraio. A vital iron ore port, the naval basin was a center for repairing marine vessels. Two groups of Liberators made for a crowded takeoff but at target, deadly shrapnel met the ships as bombs were dropped. And although "eighteen ships were damaged by heavy flak with three unable to fly the following day," Bob's crew returned unharmed. *Another day closer to fifty . . .*

EIGHTEEN MAY. Xenia Oil Refinery . . . *We were briefed on Ploesti. The target had put the fear of God in us.* Aircrews readied their ships for the same dance. Takeoff and rendezvous went as planned. But on the way over, there was a ten-ten cloud cover. With weather closing in over Ploesti, the group turned to the alternate target: Belgrade. Relief wasn't exactly Bob's response. At target, they dropped their *eggs* and returned to base. It would seem that all was becoming routine. Or was it?

May 19, 1944

Mother and Dad,

. . . I missed writing you last night because I had a rather tiring day. I located some instruments and am organizing an orchestra. It will afford diversion & relaxation for the fellows & will be entertaining to the rest of the squadron . . . it ought to be a pretty good morale factor as there is not much else to do.

. . . I am living a very interesting life although it is a rather fast one. However, I don't think this is going to change me too much . . .

TWENTY-TWO MAY. Target was Piombino. Bombs were dropped on blast furnaces of a steel mill. Their brother group lost a Lib. The job was becoming a daily grind and taking its toll. But Bob kept going.

TWENTY-FOUR MAY. Based at Manduria, Park Chetwood, Bob's best friend from advanced navigation school, was on his ninth mission but his first over Wiener Neustadt. The air over the target was just as fierce, if not more as when Bob visited in the days prior.

Out of the overcast, the enemy fighters appeared from nowhere. Me 109s met the armada swarming and hungry. Chetwood's ship trailed formation. Fighters got a lock on his bomber, battering her from nose to wings to tail.

As they made a second pass, strafing pierced the Plexiglas greenhouse in the nose. Park and his bombardier each took a lethal hit. The only child of a grocery store owner, Park paid the biggest price for war. What might have been will never be known. The immeasurable cost of war.

As Park ventured to Wiener Neustadt, Bob flew to Zagreb. *Screamin' Demon* targeted an airfield before returning to base. Bob didn't know it then, but he was the lucky one that day.

TWENTY-FIVE MAY. Needing new tires, *Screamin' Demon* was grounded for maintenance. Her crew stood down. Short a navigator, Bob was awakened early to substitute on the Watts crew. *Captain Watts was a West Pointer, the second in command of our group and a stickler to the rules. He was the type of leader that you didn't speak with unless spoken to.*

Bob took a seat with familiar faces. As the curtain was drawn, the target was revealed. The Fifteenth had abruptly changed course from Italy and other eastern objectives. Aim was redirected to French targets: Carnoules marshaling yards at Toulon.

It was a long trek north but by the time he returned to base, attended the debriefing, cleaned up, and ate dinner, Bob was finished. Almost. He had just enough energy to stop by the Officers' Club for a single drink. It had been a lengthy two days in a month of long days but no longer than what was to come.

TWENTY-SIX MAY. At 0230, Bob rolled out of bed knowing the early hour meant a long day. As the curtain was pulled, the red yarn stretched to Lyon, France. Vaise marshaling yards. It was another marathon flight as *Screamin' Demon* flew alongside a hundred ships or more. Bombs dropped, damaging the main transport lines before the ships reversed course and returned to base.

TWENTY-SEVEN MAY. It was Bob's third time over France and his fourth day in a row of flying. The target was an airfield at Salon-de-Provence. As the ships reached the southern coast of France, they were met by heavy flak. At the aerodrome, Liberators damaged hangars, the control tower, and "a nest of German Junker

88s" that had been menacing Mediterranean shipping lanes. Before leaving, the group cratered the enemy's landing field.

The days had been busy and at night, Bob melted into his cot but not before writing.

May 27, 1944

Polley,

. . . You can't guess what I am making for you—a ring out of some Plexiglas. Plexiglas is a type of non-shatterable glass we have for windows in the nose of our plane. This glass is quite significant since the ring will be made from the first window shot out of our plane . . .

I got your letter asking me not to knock myself out by trying to get my missions over too soon. Well, don't worry too much, I can get a rest leave by requesting it. I will take care of myself and will come back to you just as we were together last . . .

TWENTY

Leading the Wing

TWENTY-NINE MAY 1944. Park Chetwood's final mission was to this city. Bob had made a prior visit. And the Air Force vowed to return. Wiener Neustadt. A dreaded objective with air defense fortifications arguably second to Ploesti.

The run to the ball bearing factory was known as *Flak Alley.* Derived from the German word *Flugabwehrkanone*, it translated to Flight Defense Cannon. Shortened to *flak*, the term became synonymous with explosive projectiles flung high into the path of oncoming bombers.

Facing powerful defenses, it was a tough mission. The enemy's rolling stock replacement parts were damaged but not without a fight. And at the price of men and aircraft.

When the group rallied away from target, a dozen fighters swooped in from out of nowhere. Flying to within fifty yards, they peeled away before circling back. Speeds were lightning fast. Barreling in at well over 350, a lone *Messer* aimed his sights to the side of formation, strafing one unlucky bomber. Captivated out the window, Bob followed a ship as she fell from the sky. Out of control, her nose dropped before spiraling toward the Austrian countryside. Flames followed her until she burst into nothingness. *I saw their plane blow up. I don't know how many guys got out. It was a terrible feeling . . . you'd see the wing blown off . . . And you realize, this can happen to you.* Fighting the urge, Bob retched into his oxygen mask. It was real. His friends were gone. Weeks before, the periled airmen had arrived in Italy when Bob had. Both crews had set up camp at the same time. Bob's tent was next to theirs. They played cards and drank together. He knew the officers well. And he knew the enlisted men.

In that instant, his eye caught another flash. A second Lib was hit and exploded. The Messer was firing rockets. As they left the target, another ten men suffered a fatal blow.

While the *Screamin' Demon* sustained battle damage, she made it home. She was the lucky one that day.

Bob, like the others, returned exhausted and defeated. And visibly upset by the loss of a leader, their lieutenant commander. It was a solemn debriefing. A jigger of whiskey was offered to comfort tensions. But the taste couldn't mask the day. Emotions hit rock bottom.

That night the Group Commander pulled Bob aside. *Colonel Keese took great interest in me. He was afraid I was going to be made squadron navigator and he would lose me, so after this mission, Colonel Keese came to me and said, "I want you on tomorrow's mission—we don't know the particular target but you will be my navigator." It was a huge honor to fly with the colonel.*

THIRTY MAY. Bob first learned at briefing that *I was not only lead navigator of my group, which was 36 planes, but our group was the lead for the entire wing, which was 108 planes.* (Similarly, John B. had been the wing leader over the initial mission to Rome, a last mission before he went to Ploesti.)

I guess the reason I drew the job is because I was flying with the captain, who dropped back to cover a wounded ship, and I brought us in from pretty deep in enemy territory. The captain is second-in-command of our squadron and is flying copilot for the colonel tomorrow. He is the one who chose me to navigate for the lead ship. Gosh, Polley, I hope I do well.

The target was Wels, Austria. A jet engine factory. It had recently opened and, while anti-aircraft was anticipated, fighter opposition was unknown. Once the ships met in formation, Bob set the heading north. With over a hundred Libs in tow, he altered the course just enough to confuse Axis tracking. *Once at altitude, you don't go directly to the target, but you take a dog leg here or there to throw off the Germans who were trying to track you.* When the B-24 convoy flew over the target, the Luftwaffe had failed to identify the bombers' objective. "The mission encountered accurate flak and the 484th Bomb Group, and the [friendly] escort, tangled with [enemy] fighters." The mission was no milk run.

When we got back down, Colonel Keese told me, "This is the most perfect mission we have ever flown."

Upon landing, each airman was greeted with a shot of whiskey, a regular attempt to calm jittery nerves from the day. Bob would have taken a long swig, recognizing he had made it back. Again.

It was another long mission. *I was in the air fourteen hours.* From an early-morning briefing to takeoff; covering the miles to target; entering flak-erupting skies; dropping the bomb load; and routing the return trip home—all the while, Bob was making minute-by-minute calculations of the Wing's course. Debriefing punctuated a grueling day. It was another huge responsibility that he would shoulder.

Unbeknownst to Bob, in an official ceremony commending the Wels mission days later, the colonel declared, "So ably was the Wing led, so perfect the navigation and bombing, that the Wels aircraft factory installations are but a memory to the Germans. All our bombers returned unharmed. So fine a job was done that this highly successful raid is an inspiration and has pushed the Group to first place in the Fifteenth Air Force." Brigadier General Atkinson, Deputy Commander of the Fifteenth Air Force, awarded the *Distinguished Flying Cross* to the flight officers on the Wels mission who were present on the day of the ceremony.

Bob's first mission had been April 29. A month. Since then, he had flown over sixteen targets with a few counting as double missions. When he wasn't flying, he traveled to headquarters for continued navigation training, cracking more nav books and absorbing advanced applications on novel instruments.

After the Wels mission, Bob was exhausted. *I had flown more missions than anyone in my group, and at least three more than anyone on my crew. I went to the infirmary to tell the flight surgeon that I needed time off. But the colonel had also stopped by and asked me, "What are you doing in here?" and I said, "I just wanted to get something to help me sleep." I couldn't admit to being exhausted. The colonel was going over my mission papers and said to the medic, "Lieutenant Cress should be set up for time off at the Isle of Capri." Colonel Keese looked at me and said, "Now, you have to fly the mission tomorrow—it's an all-out effort by the Fifteenth Air Force . . . when you get back, you'll be going to the Isle of Capri for rest and recreation camp." So I had that to look forward to.*

Polley would be graduating from the University of Illinois the following day, May 31, 1944. Bob would have been too, but for the war. That night, the moon was half full. In a letter to Polley, he wrote, *In about seven hours you'll be looking at that same moon.* Surely, the thought would have brought on a missing-Polley smile as he readied for his next flight only hours away.

TWENTY-ONE
Ploesti

THIRTY-ONE MAY 1944. The aviators were *awakened by the squadron CQ*[*] *at 0300*, as memorialized in Bob's diary. *We knew the earlier they got us up the longer the mission was going to be. Sleepy-eyed, we entered the briefing room, but our sleepy minds and bodies suddenly became very much awake when we heard that our target was to be Ploesti. We all knew that Ploesti was a tough target, and it put the fear of God in us.*

But for me, Ploesti also conjured thoughts of John B. Certainly not a place Bob wanted to revisit, but after all, the Isle of Capri, a rest camp, was just a day away.

At briefing, the operations officer described Ploesti's defenses. *It was a target that furnished 35 percent of fuel for the German war machine, 50 percent of aviation fuel, and they had a cracking plant that made high-octane aviation fuel. They defended it to the bitter death* with unmatched anti-aircraft fire and first-class fighter strength.

Concluding the briefing, Bob recalled Colonel Keese's words:

* "CQ" stands for "Charge of Quarters," the person responsible for waking up crews for missions.

"Today is an all-out maximum effort. The Fifteenth Air Force is sending up every damn plane available. We're going to knock the hell out of those oil refineries!" With the prelude delivered, a powered armada of hundreds of ships awaited takeoff.

Before leaving for the flight line, *we went back to our tent and put on our heavy flying equipment.* Grabbing his briefcase, Bob pulled at the tent opening when something made him turn around. He had left his leather gloves, a Christmas gift from Polley. As he picked them up, his eyes would meet her portrait, which sat on his footlocker next to his cot. *Often when I looked at her picture, I was reminded of our time in Chicago and the melody "I'll be seeing you," so I said, "I'll be seeing you, Polley."*

Bob was not only the ship's navigator but also the crew's intelligence and morale officer. Before each mission, he would stop by his enlisted men's tent to share details of the mission, hustle them out the door, and generally provide encouragement—*a pep talk*. Sticking his head through the canvas entrance, Bob recalled the bond of nine airmen that had formed before he joined the alliance at Harvard. *When I first met the group, Harry had been particularly skeptical of me. In his eyes, I was the college pretty boy turned navigator.* But in the missions leading up to this day, a mutual respect had grown between Bob and the crew. In a month of combat, his crew had faced battle about every other day. There was stress. But what made his crew extraordinary was the gravity within which they handled their job. A team Bob was proud of.

That morning, *Buzz Shuttleworth, the crew's radio operator, was missing. He had been sick the night before and they sent James Bell to replace him. Little was known of Bell other than being a replacement radioman from Avery, Oklahoma.* It was his first flight with the Crumbliss crew.

Crew membership was a brotherhood. Months of rigorous training, unexpected hardships, and reliance upon one another forged a bond, a unit that strengthened through combat. One could not simply be replaced like some mechanical part to an engine. Substitutes didn't have a history. Many came from crews lost in combat, and with that brought superstition. *I saw the look in the guys' eyes . . . then told them, "Let's get cracking"—I'd see them at the plane.* The crew would jump up on a truck that took them to the flight line.

A jeep spewing rocks and dust rolled up with a quick stop. As Bob's ride to the hardstand arrived, his crew officers would motion their navigator to hop on. Bob shared the news of the substitute radioman. *Name's Bell. Dick, my bombardier, had a funny sense of humor. He said, "like a ringer?" The term* dead ringer *came to mind so I said, "Yeah, a stand-in for today's horse race."*

At the hardstand, *our crew chief, Staff Sergeant Albone, was at the plane warming up the engines and making sure that everything was in tip-top shape for the mission.* As was standard procedure with the crew on board, the pilot looked down his checklist, the navigator confirmed course, while the bombardier checked his bombsight and the gunners began pre-combat procedures. *In the tail gunner's walk-through, Chinn asked, "Where are the chutes?"* No one had responded and another hiccup, a notion of things to come, was tallied. But with only minutes before departure, the parachute distribution truck rolled to a stop. The ship was now ready, and all members of the crew positioned at their respective stations.

As we taxied to takeoff, we waved to the ground crew, which meant "we'll see you in a few hours, fellas." Once again, *Screamin' Demon* was slated to be tail-end Charlie, trailing formation and guarding the back ass of the group. Vulnerable to enemy attack, odds wouldn't be in their favor. But *just as the wheels started to roll, we were notified the plane scheduled to fly the number two slot had aborted.* With a change in flight assignment, *Screamin' Demon* moved in to fill that position.

Curbing suspicion of another last-minute hitch, the crew readied for the long journey.

At half-minute intervals, the big ships roared down the pierced steel plank runway. Because *Screamin' Demon* was heavily loaded with bombs, full fuel, and bullet cartridges, Jack struggled with the column before the ship's wheels pushed from the ground. The bomber quaked before becoming airborne. Climbing to meet formation, *rendezvous went as usual.* "Over 700 ships" would target several Ploesti facilities that day. Of the seven or so refineries, Bob's crew would target the Vega Concordia. (Coincidently, John B. had been assigned to target the same Vega Concordia refinery in his mission to Ploesti.)

Over the Adriatic, the course advanced beneath them as gunners test-fired their fifties. A rattling of spent casings echoed as Bob returned to the nose. The route took them to a foreign coastline and farther, over majestic mountains. As they reached enemy territory, radio silence was mandated. Talking on the interphone was minimal. Nerves tightened.

At altitude, the air temperature dipped to minus thirty. Bob adjusted his headset as he pulled the strap to tighten his mask. He checked lines to the oxygen canister, the interphone, and his heat source. As navigator, he had to move easily between the nose and the flight deck. That also required unplugging and finding outlets to re-plug at least three devices at any one time. Keeping his electric suit plugged in was not always an option. But anticipation of the battle ahead, compounded by a rush of adrenaline, suppressed any concerns of warmth as they moved closer to target.

Looking at maps, calculating speed and heading, wind drift and dead reckoning, Bob was constantly reconfirming position. *But as the winding Danube River appeared beneath our wing, I came to the conclusion that someone had a very big imagination to call a muddy brown river the "blue" Danube.* But his attention would soon return to the mission as *Screamin' Demon* closed in on Ploesti.

The ship carried nine 500-pound bombs shackled in racks on either side of her belly. Through the center, linking the flight deck to the waist section of the ship, was a twelve-inch-wide catwalk hung by vertical steel girders. Bombardier Parsons would inch his way across the skywalk to arm each bomb by inserting a long wire to the fuse, readying the explosives.

At Câmpina, Bob would alert his pilot of the turn. Before reaching the target, Bob grabbed his helmet and threw on his *flak suit, an apron of steel links.* But not before heading across the catwalk to motion the crew to do the same. Flashing a *thumbs-up* to each gunner, he confirmed each one's readiness. Then Bob moved upstairs.

As we approached the target, we saw all things that signify a tough target. Friendly and enemy fighters were dogfighting. And up ahead, flak covered a wide area around the oil refineries. It was the heaviest I had ever seen. Flying straight and level, formation tightened into a fierce bombing front. Due to the closeness of the wings, no evasive maneuvers were possible. Advancing, *we moved closer to the sound of exploding flak.* No doubt there was tension in the cockpit. *Jack's gaze remained ahead as he pressed his throat mike and said, "Pilot to crew: Assume battle positions." We knew that in a matter of minutes we would be right in the middle of those black mushrooms of exploding flak.* Intensity increased.

The enemy had as many big guns protecting Ploesti, a town of 100,000, as they had in Berlin. And they were shooting to kill. German strategy set up a cube of blasting flak that the entire flight of bombers would fly right into. The enemy's cutting-edge anti-aircraft sensors tracked the bombers' exact altitude. Avoidance was not possible. *At eye level the flak, bursting black puffs of deadly shrapnel, was so thick that you were flying into a total black cloud with flashing all around you. You'd feel the plane lurch forward and if it was close enough, you'd get clobbered with metal pieces.* Shrapnel penetrated the thin aluminum skin of the fuselage. Chaos fronted the course. Waist gunner *Moe Bayer called out, "I'm hit!"* A jagged piece of metal shard ripped through his pants, gouging his thigh. From New Jersey and tough as nails, Bayer held firm his post. There was nothing anyone could do for him in the moment.

The crew of *Screamin' Demon* was flying 160 mph at 24,000 feet over the Vega Concordia Refinery when the pilot handed the controls to the bombardier. *With the target framed in the crosshairs, Parsons toggled the switch and said, "Bombs away!"* Nearly five thousand pounds of demolitions dropped. The crew could feel the surge of the plane following the release of her heavy load. It *was 1030*.

Turning from the target, Chinn let out his customary phrase. "Let's get the hell out of here!" Jack took back the controls and dropped the nose of the bomber to gain speed in a rallying turn from target. Bob called out the heading home. The seasoned crew would recognize the enemy had calculated for this run-for-home maneuver. Enemy anti-aircraft settings were adjusted to compensate for the increased speed and altitude change. Another hit was followed by the smell of burnt phosphorus, confirmation that the Germans had made renewed calculations with alarming precision.

Hours earlier, German radar had picked up signal tracking of a great number of American *heavies* headed easterly over the Yugoslavic mountain range. Unsure of their destination, Ploesti and Bucharest would be put on high alert. Romanian and Luftwaffe pilots were given orders to stand ready.

Lieutenant Erich Gehring would pilot his *Messer*, an Me 109. Archives indicated that he "had claimed at least two prior kills," or victories, of Allied aircraft. No doubt he was cocky and hungry for more. And he would have been ready to take on the American bombers.

According to his dossier, German-born Gehring was Bob's age. Before the war, he lived in "Munich with his parents in a multi-residential housing complex." In technical school, he studied mechanics and apprenticed at an aircraft manufacturer near his hometown. Scarcely eighteen, the military recruited him in the summer of 1941. With an "aeronautical proficiency," the Luftwaffe decided he would be best suited flying airplanes.

On January 31, 1943, he earned his commission as a German officer, a fighter pilot. He was assigned to Jagdgeschwader 53, or JG 53. One of the oldest fighter units, it was best known as *Pik As*, or Ace of Spades. His first assignment was coastal patrol over the Bay of Biscay, coinciding with John B.'s flights over the same waters. One can only wonder if they crossed paths. Later, Gehring's tour would move to missions over southern Italy.

In January 1944, he was transferred to a base at Cesena in northern Italy. By that time, he had logged over eighty combat missions. While the number was medal worthy, it didn't come without reprimands for hard landings and damaged gear. Early on, he was jailed for one such offense. But by March, he was awarded the Iron Cross first class.

In May, he would be up for promotion. Consistent with a performance evaluation, Gehring was a quick learner with command of his aircraft. A pilot with ambition, he had an honest character; respected by his peers, he was also recognized by authority; and his feet were solid in the ideology of the National Socialist Party. The Reichsadler, the official seal of the Third Reich, glittered on his dossier. Headquarters at Bologna didn't blink at the promotion. With his Italian tour of duty ended, transfer papers to Romania were signed. Late on May 12, 1944, Lieutenant Gehring took off from Cesena, just missing Bob's mission to the city hours later.

"Assigned to Popesti aerodrome," Gehring took great care of his *Messer.* He would have scavenged fuel and sandpaper to remove blackened streaks spit from the engine as he polished the aluminum skin to a mirror finish. The result, he surely believed, increased speed just enough. When it was time for a photograph, he would stand at the nose of his Me 109, proud as a papa of his baby.

Each morning, he would await the Allied aggressors, including the US bombers and fighter planes of the Fifteenth Air Force.

Then, on May 31, the siren sounded. German tracking still had not pinpointed the destination of the incoming American heavies. But at 0905, defenses would engage. Lieutenant Gehring certainly ran to the flight line and jumped up on the wing of his fighter before hurdling into the cockpit. Not testing fate, he likely secured his talisman to the side of the instrument panel. After going over his checklist, he would have taxied to takeoff. Initially he would circle over the French-inspired architecture of Bucharest until word came over his radio. He would then bank northward to Ploesti.

Screamin' Demon had just cleared the black smoke when she initiated a wide bank, rallying southwest of the target. *From all appearances we were through the flak when big white puffs appeared and WHAM! WHAM! WHAM! We were hit three times. One of the hits was on the left wing between engines one and two, knocking out and setting fire to the number one engine. Copilot Martin turned on the automatic fire extinguisher to the number one engine. Another burst struck just inboard of the number three engine, damaging radio equipment. The jolt threw radio operator Bell across the cabin. The same hit severed some oxygen and fuel lines.* "Fed by the high-octane fuel, the broken oxygen line created a welder's torch of fire." *In an instant, the rear part of the flight deck was a mass of flames. Fuel was leaking out of the gasoline control valves. I grabbed a fire extinguisher to battle the inferno on the flight deck. The third hit set fire to the bomb bay, right at the end of the radio deck.*

With smoke rising to his feet, Harry jumped down from the top turret. He would write, "Jack got on the intercom and ordered, "Turn off the gas . . ." but the rest of the message was lost." With smoke obscuring his view, Harry located the four red valves and complied with his pilot's demand. He grabbed another extinguisher to fight the flames roaring over the bomb bay. His battle readied the bomb bay for a bail out, but in doing so the fire damaged his parachute.

With the firestorm blazing through the fuselage, gunners Chinn, Tatum, and Bayer were busy shooting their *fifties* to "ward off fifteen to twenty" incoming attacking fighters who were trying to finish off the wounded plane. The action intensified as Bob said *a group of six German pursuit planes swarmed our bomber. Seconds before colliding with the B-24, the fighters split, making a wide, sweeping turn while gaining speed. They circled around. Three came in at one o'clock and the other three attacked from the rear.* After taunting the burning warbird, the fighters were lost in the distance, likely believing the ship was already doomed.

Bayer got on his mike. "Jerry coming back at three o'clock high!" The Me 109 was closing in fast. Ignoring the serious wound to his left thigh, Bayer continued shooting.

The German pilot, Lieutenant Gehring, was at the controls. Doubtlessly mindful of the bomber's fuel tank in the wings, he positioned his Messer to the starboard side. His twin machine guns would deliver a stream of bullets to the right wing before strafing that side of *Screamin' Demon.* A tinny sound peppered that side as slugs spit through the bomber. Closing in, the German pilot would have pulled the stick back, gaining just enough altitude to avoid a collision as he zoomed over *Demon*'s top turret. Surely knowing a lethal punch had been thrown, Gehring would bank away out of sight, claiming a victory over the warbird.

Demon's cockpit filled with smoke. Muscling power over the ship, Jack remained at the helm. He was "hand-working the trim controls" when he ordered the crew to bail. The alarm blared. Bell would confirm the destruction of radio equipment to ensure no recovery could be salvaged by the Axis. *Bombardier Parsons and nose gunner Townsend had come out of the nose through the passageway under the flight deck ready for a bail out.* Harry pulled the hatch lever to the bomb bay, but the doors jammed. With one foot on the radio deck, he repeatedly kicked his other foot "to actuate the hydraulic cylinder" until it opened the door.

Bob handed chutes to Harry and copilot Bill Martin. With his hand on Harry's shoulder and a shove, he drilled, *"Get out of here, go! Now! GO!" Townsend, Parsons, Martin, and Harris bailed through the bomb bay, while gunners Tatum, Chinn, and Bell, who assisted the wounded Bayer, bailed out the camera hatch in the waist.*

Bob looked back and saw that Jack was still at the controls. As soon as Jack started to leave the cockpit, the ship began to dive, so he went back to right it. Jack was still hands-on powering the controls to keep the plane level when Bob pleaded, *"JACK! GET OUT OF HERE, GO!" Jack motioned me as if to say, "Right behind you!"*

Bob knew they were on the edge. *This ship is going to blow! I had seen too many planes explode before me.* He moved toward the bomb bay. *No chute!* Bob looked around. The flak concussions had thrown items, not tied down, out of place. Any hope of finding an extra chute was lost as he scanned the walls of the fuselage. As luck would have it, a spare chute had fallen to the corner. But with the ship spiraling, centrifugal force would pull him away. With an unsteady gait, Bob grabbed what he could to move toward the parachute. Reaching for a loose strap, he wasted no time hooking into the chute.

With eight of the crew confirmed out, he made a last plea to his best friend. *"C'mon, Jack!"* Moving toward the catwalk, loosened tools launched overhead as spent shell casings were thrown about and ammunition tumbled from overturned boxes. Smoke and dust clouded his view as the tail end of the ship rose. Losing his balance, Bob fell back again. At that altitude without oxygen, he fought to maintain focus.

TWENTY-TWO

And Then the Letters Stopped...

KNOCKING HIMSELF OUT was exactly what Polley had asked Bob not to do. Hidden between the lines, it seemed he was flying every day. His positive spin on the military made it difficult to know what his life was really like.

May 31, 1944, was her college graduation at the University of Illinois. Bob would have been sitting with her, but for the war. Entering adulthood, Polley would be embarking on her first real job. With a degree in sociology, she had taken a public health position at the state capital. And she had a prince of a boyfriend that she would marry when this mad war was over. Her life was set.

Bob was a dream about writing. As Polley recalled, he wrote almost every day. But then his letters stopped arriving in the mailbox. A last letter touted being Wing navigator. Just like John B. And while she followed the Fifteenth Air Force's course in newspapers, at the time, D-Day headlined the warfront. With Normandy plastered all over the news, it was difficult finding information on Bob's group. Although it gave her pause, Polley figured he was busy.

Weeks passed.

As she recalled, Polley's mother called her in Springfield. Not unusual, Polley jumped into conversation when her mother interrupted her. Bob's mother had called. Her premonition. A telegram. Bob was missing. Her mother choked when she said, *It was the same telegram.* Mrs. White would be reliving the same cruel moment when she first learned John B. went missing. And now Essie was facing the same words.

With the news, Polley was no longer steadied in a planned orbit. *Missing? I was knocked off-kilter.* Polley's world had stopped while her head was still spinning. With Bob lost, she was free-falling, perhaps even unable to breathe. First it was John B. And now Bob.

Hoping for good news, the coming weeks would no doubt be difficult.

Time moved on. It had been a month since Bob's plane was reported missing. As Bob's sister recalled, Mrs. Cress found it difficult to release the heartbreak of Bob's last moment. Eventually, she ventured into town where running errands meant a last stop at the post office. Thumbing through mail she spotted an official-looking letter. It was from General Twining from the Fifteenth Air Force Headquarters in Bari, Italy.

According to the general's letter, "observers on other planes counted eight parachutes." There were ten on board. Intel had "no knowledge of the number or the identity of the survivors as they came down in enemy territory." He acknowledged news would likely be long in coming. And while his letter touted all the confidence in Bob as a navigator, he offered his deepest sympathy in the days of anxiety ahead.

Mrs. Cress again would call Polley's mother, who then relayed the news. At the same time, Polley was getting a taste of reality from another source. The letters she had written to Bob were returned unopened. Undeliverable. *That rude stamp,* Return to Sender, *was scratched all over the envelope.* Hurtful, it was the postmaster's statement that echoed Bob was still missing.

Bob's mother made inquiries to anyone she could think of. She reached out to family members of the crew. No one had anything to add. After making several inquiries to the governor, Illinois senators, the Red Cross, and Air Force officials, she received a response from Washington, DC.

Again, Polley's mother called Polley with the news from Mrs. Cress. Two months in, other than noting "your son's ship sustained damage from enemy anti-aircraft fire," the news was no different. All reduced to "eight parachutes." With ten men on board, it was John B. all over again. And now Bob was still missing.

By August, Mrs. Cress wrote to Polley in Springfield. Still no word about Bob, but families from five of his crew had recently received telegrams of their survival, although they were imprisoned. Her letter went on to say they were hit "near the Ploesti oil wells—heavy anti-aircraft. As soon as they were hit, they dropped out of formation—circled several times and fell. All reports said Jack had perfect control." The letter went on to describe that "the American Red Cross had a list of POWs in German prison camps but as yet none for Roumania." Mrs. Cress closed her letter with, "The War Department continues to say eight chutes. We hope they didn't count correctly."

Polley tried to focus on good thoughts. Bob would want that. Chicago. A long walk at the water's edge of Lake Michigan. Together, they looked at its vastness, where their future rose beyond dark waves. Love. Drowning and then coming up for air. It's frightening to think of the things you love. Of those who make you happy. And in a moment, all is gone. *Missing.*

A bit lonely, Polley always found comfort in home. By summer's end, her parents' anniversary was an excuse for celebration. High on the third floor of the family home, she slept on the sleeping porch. It was a corner room with screens hung from ceiling to waist on two walls that opened onto the garden below. There, she could breathe. The wind breezed just enough to counter the August heat.

Mourning doves kept her awake with their *coo-OOO-woo-woo-woo.* She remembered what her mother said, *"Talk about it, think of it, and keep hope alive. But move on."* Polley tried.

Drawn to the window, she would look over the dark landscape. A block away, blackened trees hovered all borders of Oak Grove Cemetery. Hope Cemetery. A nighthawk passed in the distance. The sound of critters beckoned as old souls tarried. Polley wasn't alone.

She moved to get a better look; the moon emerged from behind silhouetted trees draped in the shadows of thick summer air. Often mentioned in Bob's letters, the moon had been a source of conversation between the two. The orb was waning, but its expression sharpened. Its craters and valleys somehow comforted her. It seemed to smile back. Polley could *hear* Bob. *Don't lose hope. Don't you dare give up hope for a minute.* She believed he was somewhere under that moon—and he would come back.

TWENTY-THREE

The Same Blue Gaze

FLYING AT FOUR MILES HIGH, freezing temperatures, deadly flak strikes, fighting fires on board, and enemy fighters shooting to kill, it was fearsome. And now to jump? There was no time to think. In his spiraling Liberator, Bob got up and fought to reach the catwalk above the bomb bay to his bail-out platform. Looking down through the open belly, the wind was fierce as the earth drew closer. Before leaning into the slipstream of the bomber, Bob prayed for Jack, and life itself. As he jumped headfirst, he hurdled the window between life and death. Beyond the relative safety of his ship, a fall into the unknown.

Hurled like a rocket, Bob would be free-falling at 120 mph.

At altitude, anoxia, the lack of oxygen to his body, had taken over. *Falling through space was the most peaceful feeling I had ever experienced.* As he descended, the fear of *what next* crossed his mind. With little or no basic airborne instruction, he had never been to jump school or paratrooper training. This was his first time jumping from an airplane. *I had seen dramatic play-acting from movies, land downwind and roll,* but this was not Hollywood. *Even if this parachute fails to open, I thought, I'm no worse off than in a burning plane.*

Coming down from altitude at about 8,000 feet, I said a short prayer before pulling the ripcord. Twenty-four feet of chute was forced from his parachute pack. A tremendous jolt followed. Despite the terrific jarring, *it was a beautiful sight to see the silk shoot up above me [and] blossoming into a huge canopy.*

And then, it became serenely quiet.

Dangling from the chute, *I looked around and could see our plane making a slow downward spiral while losing altitude.* As if putting off the inevitable, the ship's course followed an unusually "wide spiral to the left at about a 30-degree dive." With engines dead, her props turned in a ghostlike defiance. She nosed down under control as black smoke and flames billowed rearward from her top turret and the flight deck. The crew's prized machine, now broken, was plummeting toward earth. *I worried. Did Jack get out?*

When our plane was about 800 feet above the ground, she blew up. Parts were thrown slipshod. It was emotional. *Demon* had carried Bob and his crew from home to war. And now she was gone. *Tears came to my eyes as I saw our plane explode because she had been the pride and joy of our crew since last February and had seen us through some very trying experiences.* But now, only metal crumbs scattered across a rolling hillside offered a trace of what she had once been.

I didn't have time to pull a mourning act as I could see a small dot rapidly approaching. As it became larger, I realized it was an enemy fighter. A German Me 109, the same one that had relentlessly battered *Screamin' Demon*. The fighter had surely come to defeat any remaining crewmembers. *He's going to strafe me. Rumors had spread that Germans cruelly used chutes of falling airmen as target practice.*

There was no reason to believe this would be different. With the fighter steering directly into his path, Bob was powerless to make any defensive move. Surely an easy score for the advancing German pilot, Bob prepared for a pivotal duel between mismatched rivals. With nothing to lose, he turned to face his oncoming combatant. His crystal-blue eyes aimed at the windshield through to the pilot's same blue gaze.

The enemy pilot, Lieutenant Erich Gehring, steered his fighter toward the airman helplessly dangling in the breeze. In the instant before reaching Bob's position, the fighter *ducked under* him. As Bob looked down, Erich looked up. Through the clear canopy of the fighter plane, *the pilot saluted me as he came underneath.* Bob's eyes widened. No longer combatants. Now officer to officer. *Was that a smile on the pilot's face?* Whatever it was, Bob survived.

The wind from the fighter whirled the chute nearly out of control before Bob continued his plunge toward earth. In those vanishing seconds, Bob reflected on the airman, grateful for the pilot's momentary act of humanity.

With the German fighter gone, Bob's troubles didn't end there.

I began looking over the territory beneath me for a hiding place. He was already thinking which direction his bolt for freedom would be. His chute drifted toward a village, definitely not his first choice. In the distance stood several villagers pointing at him. There would be no way to conceal his landing.

The last 300 feet raced up all too rapidly. It seemed like a mighty force hoisted the ground up to me while jamming my body into the earth. I went down straight on my feet first, like a standing jump. I hurt the devil out of my back and knocked the wind right out of me. My parachute was dragging me across the field until I was able to pull it in. Pain shot up my spine, surely I'd broken my back. But as he wiggled his fingers, he voiced a relieved *I made it.* Still struggling from the fierce impact, Bob said another short prayer. His leg was hurt badly but he dismissed the pain. His heart pounded wildly. Slowing his breath, he marshaled orders to himself. *Calm down. Get hold of yourself.*

Bob's instincts kicked in. Looking around, he assessed escape options while bundling his chute. *Walk to Italy? Find the underground?* He was hundreds of miles behind enemy lines. No equipment or friends. *Slim chance but what are my choices?* Then voices became louder. He looked around. There was no place to hide.

People were running toward me from two directions, cutting off my escape. They were calling "Comrade, comrade." About to make a run for it, I saw a home guard down on one knee aiming a rifle in back of me and a peasant with a pitchfork trying to cut off my escape from the front. Surrounded by villagers, I said, "Americanski." The people laughed and one fellow said, "Nix Americanski! Americano!"

Bob had landed near the village of Slobozia, Moară a name whose English translation means Freedom Mill. Certainly, had he known this, he would have conjured the underground.

I did everything to make friends with them by smiling, shaking hands, and giving the small boys a hair tousling. With the exception of this peasant with the pitchfork, everyone seemed over-friendly. I thought I must be in the underground. They like Americans. A young girl came over and looked at my silver wings. I wore a miniature pin on each collar and a larger one on my chest. Believing I had a chance to get to the underground, I gave her my smaller prop and wings pin.

The girl took me by the arm and started to escort me to her house when some other fellow grabbed my other arm and claimed me. About three others tried to claim me and quite an argument started. I later found out any Romanian civilian that captured an American airman would get an acre of land. The windfall meant great wealth to a peasant. *While they were arguing, an Fw 190 came flying low overhead. I jumped on top of my parachute to camouflage it because I had an optimistic hope that these peasants might help me escape. Some of them helped me to camouflage my equipment and my hopes rose.*

Bob was marched forward where, up ahead, another crowd had gathered. A light head of hair peeked above the others. *Harry! I was damned glad to see my engineer and gave him the most sincere handshake I have ever given.* The two were taken to a village post, *a new little jail with three cells, one pretty big with bars.* As the day progressed, four airmen were brought in. Now they were six. But where was Jack? And the three gunners?

Although under local Romanian control with unstructured rights, they didn't feel like prisoners subject to enemy jurisdiction. But with no common language, the guard urged the airmen by the point of his rifle to the front porch as if creating a sideshow featuring the aviators. Villagers paraded by the new celebrities. Smiling, Bob would *wink at the girls* who came to get a closer look at the handsome Americans who before had only been seen at the cinema.

Each government facility had a *great big photograph of King Michael,* the twenty-year-old monarch of Romania. Although he lost all authority when the Germans occupied Romania, his people loved him. *The villagers pointed to the king's picture and then back to me.* Bob wondered why they were pointing. Getting a closer look at the portrait, he noticed *we parted our dark hair the same.* Their expression, light eyes, and ears appeared similar. *Wonder how tall he is?* Bob was taken aback by the similarities. German, or perhaps English roots, must have crossed somewhere along genealogical lines.

An English-speaking girl of about 15 or 16 was brought in to talk to us. A refugee from Bucharest, she was very shy, and I did my best to put her at ease. When asked, I told her I was from Chicago. That was a big mistake because she had read about Chicago gangsters and Al Capone. I assured her that I was not a gangster but then she asked me, "Why did you bomb Bucharest?" I told her the Bucharest railroad yards were helping the Germans. But Bob had no compelling response when she asked about the bombing of hospitals and schools, accidental targets hit by the Allies. He was in her territory and needed to gain her confidence. She was his only link to escape or get to the underground. But as the guard returned, she abruptly ended the conversation.

I had been burned at my forehead, eyebrows gone, hair singed on top, and it was hot and I was still in my flying suit. Burned and dirty, I got permission to get cleaned up. Stripping down to his underwear, Bob left his clothes on a chair before being taken to another room to wash from a sink basin. When he returned, his pants were gone, as were provisions tucked away in the pockets. *Son of a bitch! I had my escape kit, my dollars, everything in my pants.* And Bob was on parade. Fortunately, his copilot had worn a summer flying suit over his standard uniform and gave Bob his extra pants. Once dressed, Bob became more amicable as groups of peasants, sometimes as many as thirty, were ushered past the airmen. Aside from the thievery of his belongings, Bob was surprised at how nice the villagers were.

For that short time, the men enjoyed an open-door detention. *We believed we must be in the underground as these people were so nice to us. We were celebrities there.*

The mood quickly turned when the rumble of a *motorcycle came to an abrupt stop.* Gone were the smiles of the villagers as the airmen were quickly shoved into the holding cell. Through the window, Bob could see an armed soldier swing his leg over the back of his bike, being careful not to jostle its sidecar. By the looks and condition of his uniform, Bob reasoned he was a low-ranking driver for a German officer. Perhaps he had left his superior at a bar or brothel. Bob whispered, *Fellas, keep your shoulders back—he may be a loose cannon.*

Through the open door, Bob studied the squaddie. He wore

neither clasps nor medals of rank. *A corporal at best*, he thought. Of average height, his leather jodhpurs accentuated hips topped by a belt-line paunch. *Definitely not a typical Aryan look*.

As he entered our cell, the German corporal very arrogantly raised his right arm and came out with a "HEIL HITLER." He stood there sneering, trying to outstare us. He asked if we spoke German. None of us admitted anything, although I could understand most of what he was saying. From an anti-aircraft outfit, he started boasting of knocking down 29 of our planes over Ploesti. The German corporal dropped his gaze to Bob's right collar. *My wings*, he thought. Bob was ordered to step forward. Words from his father came to mind: *A broad stance makes an impression*. Concealing the pain in his back, Bob straightened his spine to maximum height. He had a good three inches on his adversary.

Stepping closer to the navigator, the German spit his demands and threatening directives. Bob knew what he was saying. Face-to-face with his enemy, he allowed him to ramble on with insults and ego. The German was searching for information. The crew. Their Italian base. The mission. Bob gave no indication that he understood anything.

Reaching back to lessons learned, Bob contemplated the correct German words. Inflection. He had to get the delivery right. Project a strong front. He was not going to let the German's tough-guy ruse interfere with his confidence. Not in this moment. When the corporal appeared to be finished, *I looked him in the eye and said in German, "I am an American Air Force officer. You are ONLY a corporal; I will not speak to you—I will only speak to your officers!" The discipline in the German military was such that this took the wind right out of him. He got mad and ran out to his motorcycle before taking off.*

Hardly believing his own bravado, Bob was clueless as to how the soldier would respond. He had never confronted anyone with such indignation, much less an unknown enemy. He was just glad his act had worked. *From that point on we knew we were prisoners not merely of Romania but soon under German authority.* But in the exchange, the villagers no doubt gained a glimpse of America. Bob had held his ground with the German thug.

At about 1500 hours, the enlisted men were put in a horse-drawn cart and the officers . . . in a 1938 Mercedes touring car. Taken to a home-guard garrison in the town of Gaesti, we were made very happy because Bayer, Chinn, Tatum, and another airman were already there. That left only Jack unaccounted for. But for now, they were nine plus one. The other airman was Ed Ulrich, a P-38 pilot from Hollywood, California. In evading capture, he buried his equipment, insignias, and any trace that might identify his rank. The captors likely believed he was a high-ranking asset aboard Bob's ship.

Again, townspeople paraded past the airmen's cell. When old men passed, they expressed hostile doubts of the airmen's purpose.

But by early evening, the guard in charge motioned the townsfolk to leave before pulling Bob aside. There was a lot of hand signaling coupled by a crude Romanian-to-German exchange. Dumbfounded, Bob wasn't sure he got the conversation right. But in turning to Dick and Bill, he believed they had been *invited to the commanding officer's house for dinner.*

Over a meal of wild game and wine, the host, in proper English, described a friendly Romania before the Germans took hold. Having worked for a British oil company, he took kindly to Westerners. *That night we had quite a gay time singing and visiting with the CO and his family.* But as the evening went on, the aviators began to show signs of the day's fatigue. Their hosts wished them well before escorting them back to a holding cell where they were locked in for the night.

ONE JUNE. *After breakfast, the CO marched us all down to the village tavern and we drank a number of wine toasts to our friendship.* Townsfolk stopped to gawk as communications were shared through expressions driven by gestures and hand motions. *We were in this outdoor restaurant toasting with wine and laughingly saying, "When the war is over, we'll be back . . ."* It was an extraordinary exchange with their captors who, it seemed, through loyalty to their homeland, were forced to side with Nazi Germany.

The airmen were later transported *in an old beat-up truck to Targoviste, the same checkpoint as John B.'s mission*, where they spent a second night in captivity.

TWO JUNE. Nine plus one loaded onto *the back of a flatbed truck*. Headed to Bucharest, there would be a detour. The truck driver downshifted as he stopped in the village square. Deep laughter came from an outdoor café marked by colorful umbrellas. Bob turned to see a gaggle of girls and arms toasting wine. Right at that moment his smile would have grown wider. *I know that laugh.*

Lifting a glass, Jack commanded the scene. Surrounded by locals, a half-dozen empty bottles littered the table. Before Germany occupied Romania, the people reveled in their relationship with the Brits. The gathering took them back to a time when the oil fields brought much prosperity and connections to Westerners. Whether Jack's language was understood was of no moment; he was a charming American pilot. Holding his glass high, his gaze met Bob's as if to say *come join us*. Knowing the impossibility of the situation, Bob smirked in his pilot's direction.

But Jack's ride was waiting. With a tug at his arm, Jack pushed his chair back to get up but not before women hovered with hugs as old men patted his back. Escorted to the truck, Jack waved a farewell to his new friends. Bob would ask Jack, *"What the hell stories have you conjured this time?" and he responded, "They thought I was Clark*

Gable." It was no surprise that Jack had courted these girls saying he was looking for talent for his next screenplay.

The crew was complete. In this happy moment, they showered their pilot with victorious slaps. Together again, they were on the road to Bucharest.

TWENTY-FOUR

A Change in Status

ON A POCKMARKED ROAD TO BUCHAREST, the airmen bobbed on the back of an *old flatbed truck* as they moved through nameless villages. With a change in status, they fell under the supervision of another guard, "a German subofficer fancied by his newfound control," wrote Harris. As they approached populated areas, the truck would stop. It was Hitler himself who wanted downed airmen to be surrendered to public fury. The men were paraded as if rabid dogs taken off the streets.

The Romanian sergeant in charge of us would stop at every village and try to incite the villagers as if saying, "These are the Yankee gangsters, the Capones, they bomb our women and children." The taunt fueled a high-pitched babble. The guard would continue, *"They have bombed the hospitals in Bucharest."* The airmen didn't understand the language, but the hostility was clear. Jeers, stones, and spit were hurled toward them. *Or brandishing an American pistol*, the captor's self-importance bolstered his threats. *With the barrel at one airman's head, it was as if he said, "Should I shoot him with his own gun?" Wag-gling the weapon toward others, he added as if [saying], "Should I shoot them all?"* The aviators were characterized as *terror flyers* and war criminals. When the crowd was worked up enough, the squaddie stepped up on the running board of the truck before motioning the driver to the next village where he repeated the performance.

In Bucharest, the guard took us right down to the marshaling yards where we had bombed it out and sure as hell, we had hit a hospital and a school. We had devastated some of the places around the marshaling yards, which was the target. I will tell you that the people down there were mad, they did not like the Americans one bit. It was very fearsome. According to Air Force archives, other POWs mirrored Bob's sentiment in that the local Romanians at the railroad station also "wielded axes, threatened in attitude or tried to kill [them]."

Bob described his change in status. Combat aviator to war *captive; absolutely no freedoms; and hundreds of miles within enemy lines.* Before, as navigator he believed he was a person of importance, honored by his country. A free man. Suddenly, an unlucky moment reduced him to a hated man with no status. As they motored on, the unknown worried Bob the most. *Will we be separated? Will we be killed?*

Bucharest was once known as *Little Paris*. As they entered the city, the influence of French architecture surrounded them—charmed evidence of its Western ties. But the tree-lined boulevards quickly turned to bombed-out railways and crumbling structures. The Allies had done a number on the industrial sites, but stray bombs had hit civilian buildings.

They were taken to a garrison that was architecturally appealing with *crosshatches of a Bavarian villa*. Two stories high, it was a large structure with a grass-green courtyard. Down from a dividing hill, Bob saw a playing field surrounded by a running track. *Wonder if we'll be able to use it?*

Considered the Royal Garrison, *Sublagarul 6 Mihai Viteazul*

(Interim Camp Number Six *Michael the Brave)* became Bob's new home. Marshaled for processing, the prisoners of war were stripped of personal belongings and placed in a holding pen near the main compound to await interrogation. The Germans had strong intelligence but banked on weaknesses. Dossiers had already been compiled; information likely garnered from papers scattered from the wreckage of downed planes.

Bob's waist gunner, Moe Bayer, was called in for interrogation. *It was a rough one.* His flak injury caused him to limp into the Aryan's office. Moe was offered neither a chair nor introductions as the officer began by asking about the crew. *They told Moe to tell them everything they wanted to know or they would send him to Germany. The German emphasized, "You know what they do to Jews up there, Sgt. Bayer." Moe came back to me very scared and asked me what he was supposed to do—Moe said, "They kill Jews in Germany and if they send me there, I won't have a chance." I told him to keep saying, "Moe, name, rank, serial number, that's all you tell them."* Bob fully understood the consequence Moe faced but he believed, right or not, that the Germans would follow the Geneva Convention. Bob added, *"You're an American. They'll keep you here with the rest of us."*

It was time for Bob's interrogation. As he entered the room, a handsome Aryan officer sat at an oversized desk. Behind him *hung a large swastika.* The man exuded confidence and authority. *The officer articulated in proper English, "Now talk to me for a minute."* His accent struck an interesting chord. Bob wondered, *Does everyone here speak English?* He sat at attention as the interrogator flipped through pages inside an ash-colored dossier. Bob responded with *"Robert William Cress, lieutenant, serial number O-703711."* The major offered a dismissive smile.

After a protracted minute, *the major asked, "Your home, you are from the Midwest, are you not?"* Again, Bob responded with name, rank, and serial number. Ignoring the response, the Aryan continued, *"It's not Chicago . . . but somewhere near there." I was intrigued, fascinated, but tried to maintain a stoic presence. Then the German said, "I took my graduate studies in languages at the University of Chicago; lived there for eighteen years. I can pick out dialects, I would guess yours [is] from southern Illinois."* Bob sat quietly while wondering, *Was the girl from the first town a plant?* As the Aryan continued, *he seemed pro-American, even courteous, and named places around Chicago that a foreigner would likely not be aware of. But then his tone shifted. "No need to get into your trivial background. I know you are the navigator."* Bob knew the wings on his collar would be no surprise to an educated adversary. *"I know you are part of the 484th Bomb Group. We found your plane."* Bob questioned the comment. He saw *Demon* blow before impact. Was anything left? *"And we know you operate out of Torretta. We know you arrived in Italy on April 14. And we know May 31 was not your first visit to Ploesti."* Bob thought the interrogator had to be guessing about the prior visit. But still the Chicago connection was curious. *How much other dope do they have on me?* The guy knew things. He was pressing for details about units, the base, the officers, and future plans. Likely intelligence he already had but still he probed.

The major asked, "Why were there eleven on your plane that day?" The German interrogator, likely wanting to enhance his dossier, believed Ed Ulrich, the P-38 pilot who joined Bob's group of captives early on, was an extra passenger on board *Demon*, perhaps a top asset or high-ranking official. *"It will be easier if you talk to me now. Otherwise, you give me no alternative than to turn you over to the Gestapo."*

Stories had spread of excessive cruelty by the Gestapo (Nazi secret police). Wanting to end the examination, Bob said, *"You, as an officer, should understand honor and that my duty as an American airman prevents me from saying more to you than I am permitted."* The major reiterated his demand of the eleventh man. Bob's response was: *"In compliance with the Geneva Convention, Robert William Cress, lieutenant, O-703711."* Frustrated, the German ended the interview. Bob was dismissed.

Never before had he realized such levels of fear. At home, even if considered as fear, it meant a misplaced step off the barn's roof or standing duel with the Guernsey bull. Or at Ellington, holding down a trainer plane while a hurricane ripped through the base. There, he had some control over his fear. Flying into clouds of exploding shrapnel evoked real fear. At 24,000 feet, fear was fighting for one's life. Bailing out of a burning bomber raised fear a notch or two. All control released to fate. On the ground, he faced fear of being torn to shreds by a peasant's pitchfork, shot by a home guard's rifle, or stoned by an angry mob. And fear of not knowing what followed his visit with the major. With no control over the outcome, fear rose at each turn.

With the transition to imprisonment, Bob was registered as prisoner number 485.

A week into captivity, Bob's focus turned to John B. *Captured? Perhaps here just like me. He's gotta be!* Bob would write, *John B.'s experience and mine are exactly similar and I will do my best to see if I can find him in the prison.*

Bob met a pilot who was shot down on April 4. Listening, he waited for a pause before asking about the guys on the first Ploesti raid. The pilot had heard the *Tidal Wave* boys were interned in Brasov, a town about seventy miles north of Ploesti, but that was all he knew.

Bob remained certain he would find John B. He had recalled the headlines published a month after John B. went missing: CAPTAIN JOHN B. WHITE BELIEVED TO BE WAR PRISONER. Now that Bob knew the *Tidal Wave* boys were interned at Brasov, the article made more sense. Romania's King Michael had visited Brasov and, according to the newspaper article, had promised to write to each of the prisoner's families. The news account quoted *one prisoner* asking the king, "Couldn't you *cable* them instead?" Ever since John B. had been overseas, Polley had mentioned to Bob that many of his communications had been by cable. Bob felt in his heart that the "*one prisoner*" mentioned in the story must have been John B. The thought offered hope. In the following weeks, Bob didn't discover any more details on John B. but he never stopped asking.

Settling into prison life, Bob often gazed through the iron bars out the window. When Ulrich joined him, the two bantered fanciful plans of escape. How they'd be featured in *Life* magazine. Harrowing stories of reaching freedom. They'd become celebrities. It was all talk. From the first floor, a slight jump would give the two the initial momentum for the break. Beyond the courtyard was a six-foot-high concrete wall. Scaling it, they would run whatever direction of least resistance. Once out of town, they'd form a new plan. *One of the guys had a coiled hacksaw that when stiffened out, you could saw through the metal bars at the window.* They started sawing.

The Romanian guards *made nightly counts of the 40 to 50 guys in a room. Whenever someone wanted to escape, we all would switch beds so the guards couldn't get an accurate head count—it would confuse the devil out of them.* The guards usually just gave up. One evening after the count, Bob and Ed agreed this was the night. Overhearing their plan, Parsons joined in. With bars sawn off at the base, Bob pushed them out before helping Ed and Dick through the window. Bob was the last out. By the time he turned, the two had already made it over the block wall when all hell broke loose.

There was yelling. *I could hear tapping of hobnail boots on the street and the shrill of whistles.* Searchlights zigzagged a path. Before hearing more, Bob hurdled back through the window, getting help from fellow prisoners. As soon as he fell into the room, the Romanian guard switched the light on. Prisoners surrounded the window, trying to see what was going on. Bob would later learn, in the open field darkened by nightfall, Ed and Dick had fallen into a battery trench of sleeping Germans. A commotion started. Guns flared. The two were put in solitary confinement. As a result of attempted escapes, privileges were taken away.

With the full moon brightening the landscape, out of nowhere the air-raid siren wailed. Bob rushed to the window to see what was going on. That night he wrote in his diary.

TEN JUNE. Air-raid siren at 0805. The raid consisted of P-38s dive-bombing and strafing airfields. We saw a P-38 go down from flak.

In the following days, the air-raid siren awakened the prisoners from sleep. The RAF made nighttime raids, hitting targets not far from the garrison. While flak bursts went off in the sky, distant bombardments were heard. At the camp, shots also flew as Bob's sarcasm slipped out in his journal.

THIRTEEN JUNE. Just after going to bed, the men were awakened by a shot. Germans slept above the prisoners. The guard accidentally shot through the ceiling. It would be tough if one of them was hit.

With conditions not getting any better, a guard singled out twenty American officers. Bob was one of them. They were directed *to the garrison theater to this Romanian production. We were put on back rows; about ten rows in front of us were Romanian officers, then the two front rows were reserved for the German officers. I wondered what in hell was going on? Then we were all called to attention and some high-ranking Germans came up in chauffeur-driven cars and sat in the front.* Bob likened it to an American *USO show*, entertainment aimed at boosting the morale. Similar productions were put on for the Axis forces.

With a backdrop of the Reichsadler, Romanian entertainers took to the stage. *We were in the back clapping to the music and the Germans would turn around and look at us sternly. The Romanian officers got a kick out of it. Then they brought out the sultry star of the night who sang "Lili Marlene." It was quite frankly very emotional for us to hear her sing, particularly since this was a German song. When she finished, we stood up, cattle-whistling and applauding. These entertainers had never seen applause like this, so they were really playing it up to us. That's when the Germans got so mad that they walked out. Afterward, we were punished with room confinement and followed to the toilet with machine guns. That got our attention.*

That was a Sunday. A taste of confined freedom, short-lived.

> *TWENTY-ONE JUNE. Six men escaped the night before and for ten hours the remaining prisoners were subjected to roll calls. Their bookkeeping was very poor, but they finally got the fellows' names. At 1600 hours, a guard took a shot at one of our boys in the courtyard. A riot started and some boys were hit with rifle butts. After quelling the riot, they set up a machine gun to impress us. It impressed us.*
>
> *TWENTY-THREE JUNE. Winnie* blew at 0900. We saw a B-17 blow up in the air and two enemy fighters come down in flames.*

By the end of the month, food was scant and inferior. Prisoners refused to eat in hopes of improvement through striking. But

* "Winnie" or "Wailing Winnie" refers to an air-raid siren announcing the impending arrival of enemy bombers.

nothing changed. Food worsened. Men got sick. Conditions were cramped, made worse with bedbugs. Diphtheria was spreading among the POWs with little treatment offered.

> *TWENTY-EIGHT JUNE. At 0905 the siren blew. The planes came right over us and three of the bombs dropped within a hundred yards from where we were. We had no shelter from the bombs whatsoever and we dove beneath our beds for a very false feeling of security.*
>
> *We began sweating each time a new wave of bombers came over. One group of bombs swished over our heads, and I was almost sure that we had it. Four attack units came over and finally the all clear sounded. We were all pretty well unnerved but were very thankful for the results.*

Circling Bucharest that day, Lieutenant Gehring, the same pilot who had claimed Bob's B-24 yet spared him, would spar with another B-24 Liberator. The German prevailed. And a sixth victory of an Allied plane was added to his score. But at the same time, American fighters swarmed in to return the favor. Gehring's luck would run out. Payback.

Wounded in action, the German pilot would never return to combat skies.

TWENTY-FIVE

Lagarul de Prisoneri #13

A GERMAN PRESENCE BECAME MORE NOTICEABLE, and the Romanian guards were no longer friendly. A small infraction was met with a harsh response.

The number of captives was increasing.

It had been thirty days since Bob's ship went down. Lists of prisoners were reworked. Room assignments were adjusted. Crews would no longer mingle with one another. The enlisted men were singled out, lined up, and prodded by a machine gun through the long corridor before going outside. Craning his neck through the bars of the window, Bob followed a line of men, his friends, as they trudged away from camp. He wondered, *Where are they taking them?* Prisoners were again marched through town parading the consequences of acts against the Third Reich. Americans portrayed as terrorists. Crowds responded with malice. Spit and sticks were hurled. It was a repeat of the trip into town only now they were within arm's reach of angry townspeople. Already showing signs of stress, fear of the unknown intensified.

The officers were also relocated in the same manner. Led to a former girls' school, Bob scanned upward to its two and a half stories. Overlooking its classical Beaux Arts design, he was drawn to the barbed-wire fence surrounding the stone building. Sentry posts were placed on each bend of the yard and manned with a searchlight and machine guns. The tall towers were imposing. And at ground level, iron grates covering windows blocked any thought of liberty. The airmen were ushered through heavily carved doors topped by an ornate pediment. Much care had been taken in building the structure. The wood floors were painstakingly laid in a herringbone pattern. At the top of the walls, crown molding met a lofty ceiling. In the vestibule, railings of scrolled iron flanked a wide marble staircase, grand and beautiful. It was an impressive sight of architecture he hadn't expected. But the illusion stopped there.

Armed enemy soldiers patrolled the corridors at every turn. Lagarul de Prisoneri #13, a stockade for Allied prisoners, was now his home. Weeks, months, or a year was anyone's guess. Assigned to the second floor, some twenty prisoners crowded into a former classroom. Bob worried for the enlisted men of his crew taken to *God knows where* as he reckoned an uncertain future.

> *TWO JULY. Winnie blew at 1000. The air is quite excited with flak and bombs and the droning background of bomber engines. They hit both marshaling yards and an airfield. From the billowing fires it looks like a very good job.*
>
> *THREE JULY. Winnie blew at 0130 and the British are hitting town. They hit marshaling yards, but the flak guns were booming all around us and it wasn't too pleasant.*

Captivity formed Bob's every day. *Being a POW, you had no control. And in a war prison hundreds of miles within enemy lines, all freedoms were lost. We were at the whim of an enemy who carried a machine gun. Still under Romanian control, we worried the Germans might take over and make it even more miserable. That always hung over us.* It was also the waiting. Separated from home. Boredom triggered irritability. Crowded conditions didn't help. Bob tried to keep occupied but reliance on limited resources was challenging. Hard as he tried, he wasn't going to let imprisonment get the better of him.

> *TWENTY-ONE JULY. We were subjected to 2 roll calls today by the Romanian colonel. Two of our boys beat up a Romanian last April in an escape attempt and their court-martial trial was due today. They succeeded in evading the roll call and now the Col. is perturbed as he thinks they escaped.*
>
> *Also, we got the news or "rumor" that an attempt was made on Hitler's life and he was injured.*
>
> *TWENTY-FOUR JULY. Air-raid alarm at 0035. All clear at 0200. The British hit the marshaling yards and there was quite a colorful show of flak, flares, and searchlights.*

Airmen gathered in the basement for meals. Russian prisoners were charged with cooking. Food was basic. If lucky, breakfast was a cup of ersatz tea, a synthetic brew of burnt flavors lukewarm to taste, and hard bread with a slice of raw onion. Dinner chow was a nightly repeat.

One day, Bob was last out of the basement. As he stepped up to the main floor, the guards were making a fuss down the hall. Past the front door, he looked out. And then he did a double take. An American sedan, a deluxe model, was parked at the curb. Bob would have wondered, *Here in Bucharest?* From a cracked door, he could hear a female voice commanding authority in a language he couldn't understand. He could see the Romanian corporal bowing. He heard "*prinţesă.*" Meanwhile, the sentries quickly prodded the prisoners upstairs, pushing them into their rooms. Bob's hopes rose. *Did the guard say princess?* He was bowing. Royalty? Jokingly he thought, *Maybe she'll see I look like the king* but at the same time the guard slammed the door on his back. Not long after, a middle-aged woman entered the airmen's room. She made introductions in perfect English.

She addressed herself as Princess Ecaterina Caradja. Born to aristocracy, her maternal grandfather, Prince Gheorghe Cantacuzino, was Romania's former prime minister and an oilman, having developed much of Ploesti. Before the war, the family was considered the richest and most powerful in the country. While the princess was strongly opposed to Romania's alliance with Nazi Germany, she would have to put up with them in some regard. According to Air Force archives, "she was feared by certain Romanian officials and did the most to help American POWs." According to Schultz in *Angel of Ploesti*, and many POWs themselves, she was "instrumental in keeping the Allied POWs in Roumania" and not shipped to Germany.

Despite having no freedoms, the POWs believed the princess's visit made coping more tolerable. She expressed to the airmen that she was there to ensure they remained under Romanian authority. Her insistence upon compliance with the Geneva Convention opened opportunities for the prisoners. Princess Caradja supplied them with basketballs and instructed the corporal to give the POWs time on the court. At the same time, she delivered books written in English. As noted in the National Archives, "Her efforts did more for their morale than any other one thing." It was at her impetus that many of the POWs spearheaded a variety of activities. Writing supplies came in. A few boys who had been on Broadway put on skits. They played cards, gin rummy, and bridge. Calisthenics began daily. And they played basketball.

To keep prisoners informed, and to quell rumors, a POW

newspaper was created. A few airmen who had worked as editors in civilian life produced the publication. They enlisted help from prisoners who were former journalists, artists, and letterers. Posted daily on the wall for everyone to see, the paper was filled with editorials, illustrations, and updates on sports as well as goings-on in camp.

The same day the newspaper came out, a basketball tournament was held. Rooms recruited their best players for daily games, rivaling one team against another. Headlines boasted HOOP LEAGUE OPENS PLAY! Singled out were winning rooms. On the opener, Bob's top score headlined, "Cress helped put score on the board for Room Twelve to trounce Room Eleven, 38 to 18." There was reason for optimism.

By day's end, Bob was tired. So were the other guys. At lights-out, banter was quieter than normal. Settling into cots, the airmen drifted. Suddenly, *Wailing Winnie* jerked them awake. The business of war had returned. *The first air-raid siren was a warning, meaning planes were headed in our direction. Then the second went off and the bombers had crossed the Adriatic, and it was looking like they were coming our way.* The prisoners hurriedly put on their pants and shoes. Being a nighttime raid, the airmen knew it was the RAF. All they could do was wait.

And then, once they hit the Danube, they had their heading figured out and a third and final siren wailed. Lights were blackened. Soon the rumble of incoming ships would be heard. Prisoners jumped from their cots and ran, skipping steps down a crowded stairway. Reaching the basement, they huddled in place. *I thought if the building collapsed, the wall sink might offer some protection.* Others hid under the heavy tables. Still, no matter what location, being in the basement provided a false sense of security.

The British RAF bombers came over with a vengeance.

Just before midnight on July 27, the British RAF aimed its might on Bucharest at a location very near the prison schoolhouse. *From* *a Pathfinder,*[*] *the Brits dropped a green parachute that hung right over the prison schoolhouse. The other planes used the flare as an aiming point. Screamers were added to the bombs to scare civilians and us. It did. Bombs would explode. Our building shuddered and plaster fell off the ceiling. Briefly, there'd be all quiet before another round of bombs hit.*

We all wondered, Don't those guys know we're in this building?

After that, the ack ack[†] *started, which was terrifying. Anti-aircraft batteries were all around us. Again, you'd hear the bombs come down, the building shudder, plaster falling, etc. We were scared as hell. When it finally ended, we went up and looked out the window to see raging fires in all directions around our building.*

> *TWENTY-EIGHT JULY. Air raid last night at 2300 and I thank God that they didn't come any closer than they did. Many bombs hit so close to our building that it felt like [we'd] actually been hit. We could hear the bombs scream overhead & then the explosion. All clear sounded at 0115 and we came upstairs to see where the bombs hit. We could see 9 raging fires, 4 of which formed a circle around our building & about 200 yards away. Plaster and glass [were] knocked out of our building.*
>
> *0910 Air raid sounded & we went downstairs quite nervously as a result of last night's experience. The 15th AAF hit somewhere close as we could hear the flak and heard the bombers drone. The all clear sounded at 1105.*

After that, every air raid would get us all completely tense and scared—the Brits didn't care where they dropped the bombs because the

---

* Pathfinders were target-marking squadrons in RAF Bomber Command. They were a specially trained elite unit of pilots and navigators who flew ahead of the main bomber force to locate and mark targets with flares and visual indicators.

† "Ack ack" refers to the sound of artillery fire coming from German ground defenses—anti-aircraft gunfire.

Germans had bombed London indiscriminately—it was payback. While the Brits were there to get military targets, they were also there to level the doggone city. This went on night after night and was pretty terrifying.

> *THIRTY-ONE JULY. Air-raid alarm sounded at 1030. Libs came over and hit the marshaling yards. The all clear at 1230.*
>
> *We now have a basketball league with 16 teams according to the rooms. Our team played our second game yesterday & won. I made 16 points in the first game & 10 in the second.*

Air raids were picking up in intensity and regularity. There was plenty of close flak and bombs but none as close as the RAF's mission in the days before. It was a fearsome experience. But with his brothers of the Fifteenth Air Force flying over, they were headed to targets north of Bucharest. Bob was proud knowing their power just might shorten the war. And perhaps end his captivity.

In camp, life went on. While the current political situation was reported across the pages, POW newspaper headlines trumpeted the cage game. Bob's team, Room Twelve, remained undefeated as they headed into basketball finals.

> *THIRTEEN AUGUST. We lost the championship playoff this morning by a score of 34–26. I made 19 points. I also played in the all-star game this afternoon and again our league was beaten.*
>
> *FIFTEEN AUGUST. This evening we had quite a good program put on by the POWs. We had a clever Bob Hope skit, some amateur act, a truth or consequence act, and several numbers by the glee club.*

Attempts to escape picked up. On the evening of the seventeenth, *two fellows escaped but were caught in a rather novel way. They succeeded in getting away from the schoolhouse but as they walked down the street, a prostitute stopped them and started her proposition. The boys understood her gestures, but they didn't respond with the right answers. Suspicious, the prostitute called the gendarmes.* Once caught, they were put in solitary confinement.

Beyond the confines of the camp, the political landscape was changing. Romania, through its sovereign King Michael, was making secret overtures to Western powers for protection in exchange for breaking with Germany. The Allies insisted on an unconditional surrender to the advancing Russian troops. At odds with the king, Romania's Prime Minister Antonescu made it clear he would never capitulate to Soviet powers.

But Nazi control of the Balkans was falling to the Russians. Romanians, fighting on behalf of Germany, were outnumbered and outgunned. Vast numbers were dying at the hands of Russian troops. And the Red Army was knocking at Romania's doorstep.

By August 20, the Soviets broke through Romania's eastern border at Iaşi.

TWENTY-SIX

Romania Capitulates

LONG BEFORE THE WAR, Romania prospered and Bucharest blossomed. Young girls had sought higher education and young men had fashioned careers for bright futures. Her people were hardworking and lived happily under the monarchy. However, when the Germans arrived, things changed. The rising power of Prime Minister Ion Antonescu, a loyal follower of Hitler, had imposed a restricted lifestyle on the Romanian people.

Deprived of any meaningful authority, King Michael detested the forced relationship with his Axis partners. According to an Associated Press report, to annoy the High Command, he "communicated in English" with the German minister. Flaunting Yank indulgences, he openly "smoked Lucky cigarettes." At times, he would "park his American jeep" in front of Luftwaffe headquarters. And he made no secret in visiting Allied prisoners as the Reich watchdogs looked on.

Seeing that countless Romanian soldiers had perished fighting on behalf of the Third Reich, King Michael forged a scheme to break from Germany. Secret communications were exchanged with the

Allies. It was a stealthy gamble. But after weeks of intense preparation, the monarch's plan began to unfold.

TWENTY-THREE AUGUST 1944. An article from the *Chicago Tribune* outlined the plan. King Michael summoned Antonescu to the palace. Once the prime minister was secured in the king's study, palace guards were placed outside the door to prevent the minister's unexpected departure. According to Associated Press correspondent Joseph Morton, King Michael said, "I have a wire from the front and the situation looks disastrous. What are you going to do about it? Are you or are you not going through with the armistice?" Antonescu's response was "Yes . . . but there are some conditions to be met. I want a guarantee from the Allies . . . for us and against the Russians." King Michael replied, "That is so absurd . . . How do you expect the Allies to guarantee us against their own allies?" Hanging on the coattails of Hitler, an emboldened Antonescu dismissed the king's suggestion. Then, the monarch tendered his challenge for the prime minister to "make an armistice with the Allies or resign. At that point, Antonescu's rising temper overcame him. White with rage, he was unable to speak." King Michael anticipated such a response and reached "his foot for a push-button under the carpet to summon his loyal soldiers." With guns drawn, guards strong-armed Antonescu to the palace vault. But not before Antonescu screamed, "You will pay for this; you will all be shot in the morning."

The plan progressed. In anticipation of a contentious meeting, King Michael had set in motion a few distractions. Serving refreshments to Antonescu's bodyguards, so-called "servants slipped pistols from their holsters and pointed them at the guards who immediately surrendered." With Antonescu's security detail detained, one by one, senior members of the Iron Guard were lured to the palace, arrested, and imprisoned on the premises. Meanwhile, "the palace troops took up positions on high buildings overlooking the grounds" and motored tanks to strategic positions. To impair the city's communications, particularly those between German barracks and Axis headquarters, an engineer was readied to cut central telephone lines.

Later that evening at the prescribed time, the king's proclamation was broadcast over national radio. He confirmed an armistice had been entered, ending Romania's relationship with Germany. Enraged, the German command calculated ways to punish the palace loyalists. Correspondent Morton went on to write in his news article, "General Gerstenberg ordered one of the most savage and ruthless German air attacks of all time." Hitler had sanctioned bloody days to follow. By day's light, an avenging hell would descend upon Bucharest.

At the schoolhouse prison, an airman pulled out a radio set hidden in the chimney. According to the Air Force archives, "two officers transferred from another camp had smuggled a radio." Through a crackling transmission, the dials were adjusted until the BBC was heard. The broadcast was interrupted with an alert from Romania. Ears perked up as the prisoners leaned in and heard: "Romania has capitulated."

At 2300 on the night of August 23, I was just going to bed when we heard a commotion outside. I went to the window and saw a lot of people running around on the street. I assumed it was a radio alert, but they were not going into the shelter. Instead, they were surrounding our prison and hollering, "Peace! Peace!" and "You are free! You are free!" to us. Naturally we started cheering. At the same time, a fellow prisoner burst through the door saying, *"Romania quit the war! We are free!"*

A wave of hope swept through the camp. Cheers belted out.

But *we were confused by the sudden news.* Although the doors of the schoolhouse prison had opened, what would await them on the streets? German troops were still in the area. That night, life at Lagarul #13 changed dramatically. *We went to our commanding officer Gunn to see what they were all talking about.* Concerns and uncertainties of freedom were aired. Gunn quieted the outbursts, redirecting focus until he could confirm the situation. *Later that night, a high Rumanian officer with an interpreter read to us that Rumania had broken relations with Germany, that we were no longer prisoners, and that Rumania was now on the "right" side. With the heavy German presence still around, he suggested we better get out of the prison camp as they were very mad about this freedom done unilaterally.*

To escape, the airmen needed weapons, safe passage through the city, and a big idea. With an ample supply of high spirits and determination, the gears were set in motion. Communications and safeguarding the airmen became top priority. Phone lines were out in the schoolhouse. At day's light, two officers would be tasked with finding a Romanian outpost to make contact with the Fifteenth Air Force headquarters. Another two officers would locate the Romanian command and arrange to move the airmen to a safe location outside of the city. Armed with the idea of freedom, the airmen were prepared to make a move at a moment's notice. It would be a sleepless night.

Wedged between Hitler and Stalin, the Americans would face danger at every turn. *The Romanian civilians told us that German snipers were perched on rooftops all around town. Rumors had spread that the Germans were singling out the POWs.* The prisoners were subject to recapture and relocation to camps in Germany. And with the Red Army approaching Bucharest, there was concern the prisoners would be used as Soviet pawns. Could Stalin be trusted? It was rumored that Russia wanted the designs of sophisticated aircraft, perhaps the B-29 Superfortress. What better trading token than an American? Or a prison full of them? And given the turmoil in town, death was not beyond reason.

A decision was made to fight back. To give the airmen any chance, they needed to be armed. After some coaxing, the Romanian corporal opened the gun stockade. Sidearms, some of which had been seized when the prisoners were initially detained, were distributed. A German Luger was handed to Bob. Armed with confidence, he ventured outside. A paperboy was hawking the *Ecoul*, Romania's primary newspaper. Bob picked up a copy. Headlines proclaimed RUMANIA A INCHEIAT ARMISTITIUL CU NATIOUNILE UNITED—PACE SI LIBERTATE (Romania signed the armistice with the United Nations—Peace and Freedom).

The prisoners gathered in the courtyard to commemorate the new alliance—Romania and the Allies. When the flags were raised, tears welled in Bob's eyes as Old Glory climbed. He was proud to be an American. As the men exchanged sentimentalities on the ground, fighter aircraft loomed overhead. With German markings on them, the airmen believed friendly Romanians must have been piloting them. But as the drone of planes increased, prisoners would point to the skies. Closing in fast, one fighter was headed for the schoolhouse. The airmen scattered from the courtyard. Leaping to skip steps upward, they funneled through the doorway before sprinting downstairs to reach the basement.

All hell broke loose—the bombing went on continuously for 48 hours. German malice released a battering assault on Bucharest. Although the primary target was the Royal Palace and the government buildings, the American internment camps were not ignored. The walls reverberated as bombs were dropped. With each hit, the POWs became *even more jittery.* The airmen had not only experienced being shot down over the hottest target in Europe, captured at the enemy's hand, but also suffered through horrific Allied bombings. And now, their newfound freedom was thwarted by Axis bombardments and the potential from Russian aggressors. No real protection was guaranteed them.

If the POWs scattered into the city, repatriation would be further complicated. But the schoolhouse remained a target of a vengeful Luftwaffe. Safety of the airmen depended on finding other refuge. Fighting played out on the roads surrounding the prison block. Romanian peasant troops would retaliate against German soldiers. With the POWs gathered in the basement, Bob *stepped up on the sink to look out an overhead window. Skidding tires ripped around intersections. Street fighting escalated.* A break in the bombing revealed skirmishes on nearby thoroughfares. Machine guns from both sides were rapidly firing away.

They couldn't stay in the schoolhouse for fear of being the target of a German bomb. With barricaded checkpoints, German forces controlled every road out of the city, making it near impossible to flee. The short-term plan proposed pairing up, finding a break in the action, and disappearing in the surrounding area. While on the move, the POWs were reminded to check back at the prison regularly so as not to miss the next status of getting out. *Down from the sink, I grabbed a friend's arm, a navigator from Indiana, Swede Samms, and said, "C'mon, let's go!" We had made a pact of escape between us* before Romania's capitulation. They exited a back door used for deliveries. Outside and sighting clear passage, they tore across the street. Bob motioned Swede down an alley. No words were exchanged. No corner or rooftops were overlooked before moving on.

Flanked by four-story buildings, they heard gunshots echoing through backstreet corridors. The two moved away from the pattering sound. With their backs to the walls, they kept to the side alleys as they sought safe haven. Having crossed a major boulevard, Bob's attention turned to the sky. He described the *shrill of a fighter was descending to earth*. Peering around the corner, he watched as a German Stuka* released a bomb, leaving a path of splintered concrete. The Stuka circled back. Just above the rooftops, the fighter shadowed the street. Battering away, he strafed a path of shells. The dive-bomber rumbled past his position before returning to the skies.

By day, the Axis dominated.

Another siren blew. A Heinkel, a German fighter plane, was in the distance making its way toward them. Civilians were storming a dugout hole under a large building. With no other option, Bob and Swede followed them into the darkness, not knowing for sure whether the choice had been a wise one. The shelter, while rudimentary, provided relative safety but for a direct hit. With a low ceiling, *we crawled through the shelter just like a groundhog in a burrow in the ground. You'd fall over live bodies because it was so dark.* The farther in they went, the darker it became. Bob recognized a two-pitched sound, higher then lower. *"CLICK-click. They were old ladies that had 'clickers' like from Cracker Jack boxes."* But as his eyes adjusted to the darkness, "the clicking was a means of communications between two older women," said Samms.

As the pounding subsided, the two POWs made their way out of the hovel. *Swede and I decided to go near the outskirts of town to see the situation*. But with the barrage continuing, it was difficult to cover much ground. Besides, they didn't want to wander too far lest they lose track of updates coming from the schoolhouse. At dusk, Bob returned to the school's basement. Although planes were heard throughout the night, no hits were scored. The night was long. He took refuge under the same wall sink on the chance it offered enough protection for time to duck and run.

---

* The Stuka was a German dive-bomber and ground-attack aircraft used in WWII.

The airmen awakened on Day Two of their ostensible freedom. The city remained a war zone. A repeat deluge of German bombing returned. Fires broke out. Smoke and dust filtered through the streets. Rumors spread that the king's palace was ravaged; intricately designed structures crumbled; architectural marvels were lost. Reduced to piles of rubble, the city was maniacally ruined by the Nazis.

Romanian ground forces fought to keep the rail and communication lines from German demolition squads who were destroying important assets, including the electrical grid and telephone cables, while retreating from the city. In further retribution, *the Germans poisoned the city's water supply and disrupted utilities. The schoolhouse prison was without drinking water except for a single barrel stored previously in the kitchen*. Water was sparingly doled out.

Hitler would turn the battle into a personal vendetta, ordering nothing less than a barbaric bombardment over Bucharest. His intent was to destroy Romania at its heart. If the Führer was denied the country's resources, no one was to have them.

As the Axis had not honored a peaceful departure, Romania declared war on Germany.

As Day Three dawned, German bombing resumed. But by midday, the skies became quiet. But not for long. Looking overhead, *we saw our American bombers and we were outside cheering.* Their brother heavies of the Fifteenth Air Force *were headed over to hit the German troop concentration north of Bucharest.*

Much earlier that day, an armada of American bombers with fighter escort took off from bases in Italy. As they crossed the Romanian capital, they hit the remaining German aircraft at Otopeni aerodrome. Bob didn't know it at the time, but it was his brothers of the 484th who were leading the raid. The heavies had devastated German communications, administration buildings, enemy barracks, hangars, and runways at the aerodrome just north of Bucharest. By day's end on August 26, the Air Force had evened the score. No longer was the Luftwaffe able to make any strikes. Forced to retreat, German ground troops soon backed out of the city.

Bob could hear the bombardments to the north of town. The welcome sound bred hope. But still, there was the question of *What now?* Happy with the US strike on the German-controlled bases, the Romanian general agreed to evacuate the US airmen to the countryside. With outside communications damaged in the German air strikes, efforts to contact Allied commanders failed. Desperate, American colonel Gunn asked for a plane to fly back to Italy. After consideration, it was agreed. Gunn would have a plane to fly to Fifteenth Air Force Headquarters in Bari, Italy.

Returning to the schoolhouse for the latest advisory, no doubt Bob had a grin across his face. Change was coming. Transport had been arranged to take the POWs out of the city. But still, vast enemy territory and the Adriatic Sea lay between him and freedom.

While Romania's provisional government now sided with the Russian ally, her people remained fearful at the prospect of a Soviet occupation. The country had experienced a brutal dictatorship, not unlike the rule imposed by Stalin. Although the Soviet leader offered assurances Romania would be left to govern itself, doubt lingered.

And the Red Army tromped closer to Bucharest.

TWENTY-SEVEN

A Garrison in the Forest

TWENTY-SEVEN AUGUST 1944. Across from the schoolhouse, the church belfry chimed six bells. All else was quiet. As the POWs awakened, thoughts of returning home would nurture the morning optimism. While transport was expected, no buses were seen. They waited.

By afternoon, city buses and military lorries began arriving at the schoolhouse prison. Nearly four hundred airmen crowded on. (In a separate journey, several hundred enlisted airmen would come from a POW camp near Bucharest's north railroad station.) As the vehicles traveled the tree-lined boulevard, townspeople lined the sidewalks greeting them with cheers. *How different that day's reception was.* As they rolled over roads ravaged by war, Bob kept his gaze to the sky, wary of a lone wolf. His nerves, still frayed, were aware of the potential for the enemy to pack a final punch.

Out of town, a dirt road led to an area hidden deep within an overgrown forest. They arrived at Bragadiru, a garrison southwest of Bucharest. Before, the location had been a training camp for

Romanian officers. But now it was a temporary stockade for the Americans.

Romanian troops that remained at the compound, surely uncertain of their future, surrounded the incoming trucks. In the months prior, they had battled the American *heavies*; perhaps a few encountered one another in the skies. But now Americans stood side by side with former enemies joined at a camp in the woods.

As the American officers arrived, the enlisted men who had been interned at another camp were already there. Bob worked his way through groups of men. Above a sea of heads, he saw a familiar sight—Harry, Bob's flight engineer, stood inches above the others. Bob's gait picked up. Others made their way over. The former crew of ten gathered and they stood just as they had the morning they were shot down, not sharing stories of captivity but joking as they had on long training missions back in Nebraska. Together again, confidence soared.

While the POWs gathered at Bragadiru, the plan was unfolding at Popesti, an airfield southeast of Bucharest. With communication lines out, two Romanian pilots awaited their newly allied passenger to fly him to Air Force headquarters in Italy. Colonel Gunn would have looked guardedly at the plane that offered him passage. With treadless tires, smoking rivets, and leaking oil, there was no way the plane would make it out of Romania. Despite its worn appearance, the Savoia-Marchetti defied gravity as it took to the skies. But before reaching altitude, whether lost nerve, mechanical failure, or ordered to return, "the Romanian pilot made an unexpected turn back [to Popesti]."

As Gunn deplaned, he was greeted by another Romanian pilot. In perfect English, Captain Bâzu Cantacuzino extended an offer to take Gunn to Italy.

"Handsome and dashing," Cantacuzino was Romania's leading ace and the commander of its fighter group. Days prior, he had been flying on behalf of Axis forces. He had thousands of hours in the air and Allied victories to his credit. With royal blood running through his veins, he was cousin to Princess Caradja, who had earlier used her influence to improve conditions for the POWs.

Colonel Gunn followed the pilot to a German fighter aircraft. The plane was fitted with only one seat in the cockpit. "Cantacuzino offered to fly Gunn in the radio compartment of his Me 109." Gunn would ride supine in the waist-to-tail section where the radio equipment had been removed. With final arrangements made, as an added precaution, an American flag was hastily painted on both sides of the plane and a single star on each wing. But before the paint had a chance to dry, Cantacuzino pulled Gunn aside. Word had spread of their trip the following morning. With Germans still operating in the area and with many Romanians in flux, there was no guarantee of secrecy. On the pretext of a practice run, the two men readied the plane for an immediate departure.

Gunn was helped through the eighteen-inch opening of the radio compartment. Feet first, he wormed his way through the tail until he was stretched out. The plate was repositioned, and fasteners were screwed down, securing the colonel inside the fuselage tail section.

At 1720, Cantacuzino turned the plane to the length of the grassy airstrip before throttling up. Gunn likely wrapped his arms around his tucked knees, working his body into a fetal position, affording a balanced weight toward the front of the plane to aid the center of gravity for takeoff. Once at altitude, he would straighten out and fly in a corpse-like position.

As the small fighter approached San Giovanni AFB in Italy, Cantacuzino lowered the landing gear. With wheels down, he made a pass around the field, rocking his wings as a friendly gesture to avoid any ground opposition. Despite seeing guns at readied attention, the pilot approached at deck level before setting the plane down and taxiing to a stop. The German fighter aircraft "was surrounded by a curious throng" of armed American soldiers circling the small plane as the Romanian pilot sat in the cockpit.

"Cantacuzino, obviously enjoying himself, stood up in the cockpit, announced that he had a surprise for them, and called for a screwdriver," according to Air Force archives. Increasing their alert, the Americans would look incredulously at one another before the pilot added, "I have somebody here you'll be pleased to see." As the panel of the radio compartment was removed, Colonel Gunn, likely dizzy from hypoxia, slithered through the opening. Within minutes, he requested to see the commander. Both airmen were immediately transported to headquarters at Bari where "Gunn sat down with Brigadier General Born, Director of Operations for the Fifteenth Air Force, to evolve a rescue plan."

Special Ops worked feverishly through the night. A detailed analysis was reduced to three concerns: the remaining German strength in the area, the intended objective of the advancing Red Army, and a feasible plan to evacuate some 1,200 airmen.

The following morning a plan was presented. By late afternoon, the supreme Allied commander over the Mediterranean Theatre would grant approval. Within twenty-four hours of Gunn's landing, the operations order was completed.

As with the many details requiring immediacy, transport was the key element. Due to logistics, the airmen could only be evacuated by air. No transport troop carriers were immediately available. After analyzing aircraft loads and capabilities, the B-17 Flying Fortress, also referred to as a *Fort*, was deemed best suited for a heavy takeoff from a short, grassy field.

Adapting the B-17 Forts into a troop ship was the next order of business. Ground crews were briefed on converting bombers to accommodate an additional twenty men while mechanics hastily gathered the necessary tools and materials to retrofit the bombers.

Two modified B-17 Forts would be requisitioned for the following morning. Working around the clock, they made the necessary modifications. All nonessential equipment was removed, leaving only gun emplacements and bullet cartridge boxes should enemy resistance be encountered. Bomb racks were replaced with plywood benches. A layered floorboard was secured onto the belly of the bomb bay to avoid a misplaced step.

The carpentry was followed by a good *going-over* of the engines. Spark plugs were replaced, oil reservoirs filled, and tanks topped off. The chief mechanic gave a final *once-over* to ensure the integrity of transporting its returning cargo.

While the two B-17s were being finalized, another thirty-four waited to be retrofitted. It was a frenzied couple of days.

TWENTY-EIGHT

Operation Reunion

TWENTY-NINE AUGUST 1944. According to the Air Force Historical Research Agency archives, *Operation Gunn* was a preparatory phase. It was followed by the prisoner repatriation, the evacuation itself, which was dubbed *Operation Reunion.* The mission required verification that Popesti airfield was, in fact, in friendly Romanian hands. Given a P-51 Mustang to fly, Cantacuzino was charged with confirming a safe military situation. Alongside him flew two experienced American pilots, each in a Mustang. While flying escort to the Romanian, the Mustang pilots were also prepared to take immediate offensive action should he prove to be a double-cross. The flight over went as planned. As Cantacuzino landed at Popesti, the other two circled above. After seeing a flare signaling an *all clear,* "the two P-51s climbed to altitude and flashed a signal to a weather plane halfway over Yugoslavia, which then relayed the *go ahead* to Headquarters in Bari."

Earlier in the day, military trucks were dispatched to Brasov, a town north of Ploesti. Deep in the Carpathian Mountains, the airmen from the *Tidal Wave* raid of August 1, 1943, had been imprisoned at Timisul de Jos, a converted holiday resort. Boarding lorries, they were now headed for freedom.

As the trucks carrying the *Tidal Wave* POWs made their way south, a German convoy was driving north, away from Ploesti. The two groups were headed toward one another. At the sight of the oncoming Germans, the truck carrying the American airmen pulled off the roadway. According to the National Archives, "the trip was harrowing" for the Americans. Concealed by heavy canvas on the back of lorries, the airmen were "prepared to fight for their lives." But the German troops, likely determined to flee the Red Army, continued on without incident.

When the Eighth Air Force *Tidal Wave* POWs arrived at Bragadiru, stories of confinement were shared with their Fifteenth Air Force brothers. While Bob went person-to-person searching for John B., Jack mingled with some of the pilots. When he met an airman from the 93rd Bomb Group, John B.'s group, he went looking for Bob. Jack made introductions of a pilot who flew on *Tidal Wave.* His name was Worthy Long. Extending his hand, Bob immediately broke into interrogation, asking if he knew John B. Long did. Their huts had been next to one another's in England. Long said John B. was a likable guy; back at Hardwick, he had those high-nosed Brits eating out of his hand, even captured the ear of General Devers. When Bob said John B. had gone missing that day, Long described his shot-to-hell story, before adding . . . *and after that turn, some pilot or navigator, he wouldn't have doubted if it was White, started squawking, "Wrong turn."* Course correction had brought them in right where the hottest guns were. After Long's disabled ship dropped next to a German bunker, his crew was picked up and he didn't know anything more about John B.'s ship.

Since capture, Bob had hoped to find John B. in Brasov. Thoughts now turned south of Ploesti. *How far? Who picked him up? Maybe he was in a Bulgarian prison? Or somebody's basement?* Bob thought of the parachutes reported. There was still reason to believe John B. had made it to the underground. *Maybe injured?* Just maybe there was something to hold on to.

The Allied attacks by air allowed an easy Soviet occupation into Romania. According to an Army Air Force press release, "By August 29, the Red Army had crossed into the easternmost city limits of Bucharest driving American-made trucks, jeeps, and tanks, which had played an important role in their victory." The Russians conquered the city without a trace of opposition. As the militia rolled in, throngs of Romanian civilians lined the boulevards to welcome the invaders. But beneath the cheers, apprehension of a future under Soviet occupation percolated. Air Force archives noted, "From some [Romanians], we heard expressions of fear concerning the Russian troops."

Concern remained that the Russians might use the American POWs as pawns. Stalin was unpredictable and wanted more from the Allies. He wanted US intelligence. American ingenuity. And he wanted expansion of territory.

Urgency dictated a successful operation of repatriation, "a quick evacuation arranged by the American and Romanian governments" before Soviet forces took control of the country.

Back at Air Force headquarters in Bari, Italy, something big was in the works. Wings of B-24s were grounded. Fighter groups were put on alert status as were B-17 crews. Airmen were ordered to stand by for an assignment still in the making.

THIRTY-ONE AUGUST. At briefing, the day's mission was outlined: a mass evacuation of POWs, some 1,200 hundred airmen, from Bucharest back to Italy. Three dozen B-17 Flying Fortresses had been prepared for the job. Thwarting any resistance, a hefty escort, some "ninety-four P-38 Lightnings and 158 P-51 Mustangs were dispatched to provide cover." Following a good luck and Godspeed message, the rescue was set in motion.

At daybreak in Romania, some "twenty-seven buses and military lorries" stormed into the forest camp. The rumbling motors must have certainly interrupted Bragadiru's morning stillness, but the men had awakened earlier in anticipation of the day. Airmen piled into vehicles that would take them to a staging area to await departure.

Bob waved off his crew as he boarded the last bus filled to half capacity. The route took him back through the city to pick up stray airmen. With the driver rolling slowly to avoid bombed-out craters, a somber expression on the window would have reflected back to Bob as he faced the train station. Devastation. A crumbling mess, the transportation hub would no longer transport Hitler's crude oil. And it offered no immediate use by the Soviets. But sadly, it also offered no transport for refugees. As the bus motored through the economic center of the city, Bob witnessed unbelievable ruin. Ornately built banks were trashed. Cathedrals were damaged. But in futile attempts to restore the beauty to fallen structures, Romanians busied themselves picking up stones and moving debris.

The bus would stop long enough to board a few airmen before resuming. They entered a roundabout where they circled the *Arcul de Triumf*. The monument had been patterned after the Arc de Triomphe in Paris and luckily escaped severe damage. Constructed of granite, the Triumphal Arch was built to commemorate troops returning from the First World War. Passing the arch, Bob would imagine his own homecoming.

As the road straightened out, his thoughts turned inward. About his future. After months of imprisonment, what would it be like at home? *What about Polley? Did she even know he was alive? Did she still care?* As he put it, *time tended to soften passions. Would she still be there for him; had she found someone else?* He had to shake the thought. For now, his focus would be getting out of this *goddamn* country. Everything else would play out on its own.

Reaching *an airfield south of town*, Bob had arrived at his point of embarkation. Popesti aerodrome was a former enemy fighter field, now staging American airmen. *We hid beneath the canopy of an apple orchard in clusters of twenty airmen at intervals of 150 feet along the length of the airfield.* Bob would have craned his neck searching the western skies for transport planes before looking to the men around him. Their thin bodies were exhausted from the past seven days, compounded by prior months. A year for some.

Beneath a high ceiling of scattered clouds tiny dots emerged, enlarging on approach. First to come over the field were the P-51 Mustangs. *The fighters gave us a terrific buzz job zooming overhead at tree level before circling above to watch for German planes.* It was a thrilling and appreciated show of American airpower. Any indication of fatigue vanished at the appearance of brother airmen from the US Army Air Forces.

With a confirmed friendly status of the field, twelve B-17s escorted by a swarm of fighters came into sight. Their faint hum amplified to a roaring rumble as an American armada of rescue ships circled overhead. Channeled by his university days, Bob conducted cheering chants of freedom: *"USA! USA!"* The mantra led the men to focus on the next phase of the mission—the largest evacuation by air ever undertaken by the US military.

While the repatriation mission was a humanitarian undertaking, the bombers flew a perilous journey, passing German fighter bases along the route. As added insurance, P-51 and P-38 fighters flew escort for penetration and withdrawal, patrolling the skies overhead.

The first group of twelve B-17 Flying Fortresses, *Fort* for short, initiated the sequence. But the airfield could only handle six planes at a time. Bob watched as the first Fort lowered his gear and landed. The ship taxied to the farthest point along the orchard. When it came to a stop, engines idled as propellers remained in motion. Wasting no time, the rescue unit loaded the wounded, some on litters, into the first readied ship. Directly following, a second B-17 rolled to a stop behind the lead ship. With props in constant rotation, additional wounded airmen were loaded. As a third *Fort* rolled to a stop, twenty airmen waited to board. With blades spinning, the hatch was opened. It took no coaxing for the airmen to bolt to the bomber. One at a time, they climbed aboard and within minutes, a count of twenty was confirmed. The pilot released the brake to move forward to his takeoff position.

Meanwhile a fourth B-17 rolled to a stop. Props spinning. Door opened. And the next group of twenty airmen rushed the ship. Count was confirmed and as soon as the access was securely shut, the ship readied for takeoff. A fifth Fort rolled to a stop. Engines remained engaged while another group of twenty advanced the plane. And a sixth Fort mirrored the same routine. All ships pausing only moments to fill the bay with the freed airmen before rolling forward as the last of a half-dozen ships closed the gap for takeoff.

As the lead six took to the skies, the next column of six Forts landed and repeated the same procedure. From landing to loading to takeoff, the process for six of the B-17s "took fifteen minutes." With formation headed back to Italy, some 240 former prisoners of war, packed on twelve B-17 bombers, were finally headed home.

Still waiting his turn, Bob followed the first group of twelve Fortresses as they lifted from the grassy airstrip and climbed into the air. Freedom was just a flight away. Counting the airmen ahead of him, his number placed him on the second round of the next B-17s to land.

True to schedule, a second group of twelve Forts entered the skies over Popesti. Fighter escorts circled above. The first six ships of twelve landed in succession, rolling to a stop with props rotating as clusters of twenty men each dashed from the orchard into the awaiting planes. Shy of fifteen minutes, the six ships rolled forward for takeoff.

Another six Fortresses landed and taxied adjacent to the orchard. As the ships stopped, props spinning, the men bolted to the aircraft.

As Bob entered the fuselage, he went straight to the flight deck. It had been his habit to hover over Jack's shoulder to call out speeds and altitude as the ship lifted. He didn't want to miss anything about this takeoff. With the Fort heavily loaded, the pilot used every bit of distance and flaps as the ship bounced down the grassy terrain to capture the wind. As the taildragger bobbled to gain air, Bob held his breath until liftoff was complete. The shaking and rumbling of the B-17 didn't worry him because he knew the warbird would take him home.

Bob stretched over the pilot's shoulder to get a last glimpse of Romania. Below, divided fields came into view, a colorful display of greens and golds. As he moved his gaze forward, they passed *the last mountain range, and the Adriatic soon came in view.* Bob would have turned to his nineteen buddies, motioning a thumbs-up as all surely responded with smiles.

As the B-17 Fortress made its way over the sea, Bob crawled to the navigation station in the nose section. As he looked out the astrodome, he saw the fighter escort, P-51 Mustangs, cross overhead. *The Tuskegee Airmen* of the 332nd Fighter Group had flown from Italy and back, protecting the bombers throughout Operation Reunion. What a thrill to see the *Red Tails*, nicknamed for the red paint on the tails of their aircraft, bank away, roaring a path to safe haven. In friendly territory, Bob was out of harm's way. Seeing the coast of Italy, unbridled joy consumed him—he was headed home.

While the returning B-17s were landing in Italy, a final group of twelve Forts descended on Popesti aerodrome to repeat the process. It was a perfectly synced orchestra.

As Bob's group landed at the American air base, throngs of fellow airmen were waiting along the tarmac with arms waving and hailing cheers. As the plane rolled to a stop, free men exited the ships, some falling to their knees and kissing the ground.

A jubilant General Twining greeted the returning heroes of the Battle of Ploesti. "Your safe return to my command marks the culmination of an outstanding campaign in the annals of American military history . . . Thank God you're back." All the while, newsreel cameras memorialized the reunion.

By the end of the first day, over 700 former prisoners of war had reached the American base at Italy. In the following days, a repeat of the rescue mission was performed. Over 300 men were repatriated on September 1. The planes were grounded on September 2, perhaps not to show a pattern to enemy eyes. But on September 3 and 4, the Air Force returned for the remaining hundred or so *missing in action*.

By operation's end, some 1,162 airmen had been repatriated.

As the excitement of *Reunion* quieted down, the evacuees moved through a reception of sorts. Once cleared medically, OSS officers conducted a lengthy debriefing. And war correspondents would spend much time gathering information and taking photographs, sending their notes to hometown newspapers hungry for upbeat human-interest stories.

TWENTY-NINE

Reaping the Hill's Harvest

JIM AND ESSIE CRESS HAD JUST FINISHED DINNER. It was 6:15 p.m. on a Friday night. September 1, 1944. According to the *Hillsboro Journal*, Bob's parents "had tuned their radio into a foreign news broadcaster speaking from an Italian air base where former prisoners had just landed from Bucharest." Incredibly, the speaker was interviewing Warren Townsend, Bob's nose gunner. Well aware of his name, Essie had remained in touch with family members of the crew since Bob went missing. His parents continued to listen in hopes some mention would be made of Bob's survival. The news article went on to say, "Never had the [Cress] family received confirmation of their son's capture, demise or escape to the underground from the government or from any of the men's families who went down with him. Numb from anxiety and shock," Bob's parents had lived under such strain of not knowing what the ultimate outcome might be. Although they hoped good news would someday arrive, it was still a tough go grasping the unknown.

Still no definitive information was available.

A few days later in an attempt to divert focus, the Cress family made plans to table summer's harvest with friends and family on the *Hill.* Heads surely turned as a delivery van drove up the winding driveway to the residence before finding a place to park. Jumping out of his truck, the messenger went person to person asking for Mrs. Essie Cress. A cousin pointed over to the back door. Bob's sister let him in. Essie, posed at the sink, was asked to sign for the cablegram. No doubt she froze in fear, but she signed her name. Her husband had skipped up the four steps into the kitchen. He would look into her eyes, seeing his son's same blue gaze. Welling up with worry, she opened the telegram.

> *ALL WELL AND SAFE. PLEASE DON'T WORRY. ROBERT WILLIAM CRESS.*

Essie would have held the message to her heart, nearly collapsing with joy as her husband let out a jubilant *Thank you, God!*

The news quickly spread to Polley, who was ecstatic beyond all dreams. After years of indecision, she would soon reunite with Bob, having finally realized he was her true love.

Bob eventually returned to Torretta Airfield. Time was spent exchanging stories when orders came for the final leg of his journey—transport from Naples back to American soil. On September 12, a thousand or so men boarded the *Athos II*, a German-built cargo steamer that had become the property of the French government. In his twenty-one years, a lifetime of experience had been crowded into eighteen months for a young man repatriated from a war prison. Much of his boyishness had gone. In its place, manhood came at the price of lost friends and battle scars. Bob survived.

Arriving in New York Harbor, the city skyline created a backdrop for their escort—a Navy blimp. Fireboats spraying plumes of water offered a grand welcome salute to the returning airmen. Bob leaned against the handrail gazing toward America's symbol of strength, freedom, and peace—the Statue of Liberty. Brushing a tear from his cheek, he took joy in standing with his crew.

Bob reflected on the course that got him back to US soil. Farewell to celestial navigation over a vastly dark Atlantic, to ancient artifacts of Africa, to a tent city at Torretta Airfield in Italy. A heartfelt farewell to *Screamin' Demon*, which vanished over Ploesti skies, and a mammoth farewell to captivity at Lagarul #13.

With his eyes set to a higher horizon, he thought of Polley. Giddy with joy, he was thrilled to be returning to his parents and his home, *Cress Hill*.

EPILOGUE
Luck and Fate

WHEN JOHN B. WENT MISSING, the Whites were devastated. Months later, Bob went missing over the same target. Two families from the same small community experienced the same overwhelming grief—the loss of a child.

But Bob came home. Being a former prisoner of war, he didn't return to combat. He was assigned to Intelligence, a desk job, for the remainder of the war. It put him in perfect position to continue searching for John B. He set out to find what happened. He asked questions. Followed up on leads. He used whatever resources available to deliver answers to the Whites. But still, he felt it wasn't enough.

His experience would have its scars. Years later, the reality of war still haunted his dreams. An accurate flak strike. Falling out of control. And disappointment of lost friends. Good guys doing their job. Bob was told he was the lucky one. He didn't exactly feel that way. Rather, he carried the loss of those who didn't return. Survivor's guilt.

The burdens of captivity would change anyone. And so would

combat. Seeing friends lost in enemy skies. As life went on, he was good at concealing the toll. Never did he forget what and whom he'd left behind.

Bob returned home to a hero's welcome, more than he felt he deserved. Among his commendations, he was awarded the *Purple Heart* for injuries and the *Distinguished Flying Cross* for gallantry—fighting fires on board a burning ship and enabling precious moments for his entire ten-man crew to safely bail.

And if not for the day he was shot down, May 31, 1944, he might have received a second *Distinguished Flying Cross*. The day before, May 30, 1944, Bob led the Wing to and from Wels, Austria. According to the National Archives, the mission was deemed "so perfect in navigation, the Wels mission pushed the 484th into a first-place standing in the Fifteenth Air Force." As a result, the officers that flew to Wels that day were each awarded the *DFC*. But the day following the Wels mission, Bob went missing in action over Ploesti. One presentation may have been overlooked. A commendation Bob neither knew existed nor would ever see.

Although Germany surrendered in May 1945, the war in Japan didn't end until August. Upon discharge, Bob passed the torch of finding John B. to the military. In subsequent speaking engagements, he whitewashed some of his service experiences—the military had sworn airmen to secrecy for fifty years. Never did he divulge the true burdens of war. Loyal as a soldier, he safeguarded their secrets.

At the close of war, in a promise to his mother, he returned to college and graduated a year and a half later. Perhaps the reason he didn't pursue law school was because of the soaring pace through navigation and combat or his experience in captivity. Or maybe he just wanted to settle down.

During that time, Bob was brought into the White family as a son—perhaps a replacement, of sorts. High expectations were put on him. Or perhaps those expectations were his. Three years to the day that he parachuted from a burning plane, on May 31, 1947, he married Polley. With a checkerboard as life's landscape, he was her knight.

Bob considered himself a survivor, dismissing the hero talk. He believed John B. was the real hero, giving a lifetime of service in those few moments over Ploesti.

Early on, the White family received letters indicating multiple chutes had been seen that fateful day. They believed that *surely, he hid out in the Underground.* Airmen who knew him sent letters of assurances that John B. was hiding out with some guerilla band in the mountains. They banked on those letters. But with time, the not knowing was their burden.

In a military show of pomp and circumstance, a still-missing John B. was awarded the *Distinguished Flying Cross* for his mission over Ploesti. On his behalf, the family accepted the commendation. It was John B.'s second *DFC* award. Years later he was awarded the *Purple Heart.*

With the war still ongoing, the military couldn't enter enemy territory to get answers. His designation remained an "unresolved casualty." As the Allies gained ground, efforts were made to locate other *MIAs* in Eastern Europe.

Luck had seen John B. through multiple daring missions but fate ended the streak.

After surviving the hell of Ploesti and well on his way back to Benghazi, Hillsboro was, quite literally, on the horizon. Having reached quota, his twenty-fifth mission, he was to be rewarded with a trip stateside. John B. only lacked "a few miles of enemy territory and the sea" before earning a ticket home to Hillsboro. But then, two American bombers collided. In a milky haze, his ship had been hit by surprise or vice versa (no one will ever know for sure). One letter indicated his ship was "rammed from the rear." A sudden free fall as no one on his ship had time to hook into a parachute. The "tail section dropped from the clouds" as the nose barreled into the mountainside. No one from John B.'s ship survived. From the other, only three survived.

Two and a half years after he went missing, report of his death was issued. Letters from the War Department called it "an unfortunate consequence of battle" and US Senator Lucas wrote, "John B. made the supreme sacrifice in defense of his country."

And then it hit Polley, *I'll never hear John B.'s voice again, booming with depth as he called my name.* Looking back to her August train ride, when she was reading his letter from *Somewhere in Africa*, John B. was already gone.

In April 1949, the Quartermaster's office followed the crew's course to eastern Europe. Their remains were buried in present-day Serbia, in the tiny hamlet of Crna Trava. The name of the village translates to *black grass.*

Initially buried in a peasant cemetery, John B.'s remains, and that of his crew, were disinterred and reburied in Belgrade, Yugoslavia.

Yet again, the remains were disinterred. The American Graves Registration Service was unable to confirm an individual identification. Only a group ID was possible. There was no DNA tracing then, only a presumption made as to each airman.

Nearly six years after *Tidal Wave*, the remains of eleven men's lives of *Exterminator* were brought back to the States.

A military funeral was held. There's a bevel marker naming the deceased crewmen from both planes at Jefferson Barracks National Cemetery in St. Louis. The Whites later had their own service at Oak Grove Cemetery, a stone's throw from their home in Hillsboro, and placed a large cenotaph in the family plot marking John B.'s life.

We may never know what John B. would have accomplished, but we know he had an indomitable spirit.

How are lives coursed? Luck? Fate? Perhaps divine intervention?

For certain, John B. and Bob responded to the call to serve. They did what they were told to do. Flying in a heavy bomber at *freezing temperatures* while *facing flak, fire, and enemy fighters was pure hell. It was fearsome.* But looking at what those airmen did, it was also courageous. They were tested in ways we can't understand. Love of country was a big deal. And so was family. *The war years were times when the pendulum of life swung wide and rapid. Lives were put on hold.*

As depriving Hitler's fuel source became a top priority, the War Department set its sights on destroying the Ploesti Oil Fields. They used bombers driven by airmen from the Eighth (loaned to the Ninth) and the Fifteenth Air Forces to accomplish the task. Before the war, these young men worked on family farms, in coal mines, and in small towns, helping their families recover from the Depression. But when called, they were dispatched to free nations from Axis aggression.

Unselfishly, John B. and Bob believed their efforts would shorten the war and make the world a better place. But in missions to destroy Ploesti, "2,432 US bomber crewmen were killed, missing or became POWs in Romania." John B. and Bob became statistics.

The War College concluded the first air raid on Ploesti was "one of the bloodiest and most heroic missions of all time." And to think, the Air Force returned. War is a notion born of opposing powers, but mostly it touches individuals.

Lives forever changed.

AFTERWORD

My husband, Beda's, hobby is building experimental airplanes. Currently, he is building his second plane, a 72 percent scale all-carbon replica of a P-51 Mustang, the WWII fighter aircraft that significantly impacted the air war. His first plane was a single engine two-seater—the Alvarez Polliwagen (look it up on Wikipedia—that's his plane pictured). We call her *Miss Polli*.

Regularly, when my parents visited from Atlanta, my father, Bob, (the same B-24 navigator in this story) helped Beda in the garage with the construction of *Miss Polli,* offering suggestions for calculations or hashing out design ideas. Years into the project, while at home in Atlanta, Bob passed away.

Eventually *Miss Polli* was moved to Pompano Beach Airfield. At my request, Beda was to hire a test pilot for the first flight. But when the so-called pilot arrived at the hangar in flip flops, and with the rudder pedals crucial to flight, Beda lost confidence in the other pilot's abilities and canceled the appointment.

Days later, Beda came home after a visit to the airport. He had one of those *Cheshire cat* grins smeared across his face. It didn't take much to recognize that he had flown the plane. Tossing a few expletives, I was steaming mad.

Then he said, "But I've got a story to tell you . . ."

No *story* was getting him off the hook. Still, I listened.

"Testing the plane's lift down the runway, it just felt right, and I took off. Surprised the hell out of me, but I went with it. As I headed east to the Atlantic, the tower got on the radio and said, 'Two-Three-Five Bravo Delta, be advised there's a heavy bomber to your north headed down the coast.' At the moment, I was more concerned with looking ahead and what my flight instruments were doing, but with a glance to my left, I knew it was a B-24."

For me, tears and emotion followed . . . With only two or three airworthy B-24 Liberators on the globe, I was sure my father's spirit was watching over Beda on that first flight.

The next day, with a camera over my shoulder, I headed to Executive Airport. The year before, a couple warbirds with the Collings Foundation had stopped there on tour. As I went up to the operations desk at Banyan Air, I said, "I'd like to see the B-24." The guy looked at me curiously, so I began to explain what a B-24 was. "You know, it's a WWII bomber . . ."

Needing no explanation, the guy said, "I know what a B-24 is . . . but it hasn't been here for a couple weeks. It's up the coast—in Jacksonville." Mind you, Jacksonville is 330 miles north of Fort Lauderdale. As I looked at him incredulously, he added, "But for some reason, it was seen flying in the area yesterday—shouldn't have been, but it was . . ."

What do you think? Coincidence? Perhaps. Beda should not have been flying *Miss Polli* on her maiden flight; the B-24 should not have been flying in the area that day—much less at the same time the small single engine was taking off across the coast. Since Bob had spent so much time in the garage with Beda constructing the experimental aircraft, one can only imagine that Bob would have wanted to see that first flight of Beda's new plane. Seriously, what are the odds of *Miss Polli* in the same airspace as a B-24 Liberator?

As a side note, the next year I took an unforgettable ride in that very same B-24 Liberator—*Witchcraft*.

ACKNOWLEDGMENTS

This project began as a personal story for my cousins—a way to honor the courage and sacrifice of two of their uncles during WWII. But it grew into something larger, thanks to an incredible circle of support.

Peter McGuigan has been the greatest advocate I could have ever hoped for. From the get-go, he recognized this was a story worth telling and took me on as an unpublished author. I am deeply grateful for his faith in the manuscript and for taking a chance on me. And to his team, Joanna Rasheed, Lillabeth Brodersen, and Elizabeth Aaron, heartfelt thanks for their invaluable support navigating the publishing world.

And to Claire Wachtel, I count myself fortunate to have worked with such a masterful editor. Her style was demanding but always smart, pushing me to hone the narrative to its best version—so grateful for her insight and steady expertise. Much appreciation to Juliana Nador, Alison Skrabek, and Sandy Noman for their tireless attention to detail; to Patrick Sullivan for the spot-on jacket design; and to Diane João for her meticulous copyediting. My sincere thanks to all the folks at Union Square and Hachette for bringing to life the words of two navigators whose journeys deserved to be remembered.

John B. and Bob guided the narrative and formed the foundation of this book. But also, details were compiled from many others.

Polley saved hundreds of Bob's letters, his diary written while a POW, newspaper clippings, and scrapbooks. Likewise, she saved scores of letters from John B., her mother's dailies, and other verities. Polley's sister, Anne, saved family letters from John B., journals, and photographs—Cousin Bev graciously loaned those materials to enhance the accuracy of the story. Together with conversations and memories preserved on tape, these resources directed the lion's share of the story.

While personal materials prompted the journey, Beth McCormick, also a daughter of a former Romanian POW, provided the kick-start. She connected me with Dan Melinte, a historian with expertise in WWII aviation archaeology, who led me on Bob's journey in Romania from bail out to prison camp to the pilot who claimed the downing of *Screamin' Demon*. A visit to the Military Archives at Freiburg, Germany, provided records on the German pilot. And a flight on one of the last airworthy B-24 Liberators in the world was unforgettable. Colonel Gunn's son, Bill, shared his father's story while we were in Romania. Harry Harris's son, Harry, shared his father's memoirs. The 484th Bomb Group provided a look into operations at Torretta Airfield in Italy. And a visit with Swede Samms, gentle and kind like so many from his generation and who served as a POW with my father, shared his firsthand experiences.

Eric Neagle, Chicago Kent School of Law, discovered transcripts of John B.'s *radio debates*. A published version of Hugh Roper's diary corroborated mission histories. Russ Longnecker, words preserved in *Ploesti* by Dugan and Stewart, provided insight into John B.'s final mission. With an emotional visit to the Hardwick Airfield in Great Britain, the base also offered a glimpse into military life on the English countryside. The 93rd Bomb Group was an invaluable resource as was Michael Sellers (director) and John Marx who connected me with the Defense POW/MIA Accounting Agency. And fifties television personality Mary Hartline, surprisingly after so many years (and four husbands), saved and shared her memories and scrapbooks on John B.

Discoveries through research were the most rewarding aspect, especially sharing them with friends. Liz listened to new connections and encouraged finishing the first draft. Having known Bob and Polley firsthand, lifelong friends Becky, Kathy, and Johnet provided the support I needed to keep moving ahead. For these women, I'm enormously grateful.

And always available, cousin Nancy kept me focused on the objective, offered feedback and combed through drafts of the story, polishing words on the page—my heartfelt gratitude for her tireless help, loyalty, and brilliance.

My husband, Beda, was always game for another travel adventure having underwritten this entire project but also, being an aviation enthusiast, he explained the workings of flight that helped me immeasurably in writing this story. I couldn't have done it without him. To my cousin Ron, for his interest, expertise, and unwavering guidance, and to my brother, Bob, who enhanced memories of our father while sharing some special anecdotes—much love and appreciation go to these guys.

I never met my mother's brother. But with his military portrait prominently displayed in my grandmother's music room, I always knew who he was. Or thought I did. He was *Uncle John B. who died in the war.* I didn't need advanced explanation. As a young girl, that was enough. I don't remember when I learned of his connection with my father, but again, it seemed I always knew of it. Just like I always knew my father was a POW, albeit a foreign concept. And for whatever reason, at the time, I didn't need to know more.

When I was young, my father told me bedtime stories laced with dive-bombing *Stukas*, daring escapes, German interrogations, and his take on *Oy-Oy-Seven* adventures. He took me for long walks in the park, pointing out star formations and always the moon. Hints of his past? Perhaps.

At the time my father passed away, I didn't deliver his eulogy. I've often wondered why. I like to think time was needed to follow his journey. Their journeys. I understand a lot more now.

SOURCE NOTES

Introduction

xi **Each generation:** Cress, Bob, Living through the WWII years, 1988.

xi **I listened to the theme songs . . . would memorize the lyrics . . . whistle . . . play it on my horn:** Cress, Bob, *Growing up on Cress Hill Farm*, (1988), 1.

xiii **1939 . . . primary trading partner:** *USAF Historical Study—The Ploesti Mission*, AFHRA Reel K1012 (June 1944), 519.

xiii **In modern warfare . . . "essential than oil":** *USAF Historical Study No. 103*; AFHRA Reel K1012 (6/15/44), 509.

xiii **60 percent of Axis crude oil:** *Discussion of Ploesti oil fields as a target*, US Air Force Historical Research Agency (AFHRA) Reel 25087 (4/18/43), 338.

xiii **blueprint for the strategic bombing. . . . priority target:** Truxal, Luke W., *The Failed Bombing Offensive: A Reexamination of the Combined Bomber Offensive in 1943*, University of North Texas (Dec. 2011), 11, 25.

xiv **zero altitude:** *USAF Historical Study No. 103—The Ploesti Mission*, AFHRA Reel K1012 (June 1944), 538.

xiv **"height of fifty to one hundred fifty feet":** 1st Lt. Bert Case Interview with Lt. Gen. Edward J. Timberlake, *Summary of Air Force Experience*, NARA NAID 72114, 342-USAF-49697, (9/26/47).

Part One

Prologue: *Making It Through Hell*

4 **Not one to be:** interview with Anne White French, 1995.

4 ***mixed bag of tricks:*** John B. letter (11/30/42), 1.

4 **Ploesti was pure hell:** "closest thing to Dante's inferno," *USAF Historical Study No. 103—The Ploesti Mission*, National Archives, AFHRA Reel K1012 (June 1944) 613, 563; "Roper made it through hell": 330th BS History—August 1943 Notes (8/2/43), AFHRA Reel B0183, 1846; "at 100 feet you see too damn much . . . it scares the hell out of you": *USAF Historical Study* (8/1/43), AFHRA Reel K1012, 611; all hell over the target: 330th BS History (Aug. 1943), AFHRA Reel B0183, 1848.

4 **"auxiliary fuel tanks":** *USAF Historical Study No. 103*, AFHRA Reel K1012, 563; Dugan and Stewart, *Ploesti* (1962), 65.

4 ***I've had some of:*** John B. letter (1/13/43).

4 **0200 hours:** Dugan and Stewart, *Ploesti*, Random House (1962), 78.

5 **zero altitude:** *USAF Historical Study 103—The Ploesti Mission*, AFHRA Reel K1012 (June 1944), 538.

5 **"shortening the war":** Dugan and Stewart, *Ploesti*, Random House (1962), 36.

5 ***It was a huge risk:*** John B. letter (7/30/43), 1.

5 **"Expected losses":** *Report of Attack on Ploesti*, 9th USAAF, National Archives, AFHRA Reel A6539 (9/20/44), 234.

6 **"group was also":** SECRET HQ Mediterranean Allied AF APO 650, 9th AF, AFHRA A6539 (9/20/43), 235.

6 **some 21,000 pounds of fuel** (3,100 gallons): Dugan and Stewart, *Ploesti*, Random House (1962), 83.

6 **"the first, and possibly suicidal":** Dugan and Stewart, *Ploesti*, Random House (1962), 83.

6 **Hitting the target:** Roper diary (7/19/43).

7 **Olliffe:** Dugan and Stewart, *Ploesti*, Random House (1962), 93.

7 **"combat box"** (footnote): *Combat Box: Bomber Formations*, National Museum of the USAF online (date unknown).

7 **"very muscular man":** Longnecker in Dugan and Stewart, *Ploesti*, Random House (1962), 93.

7 **"his B-24 as if":** Longnecker in Dugan and Stewart, *Ploesti*, Random House (1962), 93.

7 **"recent outbreak":** Dugan and Stewart, *Ploesti*, Random House (1962), 81; Miller, *Masters of the Air*, Simon & Schuster (2006), 188.

7 **three hours out:** Dugan and Stewart, *Ploesti*, Random House (1962), 93.

8 **radio silence:** *USAF Historical Study No. 103—The Ploesti Mission*, AFHRA Reel K1012, 602.

8 **An error:** *93rd BG Tactical memo*, AFHRA Reel B0185 (8/1/43) 229.

8 **"several minutes and tens":** turn by Compton, 376th BG Commander at Targoviste was an error: *USAF Oral History of Genl. Jacob Smart*, AFHRA 1041988, 95 (November, 1978).

8 **turned too soon:** *330th BS History* (Aug. 1943), AFHRA Reel B0183, 1845; *RAF form 441A Sortie* reports for 93rd BG on *Tidal Wave* (8/1/43), American Air Museum online, 21 of 38.

9 **dark haze rising:** Dugan and Stewart, *Ploesti*, Random House (1962), 111.

9 **communications between aircraft:** *USAF Historical Study No. 103—The Ploesti Mission*, AFHRA Reel K1012, 602.

9 **navigator broke . . . silence. "Mistake!":** Miller, *Masters of the Air*, Simon & Schuster (2006), 190; Dugan and Stewart, *Ploesti*, Random House (1962), 107.

9 **"Discovering the mistake":** *409th Historic Narrative*, AFHRA B0183 (Aug 1943), 1862.

9 **as low as fifty feet:** *USAF Historical Study No. 103*, AFHRA Reel K1012, 238; *USAF Experience* video interview of Lt. Gen. Timberlake (9/26/47) (NARA).

9 **"We were going in":** Longnecker in *Ploesti*, Random House (1962), 115.

9 **fast-firing cannons:** Dugan and Stewart, *Ploesti*, Random House (1962), 115.

10 **"an eight-minute road to target":** *RAF form 441A Sortie* reports for 93rd BG on *Tidal Wave* (8/1/43), American Air Museum online, 33 of 38.

10 **"An *eighty-eight* cannon":** Longnecker in *Ploesti*, Random House (1962), 115.

10 **"hole ripped through":** Freeman, *The Ploesti Raid*, 124.

10 **a detonating cable:** Dugan and Stewart, *Ploesti*, Random House (1962), 116.

10 **smashed into a storage tank:** Dugan and Stewart, *Ploesti*, Random House (1962), 118.

10 **"A huge oil tank exploded":** Longnecker in *Ted's Traveling Circus*, 177.

11 **Olliffe . . . dropped his B-24:** Longnecker in *Ploesti*, Random House (1962), 118.

11 **smudge pots:** *USAF Historical Study* (8/1/43), AFHRA Reel K1012, 639.

11 **black smoke:** *93rd Sortie Report of Longnecker*, AFHRA Reel B0185 (8/1/43), 235.

11 **Luftwaffe fighter:** Dugan and Stewart, *Ploesti*, Random House (1962), 71.

12 **outer ring:** Dugan and Stewart, *Ploesti*, Random House (1962), 193.

12 **Libs were passing them:** Dugan and Stewart, *Ploesti*, Random House (1962), 127.

Chapter One: *Hillsboro, Illinois Years Before*

13 **watercourses. . . . rising bluff:** *Montgomery County*, Historical Encyclopedia of Illinois, Chicago, 1918.

13 **an arrowhead:** Bob video (1991); conversations between Bob Cress and Jan Cress Dondi, Hillsboro, IL, and on Cress Hill Farm (summer 1991).

13 **proud:** Cress, Bob, *Growing up on Cress Hill Farm* (1988), C6.

14 **population of 4,435:** *Montgomery County*, Historical Encyclopedia of Illinois, Chicago, 1918.

14 **John White, Sr.:** Lawrence, *A Celebration of the Brown and White Legacy* (2001), 143–171; White family archives.

14 ***Hillsboro's version of:*** conversations between Bob Cress and Jan Cress Dondi, Atlanta (1997).

15 **delegate:** Ada's journal (1940).

15 **homesteaded . . . in 1818:** Hershberger, Beckemeyer, *The Story of Cress Hill Farm* (2017), v.

15 ***The old road. . . . During Abraham Lincoln's:*** Cress, Bob, *Living through the WWII years*, 1988, C4.

16 ***showplace,* using cutting-edge:** Cress, Bob, *Growing up on Cress Hill Farm* (1988), C4; Hershberger, Beckemeyer, *The Story of Cress Hill Farm* (2017), 310.

16 **"best farm-to-market":** Hershberger, Beckemeyer, *The Story of Cress Hill Farm* (2017), 260.

16 ***early prototype for:*** Cress, Bob, *Growing up on Cress Hill Farm* (1988), C7; Hershberger, Beckemeyer, *The Story of Cress Hill Farm* (2017), 310.

16 ***"live from the":*** Cress, Bob, *Living through the WWII years*, 1988.

16 **John B. White, Jr.:** Lawrence, *A Celebration of the Brown and White Legacy* (2001), 175–183; White family archives.

17 **"He imagined a":** White family archives; Interview with Mary Hartline, 2016.

17 **"senator one day":** White family archives, sympathy cards, 1943; Interview with Mary Hartline, 2016.

17 **absentee ballot**: John B. letters (4/2/42, 9/12/42).

18 **Growing up on:** Cress, Bob, *Living through the WWII years*, 1988; Bob video (1991).

19 ***Working the tractor:*** Cress, Bob, *Growing up on Cress Hill Farm* (1988), C1-2.

19 ***I was sitting with him:*** *Growing up on Cress Hill Farm* (1988), C1.

19 **"Well, you saw Tom":** Cress, Bob, *Growing up on Cress Hill Farm* (1988), C2.

19 ***That was the end:*** Cress, Bob, *Growing up on Cress Hill Farm* (1988), C2.

19 **Life's lessons were:** conversation between Bob Cress and Jan Cress Dondi, Atlanta (1995).

19 ***blending of breeds:*** Cress, Bob, *Growing up on Cress Hill Farm* (1988), C7. Hershberger, Beckemeyer, James W. Cress, Sr.—*1911 European Trip, Story of Cress Hill Farm*, 364–370.

19 **trip to Europe:** Bob video (1991); Hershberger, Beckemeyer, James W. Cress, Sr.—*1911 European Trip, Story of Cress Hill Farm*, 364–370.

20 **ambassador, Whitelaw Reid:** Independence Day Gala Invitation No. 2937, Photograph, Hershberger, Beckemeyer, James W. Cress, Sr.—*1911 European Trip, Story of Cress Hill Farm*, 366.

20 **Dorchester House:** Hershberger, Beckemeyer, James W. Cress, Sr.—*1911 European Trip, Story of Cress Hill Farm*, 366; also found at https://www.edwardianpromenade.com/holidays/a-fourth-of-july-reception/.

20 **"Amongst these elegant":** conversation between Bob Cress and Jan Cress Dondi, Atlanta (1995).

20 **German military intervention:** London's *The Guardian* (7/3/1911), 7.

20 ***Bob Seymour said:*** Bob video (1995).

20 **Britain Goes to War:** *Chicago Sunday Tribune* (9/3/1939), 1.

20 ***The rest of the day:*** Bob video (1995).

21 **Bob considered what the headlines**: Bob video (1995).

21 ***Just maybe this:*** Bob video (1995).

21 ***boyfriends list:*** Bob video (1995).

21 ***beau-of-the-week:*** Bob video (1995).

21 **adored her oldest brother:** conversation between Polley White Cress and Jan Cress Dondi, Fort Lauderdale, FL (Thanksgiving 2012).

22 **"Mother thought you played well":** Bob video (1995).

22 ***Polley had always kept:*** Bob video (1995).

23 **editorial cartoon:** *Chicago Sunday Tribune* (2/11/40), 1.

23 **"Mrs. White and I watched":** Bob video (1995).

23 **"conference championship":** *Montgomery County News* (February 1940).

23 **exchange . . . debate:** Ada's journal (February 1940); conversation between Bob Cress and Jan Cress Dondi, Atlanta (1995).

24 **Prairie Farmer Radio:** Chicago-Kent School of Law, *Radio Debates 1940* (transcripts), Chicago (Foreword).

24 **"Tonight's program":** Chicago-Kent School of Law, *Radio Debates 1940* (transcripts), Chicago (4/13/40), 10.

24 **"International relations":** Palasz in Chicago-Kent School of Law, *Radio Debates 1940* (transcripts), Chicago (4/13/40), 11.

24 **"Now, the affirmative":** Ibid., 12.

25 **"Since our shores":** Ibid., 13.

25 ***The question now is:*** John B. White, Jr., in Chicago-Kent School of Law, *Radio Debates 1940* (transcripts), Chicago (4/13/40), 15–16.

27 ***No, I'm not playing:*** (tumbling episode) conversation between Polley White Cress and Jan Cress, Atlanta (summer 1973).

27 **She suggested they see others:** Bob video (1995).

28 **"Youth of today":** Bob video (1995); Bob scrapbook; *Award Diplomas*, Montgomery County News, Hillsboro, IL (6/3/40), 1, 6.

28 **work on the farm:** Bob video (1991 & 1995); conversation between Bob Cress and Jan Cress Dondi, Hillsboro (1991).

29 **July Fourth:** conversation between Bob Cress, Polley White Cress, and Jan Cress Dondi, Atlanta (1995).

Chapter Two: *A First Call to Serve*

30 **Denmark, Norway, Belgium:** *The History Place—WWII in Europe* (1996), https://www.historyplace.com/worldwar2/timeline/ww2time.htm.

30 **"certain eventuality":** Owen, David, *British Strategy in the Near Future* (May 1940), https://blog.nationalarchives.gov.uk/vital-words-of-hope-26-may-1940/.

30 ***the Blitz:*** from the Imperial War Museum, https://www.iwm.org.uk/history/the-blitz-around-britain.

31 **Congress enacted the first:** FDR fireside chat, 9/16/40; Bob video (1995) and interview.

31 **Christmas break:** Cress, Bob, *Living through the WWII years*, 1988, B3.

31 **New Year's Eve:** Cress, Bob, *Living through the WWII years*, 1988, B3.

31 **Christmas dance:** Cress, Bob, *Living through the WWII years*, 1988, B2.

31 **lyrics in her ear:** Cress, Bob, *Living through the WWII years*, 1988, B2.

31 **Bob memorialized:** (NYE episode) Cress, Bob, *Living through the WWII years*, 1988, B3–6.

32 ***She seemed so appreciative:*** Cress, Bob, *Living through the WWII years*, 1988, B3.

32 ***I know from personal:*** Cress, Bob, *Living through the WWII years*, 1988, B3.

32 ***I explained I didn't:*** Cress, Bob, *Living through the WWII years*, 1988, B3; Bob's video (1995); conversation between Bob Cress and Jan Cress Dondi, Atlanta (1995).

32 ***I could have resolved:*** Cress, Bob, *Living through the WWII years*, 1988, B3.

32 **Immature at seventeen:** Cress, Bob, *Living through the WWII years*, 1988, B3.

32 ***Dear Bob. . . . What kind:*** Cress, Bob, *Living through the WWII years*, 1988, B5.

33 ***Dizzy dame:*** Cress, Bob, *Living through the WWII years*, 1988, B3.

33 ***For the next week:*** Cress, Bob, *Living through the WWII years*, 1988, B5.

33 ***Dizzy dame:*** Bob's letter (1/22/41); Cress, Bob, *Living through the WWII years*, 1988, B5.

33 ***You referred to me:*** Cress, Bob, *Living through the WWII years*, 1988, B6.

33 ***"Polley used the word":*** Cress, Bob, *Living through the WWII years*, 1988, B6.

33 ***Brrr-rr-rrr. I'll bet they:*** Bob letter (2/17/41).

33 ***Last summer, Allan:*** Cress, Bob, *Living through the WWII years*, 1988, B6.

34 ***I am afraid:*** Bob letter (3/6/41), Cress, Bob, *Living through the WWII years*, 1988, B7.

34 **"Unless the advance":** President Roosevelt, Fireside Chat #17 (5/27/41).

34 **Hillsboro's Main Street:** (John B.'s law practice) Interview Mary Hartline (2018).

35 **Omer Poos:** Lawyer and Judge, US District Court for Southern District of Illinois.

35 **friends at the Ariston:** Bob letter (5/18/40); Bob video (1995); conversation between Bob Cress and Jan Cress Dondi, Atlanta (1995).

35 **Linxwiler:** Bob letter (5/18/40); Bob video (1995).

35 ***"You heard Roosevelt's":*** Bob letter (10/29/40).

36 **Harvard Law:** Bob video (1995); Bob letter (8/23/43), 1; Hershberger, Beckemeyer, *The Story of Cress Hill Farm* (2017), 243.

36 **Colonel Linxwiler:** Bob letter (4/19/43); White family archives; *Jefferson City Post-Tribune* (4/15/43), 1; https://www.warhistoryonline.com/articles

/mutual-helpfulness-co-founder-of-american-legion-post-leaves-legacy-of-public-service.html?safari=1.

36 **wasn't exactly thrilled:** interview with Anne White French (1997); conversation between Polley White Cress and Jan Cress Dondi, Atlanta (1995).

36 **Air Corps:** Bob video (1997); conversation between Bob Cress and Jan Cress Dondi, Atlanta (1997).

37 ***I was out with John B.:*** Bob letter (5/18/41).

37 **he had apprehensions:** interview with Anne White French (1997).

38 **"tribe":** John B. letter (3/15/42).

39 **game of chess:** conversation between Polley White Cress and Jan Cress Dondi, Atlanta (1995); interview with Anne White French (1997).

39 ***Always reason one:*** John B. letter (3/15/42).

39 **of course, John B.:** interview with Anne White French (1997).

40 **call to service:** conversation between Polley White Cress and Jan Cress Dondi, Atlanta (1995); interview with Anne White French (1997).

40 **question of deferment:** conversation between Polley White Cress and Jan Cress Dondi, Atlanta (1995); interview with Anne White French (1997).

41 **departure:** interview with Mary Hartline (2016, 2018).

41 **June 24, 1941:** *Montgomery County News* article (Mary Hartline scrapbook), (June 1941).

41 **He memorialized the:** dialogue with Polley White Cress regarding Dagon episode and Bob, *Living through the WWII years*, 1988; Bob letter (6/5/43); Bob video (1995).

42 ***Given the rise:*** Bob video (1995).

42 ***loud music in:*** Bob video (1995).

42 **"Will you come get me?":** (walkout exchange) Bob video (1995).

43 ***twenty of the prettiest:*** Bob video (1995).

43 ***walkout rules:*** Bob video (1995).

43 ***"Herman the German":*** Bob video (1995); Book Review *The Luftwaffe*, Reiss, Hermann the German, AFHRA Reel A1271, 916.

43 **The Hillsboro brood had:** Bob video (1995).

44 ***Between Champaign and school:*** Stamm, Caitlin, *Campus Memories:* University of Illinois Urbana-Champaign Library archives (7/2/15) at Archives.library.illinois.edu; Bob video (1995).

44 ***With the three of us:*** Bob video (1995).

44 ***Polley called me:*** Bob video (1995).

Chapter Three: *America Joins the Fight*

46 **wanted to fly:** John B. letter (7/5/41); White family archives.

46 **"I have to disqualify you":** John B. letter (9/20/41).

46 ***Hay fever. Anyone:*** John B. letter (9/20/41).

46 ***I talked some more:*** John B. letter (9/20/41).

47 ***met the government train:*** John B. letter (11/14/41).

47 ***Planes flew overhead:*** John B. letter (11/14/41).

47 ***nine squadrons from:*** John B. letter (12/3/41).

47 ***I saw upward:*** John B. letter (12/3/41).

47 **airshows in St. Louis:** Lawrence, *A Celebration of the Brown and White Legacy* (2001), 178.

47 **touch football:** John B. letter (3/23/42).

48 ***Most of the Illinois:*** Bob video (1997).

48 **Ward Quaal interrupted:** Bob video (1997); Television Academy Foundation, oral history interview of Ward Quaal, Chapter 1, 2004; Fink, John, WGN, World Radio History, A Pictorial History, 1961, 60.

48 ***We knew at that:*** Bob video (1997).

48 ***Later that night:*** Bob video (1997).

49 **January 28, 1942:** 8th Air Force Archives (8af.af.mil).

49 ***I'm in very low:*** John B. letter (1/10/42).

49 **transfer to navigation:** John B. letter (1/15/42 & 2/28/42).

50 ***Navigators are the ones:*** John B. letter (2/28/42).

50 ***been moved again:*** John B. letter (2/28/42).

50 ***A right handy system:*** John B. letter (4/7/42).

50 **radio compass. . . . Atmospheric:** John B. letter (4/7/42).

50 ***By week six, the exams:*** John B. letter (4/14/42).

50 **a photographer was:** Lt. White in *Life* magazine, *Montgomery County News*, Hillsboro, IL (undated); *Aerial Nav. Guides U.S. Planes on World's Longest Flights, Life* (9/28/42), 92–3.

50 ***Aerial Navigation***: *Life* magazine. September 28, 1942, issue.

51 ***course a heading***: John B. letter (4/19/42); Bob letter (10/2/43).

51 ***We were given a course to fly:*** John B. letter (4/19/42).

51 ***Ground speed, direction, force of wind:*** John B. letter (4/19/42).

51 ***The second problem was:*** John B. letter (4/19/42).

51 **western travel with:** John B. diary (1927); Lawrence, *A Celebration of the Brown and White Legacy* (2001), 175–182; White family archives (1928).

52 **Her keen interest:** conversation between Polley White Cress and Jan Cress Dondi, Fort Lauderdale (2012); Nellie's scrapbooks in White family archives.

52 ***I wish I had gotten Grandmother:*** John B. letter (4/14/42).

52 ***Celestial navigation is no cinch:*** John B. letter (4/19/42).

52 ***If I put my mind:*** John B. letter (4/19/42).

52 ***It's all right to make:*** John B. letter (5/1/42).

52 ***13,500 feet was the highest:*** John B. letter (5/17/42).

53 ***a transport plane had flown:*** John B. letter, (5/31/42).

53 **General Doolittle:** "Shangri-la Has Nazis Guessing," *Austin American* (5/20/42), 1; "Terror on Jap Faces Related—Numerous Details of Attack on

Tokyo Are Disclosed as Doolittle Revealed as Leader," *Fort Worth Star-Telegram* (5/20/42), 2; "Yanks Slapped Japs" *Austin American* (5/20/42), 1; "War Dept Promises Tokyo Additional Raids—Veil at last torn from famed 'Shangri-La' bombing base," *Corsicana Daily Sun* (4/21/43) 1; "American Bombers based in Carrier for Raid on Tokyo—Famed 'Shangri-La' location finally given out by Tokyo," *Corsicana Daily Sun* (4/20/43), 9; "Henry McLemore on Shangri-la," *The Macon News* (5/23/42), 4; newspaper interviews with Doolittle.

53 **"Fifteen minutes and fifty miles":** "Plenty of Texans Accompanied Doolittle in Bombing of Japan," *Austin American* (5/20/42), 3; "Repeat Bombing of Japan Hints If American Base Remains Secret," *El Paso Herald-Post* (5/20/42), 12; newspaper interviews with Doolittle.

53 **"to cause as much confusion":** "Yanks Slapped Japs, Escaped, Doolittle revealed as Leader of US Airmen in Daring Raid," *Austin American* (5/20/42), 1; newspaper interviews with Doolittle.

53 **1,500 feet:** "Terror on Jap Faces Related—Numerous Details of Attack on Tokyo Are Disclosed as Doolittle Revealed as Leader," *Fort Worth Star-Telegram* (5/20/42), 2; "American Bombs Fall Near Emperor's Home," *Austin American* (5/20/42), 3; newspaper interviews with Doolittle.

53 **"Later that evening":** Ada White diary (6/13/42).

53 **champagne hailed celebrations:** Ada White journal (6/13/42).

54 **"Nearly a year since":** Ada White journal (6/21/42).

54 **"how we hated":** Ada White journal (6/24/42).

55 **June 5, 1942:** Dugan and Stewart, *Ploesti*, Random House (1962), 8.

55 **Thirteen heavy bombers:** *USAF Historical Study No. 103,* AFHRA Reel K1012, 525.

55 **served to alert the Axis:** Dugan and Stewart, *Ploesti,* (1962), 30.

55 **Gerstenberg. . . . fortified loop:** Dugan and Stewart, *Ploesti*, (1962), 31.

55 **"forty separate batteries":** *RAF form 441A Sortie* reports for 93rd BG on *Tidal Wave* (8/1/43), American Air Museum online, 12 of 33.

55 **"barrage balloons trailing":** Dugan and Stewart, *Ploesti*, Random House (1962), 116.

55 **"smudge pots":** *USAF Historical Study* (8/1/43), AFHRA Reel K1012, 639.

56 **"topped oil derricks":** *RAF form 441A Sortie* reports for 93rd BG on *Tidal Wave* (8/1/43), American Air Museum online, 8 of 38.

56 **"whirling haystacks":** *RAF form 441A Sortie* reports for 93rd BG on *Tidal Wave* (8/1/43), American Air Museum online, 12 of 38; *USAF Historical Study 103—The Ploesti Mission*, AFHRA Reel K1012, 608.

56 ***Festung Ploesti:*** *RAF form 441A Sortie* reports for 93rd BG on *Tidal Wave* (8/1/43), American Air Museum online, 12 of 29.

56 ***Winning Your Wings:*** Bob video (1997).

56 **Chanute Field**: https://www2.illinois.gov/epa/topics/community-relations/sites/chanute-afb/Pages/default.aspx.

57 ***"Just picture yourself":*** Bob video (1997).

57 ***We live in fame:*** Bob video (1997).

57 ***"I'm joining the Air Corps":*** Bob video (1997).

57 ***"Airplanes? You know nothing":*** Bob video (1997).

Chapter Four: *First in Combat*

58 **the *Unterseeboot:*** *The Battle Against the U-Boat in the American Theater, Operations off the East Coast* (Dec 1941–June 1942), A.T. Warnock, AFHRA (AFD-20050429-018), 10; Murphy, *Sharks in American Waters, America in WWII,* (10/2006); Lane, "War on the Home Front," *The St. Augustine Record,* (7/19/2010), https://www.staugustine.com/article/20100719/NEWS/307199989; Schoettler, Carl, "U-boat skipper recalls good hunting off East Coast," *Baltimore Sun* (11/2/92); Captain's Log of Reinhard Hardegen, U-boat 123, Property of the Kriegsmarine; Gannon, Michael, *Operation Drumbeat: The Dramatic True Story of Germany's First U-boat Attacks Along the American Coast in WWII*, NY: Harper & Row, (1990).

59 ***There is a rumor:*** John B. letter (7/1/42).

59 **Lucille Saliba:** Interview with David Gover Rice (2014); White family archives.

59 **post chapel at Barksdale AFB:** newspaper clipping from Polley scrapbook (7/12/42).

59 **"I am happy for John B.":** Ada journal (7/11/42).

60 ***Jumping-off place, practical:*** John B. letter (7/1/42), 1.

60 ***"Hey, fellas, we need":*** John B. letter (7/1/42).

60 ***It was the first time:*** John B. letter (7/1/42).

60 ***The pilot gave me:*** John B. letter (7/1/42).

60 ***We couldn't verify:*** John B. letter (7/1/42).

60 **brother crew bagged:** www.93rd-BG-museum.org, Barksdale AAF, and Col. Timberlake.

60 ***I've talked to navigators:*** John B. letter (7/1/42).

60 **"widened to the Yucatán":** *93rd BG History*, AFHRA Reel B0183, 1491.

61 **93rd Bombardment Group:** *History of the 93rd Bomb Group*, https://www.93bg.com/history-book; USAF Experience interview of Col. Timberlake (9/26/47) (NARA).

61 ***I was in on a secret confab:*** John B. letter (7/1/42).

61 **"John B. called to tell":** Ada journal (8/29/42).

61 **"I wish I knew where John B.":** Ada journal (8/31/42).

61 **Newfoundland:** *330th Bomb Squadron Historical Record,* AFHRA Reel A0582, 1225.

61 **"Winds were stronger than":** Bowman, *Fields of Little America*, 1.

61 **Polaris:** Anderson, *The Route and Other Plans*, diary of Captain Hugh Rawlin Roper, 9.

61 ***I can't believe it:*** Roper diary (9/4/42).

61 **"Turn One-Eight-Zero":** Roper diary (9/4/42).

62 **"All during the trip":** Roper diary (9/4/42).

62 **"the sixth B-24":** John B. telegram (Ada White journal 9/7/42); Roper diary (9/6/42).

62 **Eighth Air Force:** Group Annual, *The Story of the 93rd Bomb Group*, 10.

62 **"training sessions were":** Roper diary (9/4/42).

62 **"Science, the sun and stars":** *Aerial Navigation Guides U.S. Planes on World's Longest Flights*, Life magazine (9/28/42), 92.

63 **Cambridge. The Eagle pub:** John B. letter (10/2/42).

63 ***Time has brought:*** John B. letter (9/25/42).

63 **NINE OCTOBER 1942. . . . Lille:** *93rd BG mission report*, AFHRA Reel B0184, 1940; History of the 93rd Bomb Group, https://www.93bg.com/history-book.

63 **"I know you Joes":** Bowman, *Fields of Little America*, Patrick Stephens, 4.

64 **Fifty German fighters:** *93rd BG mission report*, AFHRA Reel B0184, 1940.

64 **"Most of the fellows":** *330th BS Narrative of October 1942*, AFHRA Reel B0183, 1559.

64 **game day in Champaign:** Ada's journal (10/10/42).

64 ***My thoughts are with you:*** John B. telegram (10/9/1942).

64 **"Allied forces will soon":** *Mr. Churchill's War Survey, The Guardian*, London (11/12/42), 5.

65 **"Casablanca has just":** *Mr. Churchill's War Survey, The Guardian*, London (11/12/42), 5.

65 **"In late October":** Roper diary (11/11/42); Unknown newspaper clipping (11/26/42), John B.'s scrapbook; http://93rd-bg-museum.org/data/bomb-group-missions.htm. From historynet.com and article by Sam McGowan, *World War II* magazine (May 1997).

65 ***We're on a special job:*** John B. letter (11/4/42), 1.

65 **"making an impact":** Roper diary (11/25/42), 15.

66 **Saint-Nazaire:** *93rd Bomb History*, National Archives, AFHRA Reel B0183 (November 1942), 1572.

66 **German merchant vessel:** *Captain Hugh Rawlin Roper* (11/11/42), 12.

66 **"What a prize it would be":** *Captain Hugh Rawlin Roper* (11/11/42), 12.

67 **failed second attempt:** *Captain Hugh Rawlin Roper* (11/11/42), 12–14.

67 **six British Beaus:** *Montgomery County News & Hillsboro Journal* clipping (11/26/42).

67 **"the [enemy] ship's position":** Roper diary (11/11/42), 13.

67 **"Wrong! Wrong! Six German":** Miller, *Masters of the Air*, Simon & Schuster (2006), 190; Dugan and Stewart, *Ploesti*, Random House (1962), 107.

67 **"climb and crest":** *Captain Hugh Rawlin Roper*, diary (11/11/42) 13–14; Millard County Chronicle and Salt Lake City newspaper (11/19/42).

67 **"just above the waves":** *Captain Hugh Rawlin Roper*, diary (11/11/42) 13–14.

68 **hit a second enemy Ju 88:** *Montgomery County News & Hillsboro Journal* clipping (12/20/43).

68 **"You can't land":** Roper diary (11/11/42).

68 **"an empty cartridge":** Roper diary (11/11/42) 13–14.

68 ***Tell Bill to take:*** John B. letter (11/11/42).

69 ***intruder* missions. . . . Gee box:** *329th War Diary*, AFHRA Reel A0582, (March 1943), 472; Roper diary (11/25/42).

69 ***At a station near Oxford:*** John B. letter (11/30/42).

69 ***and some high-powered:*** John B. letter (12/15/42).

69 **English custom:** John B. letter (12/28/42); *Yanks Follow an Old British Custom*, The Liberator (12/28/42), AFHRA Reel B0183, 1632.

69 ***whiskey tenors—mellow:*** John B. letter (12/28/42).

69 ***historical trip:*** John B. letter (1/3/43); *Squadron Diary*, Jan. 1943, AFHRA Reel B0183, 1705.

69 **"first US raid on Germany":** *329th BS War Diary* (January 1943), AFHRA Reel A0582, 469.

69 ***there were about thirty-two news reporters:*** John B. letter (1/3/43).

70 **January 2, 1943:** *329th Bomb Squadron War Diary*, AFHRA Reel A0582 (1/2/43), 469, 495; *Squadron Diary—Jan. 1943*, AFHRA Reel B0183, 1705.

70 **"with heavy cloud cover":** Roper diary (1/2/43).

71 **"Abort mission":** *329th Bomb Squadron War Diary*, AFHRA Reel A0582 (1/2/43), 469.

71 **crew would return deflated:** Roper diary (1/2/43); *329th Bomb Squadron War Diary*, AFHRA Reel A0582 (1/2/43), 469.

71 **January 27, 1943, lead:** *329th BS War Diary*, AFHRA Reel A0582 (1/2/43), 469.

71 ***At 25,000 feet, the thermometer:*** John B. letter (2/2/43).

72 ***Two boys in my crew:*** John B. letter (2/2/43).

72 **pulled the mask:** John B. letter (2/2/43).

72 **"Local relatives are of the opinion":** *Montgomery County News* (6/24/43), 1; *Montgomery County News & Hillsboro Journal* clipping (12/20/43 & 7/26/43).

72 **Casablanca. The conference:** *Planning of Ploesti*, AFHRA Reel 1041988, 83.

72 **blueprint for the strategic bombing:** Truxal, Luke, *The Failed Bombing Offensive: A Reexamination of the Combined Bomber Offensive in 1943*, University of North Texas (Dec. 2011), 11, 25.

72 **"taproot of German might":** Dugan and Stewart, *Ploesti*, Random House, 1962, 3.

72 **Initial estimates . . . up to 60 percent**: *Discussion of Ploesti Oil fields as a target*, US Air Force Historical Research Agency (AFHRA) Reel 25087 (4/18/43), 338.

73 **"zero-altitude":** *USAF Historical Study No. 103—The Ploesti Mission,* AFHRA Reel K1012 (June 1944), 538.

Chapter Five: ***A Second Call to Serve***

74 **his call to serve:** Bob video (1997).

74 **long walks:** conversation between Bob Cress and Jan Cress, Bagley Park, Atlanta (summer 1970).

74 **tranquility he found:** conversation between Bob Cress and Jan Cress, Bagley Park, Atlanta (summer 1970).

74 **"Youth of today":** Judge Fred Bale, *Award Diplomas, Montgomery County News*, Hillsboro, IL (6/3/40), 1, 6; Bob video (1995).

75 **pride in his home:** Bob letters (May 1944); a lifetime of conversation between Bob Cress and Jan Cress Dondi.

75 ***Anything is possible if:*** Bob letter (8/24/43).

75 **brick-lined silo . . . milking parlor . . . serenading cows . . . skating bladeless . . . cemetery:** Bob video (1991); conversation between Bob Cress and Jan Cress Dondi, Hillsboro (1991).

75 **Report to Fresno:** Lt. Col. Porter, Sixth Service Command—Orders for Active Duty (2/16/43).

75 ***We were still good friends:*** Bob video (1997).

76 **Midway Saloon:** Bob video (1997).

76 ***Off we go into the wild blue yonder:*** Bob video (1997).

76 **gigantic patriotic display:** *Mammoth War Display Planned in Union Station*, Chicago Tribune (7/7/42), 15; conversation between Bob Cress and Jan Cress Dondi, Atlanta (1997).

76 ***jazzed by the Air Corps:*** conversation between Bob Cress and Jan Cress Dondi, Atlanta (1997).

76 **YMCA:** Bob video (1997).

76 ***orange and blue necktie:*** Bob video (1997).

76 ***Good enough for:*** Bob video (1997).

77 ***College boys clad:*** Bob video (1997).

77 **"Nothing cemented friendships":** Towles, Amor, *A Gentleman in Moscow*, Penguin Books (3/26/19).

78 ***Blackout conditions:*** Bob letter (2/26/43); Bob video (1997).

78 **Ellwood Oil Company:** Edhat staff, *The Bombardment of Ellwood in 1942*, Santa Barbara News-Press (2/24/42; upd 2/27/19) at https://www.edhat.com/news/the-bombardment-of-ellwood-in-1942.

78 ***Airplanes are going:*** Bob letter (2/26/43).

78 ***If this is the Air Corps:*** Bob letter (2/27/43).

79 ***"Tough luck, boys":*** Bob letter (3/1/43).

79 ***Honestly, the life:*** Bob letter (3/1/43).

80 ***It looks like:*** Bob letter (3/22/43); John B. letter (8/28/41).

80 ***never seen such bright:*** Bob letter (3/22/43).

80 **After a thousand miles:** Bob letter (3/22/43), 1.

80 **Polley had ventured:** Lawrence, *A Celebration of the Brown and White Legacy*, (2001), 210.

81 ***like an oversized fraternity:*** Bob letter (3/22/43).

81 **Branch Agricultural College:** Bob letter (3/22/43).

81 ***seventh-place ranking:*** Bob letter (3/23/43).

81 **ten hours of flight training:** Bob letter (5/6/42).

82 **Piper Cub assumed an L-4 military designation:** Pope, *Piper Cub, Flying* magazine (7/25/12), https://www.flyingmag.com/aircraft/pistons/piper-cub/.

82 **met his instructor:** Bob video (1997); Bob letters (5/4 & 6/43).

82 ***"Make sure the":*** interview with Beda Dondi regarding his conversations with Bob Cress (May 1988).

83 **Cedar City at an elevation of 6,000 feet**: Bob video (1997).

84 ***The instructor gave me:*** Bob letter (5/4/43, 5/6/43); Bob video (1997).

84 ***"Take this goddamn":*** conversation between Bob Cress and Jan Cress Dondi, Atlanta (1997).

84 ***I am proud of myself:*** Bob letter (5/4/43).

84 ***It will just kill me if:*** Bob letter (5/7/43).

84 ***it was cloudy. . . . At 2,000 feet:*** Bob letter (5/10/43).

85 ***throttle for altitude, pitch:*** Bob letter (5/14/43).

85 ***flying at a 30-degree angle:*** Bob letter (5/10/43); Bob video (1997).

85 ***a prince of a fellow. . . . jumped on for any move:*** Bob letter (5/13/43).

85 ***Without warning. . . . I glided down:*** Bob letter (5/13/43); Bob video (1997).

86 **fast friends:** Bob letter (5/13/43); Bob video (1997).

86 **loops or rollovers:** Bob letter (5/14/43).

86 ***While the maneuvers:*** Bob video (1997) and interview; Bob letter (5/13/43).

86 ***definitely not a ride:*** conversation between Bob Cress and Jan Cress Dondi, Atlanta (1997).

86 **approach-to-landing stalls:** (story) Bob letter (5/18/43); Bob video (1997).

86 ***stick, throttle, rudder. . . . There is quite a sensation:*** Bob letter (5/6/43).

87 **final flight evaluated procedures:** Bob letter (5/22/43).

87 ***After doing the 500- and 1,500-feet maneuvers:*** Bob letter (5/22/43).

87 ***Falcons? I thought:*** Bob letter (5/22/43).

88 ***white spots on rocks and I realized:*** Bob letter (5/22/43).

88 ***I counted mule deer:*** Bob letter (5/23/43).

Chapter Six: *Diversions Over Europe*

89 **Churchill himself had advocated:** Eaker, Ira C., *Some memories of Winston Churchill*, The Aerospace Historian (Sept.1972) p. 121; Truxal, Luke, *Failed*

Bombing Offensive: Reexamination of the Combined Bomber Offensive in 1943, University of North Texas (Dec. 2011), 21.

89 **Dunkirk. . . . *Tojo*:** *329th War Diary*, AFHRA Reel A0582 (2/15/43), 471; Roper diary (2/15/43).

89 ***We bombed all:*** *Local Attorney Bombs Nazi Bases*, unnamed newspaper clipping (handwritten 2/19/43 in JB scrapbook) published John B. letter to Omer Poos.

89 **the plane ahead:** Roper diary (2/15/43).

90 **rear of the formation:** Roper diary (2/15/43).

90 ***The tail gunner:*** John B. letter to Omer Poos found within newspaper clipping headlined *Local Attorney Bombs Nazi Bases* (2/19/43).

90 ***Three of our ships:*** John B. letter (2/19/43); Roper diary (2/15/43).

90 ***We had to shut:*** John B. letter to Omer Poos found within newspaper clipping headlined *Local Attorney Bombs Nazi Bases* (2/19/43); Roper diary (2/15/43).

90 ***Exterminator*, she was down:** Roper diary (2/15/43).

90 **diversion missions:** *93rd Narrative* (March 1943), AFHRA Reel B0183, 1738; *93rd Mission report* (5/1/43), AFHRA Reel B0185, 1944; *Story of the 93rd Bomb Group Unit History*, 37.

90 **Diversions:** McGowan, Sam, *The Traveling Circus*—WWII feature, Historynet staff (8/19/97), found at https://www.historynet.com/the-traveling-circus-may-97-world-war-ii-feature/; McGowan, *The Boeing B-17 Flying Fortress or the Consolidated B-24 Liberator*, found at https://warfarehistorynetwork.com/boeing-b-17-flying-fortress-vs-the-consolidated-b-24-liberator/.

91 **Rouen:** 93rd BG mission list.

91 **"five minutes in":** Roper diary (3/8/43).

91 **Abbeville Kids:** *329th BS Diary* (March 1943), AFHRA Reel A0582, 501.

91 **British Spitfires:** Roper diary (3/8/43).

91 **"The squadron leader":** Roper diary (3/8/43).

91 **dogfights:** *329th Bomb Squadron Diary*, AFHRA Reel A0582 (March 1943), 501.

91 ***The movies had nothing:*** John B. letter (3/18/43).

91 **Brest:** *93rd Mission report*, AFHRA Reel B0184, 1985.

91 **Diversion tunnels:** Roper diary (3/31/43).

91 **Amiens. . . . Rotterdam:** Roper diary (3/31/43); John B. letter (4/7/43).

91 ***I watched a friend:*** John B. letter (4/7/43).

91 **Hardwick:** John B. photo inscription (March 1943); Roper diary (3/9/43).

91 ***He appears:*** John B. letter (4/7/43).

92 **Vegesack:** *329th Bomb Squadron Diary*, AFHRA Reel A0582 (March 1943), 501.

92 ***This evening the neighborhood:*** John B. letter (3/18/43).

92 **Wilhelmshaven:** *93rd Mission report*, AFHRA Reel B0184 (3/22/43), 1980; John B. letter (3/23/43); Roper diary (3/22/43); 93rd BG mission list.

93 **Bordeaux:** *93rd Mission report*, AFHRA Reel B0184 (3/22/43), 1945; John B. letter (6/3/43); Roper diary (5/17/43).

93 **"the Eighth [Air Force's] longest mission to date":** Stewart, Carroll, *Ted's Traveling Circus*, Nebraska Printing Center (2007), 123.

93 **Over the Bay of Biscay:** Roper diary (5/17/43).

93 **"flew at an altitude of 2,000 feet":** Roper diary (5/17/43).

93 **"southern France was beautiful"**: Roper diary (5/17/43).

93 **"as we neared the target":** Roper diary (5/17/43).

93 **"came within fifty feet":** Roper diary (5/17/43).

93 **"The mission was":** Roper diary (5/17/43).

93 ***We picked up:*** John B. letter (6/3/43).

94 **"seventeen bombers on":** Roper diary (5/17/43).

94 **Axis Sally (Mildred Gillars):** found at https://www.britannica.com/biography/Mildred-Gillars; Roper diary (5/17/43).

94 **La Pallice:** Roper diary (5/29/43).

95 **early June:** June 16, 1943—*93rd BG Historical Narrative* (June 1943), AFHRA Reel B0183, 1779; June 13, 1943, from *American Air Museum*, Media-379228.

95 **"Following the La Pallice":** *93rd BG Historical Narrative* (June 1943), AFHRA Reel B0183, 1779.

95 **"No one can imagine":** *329th Squadron Diary* (July 1943), AFHRA Reel B0183, 1782.

95 **"the RAF brought":** *93rd BG Historical Narrative* (June 1943), AFHRA Reel B0183, 1779; same event also noted June 13, 1943, from *American Air Museum*, Media-379228.

95 ***Super-Duper:*** *93rd BG History* (July 1943), B0183, 1823; AFHRA Reel B0184, 1712, 1864.

95 **Rumors:** *330th BS History* (June 1943), AFHRA Reel B0183, 1784.

96 ***Something big was going on:*** John B. letter (6/23/43).

96 ***My ship is probably:*** John B. letter (6/23/43).

96 ***General Devers, General Eaker, General Hodges:*** John B. letter (6/23/43).

96 ***We were picked out:*** John B. letter (6/23/43).

96 ***I explained to him:*** John B. letter (6/23/43); *93rd BG Historical Narrative* (June 1943), AFHRA Reel B0183, 1795; *Story of the 93rd Bomb Group Unit History* photo, 42; Roper diary (6/23/43).

97 ***I told him about:*** John B. letter (6/23/43); *93rd BG Historical Narrative* (June 1943), AFHRA Reel B0183, 1795; *Story of the 93rd Bomb Group Unit History* photo, 42; Roper diary (6/23/43).

97 **"two fighters made":** Roper diary (5/17/43).

97 **"came within fifty feet":** John B. letter (6/3/43); Roper diary (5/17/43).

Chapter Seven: *Classification*

98 ***Reaching Hollywood and Vine:*** German Messerschmitt per Bob letters (5/29/43, 5/30/43); "Japanese Zero" per Bob video (1997).

98 **Brown Derby:** Bob video (1997).

98 **"On the house, boys!":** Bob video (1997).

99 ***There certainly are:*** Bob letter (5/29/43).

99 **battery of examinations:** Bob video (1997); NARA, WWII Air Force *Cadet Classification* movie narrated by Ronald Reagan (1943).

100 ***Truly this is the busiest:*** Bob letter (6/2/43).

100 ***Maybe it is because:*** Bob letter (6/3/43).

101 ***Triumph of the Will:*** The History Place (2001), https://www.historyplace.com/worldwar2/triumph/tr-will.htm.

101 ***As part of a series:*** Bob letter (6/9/43).

101 ***Movie actors:*** Bob letter (6/10/43).

101 ***on the athletic field:*** Bob letter (6/10/43).

102 ***the wits scared:*** Bob letter (6/10/43).

102 ***I must have:*** Bob video (1997).

102 ***In the hall were about:*** Bob letter (6/10/43).

102 ***It was really:*** Bob letter (6/10/43).

102 ***The way I feel:*** Bob letter (6/11/43).

103 **Ellington:** Bob letter (6/19/43), 1, 3; Carlson, *Ellington Field: A Short History, 1917–1963,* NASA/CR-1999-208921 (Feb. 1999), 23–34.

103 **Wake-up . . . 0500:** Bob letter (6/19/43).

103 **guy running the food:** conversation between Bob Cress and Jan Cress Dondi in Atlanta (1997).

104 ***math, ground & air forces:*** Bob letter (6/20/43, 6/22/43).

104 ***Then at night:*** Bob letter (6/22/43).

104 ***The Aragon was:*** Bob letter (6/28/43).

105 **Park Chetwood, convertible:** Bob letter (8/10/43, 9/19, 22, 28/43); video of convertible discovered in Mountaineer Archives, Dwight Watson, Skoog, Lowell, *Written in the Snows—The Ski Climbers, Part 6* (2010), htpp://alpenglow.org/written-in-the-snows/ski-climbers6.html.

105 ***Seattle Post:*** "Seattle Boy Seeking Silver Skis Trophy," *Seattle Post-Intelligencer* (4/6/41), 1.

105 ***I danced with girls:*** Bob letter (6/28/43).

106 ***I went from Barracks 868:*** Bob letter (7/4/43).

106 **"one of the group's":** *Hillsboro Journal* clipping, *Local Attorney Bombs Nazi Bases* (undated).

106 **William J. Humphries. . . .** ***squadron navigator:*** *Montgomery County News* (3/29/43), 1; reference from *Air Ramblers Bomb Nazis from Caribbean to Naples,* Chicago Sun (3/28/43); *Montgomery County News* (6/24/43), 1; Bob letter (7/9/43).

106 **Sicily. . . . Mussolini:** found at https://www.history.com/topics/world-war-ii/invasion-of-sicily.

107 ***Texas heat was:*** Bob letter (7/25/43).

107 **It *was quite reminiscent:*** Bob letter (7/25/43).

107 ***It reminded me of:*** Bob letter (7/25/43).

Chapter Eight: *The Plan to Destroy Ploesti Begins*

108 **NINE JULY 1943:** John B. letter (7/18/43); Roper diary (7/9/43); *USAF Historical Study No. 103: The Ploesti Mission* (6/15/44), AFHRA Reel K1012, 573.

108 **Boringden:** Anderson, *Captain Hugh Rawlin Roper 1915-1943*, 29.

108 **Forbes:** John B. letter (7/18/43); *Cypher Message Mediterranean Air Command to Col. Smart*, AFHRA Reel 25028 (7/4/43), 1002; *USAF Oral History General Jacob Smart,* AFHRA Reel 1041988, 86; *330th BS History* (July 1943), AFHRA Reel B0183, 1816; *OSS memo,* AFHRA Reel A1255, 832; Memo from Air Minister Whitehall (7/8/43), AFHRA 25079, 1366; Anderson, *Captain Hugh Rawlin Roper 1915–1943*, 28.

108 **Geerlings:** *Cypher Message Mediterranean Air Command to Col. Smart,* AFHRA Reel 25028 (7/4/43), 1002; *USAF Oral History General Jacob Smart,* AFHRA Reel 1041988, 85; Anderson, *Captain Hugh Rawlin Roper 1915–1943*, 28; Dugan and Stewart, *Ploesti*, Random House (1962), 60; Roper diary (7/9/43).

108 **miniature representation:** *Cypher Message Med. Air Command to Col. Smart*, AFHRA Reel 25028 (7/4/43), 1002; *330th BS History* (July 1943), AFHRA Reel B0183, 1824; Anderson, *Captain Hugh Rawlin Roper 1915–1943*, 28.

109 **"oblique drawings to show":** Dugan and Stewart, *Ploesti*, Random House (1962), 45.

109 **"a Texas-drawling New York":** Dugan and Stewart, *Ploesti*, Random House (1962), 46.

109 **"45-minute sound film":** *Cypher Message Med. Air Command to Col. Smart*, AFHRA Reel 25028 (7/4/43), 1002; *330th BS History* (July 1943), AFHRA Reel B0183, 1824; Anderson, *Captain Hugh Rawlin Roper 1915–1943*, 28.

109 **"Consequently, Intelligence had bet":** Dugan and Stewart, *Ploesti*, Random House (1962), 61.

109 ***we left England:*** John B. letter (7/18/43).

109 **Sicily:** *328th BS History* (July 1943), AFHRA Reel B0183, 1808; *9th AF Tactical Radio Net* (7/9/43), AFHRA Reel B0185, 442.

109 **"shorten the war by six months":** Dugan and Stewart, *Ploesti*, Random House (1962), 36.

109 **Thermite sticks:** *USAF Oral History Interview—Col. Smart*, AFHRA Reel 1041988 (Nov. 1978), 86 Anderson, *Captain Hugh Rawlin Roper 1915–1943*, 29.

109 **incendiaries:** *Final Report* (8/3/43), AFHRA Reel 25074, 948; *93rd Historical Narrative*, AFHRA Reel B0183 (8/1/43), 1835.

110 **"If we were hit":** Geerlings in Dugan and Stewart, *Ploesti*, Random House (1962), 61.

110 ***Since we were a single ship:*** John B. letter (7/18/43).

110 **Leslie Howard:** *93rd BG Narrative* (June 1943), AFHRA Reel B0183, 1783; Geerlings in *Ploesti*, 60; Anderson, *Roper diary 1915–1943*, 30; Dugan and Stewart, *Ploesti*, Random House (1962), 60.

110 **"Junker 88s"; "Looks like":** Brannon in *Ploesti*, 61; Anderson, *Captain Hugh Rawlin Roper 1915–1943*, 30.

111 ***We were a long:*** John B. letter (7/18/43).

111 **Timberlake flew in:** John B. letter (7/18/43); *Official History of the 93rd Bomb Group, 328th, 329th, and 330th Squadrons*, US 8th Air Force, Maxwell AFB, Montgomery, Alabama; Anderson, *Roper, The Route and Other Plans*, personal diary of Captain Hugh Rawlin Roper, 31.

111 **Terria . . . Benghazi #7:** AFHRA Reel A0582 (July 1943), 335; Memo, AFHRA Reel 25028 (6/24/43), 967.

112 **"Crawling with scorpions":** Dugan and Stewart, *Ploesti*, Random House (1962), 34.

112 ***It's hot and dusty:*** John B. letter (7/18/43); *329th BS History* (July 1943), AFHRA Reel B0183, 1808.

112 **guided Timberlake:** John B. letter (7/18/43).

112 ***At a nightclub:*** John B. letter (7/18/43).

112 ***had remarkable control:*** John B. letter (7/18/43).

113 **Rickenbacker . . . morale-boosting:** John B. letter (7/18/43); AFHRA Reel B0184 (July 1943), 1732.

113 **"claimed twenty-six victories":** https://www.historynet.com/captain-eddie-rickenbacker-americas-world-war-i-ace-of-aces/.

113 **"courage is doing":** Rickenbacker, *New York Times* magazine, (11/24/63).

113 ***spirituous talk on fighting:*** John B. letter (7/18/43).

113 ***As I look below:*** John B. letter (7/18/43).

114 **McKelvey . . . crashed:** *93rd BG Narrative* (July 1943), AFHRA Reel B0183, 1815; Anderson, *Captain Hugh Rawlin Roper 1915–1943*, 31–32; John B. letter (7/18/43).

114 ***We have dropped supplies:*** John B. letter (7/18/43).

114 ***The RAF rescue service:*** John B. letter (7/18/43).

114 **Rome. . . . leading the Wing:** *93rd BG Sortie rept* (7/19/43), AFHRA Reel B0185, 297.

114 **"This was one":** Anderson, *Captain Hugh Rawlin Roper 1915–1943*, 32.

114 **Vatican:** *330th BS History* (July 1943), AFHRA Reel B0183, 1818; Anderson, *Captain Hugh Rawlin Roper 1915–1943*, 33; John B. letter (7/22/43); Roper diary (7/19/43).

114 **"We were briefed":** Anderson, *Captain Hugh Rawlin Roper 1915–1943*, 33.

114 **112 Liberators** (footnote): from Air Force Historical Support Division, https://www.afhistory.af.mil/FAQs/Fact-Sheets/Article/459020/the-army-air-corps-to-world-war-ii/#:~:text=July%2019%2C%201943.,is%20staged%20in%20the%20afternoon.

114 **"this was a big raid"** (footnote): from *330th BS History* (7/19/43), AFHRA Reel, B0183, pp. 1807, 1816.

115 **0735; 1319 hours:** Anderson, *Captain Hugh Rawlin Roper 1915–1943*, 33.

115 **"all crews returned":** *330th BS History* (July 1943), AFHRA Reel B0183, 1818; Anderson, *Captain Hugh Rawlin Roper 1915–1943*, 33; John B. letter (7/22/43); Roper diary (7/19/43).

115 **"Photoreconnaissance indicated":** *Brereton Memo to Eisenhower,* AFHRA Reel 25079 (7/20/43), 1380.

115 **"one of the most successful raids":** AFHRA Reel B0184, (12/3/43), 1862.

116 **group leaders expressed:** Dugan and Stewart, *Ploesti* (1962), 61.

Chapter Nine: *A Storm on the Horizon*

117 ***Super-Duper:*** *93rd BG History* (July 1943), B0183, 1823; AFHRA Reel B0184, 1712, 1864.

118 ***longer & tougher & a real "Purple Heart":*** John B. letter (7/22/43).

118 **German submarines:** Fincher, Read, *The 1943 "Surprise" Hurricane*, NOAA History, 6/8/2006; *Wartime Fears Kept 1943 Hurricane Under Wraps,* Tyler Morning Telegraph (5/24/03), 28; *People were not ready for the Intensity of the Hurricane of 1943*, The Galveston Daily News (12/25/99), 20.

118 ***We got the order:*** Bob letter (7/27/43).

119 ***We are having something:*** Bob letter (7/27/43).

119 **surprise attack:** Bell, *Houston Public Media*, 5/31/2007; Fincher, Read, *The 1943 "Surprise" Hurricane*, NOAA History, 6/8/2006.

119 ***The peak of the storm:*** Bob letter (7/27/43).

120 ***The wind was blowing:*** Bob letter (7/27/43 and 7/28/43).

120 ***I got hold of a rope:*** Bob letter (7/27/43 and 7/28/43).

120 ***Swirling sand pricked:*** Bob letter (7/28/43).

120 **"clocked a speed of 132":** Fincher, Read, *The 1943 "Surprise" Hurricane*, NOAA History, 6/8/2006.

120 ***And then all hell:*** Bob letter (7/28/43).

120 ***The rope I was holding:*** Bob letter (7/28/43).

120 ***The big plane collapsed:*** Bob letter (7/28/43).

120 ***I then went over:*** Bob letter (7/28/43).

120 ***We were relieved:*** Bob letter (7/28/43).

121 ***At 9:00 p.m. we went back:*** Bob letter (7/28/43).

121 ***The second phase.... Dodging a piece.... At 2:30 a.m.:*** Bob letter (7/28/43).

121 ***All day today:*** Bob letter (7/28/43).

121 ***A hurricane is much different:*** Bob letter (7/28/43).

122 **"it was the worst storm":** "Severe Storm Hits City," *The Galveston Daily News* (July 28, 1943), 1, 7.

Chapter Ten: *Tidal Wave August 1, 1943*

123 ***Life* magazine:** Cover, *Life* magazine, July 26, 1943.

124 **first-ever film used at briefing:** *330th BS History* (July 1943), National Archives, AFHRA Reel B0183, 1824; *Tidal Wave* folder, Memo from Air Ministry Whitehall (7/8/43), AFHRA Reel 25079,1366.

124 **"the principal purpose":** *USAF Historical Study No. 103—The Ploesti Mission*, AFHRA Reel K1012 (6/15/44), 591.

124 **"Romania, a country rich":** Ploesti briefing film, USAF, found at http://www.93bg.com/#!video-polesti-film/c11ll; *USAF Historical Study No. 103*, AFHRA Reel K1012, 569.

125 **"*White Force* Section Two":** *93rd Bomb Group Sortie*, AFHRA Reel B0185 (8/1/43), 235.

125 **"This is a tough job":** Ploesti briefing film, USAF at http://www.93bg.com/#!video-polesti-film/c11ll.

125 **"heavy guns":** *Historical Study No. 103*, AFHRA Reel K1012, 568; 564; 583.

125 **"a captured Romanian pilot":** Dugan and Stewart, *Ploesti* (1962), 66.

125 **"was the most heavily":** Dugan and Stewart, *Ploesti* (1962), 66.

125 **last rehearsal:** *USAF Historical Study 103—The Ploesti Mission*, AFHRA Reel K1012 (6/15/44), 583.

125 **"fifty feet":** *USAF Historical Study No. 103*, AFHRA Reel K1012, 238.

125 **"Executed without a hitch":** *Historical Study No. 103*, AFHRA Reel K1012, 568; 564; 583.

125 **"In two minutes":** *Historical Study No. 103*, AFHRA Reel K1012, 568; 564; 583.

125 **"It was something":** Geerlings in Dugan and Stewart, *Ploesti* (1962), 64.

126 **"As far as I could tell":** Gervasi in Dugan and Stewart, *Ploesti* (1962), 68.

126 **"This is it":** Gervasi of Brereton in Dugan and Stewart, *Ploesti* (1962), 68.

126 **powerful calling card:** Dugan and Stewart, *Ploesti*, 69; Walt Stewart memories in Dugan and Stewart, *Ploesti* (1962), 68–69.

126 **unprecedented:** *USAF History*, AFHRA K1012 (8/1/43), 592; Dugan and Stewart, *Ploesti*, 243.

127 **"participating in one":** *330th BS Historical Narrative* (7/4/43), AFHRA Reel A0592, 1276.

127 **Timberlake presented John B.:** John B. letter (7/30/43); Dagon letter (8/30/43).

127 **promoted to captain:** John B. letter (7/30/43); Dagon letter (8/30/43).

128 **"unofficial estimates of the chances":** *USAF Historical Study No. 103—The Ploesti Mission* (June 1944) AFHRA Reel K1012, 593.

128 **"if nobody comes back":** *Air & Space Forces Magazine (originally Air Force Magazine), Tidal Wave* (12/1/07), Walter J. Boyne.

128 **"worth the price":** *Report of Attack on Ploesti*, 9th USAAF, National Archives, AFHRA Reel A6539 (9/20/44), 234, 125.

128 **"The raid on Ploesti":** Dugan and Stewart, *Ploesti*, Random House (1962), 79.

128 **"The armada . . . was the most":** Dugan and Stewart, *Ploesti*, Random House (1962), 86.

128 **"They flew to shorten":** Dugan and Stewart, *Ploesti*, Random House (1962), 86.

128 **Another pilot, and friend:** Stewart, Cal, *Ted's Traveling Circus*, Nebraska Printing (2007), 159-160.

128 **"Since his plane":** interview with Karl Casanova, Capt. Jack Stanley Jones's great-nephew, 2016.

129 **pilot observer:** Dugan and Stewart, *Ploesti*, Random House (1962), 206.

129 **One hundred seventy-seven heavy bombers:** *USAF Historical Study No. 103—The Ploesti Mission*, AFHRA Reel K1012, 621; *93rd BG Historic Narrative* (August 1943), AFHRA Reel B0183, 1862.

129 **"carrying a cargo":** *USAF Historical Study No. 103*, AFHRA Reel K1012, 598.

129 **"varying styles of leaders":** Dugan and Stewart, *Ploesti*, Random House (1962), 92.

129 **"wider spread between":** *USAF Historical Study No. 103*, AFHRA Reel K1012, 600.

129 **climbed to 16,000 feet:** *93rd BG History*, AFHRA Reel B0185, 1866; Dugan and Stewart, *Ploesti*, 96.

130 **"The Luftwaffe had recently":** *USAF Historical Study No. 103*, AFHRA Reel K1012, 567; Dugan and Stewart, *Ploesti*, Random House (1962), 86; 71.

130 **Germans were aware:** Dugan and Stewart, *Ploesti* (1962), 87.

130 **market day:** Dugan and Stewart, *Ploesti*, Random House (1962), 70.

130 **"waving from the ground":** *93rd Narrative report* (8/1/43), AFHRA Reel B0185, 229; *USAF Historical Study No. 103—The Ploesti Mission*, AFHRA Reel K1012, 608; RAF Sortie Report form 441 A, AAM Document 39850, Lt. Hurd, 93rd BG, 329 BS (8/1/43).

131 **"wearing headphones. . . ." "When they received":** Dugan and Stewart, *Ploesti*, Random House (1962), 87; *93rd Narrative report* (8/1/43), AFHRA Reel B0185, 229.

131 **Full Alarm:** *USAF Historical Study No. 103*, AFHRA Reel K1012, 604, 645.

131 **simultaneous attack on both:** Dugan and Stewart, *Ploesti*, Random House (1962), 112.

131 **"Damned cleverly done":** German Air Controller Zahn in Dugan and Stewart, *Ploesti*, Random House (1962), 112.

131 **nav desk:** Author's flight on a B-24 Liberator.

132 **"turned at Targoviste instead":** *93rd BG Tactical Radio Net*, AFHRA Reel B0185 (8/1/43), 229.

132 **"had no choice but":** *330th BS History* (Aug. 1943), AFHRA Reel B0183, 1845.

132 **radio silence was broken:** *USAF Historical Study No. 103—The Ploesti Mission*, AFHRA Reel K1012, 602.

132 **"Mistake! Mistake!":** Miller, *Masters of the Air*, Simon & Schuster (2006), 190; Dugan and Stewart, *Ploesti*, Random House (1962), 107.

132 **"got to within ten minutes":** RAF Sortie report, 93rd BG, Major Potts, AAM Doc 39850 (8/1/43).

132 **wingtip-to-wingtip:** *USAF Historical Study No. 103*, AFHRA Reel K1012, 558.

133 **south where defenses were heaviest:** Dugan and Stewart, *Ploesti*, Random House (1962), 107.

133 **"fifty feet":** *USAF Historical Study No. 103*, AFHRA Reel K1012, 238; *USAF Experience* video interview of Lt. Genl Timberlake (9/26/47), (NARA).

133 **point-blank range:** *93rd BG History*, AFHRA Reel B0185, 1867.

133 **"direct fire fight":** Dugan and Stewart, *Ploesti*, Random House (1962), 114–115.

133 **"I could see the muzzle flash":** Longnecker in Dugan and Stewart, *Ploesti*, Random House (1962), 115.

133 **"The shell removed":** Longnecker in Dugan and Stewart, *Ploesti*, Random House (1962), 115.

133 **"suddenly, a huge oil":** Longnecker in *Ted's Traveling Circus*, 177 and Dugan and Stewart, *Ploesti*, Random House (1962), 118.

134 **"*Circus* planes trailing":** Dugan and Stewart, *Ploesti*, Random House (1962), 117.

134 **"Going over":** *Bombing Personnel Narratives*, Walt Stewart, AFHRA Reel B0184, 1740.

134 **"wanted was to get beyond":** Longnecker in Dugan and Stewart, *Ploesti*, Random House (1962), 115.

134 **"had made it through hell":** *330th BS History* (Aug. 1943), AFHRA Reel B0183, 1846.

134 ***Thunder Mug* and *Let 'er Rip* rejoined:** Stewart in *Ted's Traveling Circus*, 177.

134 **"with *Exterminator* in the lead":** Stewart, *Ted's Traveling Circus*, 158.

135 **"Hanging from. . . ." "part of her left. . . ." "flying junkyard":** Longnecker in *Ted's Traveling Circus*, 174 and *Ploesti*, 115.

135 **"guy-wire":** Koen in Dugan and Stewart, *Ploesti*, Random House (1962), 206.

135 **"hole in her right wing":** Freeman, *The Ploesti Raid*, 124.

135 **"passed over the Danube":** RAF Sortie report, 93rd BG, Capt. Brown, AAM Doc 39850 (8/1/43)

135 **"at one waist window, waving":** Interview with Joe Avedano Duran (Oct. 2020).

135 **reached mission quota:** Dugan and Stewart, *Ploesti*, Random House (1962), 205.

136 **over southern Bulgaria:** NARA, MACR 334.

136 **"Clouds soon forced":** Longnecker in Dugan and Stewart, *Ploesti*, Random House (1962), 206.

136 **"broke away into a steep dive":** Murray in *Ted's Traveling Circus*, 211.

136 **crashing in flames east of Brod:** Freeman, *The Ploesti Raid*, 124.

136 **tail assembly snapped:** *330th BS History* (Aug. 1943), AFHRA Reel B0183, 1848.

136 **"by 1700, with no":** *USAF Historical Study No. 103—The Ploesti Mission* (June 1944), AFHRA Reel K1012, 619.

137 **At 1810, planes:** *USAF Historical Study No. 103—The Ploesti Mission* (June 1944), AFHRA Reel K1012, 619.

137 **"165 that had reached":** *Final Report* (8/3/43), AFHRA Reel 25074, 948.

137 **"seventy ships were":** National Archives, *Historical Study*, AFHRA Reel K1012, 619.

137 **"the nightmare that":** *330th BS History* (Aug. 1943), AFHRA Reel B0183, 1848.

137 **"of the 1,726":** *USAF History study* (8/1/43), AFHRA Reel K1012, 621.

137 **"of the group's thirty-seven":** *329th BS History* (Aug. 1943), AFHRA Reel B0183, 1844.

138 ***Black Sunday:*** Stout, *Fortress Ploesti*, 41.

138 **"greater losses are":** *AF HQ to AGWAR memo*, AFHRA Reel 25079 (7/30/43), 1382.

138 **failure to conduct aerial reconnaissance:** *Historical Study No. 103—The Ploesti Mission*, AFHRA Reel K1012, 564; postwar recorded interview with General Timberlake (NARA).

138 **Martin-B. . . . "impracticable":** *Memo to Smart* (6/2/43), AFHRA Reel 25079, 1259, 1260, 1275.

138 **"that his men":** *Historical Narrative of the 93rd*, AFHRA Reel B0183 (June 1943), 1779.

139 **Lancasters. . . . "impracticable":** *Historical Narrative of the 93rd*, AFHRA Reel B0183 (June 1943), 1779.

139 **"damn good navigators":** *USAF Oral History Interview of General Jacob Smart*, AHFRA 1041988 (Nov. 1978), 91–93.

139 **dummy target . . . Soluch:** *Historical Study No. 103—The Ploesti Mission*, AFHRA Reel K1012, 580.

139 **"security around . . . headquarters":** Dugan and Stewart, *Ploesti*, Random House (1962), 59.

139 **"full of people":** Dugan and Stewart, *Ploesti*, Random House (1962), 59.

139 **wandering Arabs. . . . Cretan bases:** Memorandum #39 *Handling of Arabs and Front Line Units*, by Command of Major General Bradley, AFHRA Reel 24989 (4/22/43), 103.

140 **costliest Allied air raid:** Miskimins, Airmen Memorial Museum, USAF History Support Office, *The Airmen Heritage Series*, USDoD; Axworthy, Mark (1995), *Third Axis, Fourth Ally: Romanian Armed Forces in the European War, 1941–1945*, London: Arms and Armour.

140 **suicide:** *Historical Study No. 103—The Ploesti Mission*, AFHRA Reel K1012, 580; 593.

140 **By August 16, 1943 . . . Foggia:** *93rd Historical Narrative* (August 1943), AFHRA Reel B0183, 1841.

Chapter Eleven: *The Pressure Chamber*

141 **Alabama:** conversation between Polley White Cress and Jan Cress Dondi, Fort Lauderdale (Nov. 2012).

142 **silk stockings:** Office of Price Administration, May 1942; Ames History Museum, *WWII Rationing on the US Homefront*.

142 **gas rations:** Ada White journal (9/28/42).

142 **running her fingers:** conversation between Polley White Cress and Jan Cress Dondi, Fort Lauderdale (Nov. 2012).

142 ***Somewhere in Africa:*** John B. letter (7/22/43).

142 ***The pyramids are just a few miles:*** John B. letter (7/22/43).

143 ***Cairo is a most interesting:*** John B. letter (7/22/43).

143 **Polley imagined the women:** conversation between Polley White Cress and Jan Cress Dondi, Fort Lauderdale (Nov. 2012).

143 ***still holding veil:*** John B. letter (7/22/43).

143 ***chaperone* part:** conversation between Polley White Cress and Jan Cress Dondi, Fort Lauderdale (Nov. 2012).

143 ***When you get back:*** John B. letter (7/22/43).

143 **John B.'s approval:** conversation between Polley White Cress and Jan Cress Dondi, Fort Lauderdale (Nov. 2012).

143 ***If there's anything:*** John B. letter (7/22/43).

143 ***Life* magazine:** *Aerial Navigation*, Sept. 28, 1942, 92–101; front cover, July 26, 1943.

143 **squadron navigator:** newspaper clipping, *Hillsboro Journal* (undated).

143 **John B.'s approval:** conversations between Polley White Cress and Jan Cress Dondi.

143 ***"Daddy was certainly":*** conversation between Polley White Cress and Jan Cress Dondi, Fort Lauderdale (Nov. 2012).

144 **Ellington was rebuilding**: Bob letter (7/29/43).

144 ***You can be thankful:*** Bob letter (7/27/43).

144 ***pressure chamber:*** Bob letter (8/5/43).

144 ***used to determine:*** Bob letter (7/5/43).

144 ***We had a lecture:*** Bob letter (7/5/43).

144 ***I hope that:*** Bob letter (8/4/43).

144 ***The pressure chamber:*** Bob letter (8/13/43).

145 ***it gives you:*** Bob letter (8/4/43).

145 ***At 38,000 feet:*** Bob letter (8/13/43).

145 ***We stayed there for an hour:*** Bob letter (8/13/43).

145 ***Then we dropped to 18,000:*** Bob letter (8/13/43).

145 ***Then we climbed to 30,000:*** Bob letter (8/13/43).

145 ***However, I was okay:*** Bob letter (8/13/43).

Chapter Twelve: *The Telegram*

147 **telegram:** Adjutant General to John B. White, Sr. (8/13/43)

147 **missing in action** (news): conversation between Polley White Cress and Jan Cress Dondi, Fort Lauderdale (Nov. 2012); interview with Anne White French (1997).

147 **A fear:** Ada journal (7/11/42).

148 **"What this telegram says":** interview with Anne White French (1997).

148 **positive spin:** conversation between Polley White Cress and Jan Cress Dondi, Fort Lauderdale (Nov. 2012); interview with Anne White French (1997).

148 **"John B. is resourceful":** conversation between Polley White Cress and Jan Cress Dondi, Fort Lauderdale (Nov. 2012); conversation between Bob Cress and Jan Cress Dondi, Atlanta (1995); White family archives.

148 ***"top-notch pilot and crew":*** John B. letter (1/3/43).

148 **"likely hiding out":** conversation between Polley White Cress and Jan Cress Dondi, Fort Lauderdale (Nov. 2012); conversation between Bob Cress and Jan Cress Dondi, Atlanta (1995); White family archives.

148 **John B. would return:** interview with Anne White French (1997).

148 **Alabama:** Bob letter (8/13/43); conversation between Polley White Cress and Jan Cress Dondi, Fort Lauderdale (Nov. 2012).

149 **vacant seat:** conversation between Polley White Cress and Jan Cress Dondi, Fort Lauderdale (Nov. 2012).

149 **From the sleeping porch:** conversation between Polley White Cress and Jan Cress Dondi, Fort Lauderdale (Nov. 2012); a lifetime of visits by the author to the White home.

149 **Hope Cemetery:** https://peoplelegacy.com/cemetery/oak_grove_cemetery-3r1q/c.

149 **One summer night:** conversation between Polley White Cress and Jan Cress Dondi, Fort Lauderdale (Nov. 2012).

149 ***John B.'s booming yet kind:*** conversation between Polley White Cress and Jan Cress Dondi, Fort Lauderdale (Nov. 2012).

150 ***"Oh, John B.!":*** conversation between Polley White Cress and Jan Cress Dondi, Fort Lauderdale (Nov. 2012).

150 **she could sense:** conversation between Polley White Cress and Jan Cress Dondi, Fort Lauderdale (Nov. 2012).

150 **fearing a crumbling:** conversation between Polley White Cress and Jan Cress Dondi, Fort Lauderdale (Nov. 2012).

150 **Lloyd Handshy . . . killed:** Lloyd Handshy letters to Polley White (1942–1943).

150 **Handshy . . . killed . . . in the Pacific:** Olin Handshy letter to Polley White (11/10/43).

150 ***Bob has a fine reputation:*** John B. letter (7/22/43).

150 **Had John B. known:** conversation between Polley White Cress and Jan Cress Dondi, Fort Lauderdale (Nov. 2012).

150 **"Two pilots reported":** Walt Stewart letter (8/9/43).

151 **"Fliers returning from":** *Captain JB White Believed to Be War Prisoner: Pilot Friend Writes He Saw Plane Go Down*, Walt Stewart reference in *Decatur Herald* (8/30/43).

151 **"If any pilot could":** *Captain JB White Believed to Be War Prisoner: Pilot Friend Writes He Saw Plane Go Down*, Walt Stewart reference in *Decatur Herald* (8/30/43).

151 **"When you are forced down":** Pat Dagon letter, Hillsboro paper (8/30/43).

151 **"I lost a lot of":** Pat Dagon letter, Hillsboro paper (8/30/43).

151 **war had been:** conversation between Bob Cress and Jan Cress Dondi, Atlanta (1995).

152 **a million scenarios:** conversation between Bob Cress and Jan Cress Dondi, Atlanta (1995).

152 ***I hear John B. is missing:*** Bob letter (8/19/43).

153 ***Where is John B.?:*** conversation between Bob Cress and Jan Cress Dondi, Atlanta (1995).

153 **set a course:** conversation between Bob Cress and Jan Cress Dondi, Atlanta (1995); Bob letter (6/6/44; not received in US until Sept. 1944).

153 **shipping out:** Bob letter (8/25/43).

Part Two

Chapter Thirteen: *Ut Viri Volent*

157 ***We will be going:*** Bob letter (8/27/43).

157 ***we were issued navigation:*** Bob letter (8/28/43, 8/29/43).

158 ***50 percent:*** Bob letter (9/15/43).

158 ***About half of those:*** Bob letter (9/15/43).

158 ***I think I am going:*** Bob letter (8/29/43).

158 ***Forty out of the last:*** Bob letter (8/28/43).

158 ***Last night the siren:*** Bob letter (8/28/43).

159 ***Pilotage is looking:*** Bob letter (9/24/43).

159 ***Classes were all business:*** Bob letter (8/29/43).

159 ***one small mistake:*** Bob letter (9/4/43).

159 ***I can't explain:*** Bob letter (9/5/43).

159 ***Before we can get:*** Bob letter (9/5/43).

159 ***That is one of the simpler:*** Bob letter (9/5/43).

160 ***Daily, reports come back:*** Bob letter (9/16/43).

160 ***We are living navigation:*** Bob letter (9/4/43).

160 ***The instructor asked:*** Bob letter (9/3/43).

160 ***I made my first flight:*** Bob letter (9/10/43).

161 ***Life* magazine:** "Aerial Navigation Guides US Planes on World's Longest Flights," *Life* (9/28/42), 92–101.

161 ***It was quite rough:*** Bob letter (9/10/43).

161 ***Tonight, I have to plan:*** Bob letter 9/15/43.

161 ***We drove to the University:*** Bob letter (9/21/43).

161 ***the Fiji house had been:*** Bob letter (9/21/43).

162 ***we drove to New Braunfels:*** Bob letter (9/21/43).

162 ***All this week:*** Bob letter (10/1–2/43).

162 **His letters were:** conversation between Polley White Cress and Jan Cress Dondi, Atlanta (Sept. 2011).

163 **Harvard Army Air Field. . . . 484th Bomb Group:** https://484th.org/About/About.htm.

163 ***With a final exam:*** Bob letter (10/10/43).

163 ***some seventy stars:*** Bob letter (9/3/43).

163 **stars would evoke memories:** conversations between Bob Cress and Jan Cress at Bagley Park, Atlanta (1970).

164 ***"Polaris. The North Star":*** conversation between Bob Cress and Jan Cress at Bagley Park, Atlanta (1970).

164 **this phase of navigation:** Bob video (1997).

164 ***Saturday night, Chetwood:*** Bob letter (10/31/43).

164 ***you drink one:*** Bob letter (10/31/43).

164 ***We didn't have dates:*** Bob letter (10/31/43).

165 ***"Nicht sehr gut":*** Bob letter (10/31/43).

165 **Bob had learned German:** conversation between Bob Cress and Jan Cress Dondi, Atlanta (1997).

165 **"They're gonna love":** conversation between Bob Cress and Jan Cress Dondi, Atlanta (1997).

165 **Fifteenth Air Force:** https://15thaf.org/index.htm.

166 ***One night looking:*** Bob video (1997).

166 ***I looked into train schedules:*** Bob letter (12/16/43); Bob video (1997).

166 ***I could only get home:*** Bob letter (12/16/43).

166 ***Looks like I will be:*** Bob letter (12/19/43).

166 **Class 43-18:** Announcement, Army Air Forces Navigation School, San Marcos Army Air Field (12/23/43); *Montgomery County News* clipping (Bob's scrapbook, date unknown); Formal Announcement by AAF, San Marcos Army Air Field (12/24/43).

166 ***Great guys!:*** conversation between Bob Cress and Jan Cress Dondi, Atlanta (1997).

166 ***Ut Viri Volent:*** Bob letter (12/16/43).

167 ***he parachuted, maybe . . . captured:*** conversation between Bob Cress and Jan Cress Dondi, Atlanta (1995).

167 ***I knew I was more:*** conversation between Bob Cress and Jan Cress Dondi, Atlanta (1995).

167 **Bob learned the top twenty:** Bob video (1997).

167 ***A ten-day furlough!:*** Bob video (1997).

167 ***a navigator from Carthage:*** Bob letter (12/13/43); Bob video (1997).

167 **Two newly commissioned:** Bob video (1997).

167 ***the most direct route:*** Bob letter (12/13/43).

167 ***target was an eastbound train:*** Bob video (1997).

168 ***accelerated to seventy:*** Bob video (1997).

168 ***How fitting that:*** Bob video (1997).

168 ***My driver was doing:*** Bob video (1997).

168 ***an unexpected sleet storm:*** Bob video (1997).

168 ***the incoming train:*** Bob video (1997).

168 **His folks . . . Union Station:** Bob letter (12/19/43).

168 **had not slept . . . adrenaline:** conversation between Bob Cress and Jan Cress Dondi, Atlanta (1997).

169 **Tehran Conference:** https://history.state.gov/milestones/1937-1945/tehran-conf.

Chapter Fourteen: *Combat Training Stateside*

170 **"We'll Meet Again":** Lyrics by Ross Parker and Hughie Charles (1939); Bob letter (1/3/44).

170 ***It was pretty hard:*** Bob letter (1/3/44).

171 **Hastings. . . . Hotel Clarke:** Bob letter (1/5/44).

171 ***7:10 bound for Harvard:*** Bob letter (1/5/44).

171 ***A light freezing rain:*** Bob letter (1/6/44).

171 ***That old north wind:*** Bob letter (1/6/44).

171 ***The town's name:*** Bob video (1997); Bob letter (8/23/43).

172 **Kearney Field:** http://nebraskaaircrash.com/aaf/harvard.html.

172 **Harvard Army Air Field:** http://nebraskaaircrash.com/aaf/harvard.html.

172 **Crumbliss:** Interview with Joan Crumbliss, 2015, 2018; Waters, Elizabeth, *Captain Relates Life in War Prison*, Unknown newspaper clipping, presumably September 1944.

172 ***I immediately liked Jack:*** conversation between Bob Cress and Jan Cress Dondi in Atlanta (1997).

172 ***old man on the crew:*** conversation between Bob Cress and Jan Cress Dondi in Atlanta (1997).

172 ***bending the rules:*** Bob video (1997).

172 ***I felt lucky:*** Bob video (1997).

173 ***First impressions laid:*** Bob video (1997).

173 ***A likable guy:*** Bob video (1997).

173 ***in his words:*** Bob's written description on crew photo (March 1944).

173 **military lifer:** Obituary, Bethany Lutheran Church, Fredericksburg, TX (6/5/17).

173 ***I came in as a brand-new:*** Bob video (1997).

173 **While finalizing their:** Bob video (1997).

173 ***A-grade fraternity boy:*** Bob video (1997).

173 ***skinny new kid:*** Bob video (1997).

173 **his new office, the B-24:** Bob letter (1/6/44).

174 ***From there I'll take:*** Bob letter (1/6/44).

174 ***I got the 3rd highest score:*** Bob letter (1/10/44).

174 ***I have been busier than heck:*** Bob letter (1/14/44).

174 ***we will work eight days:*** Bob letter (1/16/44).

174 ***we flew to St. Louis:*** Bob letter (1/19/44).

175 ***People unacquainted:*** Bob letter (1/22/44).

175 ***John B. was in:*** conversation between Bob Cress and Jan Cress Dondi in Atlanta (1995).

175 **met a bombardier:** Bob letter (2/1/44).

177 ***the lights burned:*** Bob letter (2/5/44); Bob video (1997).

177 ***He was carrying:*** Bob letter (1/31/44).

177 ***I pulled the crew:*** Bob video (1997).

177 ***One of the pilots:*** Bob video (1997).

177 ***I called him up:*** Bob letter (2/1/44).
178 ***on takeoff and landing:*** Bob letter (1/16/44); Bob video (1997).
178 **crawling through a narrow:** Author's flight on a B-24 Liberator.
178 ***the astrodome, a bulged window:*** Bob letter (2/14/44).
178 ***I take out my octant:*** Bob letter (2/7/44).
178 ***I am more pleased:*** Bob letter (1/16/44).
179 ***Metal boxes of ammunition:*** Bob video (1997).
179 ***Nearing the target:*** Bob video (1997).
179 ***hand the controls:*** Bob letter (6/7/43).
179 **Over the target:** Bob video (1997).
179 ***Today while flying:*** Bob letter (2/8/44).
180 ***I'd rather have him:*** Bob letter (2/9/44).
180 **With a *clever:*** Bob letter (2/9/44).
181 ***my pilot and I:*** Bob letter (2/10/44).
181 ***We pitched the flights:*** Bob video (1997).
181 **from New York to Texas, South Dakota to Oklahoma:** Bob letter (2/10/44).
181 **crew photograph:** Bob letter (2/12/44); Bob video (1997).
181 ***I was tied up:*** Bob video (1997).
181 ***The flight to Chicago:*** Bob letter (2/14/44).
182 ***How could we land:*** Bob video (1997).
182 **presented with a brand-new:** Bob letter (2/22/44); Bob video (1997).
182 ***The real deal:*** Bob video (1997).

Chapter Fifteen: *Chicago*

183–194 **Chicago:** Chicago story entirely written by Cress, Bob, *Living through the WWII years*, (1988).

192 **"Temptation":** lyrics by Nacio Herb Brown and Arthur Freed (permission requested from Hal Leonard LLC).

192, 194 **"I'll be seeing you":** Lyrics by Irving Kahal and Sammy Fain (permission was granted by Lee Phillips on behalf of Sammy Fain; permission granted by Hal Leonard LLC).

194 **creating flight plans:** Bob video (1997); conversation between Bob Cress and Jan Cress Dondi, Atlanta (1997).

195 ***I got such a kick:*** Bob letter (2/29/44).

195 ***I saw the exact spot:*** Bob letter (2/29/44).

195 **landmarks:** Bob letter (2/26/44 & 2/27/44); Bob video (1997).

195 **Zeppelin:** Hugh Sexton, "Graf Zeppelin Will Land at Chicago Today," *Chicago Tribune* (10/26/33), 1, 4.

195 ***I located the hospital:*** Bob letter (2/26/44); Bob video (1997).

195 ***Everyone wanted to do it:*** Bob video (1997).

196 ***diversion or circuitous route:*** Bob video (1997).

196 **"it became a common joke":** *Lt. Robert Cress Flies Over Home in Army Plane, Montgomery County News* or *Hillsboro Journal* clippings (likely March 1944).

196 **Jack let down to treetop:** Bob video (1997); conversation between Bob Cress and Jan Cress Dondi in Atlanta (1997).

196 **"The huge Liberator":** *Montgomery County News* or *Hillsboro Journal* clipping (March 1944).

196 **what his parents saw:** conversation between Bob Cress and Jan Cress Dondi, Atlanta (1997).

196 **Essie's fifty-second birthday:** *Lt. Cress Flies Over Home in Army Plane,* Hillsboro Journal, Hillsboro, IL (3/2/44), 1; Bob letter (2/29/44 & 3/1/44); Bob video (1997).

197 ***Who the heck:*** conversation between Bob Cress and Jan Cress Dondi, Atlanta (1997).

197 ***All the people:*** Bob letter (2/29/44).

197 ***That was the most:*** Bob video (1997).

197 **Flat-hatting:** *Flying* magazine (Dec. 1993), 120.

198 ***Undoubtedly it was the fastest:*** Bob letter (3/1/44).

198 ***we are certainly proud:*** Bob letter (3/1/44).

198 ***Fifty-five pounds:*** Bob letter (3/9/44).

198 ***It takes quite a lot:*** Bob letter (3/9/44).

198 ***I got such a yearning:*** Bob letter (3/5/44).

199 ***Like a Pen from another Planet!:*** Parker pen advertisement (1941).

199 ***I am still wondering:*** Bob letter (2/28/44).

200 ***I was given a short haircut***: Bob letter (3/13/44).

200 **staging area:** Special Order #68, Extract and Roster 5, 484th Bomb Group, (3/8/44), www.484th.org.

200 ***From there, the compass:*** Bob letter (3/9/44).

200 ***I heard a bird singing:*** Bob letter (3/12/44).

200 ***It really is a beautiful day:*** Bob letter (3/12/44).

Chapter Sixteen: *Transatlantic Passage*

201 **sworn to secrecy:** 484th Bomb Group *War Diary* (March to June 1944), AFHRA Reel 1824, 1; conversation between Bob Cress and Jan Cress Dondi in Atlanta (1997).

201 ***we were under strict:*** Bob letter (3/13/45) referencing 3/21/44 date.

201 **Waller Field:** Page, Thomas E., (Major Adjutant), 484th Bomb Group (Pathfinder) *Historical Records,* National Archives Reel 1824, (6/30/44), 6; conversation between Bob Cress and Jan Cress Dondi in Atlanta (1997).

201 ***Since I was the one***: Bob video (1997).

202 ***Dakar, French Morrocco:*** Bob video (1997).

202 ***The trip from West Palm Beach:*** Bob video (1997); Bob notations (undated).

202 ***We went past the edge:*** Bob video (1997); Bob notations (undated).

202 ***Trinidad:*** 484th BG *War Diary* (March to June 1944), AFHRA Reel 1824, 2; Bob notations (undated).

202 ***From Trinidad, I set:*** Bob video (1997); Bob notations (undated).

202 ***I confirmed I had my escape kit:*** Bob video (1997).

202 ***I was a good student of geography:*** Bob video (1997).

202 ***Belém:*** Page, 484th Bomb Group (P) *Historical Records*, National Archives Reel 1824, (6/30/44), 7; Bob video (1997); Bob notations (undated).

202 ***Showered in mosquito netting:*** Bob letter (3/23/44); Bob video (1997).

203 **Fortaleza:** Page, 484th Bomb Group (P) *Historical Records*, National Archives Reel 1824, (6/30/44), 7; Bob video (1997); Bob notations (undated).

203 **the *dot* upon which:** conversation between Bob Cress and Jan Cress Dondi, Atlanta (1997).

203 **It was a time before . . . GPS:** conversation between Bob Cress and Jan Cress Dondi, Atlanta (1997).

203 ***using a sextant:*** Bob video (1997).

203 ***the stars south:*** Bob video (1997).

203 **he would become the star finder:** conversation between Bob Cress and Jan Cress Dondi, Atlanta (1997).

203 ***Because we were heavily:*** Bob video (1997).

203 ***Mail sacks had been:*** Bob video (1997).

204 ***It was a 2,100-mile trip:*** Bob video (1997); Bob notations (undated).

204 **"another quarter mile":** Harris, *Scenes from Yesterday* (1993), 38.

204 **"C'mon, baby, lift":** conversation between Bob Cress and Jan Cress Dondi, Atlanta (1997).

204 **"mountainside":** Harris, *Scenes from Yesterday* (1993), 37.

204 ***turn-and-bank:*** Bob video (1997); conversation between Bob Cress and Jan Cress Dondi, Atlanta (1997).

204 ***It was not unlike:*** Bob video (1997).

204 **Harry Harris:** interview with Harry Harris, Jr. (summer 2014); Harris, *Scenes from Yesterday* (1993).

204 **"the superchargers":** Harris, *Scenes from Yesterday* (1993), 38.

205 ***We had to go through:*** Bob video (1997).

205 ***Sitting at my nav desk:*** Bob video (1997).

205 **"Winds clocked hurricane-force":** Harris, *Scenes from Yesterday* (1993), 37.

205 ***"Gunner to pilot: fire":*** Bob video (1997).

206 ***Is this what it looks like?:*** Bob video (1997).

206 ***"Navigator to Crew":*** Bob video (1997).

206 ***St. Elmo's Fire:*** Bob video (1997).

206 ***In celestial navigation:*** Bob video (1997).

206 ***Finally, we got through:*** Bob video (1997).

206 ***Working my tail off:*** Bob video (1997).

206 ***was the greatest responsibility:*** Bob video (1997).

206 **Jack flipped through channels:** Bob video (1997).

206 ***After long hours:*** Bob video (1997).

207 ***Jack picked up what:*** Bob video (1997).

207 ***I told Jack to adjust:*** Bob video (1997).

207 ***I made some adjustments:*** Bob video (1997).

207 ***We got there one minute:*** Bob video (1997).

207 ***From that time on:*** Bob video (1997).

208 **Dakar:** Page, Thomas E., (Major Adjutant), 484th Bomb Group (Pathfinder) *Historical Records*, National Archives Reel 1824, (6/30/44), 7; conversation between Bob Cress and Jan Cress Dondi, Atlanta (1997).

208 ***At six-foot-six:*** Bob video (1997).

208 ***The only way to circumvent:*** Bob video (1997).

209 ***We had to use celestial sun lines:*** Bob video (1997).

209 **Atar:** AFHRA, Reel 5694, Ref A3174, Doc 00189728.

209 **Tindouf:** AFHRA, Reel 00151, Ref A0147, Doc 00006873.

209 **Atar. . . . Tindouf. . . . treacherous mountain pass:** 484th Bomb Group (P) *War Diary* (March to June 1944), AFHRA Reel 1824, 3.

209 ***It started to rain:*** Bob video (1997).

209 ***Because our plane:*** Bob video (1997).

209 **Marrakech:** 484th Bomb Group *Historical Records*, National Archives Reel 1824, (6/30/44), 8.

209 ***The buildings looked like:*** Bob video (1997).

209 ***After over 1,300 miles:*** Bob video (1997); Bob notations (undated).

209 **Djedeida:** 484th Bomb Group *Historical Records*, National Archives Reel 1824, (6/30/44), 8,206.

210 ***Right around this section:*** Bob letter (4/5/44).

210 ***confiscated a jeep:*** Bob video (1997).

210 **"warnings of booby traps":** *Historical Records*, 484th Group History (6/30/44), 6.

210 ***scrubby countryside exploring:*** Bob video (1997); Bob scrapbook.

210 **"was pushed into the sea":** Page, (Major Adjutant), 484th Bombardment Group (Pathfinder) *Historical Records*, National Archives Reel 1824, (6/30/44), 8; Bob video (1997).

210 **an open compound:** conversation between Bob Cress and Jan Cress Dondi, Atlanta (1997).

211 ***We didn't have any guards:*** Bob video (1997).

211 **onboard radio:** Bob video (1997).

211 ***With a sultry voice:*** Bob video (1997).

211 ***Axis Sally:*** conversation between Bob Cress and Jan Cress Dondi, Atlanta (1997).

211 ***"Heard you boys":*** Bob video (1997).

211 ***At that point:*** Bob video (1997).

211 **Rita Zucca:** found at https://www.historynet.com/axis-sally/.

211 ***We got into the city:*** Bob video (1997).

212 ***The Germans were counting:*** Bob video (1997).

Chapter Seventeen: *Tempus Fugit*

213 **484th . . . first combat mission:** 29 April 1944, 825th BS Operations Order 4/28/44.

213 **"Crumbliss crew. Position":** 29 April 1944, 825th BS Operations Order 4/28/44; interview with Bob.

213 ***feeling much like:*** Bob letter (4/15/44).

213 **base operations:** Interview with Dick Olson, 484th historian; *Torretta Flyer* at www.484th.org; www.461st.org; Ronald V., *Abandoned, Forgotten & Little Known Airfields in Europe—Torretta* (2/2/2013), www.forgottenairfields.com.

214 ***When sleeping, we are bothered:*** Bob letter (4/15/44 & 4/18/44).

214 ***small radio in our tent:*** Bob video (1997).

214 ***I called the others over:*** Bob video (1997).

215 ***Axis Sally played good:*** Bob video (1997).

215 **briefing:** conversation between Bob Cress and Jan Cress Dondi in Atlanta (1997).

216 **boarded the B-24:** Author's flight in a B-24 (2015).

216 **takeoff. . . .** ***positions:*** conversation between Bob Cress and Jan Cress Dondi, Atlanta (1997).

216 ***Intel suggested German:*** Bob video (1997).

216 ***One day flying over:*** Bob video (1997).

216 ***Jack pushed the column:*** Bob video (1997).

217 **Emergency kits:** Bob video (1997).

217 ***first flights:*** Bob video (1997).

218 ***"Tempus fugit":*** Bob letter (4/28/44).

218 ***Will I plot:*** Bob video (1997).

219 ***Personal items are:*** conversation between Bob Cress and Jan Cress Dondi, Atlanta (1997).

219 ***No need to give:*** conversation between Bob Cress and Jan Cress Dondi, Atlanta (1997).

219 ***It was an honor:*** conversation between Bob Cress and Jan Cress Dondi, Atlanta (1997).

219 **Drniš, Yugoslavia:** Page, 484th Bomb Group (Pathfinder) *Historical Records*, National Archives Reel 1824, (6/30/44), 8; Bob notations (4/29/44).

219 **flak. . . . relative term:** conversation between Bob Cress and Jan Cress Dondi, Atlanta (1997).

220 ***"Jack, you're buying me a beer":*** conversation between Bob Cress and Jan Cress Dondi, Atlanta (1997).

220 **future plans ensured:** conversation between Bob Cress and Jan Cress Dondi, Atlanta (1997).

220 ***Oxygen canister, good:*** Bob video (1997).

220 **At takeoff:** Bob video (1997).

221 **"Let's get the hell out":** Harris, *Scenes from Yesterday*, 40.

221 ***milk run:*** Page, 484th Bomb Group (Pathfinder) *Historical Records*, NARA Reel 1824, (6/30/44), 9.

221 ***The mission fit:*** Bob video (1997).

221 **Alessandria, Italy:** found at https://484th.org/Missions/April_1944.html; Bob notations (4/30/44).

221 ***The objective was another:*** Bob video (1997).

221 ***We weren't delivering milk:*** Bob letter (4/30/44).

222 ***I often went to:*** Bob video (1997).

222 ***We covered local places:*** Bob video (1997).

222 ***Saturday Evening Post:*** Morton, Joseph, "They Call it Screaming Demon," *Saturday Evening Post*, (3/4/44), 17–19; conversation between Bob Cress and Jan Cress Dondi, Atlanta (1997).

222 **"Bomber, fighter, strafe":** Morton, Joseph, "They Call it Screaming Demon," *Saturday Evening Post*, (3/4/44), 17–19.

222 ***The Invader:*** conversation between Bob Cress and Jan Cress Dondi, Atlanta (1997).

223 ***I guess Bill and Harry John:*** Bob letter (5/1/44).

223 ***I imagine he will:*** Bob letter (5/1/44).

223 **Rumors of major amphibious operation:** conversation between Bob Cress and Jan Cress Dondi, Atlanta (1997).

Chapter Eighteen: *Corsica*

224 **La Spezia:** found at https://484th.org/Missions/May_1944.html; Bob video (1997); Bob's notations.

224 ***So Jack, there were:*** conversation between Bob Cress and Jan Cress Dondi, Atlanta (1997).

224 ***"You know, your German":*** conversation between Bob Cress and Jan Cress Dondi, Atlanta (1997).

224 **Corsica:** conversation between Bob Cress and Jan Cress Dondi, Atlanta (1997).

225 ***Flak shot up our plane:*** Bob letter (5/4/44); Bob video (1997).

225 ***Engine two received:*** Bob letter (5/4/44); Bob video (1997).

225 ***Working overdrive, number three:*** Bob letter (5/4/44); Bob video (1997).

226 ***Jack ordered the crew:*** Bob video (1997).

226 ***"Corsica!" And Jack said:*** Bob letter (5/4/44); Bob video (1997).

226 ***Down to two engines:*** Bob video (1997).

226 ***I shoved the map:*** Bob video (1997).

226 ***I was the only guy:*** Bob video (1997).

226 ***Napoleon:*** Bob letter (5/4/44); Bob video (1997).

227 ***It was complex:*** Bob video (1997).

227 ***Coming in from:*** Bob video (1997).

227 ***landing*** (episode): conversation between Bob Cress and Jan Cress Dondi, Atlanta (1997).

227 ***the ship was shaking:*** conversation between Bob Cress and Jan Cress Dondi in Atlanta (1997).

227 ***"C'mon, you mothers":*** Bob video (1997).

227 ***As the ship lumbered:*** Bob video (1997).

228 ***We didn't know what:*** Bob video (1997); Bob letter (5/4/44).

228 ***The crew positioned:*** Bob video (1997); Bob letter (5/4/44).

228 ***knelt down and kissed:*** Bob video (1997).

228 **emergency personnel:** Bob letter (5/5/44).

228 ***standing out of:*** Bob letter (5/5/44).

229 ***We were introduced:*** Bob video (1997).

229 ***Turns out we were:*** Bob video (1997).

229 ***One pilot crowed:*** Bob video (1997).

229 ***The P-47 pilots:*** Bob video (1997).

229 ***he was a famous:*** Bob letter (5/4/44).

229 **Wyler:** *William Wyler, Sur les traces d'Alto*, found at www.alto-squadron.fr/idexWylerUS.html; Harris, Mark, *Five Came Back*, American History TV C-Span3 (6/22/2014).

230 **Lou Tatum:** Bob video (1997).

230 **Because the P-47 had:** Bob video (1997).

230 ***We worked all day:*** Bob video (1997).

230 ***Immediately on takeoff:*** Bob letter (5/5/44); Bob video (1997).

231 ***Colonel Keese asked, "Jack":*** Bob video (1997).

231 ***plane number is 773:*** Bob letter (5/4/44).

231 ***We came back:*** Bob video (1997).

231 ***Our enlisted crew:*** Bob video (1997).

Chapter Nineteen: *I've Been to a Place . . .*

232 ***The sergeant said:*** Bob video (1997).

232 ***I said there must be:*** Bob video (1997).

232 ***I knew the Ploesti:*** Bob video (1997).

232 ***1st time to Ploesti*** (footnote): Bob notation on letter (5/8/44).

233 ***chaff* or *window:*** Bob video (1997).

233 ***It was not unlike Christmas:*** Bob video (1997).

233 ***Out the dome:*** conversation between Bob Cress and Jan Cress Dondi in Atlanta (1997).

234 **met with a shot:** Bob video (1997).

234 ***He's got to be hiding out:*** conversation between Bob Cress and Jan Cress Dondi, Atlanta (1995).

234 ***The moon is making:*** Bob letter (5/5/44).

234 **Bari and Foggia:** Bob letter (5/7/44).

235 ***Facing fighters was fearsome:*** Bob video (1995).

235 **Was it luck?:** a lifetime of conversations between Bob Cress and Jan Cress Dondi.

235 ***I have been to the place:*** Bob letter (5/9/44).

235 **Wiener Neustadt:** *Special Narrative* Report (5/10/44), NARA AFHRA Reel A6455, 498; www.484th.org mission list.

235 **major components:** NARA Air Force Archives Reel A6455, 633.

236 **"strong headwind":** www.461st.org, *Target: Wiener Neustadt, Nord Airdrome.*

236 **Vienna:** NARA Air Force Archives Reel A6455, 633.

236 ***I counted as chutes blossomed:*** Bob video (1997).

237 **Fifteenth Air Force lost:** Mahoney, *Fifteenth Air Force Against the Axis*, 110.

237 **group lost two planes. Twenty-one men:** 484th Bomb Group Mission #7, May 1944.

238 ***Planes were dropping:*** Bob video (1997).

238 ***I began to compile:*** Bob video (1997).

238 ***Sally said, "Hey, boys":*** Bob video (1997).

238 **Bologna. . . . Viareggio:** NARA Air Force Archives Reel A6455 (5/12/44), 934, 1077.

238 ***I am okay and going strong:*** Bob letter (5/12/44).

238 **Cesena:** NARA Air Force Archives Reel A6455 (5/13/44), 27.

239 ***I saw The Eternal City:*** Bob letter (5/13/44).

239 **"Do Not Attack Florence!":** NARA Air Force Archives Reel A6456 (5/13/44), 29; conversation between Bob Cress and Jan Cress Dondi in Fort Lauderdale (1995).

239 **Padua:** *Operations Order 440514-2*, 484th BG mission #10 (5/14/44).

239 **"dropped ninety-five tons":** NARA Air Force Archives Reel 6456, 512–513; (5/17/44), 763.

239 ***Bungdoo. An expression:*** Bob letter (5/15/44).

239 ***We saw this jeep:*** Bob video (1997).

240 **About that time:** conversation between Bob Cress and Jan Cress Dondi, Atlanta (1997).

240 **"the Fifteenth Air Force was losing":** *The Times*, Munster, IN, (3/28/45), 25; *The Atlanta Constitution*, Atlanta, GA (3/26/45), 2; *Daily News*, LA, CA (3/26/45), 8; *Star Tribune*, Minneapolis, MN (3/26/45), 3; *Daily News*, NY, NY (3/26/45) 202.

240 **Portoferraio:** NARA Air Force Archives Reel 6456, 512-513; (5/17/44), 763.

240 **"eighteen ships were":** *484th Mission report*, AFHRA Reel 6456 (5/17/44), 810.

240 ***We were briefed on Ploesti:*** Bob video (1997); conversation between Bob Cress and Jan Cress Dondi in Atlanta (1997).

240 **Belgrade:** NARA Reel 6456 (5/18/44), 937; 1042.

241 **Piombino:** Ops Order 440522-2, 484th BG mission #14 (5/22/44); Mahoney, *15th AF Against Axis*, 119.

241 **Chetwood:** NARA NND 735001, MACR No. 5190 (5/24/44).

241 **Wiener Neustadt:** Mahoney, *Fifteenth AF Against the Axis* (2013), 122.

242 **Zagreb:** NARA Air Force Archives Reel A6457 (5/24/44), 1030.

242 ***Screamin' Demon* was grounded**: Bob letter (5/27/44).

242 ***Captain Watts was:*** Bob video (1997); Ops Order 440525-2, 484th BG mission #17 (5/25/44).

242 **0230:** Leo Stark diary, (5/26/44).

242 **Lyon:** 484th BG mission #18 (5/26/44).

242 **Salon-de-Provence:** *Operations Against France*, AFHRA Reel K1023 (5/25–26/44), 210; Operations Order 440527-1, 484th BG mission #19 (5/27/44).

242 **"a nest of German Junker 88s":** *Operations Against France*, AFHRA Reel K1023 (5/25–26/44), 210; Operations Order 440527-1, 484th BG mission #19 (5/27/44).

Chapter Twenty: *Leading the Wing*

244 **Wiener Neustadt:** NARA AFHRA Reel A6458 (5/29/44), 28, 311; Operations Order 440529-2, 484th BG, mission #20 (5/29/44).

244 ***Flak Alley:*** Harris, *Scenes from Yesterday*, 39.

245 ***I saw their plane:*** Bob video (1997).

245 **The Messer was firing:** After mission *Enemy Encounters* report at IAW EO 13526, National Archives Reel A6454.

245 **loss of a leader:** Bob video; Harris, *Scenes from Yesterday*, 39.

245 ***Colonel Keese took great:*** Bob video (1997).

245 ***I was not only:*** Bob video (1997).

245 ***lead navigator:*** *Ops Order 440530-1*, 484th BG mission number 21; Bob letter (5/30/44).

246 ***I guess the reason I drew:*** Bob letter (5/29/44).

246 ***He is the one who chose me:*** Bob letter (5/29/44).

246 ***Once at altitude:*** Bob video (1997).

246 **"The mission encountered":** *Fifteenth Air Force Against the Axis*, Mahoney, The Scarecrow Press, Inc. (2013), 128.

246 ***When we got back down:*** Bob video (1997).

246 ***Colonel Keese:*** Bob video (1997); Bob letter (5/30/44).

246 ***I was in the air fourteen hours:*** Bob video (1997).

247 **"So ably was":** Page, 484th Bombardment Group (Pathfinder) *Historical Records*, NARA National Archives Reel 1824; (6/30/44), 9; Bob letter (5/30/44).

247 ***I had flown more missions:*** Bob video (1997); Bob letter (5/30/44).

248 ***In about seven hours:*** Bob letter (5/7/44).

Chapter Twenty-One: *Ploesti*

249 ***awakened by the squadron CQ:*** Bob diary (5/31/44).

249 ***We knew the earlier:*** Bob diary (5/31/44).

249 ***Ploesti*:** 484th Bombardment Group (Pathfinder), mission #22 (5/31/44); 484th BG *Narrative Statement*, USAAF (Sept. 1944, copy from Bob's scrapbook); conversation between Bob Cress and Jan Cress Dondi, Atlanta (1997); Riddle, Donald W. (Major), Plan A *Summary of Enemy Situation and Significance of Target*, HQ Operations Order No. 48 (5/4/44), 1, 2, NARA Reel A6454.

249 ***It was a target:*** Bob video (1997).

250 ***"Today is an all-out":*** Bob video (1997).

250 ***we went back:*** Bob diary (5/31/44).

250 **leather gloves:** Bob letter (5/15/44).

250 ***Often when I looked:*** conversation between Bob Cress and Jan Cress Dondi, Atlanta (1997).

250 ***When I first met:*** Bob video (1997).

250 ***Buzz Shuttleworth:*** Bob video (1997); Bob diary (5/31/44).

250 ***Crew membership:*** Bob video (1997).

251 ***I saw the look:*** Bob video (1997).

251 ***Name's Bell:*** Bob video (1997).

251 ***our crew chief:*** Bob diary (5/31/44).

251 ***In the tail gunner's:*** Bob video (1997).

251 ***As we taxied:*** Bob diary (5/31/44); Bob video (1997).

251 ***just as the wheels:*** Bob video (1997).

252 **At half-minute intervals:** Bob video (1997); conversation between Bob Cress and Jan Cress Dondi, Atlanta (1997).

252 **Jack struggled:** Bob video (1997); conversation between Bob Cress and Jan Cress Dondi, Atlanta (1997).

252 ***rendezvous went as usual:*** Bob diary (5/31/44).

252 **"Over 700 ships":** Mahoney, *Fifteenth Air Force Against the Axis,* The Scarecrow Press (2013), 129.

252 **air temperature dipped:** conversation between Bob Cress and Jan Cress Dondi in Atlanta (1997).

252 ***But as the winding Danube:*** Bob diary (5/31/44).

253 ***flak suit.*** **. . . Flashing a *thumbs-up:*** Bob video (1997).

253 ***As we approached the target:*** Bob diary (5/31/44); Bob video (1997).

253 ***we moved closer:*** Bob video (1997).

253 ***Jack's gaze remained:*** Bob video (1997).

253 ***We knew that:*** Bob diary (5/31/44).

253 ***The enemy had:*** Bob video (1997).

253 ***At eye level:*** Bob video (1997).

254 ***Moe Bayer called out:*** Bob video (1997).

254 **160 mph at 24,000 feet:** Missing Air Crew Report 5428.

254 ***With the target:*** Bob video (1997).

254 **It *was 1030:*** Bob diary (5/31/44); according to MACR 5428, it was 1035.

254 **"Let's get the hell out":** Bob video (1997); Harris, *Scenes from Yesterday*, 42.

254 **"had claimed at least":** interview with Dan Melinte, 2014; Luftwaffe aerial victories and downed aircraft (May 1944) found at http://www.asisbiz.com/Luftwaffe/Luftwaffe-aerial-victories-1944-B.html; Pilot Gehring dossier, Bundesarchiv, Abteilung Militärarchiv; translation by Peter Keel and Beda Dondi.

255 **"Munich with his parents. . . ." "aeronautical proficiency":** Ibid.

255 **January 31, 1943. . . . Jagdgeschwader 53. . . . Bay of Biscay:** Prien, *Jagdgeschwader 53 Volume 3;* email exchange with Dr. Jochen Prien (July 2020).

255 **January 1944 . . . transferred to . . . Cesena:** Gehring's Military dossier, Luftwaffe, Bundesarchiv, Abteilung Militärarchiv, Frieburg, Germany.

256 **"Assigned to Popesti aerodrome":** Ibid.

256 **Gehring:** Prien, *Jagdgeschwader 53 Volume 3*, 820.

256 **May 31:** Pilot Gehring dossier, Bundesarchiv, Abteilung Militärarchiv.

256 ***From all appearances we were:*** Bob diary (5/31/44); Bob video.

256 ***hit three times:*** *Screamin' Demon crew, Unit Citation*, Fifteenth Air Force HQ, Bari, Italy, Sept. 1944; Bob video (1997) and interview.

256 **"Fed by the high-octane fuel":** Harris, *Scenes from Yesterday,* 42.

257 ***In an instant:*** Bob diary (5/31/44); Bob video.

257 **"Turn off the gas":** Harris, *Scenes from Yesterday,* 42.

257 **fire damaged his parachute:** Bob diary (5/31/44); Bob video.

257 **"ward off fifteen":** Unit Citation, 484th BG 825th BS, 15th Air Force (5/31/44).

257 ***a group of six:*** Bob video (1997) and interview.

257 ***Bayer got on his mike:*** Bob video (1997) and interview.

258 **claiming a victory:** Luftwaffe aerial victories, German National Archives (5/31/44).

258 **"hand-working the trim controls":** Harris, *Scenes from Yesterday*, 43.

258 ***Bombardier Parsons and:*** Bob diary (5/31/44).

258 **bomb bay . . . doors jammed:** Bob video (1997); Harris, *Scenes from Yesterday*, 43.

258 **"to actuate the hydraulic":** Harris, *Scenes from Yesterday*, 43.

258 ***"Get out of here":*** Bob video (1997) and interview.

258 ***Townsend, Parsons, Martin:*** Bob diary (5/31/44).

258 ***"Jack! Get out":*** interview with Bob.

258 ***This ship is going to blow!:*** Bob video (1997) and interview.

258 ***No chute!:*** Bob video (1997) and interview.

Chapter Twenty-Two: *And Then the Letters Stopped . . .*

260 **Knocking himself out:** Bob letter (5/12/44).

260 **public health position:** Lawrence, *A Celebration of the Brown and White Legacy.* (2001), 212.

260 **Wing navigator:** Bob letter (5/30/44).

261 **difficult finding information:** conversation between Polley White Cress and Jan Cress Dondi, Atlanta (1997).

261 **telegram:** War Department, J.A. Ulio, Adjutant General (6/14-15/44); conversations with Polley and Bob, Atlanta (1997).

261 ***It was the same telegram:*** conversation between Polley White Cress and Jan Cress Dondi, Atlanta (1997).

261 ***I was knocked off-kilter:*** conversation between Polley White Cress and Jan Cress Dondi, Atlanta (1997).

261 **found it difficult:** interview with Louise Cress Beckemeyer (1997).

261 **"observers on other":** Fifteenth Air Force, General Nathan F. Twining letter (6/18/44).

261 **"no knowledge of the number":** Fifteenth Air Force, General Nathan F. Twining letter (6/18/44).

262 ***That rude stamp:*** conversation between Polley White Cress and Jan Cress Dondi, Atlanta (1997).

262 **made inquiries to anyone:** responses from various entities in Cress family archives.

262 **"your son's ship":** Major Bradunas, War Department (7/14/44).

262 **"eight parachutes":** Major Bradunas, War Department (7/14/44).

262 **it was John B. all over:** conversation between Polley White Cress and Jan Cress Dondi, Atlanta (1997).

262 **"near the Ploesti":** Essie Cress letter (8/17/44).

263 **sleeping porch:** conversation between Polley White Cress and Jan Cress Dondi, Atlanta (1997).

263 ***"Talk about it":*** conversation between Polley White Cress and Jan Cress Dondi, Atlanta (1997).

263 **Oak Grove Cemetery:** conversation between Polley White Cress and Jan Cress Dondi, Atlanta (1997).

263 ***Don't lose hope:*** conversation between Polley White Cress and Jan Cress Dondi, Atlanta (1997).

Chapter Twenty-Three: *The Same Blue Gaze*

264 **free-falling. . . . anoxia. . . . fear of *what next*:** Bob video (1997); conversation between Bob Cress and Jan Cress Dondi, Atlanta (1997).

264 ***Falling through space:*** Bob diary (5/31/44).

264 ***I had seen dramatic:*** Bob video (1997).

265 ***Coming down from altitude:*** Bob diary (5/31/44).

265 ***it was a beautiful:*** Bob diary (5/31/44); Bob video.

265 **serenely quiet:** conversation between Bob Cress and Jan Cress Dondi, Atlanta (1997).

265 ***I looked around:*** Bob diary (5/31/44).

265 **"wide spiral to":** T/Sgt. Marion G. Young, National Archives, MACR 5428.

265 **nosed down under control:** Statement of Sgt. John Canfield, Fold 3, Missing Air Crew Report 5428, (5/31/44).

265 ***I worried:*** conversation between Bob Cress and Jan Cress Dondi, Atlanta (1997).

265 ***When our plane:*** Bob diary (5/31/44).

265 ***Tears came to my eyes:*** Bob diary (5/31/44).

265 ***I didn't have time:*** Bob diary (5/31/44).

265 ***He's going to strafe me:*** Bob video (1997).

266 **face his oncoming combatant:** Bob video (1997); conversation between Bob Cress and Jan Cress Dondi, Atlanta (1997).

266 ***ducked under* him:** Bob video (1997).

266 ***the pilot saluted me:*** Bob video (1997).

266 ***Was that a smile on the pilot's face?:*** Bob video (1997).

266 ***I began looking:*** Bob diary (5/31/44).

266 ***The last 300 feet raced:*** Bob diary (5/31/44).

267 ***I made it:*** Bob video (1997).

267 ***Calm down:*** Bob video (1997).

267 ***Walk to Italy?:*** Bob video (1997).

267 ***People were running:*** Bob diary (5/31/44).

267 **Slobozia, Moară**: Romanian archives by Dan Melinte (2015); Dugan and Stewart, *Ploesti* (1962), 256.

267 ***I did everything to make friends:*** Bob diary (5/31/44).

267 ***The girl took me by the arm:*** Bob diary (5/31/44).

267 ***I later found out:*** Bob video (1997).

267 ***While they were arguing:*** Bob diary (5/31/44).

268 ***Harry! I was damned glad:*** Bob diary (5/31/44).

268 ***a new little jail:*** Bob video (1997).

268 ***wink at the girls:*** Bob diary (5/31/44).

268 ***great big photograph:*** Bob video (1997).

268 ***The villagers pointed:*** Bob video (1997).

268 ***King Michael:*** Bob diary (5/31/44); told to Bob by Princess Caradja; conversation between Bob Cress and Jan Cress Dondi, Atlanta (1997).

268 ***we parted our:*** Bob video (1997).

268 ***Wonder how tall he is?:*** Bob video (1997).

268 ***An English-speaking girl:*** Bob diary (5/31/44); Bob video (1997).

269 ***I had been burned:*** Bob video (1997).

269 ***Son of a bitch!:*** Bob video (1997).

269 ***We believed we must:*** Bob video (1997).

269 ***motorcycle came to:*** Bob video (1997).

269 **low-ranking driver:** Bob video (1997).

269 ***Fellas, keep your shoulders:*** Bob video (1997).

269 **squaddie:** Bob video (1997).

270 ***A corporal at best:*** Bob video (1997).

270 ***Definitely not a typical:*** Bob video (1997).

270 ***As he entered our cell:*** Bob diary (5/31/44).

270 ***My wings:*** Bob video (1997).

270 ***A broad stance:*** conversation between Bob Cress and Jan Cress Dondi, Atlanta (1995).

270 ***I looked him:*** Bob video (1997).

271 ***From that point on:*** Bob video (1997).

271 ***At about 1500 hours:*** Bob diary (5/31/44).

271 ***1938 Mercedes touring car:*** Bob diary (5/31/44); interview with Swede Samms (2015).

271 **Ed Ulrich:** Bob video (1997); conversation between Bob Cress and Jan Cress Dondi, Atlanta (1997).

271 **Gaesti:** Romanian archives by Dan Melinte research (2015).

271 ***invited to the commanding officer's:*** Bob diary (5/31/44).

271 **friendly Romania:** Bob video (1997); Stewart and Dugan, *Ploesti*, Random House (1962), 29.

271 ***That night we had:*** Bob diary (5/31/44).

272 ***After breakfast, the CO:*** Bob diary (6/1/44).

272 ***We were in this outdoor:*** Bob video (1997).

272 ***in an old beat-up truck:*** Bob diary (6/1/44); Bob video.

272 **Targoviste:** Dan Melinte research (2015) from Romanian Archives; conversation between Bob Cress and Jan Cress Dondi, Atlanta (1997).

272 ***I know that laugh:*** conversation between Bob Cress and Jan Cress Dondi, Atlanta (1997).

272 ***"What the hell stories"***: Bob video (1997).

Twenty-Four: *A Change in Status*

274 ***old flatbed truck:*** Bob video (1997); *Escape Statements*, AFHRA Reel K1023, 286.

274 **"a German subofficer":** Harris, *Scenes from Yesterday*, 41.

274 ***The Romanian sergeant:*** Bob video (1997); *Escape Statements*, AFHRA Reel K1023, 286.

274 ***"They have bombed":*** Bob video (1997).

274 ***Or brandishing:*** Bob video (1997).

274 ***With the barrel:*** Bob video (1997).

275 ***terror flyers:*** Bob video (1997).

275 ***In Bucharest, the guard:*** Bob video (1997).

275 **"wielded axes, threatened":** *Escape Statements*, AFHRA Reel K1023, 285.

275 **change in status:** conversation between Bob Cress and Jan Cress Dondi, Atlanta (1997).

275 ***captive; absolutely no freedoms:*** Bob video (1997).

275 ***Will we be separated?:*** Bob video (1997).

275 ***crosshatches of a Bavarian villa:*** Bob video (1997); interview with Dan Melinte (2014).

275 ***Wonder if we'll be able:*** Bob video (1997).

275 **Royal Garrison:** conversation between Bob Cress and Jan Cress Dondi, Atlanta (1997); Dan Melinte research (2014) from Romanian Archives.

275 ***Sublagarul 6 Mihai Viteazul:*** *Information Concerning POWs in* Rumania, National Archives, AFHRA Reel K1023, 284; *Op Reunion* report, AFHRA A6087 (9/5/44), 1486; interview with Dan Melinte (2014).

276 ***It was a rough one:*** From Bayer's description to Bob (1944); Bob video (1997).

276 ***They told Moe:*** from Bayer's description to Bob (1944); Bob video (1997).

276 ***"You're an American":*** Bob video (1997).

276 ***hung a large swastika:*** Bob video (1997); conversation between Bob Cress and Jan Cress Dondi, Atlanta (1997).

276 ***The officer articulated:*** Bob video (1997).

276 ***the major asked:*** Bob video (1997).

277 ***"It's not Chicago":*** Bob video (1997).

277 ***Was the girl:*** conversation between Bob Cress and Jan Cress Dondi, Atlanta (1997).

277 ***he seemed pro-American:*** Bob video (1997).

277 ***I know you are:*** Bob video (1997).

277 ***How much other dope:*** Bob video (1997).

277 ***The major asked:*** Bob video (1997).

277 ***"It will be easier":*** Bob video (1997).

277 ***"You, as an officer":*** Bob video (1997).

278 ***In compliance with:*** Bob video (1997).

278 **levels of fear:** Bob video (1997).

278 **prisoner number 485:** Batch 206, Jandarmi Dambovita County (6/2/44); also noted Prisoner 328, Strada Sfanta Ecaterina schoolhouse.

278 ***Captured? Perhaps here:*** conversation between Bob Cress and Jan Cress Dondi, Atlanta (1997).

278 ***John B.'s experience:*** Bob letter (6/6/44 received Oct. 1944); conversation between Bob Cress and Jan Cress Dondi, Atlanta (1997).

278 **April 4**: conversation between Bob Cress and Jan Cress Dondi, Atlanta (1997); interview with John M. McCormick (August 2012).

278 **"Captain John B. White believed":** Newspaper clipping, White family archives; *Decatur Herald* (8/30/43) 1; *St. Louis Globe Democrat*, Associated Press (8/30/43), 1.

279 **"Couldn't you *cable*":** *Decatur Herald* (8/30/43) 1; *St. Louis Globe Democrat*, Associated Press (8/30/43), 1.

279 ***one prisoner:*** conversation between Bob Cress, Polley White Cress, and Jan Cress Dondi, Atlanta (1997).

279 **Bob didn't discover:** conversation between Bob Cress and Jan Cress Dondi, Atlanta (1997).

279 **Ulrich** (and escape)**:** Bob video (1997).

279 ***One of the guys:*** Bob POW diary (6/10/44).

279 ***made nightly counts:*** Bob video (1997).

279 ***I could hear tapping:*** Bob video (1997).

280 ***P-38s dive-bombing:*** Bob diary (6/10/44).

280 ***guard accidentally shot:*** Bob diary (6/13/44).

280 ***to the garrison theater:*** Bob video (1997).

281 **Bob likened it:** conversation between Bob Cress and Jan Cress Dondi, Atlanta (1997).

281 ***We were in the back:*** Bob video (1997).

281 ***Six men escaped:*** Bob diary (6/21/44).

281 ***We saw a B-17 blow:*** Bob diary (6/23/44).

281 **refused to eat. . . . Diphtheria:** *Reports of POW interrogation*, AFHRA Reel K1023, 297; Bob POW diary (6/27/44).

282 ***The planes came right over:*** Bob diary (6/28/44).

282 ***Wounded in action:*** Gehring dossier, Bundesarchiv Zentralnachweisstelle LP-68214, (German Military Archives, Freibourg, Germany—translation through Beda Dondi and Peter Keel).

Chapter Twenty-Five: *Lagarul de Prisoneri #13*

283 ***Where are they taking:*** Bob POW diary (7/1/44); Bob video (1997).

284 **former girls' school:** conversation between Bob Cress and Jan Cress, Atlanta (1970); Author visit (2014).

284 **Lagarul de Prisoneri #13:** *Information Concerning POWs in* Rumania, National Archives, AFHRA Reel K1023, 284; interview with Dan Melinte (2014); Author visit (2014).

284 ***The air is quite excited:*** Bob diary (7/2/44).

284 ***British are hitting town:*** Bob diary (7/3/44).

284 ***Being a POW:*** Bob video (1997).

285 ***We were subjected:*** Bob diary (7/21/44).

285 ***The British hit the:*** Bob diary (7/24/44).

285 **Russian prisoners:** *Reports of POW Interrogation*, AFHRA Reel K1023, 294; Bob video.

285 ***Here in Bucharest?:*** conversation between Bob Cress and Jan Cress Dondi, Atlanta (1997).

286 ***Did the guard say:*** conversation between Bob Cress and Jan Cress Dondi, Atlanta (1997).

286 ***Maybe she'll see:*** conversation between Bob Cress and Jan Cress Dondi, Atlanta (1997).

286 **Princess Ecaterina Caradja:** Fili, *Biography of Princess Catherine Caradja Romania 1892–1993* found at http://www.Ploesti.net/Gallerys/Princess/index.htm; Bob video (1997).

286 **"she was feared":** AFHRA Reel A6087, 1445.

286 **"instrumental in keeping":** *Princess Ecaterina Caradja, Angel of Ploesti:* Schultz, Duane, Warfare History Network (2015); interviews with airmen at the annual reunion held by former POWs of Romania (New Bern, NC, 2012).

286 **"Her efforts did more":** AFHRA Reel A6087, 1445.

286 **put on skits:** *Operation Reunion report,* AFHRA Reel A6087 (9/5/44), 1487; Bob video (1997); conversation between Bob Cress and Jan Cress Dondi, Atlanta (1997).

286 **basketballs:** Lt. Col. Parton Memo, AFHRA Reel A6087, 1447; conversation between Bob Cress and Jan Cress Dondi, Atlanta (1997).

286 **books:** Lt. Col. Parton Memo, AFHRA Reel A6087, 1447; conversation between Bob Cress and Jan Cress Dondi, Atlanta (1997).

286 **POW newspaper:** *How Interned Airmen Got the News*, AFHRA Reel A1325 (9/1/44), 432; author archives; interview with Dan Melinte; conversation between Bob Cress and Jan Cress Dondi, Atlanta (1997).

287 **basketball tournament:** *Report of POW Interrogation*, AFHRA Reel K1023, 297; POW newspaper.

287 **"Cress helped put":** POW newspaper, Poop Sheet, *Hoop League Opens Play!*, Vol. I, No.1, Bucharest (7/27/44); Bob video (1997).

287 ***The first air-raid siren:*** Bob video (1997).

287 ***And then, once they:*** Bob video (1997).

287 ***I thought if the:*** Bob video (1997).

287 **basement provided a false sense:** Bob's diary (7/1/44).

287 **July 27, the British RAF:** AAF-RAF Press Release, *Under Bombing Attacks*, AFHRA Reel A1325 (9/3/44), 431; Bob POW diary (7/28/44); Bob video (1997).

287 ***From a Pathfinder:*** Bob video (1997).

288 ***We all wondered:*** Bob video (1997).

288 ***After that, the ack ack:*** Bob video (1997).

288 ***I thank God:*** Bob diary (7/28/44).

288 ***After that, every air raid:*** Bob video (1997).

289 ***Libs came over:*** Bob diary (7/31/44).

289 **headlines trumpeted the cage game:** POW newspaper, *Rooms 3 and 12 Tied for Cage Lead*, Vol. I, No.6, Bucharest (8/3/44); POW newspaper, *Hoop League Ends*, Vol. I, No.12, Bucharest (8/12/44), 2.

289 ***We lost the championship:*** Bob diary (8/13/44).

289 ***This evening we had:*** Bob diary (8/15/44).

289 ***two fellows escaped:*** Bob's diary (8/19/44).

Chapter Twenty-Six: *Romania Capitulates*

291 **Romania prospered:** Interviews with Alina Dumitru and Dan Melinte (2014).

291 **"communicated in English":** *Chicago Tribune* (9/12/44), 5.

291 **"smoked Lucky cigarettes":** *Chicago Tribune* (9/12/44), 5.

291 **"park his American jeep":** *Chicago Tribune* (9/12/44), 5.

292 **TWENTY-THREE AUGUST 1944. . . . "I have a wire":** Morton, Joseph, *Story of How Romania Split with Axis*, Associated Press, 9/7/1944; *Chicago Tribune*, *Tells How King of Romania Led Anti-Nazi Coup*, Moscow Sept. 2 AP (9/3/44), 5.

292 **"servants slipped pistols":** Morton, Joseph, *Story of How Romania Split with Axis*, Associated Press, 9/7/1944; *Chicago Tribune*, *Tells How King of Romania Led Anti-Nazi Coup*, Moscow, Sept. 2 AP (9/3/44), 5.

293 **"General Gerstenberg ordered":** Morton, Joseph, *Story of How Romania Split with Axis*, Associated Press, 9/7/1944.

293 **radio set:** AAF-RAF Press Release, *How the Interned Airmen Got the News*, AFHRA Reel A1325 (9/1/44), 432.

293 **"two officers transferred":** AAF-RAF Press Release, *How the Interned Airmen Got the News*, AFHRA Reel A1325 (9/1/44), 432.

293 ***At 2300 on the night:*** Bob video; Bob diary (8/27/44).

294 ***we were confused:*** Bob video (1997).

294 ***we went to:*** Bob video (1997).

294 ***Later that night:*** Bob diary (8/27/44).

294 ***With the heavy German presence:*** Bob diary; Bob video (1997).

294 **To escape:** conversation between Bob Cress and Jan Cress Dondi, Atlanta (1997).

294 **weapons, safe passage . . . big idea:** conversation with Bill Gunn (2014).

294 ***Rumors had spread:*** conversation between Bob Cress and Jan Cress Dondi, Atlanta (1997).

294 ***The Romanian civilians:*** Bob diary (8/24/44).

294 **rumored that Russia . . . B-29:** conversation with Bill Gunn (2014).

294 **German Luger:** Bob video (1997).

295 ***Ecoul:*** Romanian newspaper, August 25, 1944 (Bob's scrapbook).

295 **flags were raised:** *Reports of POWs*, AFHRA Reel K1023, 292; AAF-RAF Public Relations Release, Fox, Lt. Irving, AFHRA Reel A1325 (9/3/44), 433; Bob video (1997).

295 **assault on Bucharest:** *Reports of POWs*, AFHRA Reel K1023, 292; conversation between Bob Cress and Jan Cress Dondi, Atlanta (1997).

295 ***All hell broke loose:*** Bob diary; Bob video (1997); AAF-RAF Press Release, AFHRA Reel A1325, (9/1/44) 423.

295 ***even more jittery:*** conversation between Bob Cress and Jan Cress Dondi, Atlanta (1997).

296 ***stepped up on the sink:*** Bob video (1997).

296 ***Down from the sink:*** Bob video (1997).

296 ***Swede Samms:*** Bob diary; interview with Marshall "Swede" Samms, January 2015; Bob video (1997).

296 ***We had made a pact:*** Bob diary (8/27/44).

296 **heard gunshots echoing:** conversation between Bob Cress and Jan Cress Dondi, Atlanta (1997).

297 ***shrill of a fighter:*** AAF-RAF Press Release, AFHRA Reel A1325, (9/1/44) 423; conversation between Bob Cress and Jan Cress, Atlanta (1965 & 1997).

297 **German Stuka:** AAF-RAF Press Release, AFHRA Reel A1325, (9/1/44) 423; conversation between Bob Cress and Jan Cress Dondi, Atlanta (1997).

297 **Heinkel:** Press Release, *Under Bombing Attacks*, AFHRA Reel A1325 (9/3/44), 431; conversation between Bob Cress and Jan Cress Dondi, Atlanta (1997).

297 ***we crawled through:*** Bob video (1997); interview with Samms (Jan. 2015).

297 ***"CLICK-click":*** Bob video (1997); interview with Samms (Jan. 2015).

297 **"the clicking was a means"**: interview with Samms (Jan. 2015).

297 ***Swede and I decided:*** Bob diary (8/27/44).

297 **refuge under the same wall sink:** Bob diary (8/27/44).

298 ***the Germans poisoned:*** *50 Years Ago—Week of October 2, 1944*, unknown newspaper clipping (10/4/94); Bob video (1997).

298 ***we saw our American bombers:*** Bob POW diary (8/26/44).

298 **Otopeni:** Mahoney, *Fifteenth Air Force Against the Axis* (8/26/44), 216.

298 **his brothers of the 484th:** Mahoney, *Fifteenth Air Force Against the Axis* (8/26/44), 216.

299 **Gunn would have a plane:** *Operation Reunion*, Wharton, Don, Air News magazine, Vol. 8, No. 2, (March 1945), pp. 46-47, 72; conversation with Bill Gunn, Col. Gunn's son, Romania (2014).

299 **fearful . . . of a Soviet occupation:** interview with Dan Melinte and Alina Dumitru (2014).

Chapter Twenty-Seven: *A Garrison in the Forest*

300 ***How different:*** conversation between Bob Cress and Jan Cress Dondi, Atlanta (1997).

300 **Bragadiru:** interview with Dan Melinte (2014); conversation between Bob Cress and Jan Cress Dondi, Atlanta (1997).

301 **Harry. . . . crew of ten gathered:** Bob video (1997).

301 **Popesti. . . . Colonel Gunn:** National Archives, AAF-RAF Public Relations Release, *Col. Gunn Arranges Prisoner Evacuation*, AFHRA Reel A1325 (9/2/44), 429; Wharton, Don, *Operation Reunion*, Air Force Magazine, Vol. 8, No. 2, (March 1945), 46047, 72.

301 **Savoia-Marchetti. . . . Cantacuzino:** *Report on Operation Reunion—the Rescue of Allied Airmen from Roumania*, AFHRA Reel A6087 (Sept 1944), 1479; *Report of Interrogation of Lt. Col. Gunn*, AFHRA Reel K1023, 290; Dugan and Stewart, *Ploesti* (1962), 287.

301 **"the Romanian pilot made":** *Reports of Interrogation*, source from Lt. Gunn, AFHRA Reel K1023, 290.

302 **"Handsome and dashing":** *Report of Operation Reunion*, AFHRA Reel A6087, 1479.

302 **"Cantacuzino offered to fly Gunn":** *Summary of evacuation of ex-POWs from Rumania to Italy*, AFHRA Reel A6087 (9/5/44), 1479.

302 **Word had spread:** *Escape Statement*, Lt. Col. Gunn, AFHRA Reel A6087, 1455.

302 **American flag was hastily:** *Memo of POWs*, AFHRA Reel A6087, 1448.

302 **At 1720:** *Escape Statement*, Lt. Col. Gunn, AFHRA Reel A6087, 1479.

302 **Gunn:** *Escape Statement of Col. Gunn*, AFHRA Reel A6087, 1455.

302 **San Giovanni:** *Escape Statement of Col. Gunn*, AFHRA Reel A6087, 1455.

303 **"was surrounded by":** *Report on Operation Reunion—the Rescue of Allied Airmen from Roumania*, AFHRA Reel A6087 (Sept 1944), 1480.

303 **"Cantacuzino, obviously enjoying":** *Report on Operation Reunion—the Rescue of Allied Airmen from Roumania*, AFHRA Reel A6087 (Sept 1944), 1480.

303 **"I have somebody here":** Dugan and Stewart, *Ploesti* (1962), 287.

303 **"Gunn sat down":** *Report on Operation Reunion—the Rescue of Allied Airmen from Roumania*, AFHRA Reel A6087 (Sept 1944), 1480.

303 **Special Ops:** AFHRA Reel A1325 Operation Reunion *Special Handout for PR Release* (9/1/44), 425; conversation with Bill Gunn, Col. Gunn's son, Oct. 2014.

303 **detailed analysis:** *Escape Statement*, AFHRA Reel A6087, 1449.

303 **operations order:** AFHRA Reel A1325 Operation Reunion, *PR Release* (9/1/44), 425.

304 **Adapting the B-17s:** AFHRA Reel A1325 Operation Reunion, *PR Release* (9/1/44), 425.

Chapter Twenty-Eight: *Operation Reunion*

305 ***Operation Reunion***: Headquarters Fifteenth Air Force Public Relations Section APO 520, *Official Directive* (Bob scrapbook), 1944; *Report of Operation Reunion*, National Archives, AFHRA Reel A6087 (9/5/44), 1477.

305 **Cantacuzino was charged:** AFHRA Reel A6087, 1462.

305 **As Cantacuzino landed:** *Report on Operation Reunion—the Rescue of Allied Airmen from Roumania*, AFHRA Reel A6087 (Sept 1944), 1480.

305 **"the two P-51s":** AFHRA Reel A6087, 1462.

306 **Timisul de Jos:** *Information concerning POWs in Rumania*, AFHRA Reel K1023, 284.

306 **"the trip was harrowing":** *Data on POWs*, AFHRA Reel A6087, 1444.

306 **"prepared to fight":** *Data on POWs*, AFHRA Reel A6087, 1444.

306 **Worthy Long:** Long in *Ploesti*, 124; Bob's POW diary; conversation between Bob Cress and Jan Cress Dondi, Atlanta (1997).

306 ***and after that turn:*** conversation between Bob Cress and Jan Cress Dondi, Atlanta (1997).

307 ***How far? Who picked him up?:*** conversation between Bob Cress and Jan Cress Dondi, Atlanta (1997).

307 **"By August 29, the Red Army":** AAF Press Release, Fox, AFHRA Reel A1325, 433.

307 **"From some . . . we heard":** AAF Press Release, Fox, AFHRA Reel A1325, 434.

307 **Russians might use:** conversation with Bill Gunn (2014).

307 **"a quick evacuation":** Deane, *The Strange Alliance*, Indiana University Press (1973), 184.

307 **Wings of B-24s:** Mahoney, *Fifteenth Air Force Against the Axis*, 220.

308 **mass evacuation:** *Field Order* AFHRA Reel A6087 (8/30/44), 1465.

308 **"ninety-four P-38 Lightnings":** *Field Order* (8/31/44), AFHRA Reel A6087, 1472.

308 **"twenty-seven buses":** *Report of Operation Reunion*, AFHRA Reel A6087, 1481.

308 **The route took him:** conversation between Bob Cress and Jan Cress Dondi, Atlanta (1997).

309 ***What about Polley?:*** Bob video (1997).

309 ***an airfield south of town:*** Bob video (1997).

309 **Popesti aerodrome:** interview with Dan Melinte (2014).

309 ***We hid beneath the canopy:*** Bob video (1997).

309 ***The fighters gave us:*** Bob video (1997).

309 ***zooming overhead*:** Dugan and Stewart, *Ploesti* (1962), 292.

309 **With a confirmed friendly status:** AFHRA Reel A6087, 1462.

309 ***"USA! USA!":*** conversation between Bob Cress and Jan Cress Dondi, Atlanta (1997).

310 **P-51 and P-38 fighters:** Bob video (1997); AFHRA Reel A6087, 1463.

310 **B-17 Flying Fortresses:** Bob video (1997); AFHRA Reel A6087, 1463.

311 **"took fifteen minutes":** AFHRA Reel A6087, 1482.

311 **he went straight to the flight deck:** conversation between Bob Cress and Jan Cress Dondi, Atlanta (1997).

311 ***the last mountain range:*** conversation between Bob Cress and Jan Cress Dondi, Atlanta (1997).

312 ***Tuskegee Airmen:*** *MASAF INTOPS Summaries*, AFHRA Reel A6087 (8/31/44), 1472; conversation between Bob Cress and Jan Cress Dondi, Atlanta (1997).

312 **"Your safe return":** General Twining letter to Bob (9/3/44).

312 **"Thank God":** *General Twining in Report of Operation Reunion*, AFHRA Reel A6087, 1484.

312 **1,162 men repatriated** (total number varies): *Information concerning POWs in Rumania*, AFHRA Reel K1023, 284; 1,161: *Summary of Evacuation*, AFHRA Reel A6087 (9/5/44), 1474; 1,099: AFHRA Reel A6087, 1472 (9/2/44).

Chapter Twenty-Nine: *Reaping the Hill's Harvest*

314 **"had tuned their radio":** *Missing Flyer Cables Family of his Safety, Hillsboro Journal* (9/3/44).

314 **interviewing Warren Townsend:** *Missing Flyer Cables Family of his Safety*, unnamed (likely *Montgomery County News* or *Hillsboro Journal*) newspaper clipping in Bob's scrapbook (undated).

314 **"Never had the [Cress] family":** *Missing Flyer Cables Family of his Safety*, unnamed (likely *Montgomery County News* or *Hillsboro Journal*) newspaper clipping in Bob's scrapbook (undated); Bob video and interview.

314 **"Numb from anxiety":** *Missing Flyer Cables Family of his Safety, Hillsboro Journal* (9/3/44).

315 **telegram:** Bob, Western Union (9/4/44).

315 **jubilant *Thank you:*** interview with Louise Cress Beckemeyer (1997).

315 **ecstatic beyond all:** conversation between Polley White Cress and Jan Cress Dondi, Atlanta (1997).

315 **returned to Torretta:** Bob video (1997); conversation between Bob Cress and Jan Cress Dondi, Atlanta (1997).

315 **cargo steamer:** Bob video (1997).

315 **New York Harbor:** Bob video (1997); conversation between Bob Cress and Jan Cress Dondi, Atlanta (1997).

316 **Navy blimp:** Bob video (1997); Harris, *Scenes from Yesterday*, 80.

316 **Brushing a tear:** Bob video (1997); conversation between Bob Cress and Jan Cress Dondi, Atlanta (1997).

Epilogue: *Luck and Fate*

317 **assigned to Intelligence:** Bob video (1997).

317 **burdens of captivity:** conversation between Bob Cress and Jan Cress Dondi, Atlanta (1997).

318 **Never did he forget:** conversation between Bob Cress and Jan Cress Dondi, Atlanta (1997).

318 ***Purple Heart . . . Distinguished Flying Cross*:** Bob video (1997); *Lt. Bob Cress Home—Was German Prisoner, Hillsboro Journal* (Oct. 1944); author's personal memorabilia.

318 **"so perfect in navigation":** Major Thomas E. Page, 484th Bombardment Group (Pathfinder) *Historical Records*, NARA National Archives Reel 1824; (6/30/44), 9.

318 **sworn airmen to secrecy:** conversation between Bob Cress and Jan Cress Dondi, Atlanta (1997).

319 **May 31, 1947:** wedding day of Bob and Polley.

319 **John B. was the real hero:** conversation between Bob Cress and Jan Cress Dondi, Atlanta (1997).

319 **received letters:** Pat Dagon letter to brother Frank Dagon (8/30/43); Stewart, Walt letter to Lucille White (8/9/43).

319 **multiple chutes:** Letter to Abbie Roper and Lucille White, Stewart, Walt (8/9/43); Reports on MACR 334 and 462, IDPF file (10/13/45); subsequent statement of Clifford E. Koen, Jr., MACR 334 (date unknown).

319 ***surely, he hid out:*** conversation between Bob Cress, Polley White, and Jan Cress Dondi, Atlanta (1997).

319 **awarded the *Distinguished Flying Cross:*** Office of the Chaplain, US Army Air Forces, Letter (12/14/43).

319 **"unresolved casualty":** Acting Adjutant Lois Price, *Memorandum*, American Graves Registration Service, Africa-Middle East Zone (1/28/47).

319 **twenty-fifth mission:** Dugan and Stewart, *Ploesti* (1962), 206.

319 **"a few miles of enemy territory":** Walt Stewart in Dugan and Stewart, *Ploesti* (1962), 206.

320 **"rammed from the rear":** National Personnel Records Center / Individual Deceased Personnel (NPRC/IDPF), File relative to John B. White, Jr., American Legion to Director of Memorial Division, Washington, DC (2/20/47), 35.

320 **"tail section dropped from the clouds":** Eyewitness Bill Doerner, tail gunner of *Ready & Willing* (Roche crew), interview by Joe Duran (2003); Dugan and Stewart, *Ploesti* (1962), 206.

320 **three survived**: NARA, MACR 462.

320 **Report of his death:** NARA, NPRC/IDPF, *Battle Casualty Report*, 53, 62.

320 **"unfortunate consequence of battle":** Ada White journal; correspondence NPRC/IDPF relative to John B. White, Jr.

320 **"John B. made the supreme":** Senator Scott W. Lucas letter to the Whites, 11/3/44.

320 ***I'll never hear John B.'s voice:*** interview with Polley (Nov. 2012).

320 **April 1949:** National Archives, NPRC/IDPF *Group Burial*, 16.

320 **disinterred and reburied in Belgrade:** NPRC/IDPF, Disinterment Directive No. 9970 GB-135, 6.

320 **Only a group ID was possible:** NPRC/IDPF letter to Whites, (11/13/51), 5, 14.

321 **indomitable spirit:** Louise Campbell letter to Ada White, (8/16/43).

321 ***freezing temperatures . . . facing flak, fire, and enemy fighters was pure hell. . . . fearsome:*** Bob video (1997); conversation between Bob Cress and Jan Cress Dondi, Atlanta (1997).

321 ***The war years were times:*** Cress, Bob, *Living through the WWII years*, 1988.

321 **"2,432 US bomber crewmen":** *AAF-RAF Public Relations Release Lead-All*, AFHRA Reel A1325, 427.

321 **"one of the bloodiest and most heroic missions of all time":** Air War College, Maxwell AFB, AL (1999).

321 ***Lives forever changed:*** Cress, Bob, *Living through the WWII years*, 1988, closing words.

OTHER SOURCES*

"Aerial Navigation—It Guides U.S. Planes on World's Longest Flights," *Life* magazine, September 28, 1942 (pp. 92–101).

Air Force Historical Research Agency. www.afhra.af.mil and www.maxwell.af.mil

American Battles Monument Commission. https://www.abmc.gov/sites/default/files/interactive/interactive_files/WW2

Anderson, Garth. *Captain Hugh Rawlin Roper 1915–1943.*

Army Air Forces Historical Association. www.AAFHA.org

Ambrose, Stephen E. *The Wild Blue*. New York: Simon and Schuster, 2001.

Bell, James, *Hurricane Series: Surprise Hurricane of 1943*, Houston Public Media, 5/31/2007.

Bowman, Martin W, *Fields of Little America*: Patrick Stephens Limited, Cambridge, May 1983.

Bundesarchiv, Abteilung Militärarchiv, Wiesentalstraße 10, 79115 Freiburg. Gehring dossier, Bundesarchiv Zentralnachweisstelle LP-68214, German Military Archives, Freibourg, Germany.

Chicago Kent College of Law, Radio Debates (1940) II. *Resolved, that the United States should form an alliance with Great Britain.* (pp. 10-16)

Daraskevich, Joe, *Fiery U-boat attack off Jacksonville Beach created spectacle 75 years ago, The Florida Times-Union*, 4/9/17.

Deane, John R., *The Strange Alliance*, Indiana University Press, 1/1/1973.

Dugan, James and Carroll Stewart. *Ploesti: The Great Ground-Air Battle of 1 August 1943*. New York: Random House, 1962.

Fincher, Lew & Read, Bill, *The* 1943 *"Surprise" Hurricane*, NOAA History—Stories and Tales of the Weather Service, 6/8/2006.

484th Bombardment Group. www.484th.org

Freeman, Roger A., *The Ploesti Raid through the Lens,* Battle of Britain International Limited, London, 2004.

Gannon, Michael. Operation Drumbeat: *The Dramatic True Story of Germany's First U-boat Attacks Along the American Coast in WWII.* NY: Harper & Row, 1990.

Harris, Harry B. (1993) *Scenes from Yesterday.* (pp. 37-43)

Haulman,Daniel. *Operation Reunion*, Air Force Historical Research Agency. May 30, 2012.

Hershberger, Nancy Beckemeyer. *The Story of Cress Hill Farm.* Privately printed in Phoenix, AZ, 2017.

Hill, Michael. *Black Sunday Ploesti*. Schiffer Publishing Ltd., Atglen, PA, 1993.

Lawrence, Polley Ellen Cress. *A Celebration: Brown and White Legacy.* Privately printed in Roswell, GA, 2001.

Life magazine. July 26, 1943 (cover); September 28, 1942, 92–101.

Mahoney, Kevin A. *Fifteenth Air Force against the Axis*. Lanham: The Scarecrow Press, Inc., 2013.

Mauer, Kevin. *Damn Lucky*. St. Martin's Press, 2022.

Miller, Donald L. *Masters of the Air.* New York: Simon and Schuster, 2006.

Murphy, Brian John, *Sharks in American Waters, America in WWII* magazine. 310 Publishing, LLC, October 2006.

Murphy, Frank. *Luck of the Draw.* St. Martin's Griffin, 2023.

National Archives and Records Administration (NARA). www.archives.gov.

93rd Bombardment Group. www.93bg.com; *Tidal Wave* briefing film. http://www.93bg.com/#!video-polesti-film/c1ll

POW Newspaper, Vol. I, No.1 through 20, Bucharest, July 27, 1944 through August 23, 1944.

Prien, Jochen. *Jagdgeschwader 53*. Atglen, PA: Schiffer Publishing, Ltd., 1998.

Ramp Rooster, *484th BG Losses*, The Boys of "Ramp Rooster"—B-24 Bomber, Facebook.

Rickenbacker, Capt. Eddie V. *Fighting the Flying Circus*. Garden City, NY, Doubleday & Co, Inc., 1965.

Roper, Hugh, *The Route and Other Plans*, personal diary of Captain Hugh Rawlin Roper, 1915–1943.

Samms, Marshall N. *I was shot down over Rumania.* Sir! September 1945.

Snyder, Steve. *Shot Down*. Sea Breeze Publishing, LLC, 2017.

Sterling, Christopher H. (editor) *Biographical Encyclopedia of American Radio.* Routledge, 2011.

Stewart, Carroll. *Ted's Traveling Circus—93rd Bombardment Group (H) USAAF 1942–1945*. Lincoln, NE: Nebraska Printing Center, 2007.

Story of the 93rd Bomb Group Unit History (yearbook of group, copy obtained online from University of SW LA at Lafayette in memory of John Weeks).

Stout, Jay A. *Fortress Ploesti: The Campaign to Destroy Hitler's Oil.* Casemate Publishers, Havertown, PA, 2003, January 2011.

US Dept. of Defense, Defense POW/MIA Accounting Agency, Washington, DC.

"I'll Be Seeing You" (song); Composer: Sammy Fain; Lyricist: Irving Kahal; Published 1938 by Marlo Music Corp.

World War II History. http://www.worldwar2history.info

WWII timelines and descriptions:
https://www.pbs.org/thewar/at_war_timeline.htm
https://www.historyplace.com/worldwar2/timeline/ww2time.htm
https://en.wikipedia.org; https://www.newspapers.com
https://www.newspapers.com/image/562686393/?terms=Declaration%2Bon%2BRumania—Declaration of war on Romania
https://www.edwardianpromenade.com/holidays/a-fourth-of-july-reception/—Dorchester House
http://news.bbc.co.uk/onthisday/hi/dates/stories/september/3/newsid_3493000/3493279.stm—September 3, 1939
https://www.polk-fl.net/staff/teachers/tah/documents/floridaflavor/lessons/e-3.pdf—Hardegen log

* References to internet websites (URLs) were accurate at the time of writing. The author is not responsible for the URLs that may have expired or changed since the manuscript was prepared. The author has made diligent effort to research records relative to the missions carried out with as much accuracy based on documented evidence available at the time of publication.